Also in the Variorum Collected Studies Series:

F.E. PETERS
The Arabs and Arabia on the Eve of Islam

HAN J.W. DRIJVERS
History and Religion in Late Antique Syria

SHAUL SHAKED
From Zoroastrian Iran to Islam: Studies in Religious History and Intercultural Contacts

AVERIL CAMERON
Changing Cultures in Early Byzantium

ALFREDO MORDECHAI RABELLO
The Jews in the Roman Empire: Legal Problems, from Herod to Justinian

DAVID F. GRAF
Rome and the Arabian Frontier: From the Nabataeans to the Saracens

SEBASTIAN BROCK
Studies in Syriac Christianity: History, Literature, Theology

HAN J. W. DRIJVERS
East of Antioch: Studies in early Syriac Christianity

J.H.G.W. LIEBESCHUETZ
From Diocletian to the Arab Conquest: Change in the late Roman Empire

SEBASTIAN BROCK
From Ephrem to Romanos: Interactions between Syriac and Greek in Late Antiquity

LESLIE S.B. MACCOULL
Coptic Perspectives on Late Antiquity

T.D. BARNES
Early Christianity and the Roman Empire

JEAN-MICHEL SPIESER
Urban and Religious Spaces in Late Antiquity and Early Byzantium

VARIORUM COLLECTED STUDIES SERIES

Geography, Urbanisation and Settlement Patterns in the Roman Near East

To My Students: Past, Present and Future

Henry Innes MacAdam

Geography, Urbanisation and Settlement Patterns in the Roman Near East

Ashgate

VARIORUM

Published in the Variorum Collected Studies Series by

Ashgate Publishing Limited
Gower House, Croft Road,
Aldershot, Hampshire GU11 3HR
Great Britain

Ashgate Publishing Company
131 Main Street
Burlington, Vermont 05401–5600
USA

Ashgate website: http://www.ashgate.com

ISBN 0–86078–877–6

British Library Cataloguing-in-Publication Data
MacAdam, Henry Innes
Geography, urbanisation and settlement patterns in the Roman Near East. – (Variorum collected studies series; CS735)
1. Human geography–Arabia, Roman 2. Urbanization–Arabia, Roman 3. Land settlement patterns–Arabia, Roman 4. Middle East–History–To 622 5. Arabia, Roman.
I. Title
939.4

Library of Congress Control Number: 2001098289

The paper used in this publication meets the minimum requirements of the American National Standard for Information Sciences – Permanence of Paper for Printed Library Materials, ANSI Z39.48–1984. ∞ ™

Printed by St Edmundsbury Press, Bury St Edmunds, Suffolk

VARIORUM COLLECTED STUDIES SERIES CS735

CONTENTS

This volume contains xiv + 368 pages

PUBLISHER'S NOTE

The articles in this volume, as in all others in the Variorum Collected Studies Series, have not been given a new, continuous pagination. In order to avoid confusion, and to facilitate their use where these same studies have been referred to elsewhere, the original pagination has been maintained wherever possible.

Each article has been given a Roman number in order of appearance, as listed in the Contents. This number is repeated on each page and is quoted in the index entries.

Corrections noted in the Errata/Corrigenda/Addenda have been marked by an asterisk in the margin corresponding to the relevant text to be amended.

INTRODUCTION

The fifteen articles reprinted herein represent some of my research and publications between the early 1980s and the present. The three categories of this collection's title, i.e. Geography, Urbanisation and Settlement Patterns, are of course interrelated and interdependent aspects of the history of the Roman Near East.

Until 1985 I was resident in the modern Near East as a faculty member in the Department of History and Archaeology at the American University of Beirut. It was at that venerable institution somewhat earlier that I earned (under the tutelage of the late Roger Saidah and the late William A. Ward) a B.A. and an M.A. in ancient history and archaeology.

Long residence in Lebanon – between 1968 and 1985 – gave me many opportunities to participate in both archaeological work and field surveys in that country, in Cyprus, in Syria and in Jordan. Indeed it was numerous trips to southern Syria and northern Jordan which prompted my doctoral dissertation at the University of Manchester (1979) and the volume that (after substantial revision of the Ph. D. thesis) eventually appeared as *Studies in the History of the Roman Province of Arabia* (Oxford, BAR, 1986).

That volume focused on the frontier province the Romans called simply *Arabia*, created in A.D. 106 after Trajan's annexation of the ancient kingdom of the Nabataean Arabs. That region had previously been the subject of much scholarly attention, by both European and American archaeological expeditions, particularly between the 1890s and the outbreak of World War I in 1914. During the next twenty years – i.e. 1919–1939 – the focus of fieldwork in Syria moved north to Dura Europus, Antioch, and the coast (Ras Shamra, Byblos). In Jordan the emphasis shifted south to Amman and Petra. Not until after WWII did systematic fieldwork in southern Syria, and in all parts of Jordan, begin again in earnest.

In 1971 the publication of Glen W. Bowersock's 'A Report on Arabia Provincia', in the *Journal of Roman Studies* caught not only my attention but the attention of several other younger scholars, many of whom have since become good friends as well as colleagues. Bowersock did more than pay tribute to the prior fieldwork and major publications which laid the foundations of Roman Arabia studies; he also highlighted important areas in which new exploration and research were needed.

The response to that 'Report' was rapid and remarkable: by the time Bowersock's comprehensive volume *Roman Arabia* (1983) appeared, dozens of preliminary archaeological reports, epigraphic studies, numismatic essays and other related articles were either in press or already published. In the introduction to my BAR volume I noted that exponential increase in publications.

By the end of the 1980s 'Roman Arabia' had atttracted to itself a cadre of talented and enthusiastic scholars – North Americans and Europeans once more – but now (in contrast to a century ago) numbers of equally talented and enthusiastic scholars from the countries of the Near East itself: Israelis, Jordanians, Lebanese, Palestinians, Saudis, and Syrians. Perhaps the cumulative effect of so much work over a span of a century is best exemplified in the comprehensive new volume by D.L. Kennedy, *The Roman Army in Jordan* (2000).

It was inevitable that renewed interest in Roman Arabia would be reflected in a broader geographic context, particularly (but not exclusively) the Arabian peninsula (including Yemen) to the south and the Sinai peninsula (as far north as Pelusium) to the west. In several of the papers republished here I expanded my own research, and explored aspects of the Arabian interior (e.g. the Wadi Sirhan and the legendary oasis of Dumata/Jawf) or the Arabian peninsula as it was described or mapped or defined by ancient geographers (notably Strabo, Pliny, Ptolemy).

Within the past decade (1990–2000) more than a dozen volumes have been published on aspects of the history and archaeology of Rome's eastern imperial domains. Among those are David Kennedy and Derrick Riley, *Rome's Desert Frontier from the Air* (1990), Maurice Sartre, *L'orient romaine* (1991), Benjamin Isaac, *The Limits of Empire: The Roman Army in the East* (2nd edn., 1992), Fergus Millar, *The Roman Near East* (1993), Edward Dabrowa (ed.), *The Roman and Byzantine Army in the East* (1994), Philip Mayerson, *Monks, Martyrs, Soldiers and Saracens: Papers on the Near East in Late Antiquity* (1994), H. Lozachmeier (ed.), *Présence arabe dans le Croissant Fertile avant l'Hégire* (1995), S. Gregory, *Roman Military Architecture on the Eastern Frontier* (1995–97); John Humphrey (ed.), *The Roman and Byzantine Near East* (1995–99); David F. Graf, *Rome and the Arabian Frontiers from the Nabataeans to the Saracens* (1997); and W. Ball, *Rome in the East: The Transformation of an Empire* (2000).

My own special interests for almost two decades (1975–95) were epigraphy, geography (including toponymy), urbanisation, and social change throughout the Roman and Byzantine Near East, and to those ends most of these papers are devoted. In several instances I have bridged the Byzantine and early Islamic periods since (as those who work in either or both of these fields know) there is no definable break in the cultural continuity of Late Antiquity.

The region that became Roman Arabia had been loosely 'unified' and centrally administered by the Nabataean Arabs during the later stages of the Hellenistic period, as Seleucid and Ptolemaic control of Syria/Palestine/Transjordan gradually passed to the Romans. When Herod the Great established himself as the primary political force within Palestine (37–4 B.C.), by acceptance of a client status with Rome, he was allowed to annex to his kingdom and administer all the territory collectively called today the Lava Lands (the Hawran) of southern Syria exclusive of the northern Nabataean city of Bostra.

That was the beginning of what became a long and very gradual process of pacification and urbanisation of a region traditionally populated by pastoralists and infested with brigands who resisted – often through rebellious activity – royal and imperial encroachment. Herodian rule of the northern Hawran, and Nabataean expansion into the south of that region, provided the stability and the structured way of life which had hitherto proved impossible to effect.

Governance of that area became Rome's responsibility when the Herodian and Nabataean dynasties terminated almost simultaneously at the end of the first century A.D. and their royal domains became part of the adjoining provinces of Syria and Arabia, respectively. There is no evidence that Rome pursued a stated policy of economic and social development in the Hawran region. There is every reason, however, to believe that the provincial authorities supported, and even encouraged, the urbanisation of those rural communities.

Though few villages ever achieved the rank of formal *poleis* in the six centuries that followed the onset of Roman rule, many developed – we have abundant epigraphic evidence for this – the form and function of the larger provincial city-states (e.g. Canatha, Bostra, Philadelphia). More recently that view has been challenged vigorously by John D. Grainger ('"Village Government" in Roman Syria and Arabia', *Levant* 27 [1995] 179–195). Readers of that may judge for themselves if it is as unconvincing an argument as I find it.

One of the most significant archaeological discoveries of the 1990s in Jordan is the cache (numbering about 140) of carbonised papyri which came to light during excavations of the Petra Church almost a decade ago.

Though it will be some time before that wealth of documentation is completely available, it is already quite clear that the Petra Papyri will clarify the entire issue of land tenture in and around Petra during the period c. A.D. 535–595 (roughly the earliest and latest dated documents in the papyri hoard).

Since 1990 my research interests have led me into new areas of study in parts of the ancient Near East adjacent to Nabataea/Roman Arabia: the Persian/Arabian Gulf; Phoenicia and Phoenician culture; New Testament chronology and textual transmission. Thus the regions once the primary focus of my research are now somewhat peripheral.

Happily, fieldwork and publications by others still proceeds apace. I am confident that this will provide those who periodically produce comprehensive volumes (such as those noted above) the solid groundwork on which they can compare and contrast the development of that region with neighboring provinces of the eastern Roman Empire, as well as with other portions of the larger Roman world.

HENRY INNES MACADAM

Robbinsville, NJ, USA
19 December 2001

AUTHOR'S NOTE

The maps which appear with some, not all, of these reprinted articles were intended for the purpose of general identification of the geographical areas and also the toponyms referred to within the text. Readers requiring detailed and accurate maps must consult the best available reference source for maps of the classical world, i.e. R.J.A. Talbert (editor), *Barrington Atlas of the Greek and Roman World* (Princeton, Princeton University Press, 2000).

ACKNOWLEDGEMENTS

Grateful acknowledgement is made to the following persons, journals, institutions and publishers for their kind permission to reproduce the papers included in this volume: Vassilios Christides, Editor, *Graeco-Arabica* (I); the American School of Oriental Studies, Atlanta, Georgia (II); CNRS Editions, Paris (III); A.F. Boursac, Editor, *Topoi: Orient-Occident* (IV); E.J. Brill, Leiden (V); The British Academy, London (VI); the Editor, *Berytus* (VII, XII); Peeters Publishers, Leuven (VIII); The Darwin Press, Inc., Princeton, New Jersey (IX); the American University of Beirut, New York (X); Rudolf Habelt GmbH, Bonn (XIII); A.E. Khairallah, Editor, *Al-Abhath* (XIV); the Editor, *British Archaeological Reports* (XV).

Special acknowledgement by the author is given to Dr John Smedley and to Miss Celia Hoare of Ashgate/Variorum for their careful attention to detail and cheerful assistance in seeing this volume through to press.

I

Marinus of Tyre and Scientific Cartography:

The Mediterranean, the Orient and Africa in Early Maps

1. Marinus, Ptolemy of Alexandria and the Orbis Terrarum

> "Marinus the Tyrian, the latest of the geographers of our time, seems to us to have thrown himself with the utmost zeal into this matter [cartography]. He is known to have found out many things that were not known before. He has searched most diligently the works of almost all the historians [i.e. writers of geographical commentaries] who preceded him. He has not only corrected their errors, but the reader can clearly see that he [Marinus] has undertaken to correct those parts of the work which he himself had done badly in the early editions of his geographical maps. If we examine closely his last work we find few defects. It would seem to be enough for us to describe the earth on which we dwell from his commentaries [*hypomnêmata*] alone, without other investigations."[1]

Such was the judgment of Marinus by Ptolemy of Alexandria (c.80-c.150), prompted as much by genuine respect as by knowledge that the geographical works of Marinus were widely read and therefore a source of comparison with Ptolemy's own *Geography*. If the deference or even admiration expressed here is somewhat diluted by stringent criticisms later on, Ptolemy was clearly indebted to his predecessor and was careful to say so at the beginning.

The Introduction to Ptolemy's *Geography* (Book 1) contains all that we know of Marinus, including his name. The biographical details are totally lacking. Were it not for Ptolemy's systematic analysis of Marinus' methodology we could not even evaluate the latter's contribution to the science of cartography. But even with Ptolemy's critical essay in front of us it is impossible to know how much or how little credit Marinus is due. The difficulty is evident. The modern equivalent would be to judge a book by a solitary review in full knowledge that the work itself, apart from a quotation or two, could never be read. Marinus the geographer is today so obscured by the giant shadow of Ptolemy that he does not rate an entry in volume "M" of the fifteen-volume *Dictionary of Scientific Biography*.[2]

1 Ptolemy, *Geography* 1.6.1-2 (trans. by E.L. Stevenson, *Geography of Claudius Ptolemy* [New York, 1932]). A biographical sketch of Ptolemy appears in F. Rosenthal, *The Classical Heritage in Islam* (Berkeley, 1975) pp. 30-33 (Rosenthal's translation from Ibn al-Qittî's *Ta'rîkh al-Hukamâ*).

2 Published between 1970-78. Marinus was long ago given full and fair treatment by E.H. Bunbury, *A History of Ancient Geography* (London, 1879) Vol. II pp. 519-545; more recently (but briefly) by O.A.W. Dilke, *Greek and Roman Maps* (London, 1985) pp. 72-75. Comprehensive assessments of Marinus were published by E. Honigmann, "Marinos von Tyros," *Realencyclopädie* (hereinafter *RE*) 14.2 (1930) cols.

Neither the name Marinus nor the adjective Tyrios discloses with certainty the ethnic identity of the geographer. Marinus was a popular name among Graeco-Romans and Hellenized provincials alike (some two dozen individuals by that name are catalogued in Pauly-Wissova's *Realencyclopädie* alone). Phoenician nomenclature so far has provided only one possible attestation, *MRN* (*Maran*?). This is thought to be a misspelling of *MGN* (*Magôn, Magô*), among the commonest of Phoenician/Punic personal names.[3] Marinus is common in other Semitic languages (e.g. Palmyrene, Nabataean)[4] with closer linguistic connections to Aramaic. *MRN* or *MRN'* is Aramaic for "Lord" or "Master." In its Arabic form *MRWN* (*Marôn*) it is a name especially venerated by the "Maronite" Christians of modern Lebanon. For Hellenized Phoenicians Marinus would have been a particularly attractive name and it comes as no surprise that we find it in the Greek epigraphy of Phoenicia. *Marrinos* is attested on a tombstone from the village of Halat in the coastal territory (*peraia*) belonging to the island city of Aradus (*Ru'âd*), and Marinos is known from a dedicatory inscription at Ba'albek.[5]

By happy coincidence these transliterations evoke a Latin adjective associated with the sea and sea-faring (*marinus*) and a Greek noun for a type of fish (*marinos*). *Marinus* is thus one of several "Mediterranean" names (another is *Zenôn*) which embody aspects of bi-culturalism without the artificiality of reciprocal translations. The latter were a common feature of the Hellenistic period. The epithet *Tyrios* was used by Ptolemy in the same way that *Byblios* modified the name of Marinus' compatriot and contemporary Philo of Byblos. *Tyrios* made the necessary distinction between the geographer and his namesake Marinus, a contemporary anatomist perhaps resident at Alexandria.[6] While it doesn't prove that Marinus was a native of Tyre, it does indicate at least his residence

1767-96 (map cols. 1785-86) and more recently by N.G. Photinos, "Marinos von Tyros," *RE Supplementband* 12 (1970) cols. 791-838.

3 F. Benz, *Personal Names in the Phoenician and Punic Inscriptions* (Rome, 1972) p. 143; *MRN* in *Corpus Inscriptionum Semiticarum* I 1429.3); *MGN*: ibid. pp. 133-137. Benz is apparently following Z.S. Harris, *A Grammar of the Phoenician Language* (New Haven, 1936) p. 122, who also questioned the reading of the name.

4 In Palmyrene: J.K. Stark, *Personal Names in Palmvrene Inscriptions* (Oxford, 1971) pp. 37; 97 s.v. *MRWN'*; in Nabataean: J. Cantineau, *Le Nabatéen* Vol. II (Paris, 1932) pp. 117-118 s.v. *MR'*; in Safaitic and Thamudic: G. Ryckmans, *Les Noms Propres Sud-Sémitiques* Vol. 1 (Louvain, 1934) p. 132 s.v. *MR'*; more recently in Safaitic: G.L. Harding, *An Index and Concordance of Pre-Islamic Arabian Names and Inscriptions* (Toronto, 1971) p. 536 s.v. *MR'*, p. 537 s.v. *MR'N*. The father of the emperor Philippus Arabs (244-249) was named Marcus Julius Marinus (Aurelius Victor, *Caesaribus* 28.1). His name was variously spelled *Marinos* and *Mareinos* in Greek inscriptions; on this see R. Cagnat (editor), *Inscriptiones Graecae ad Res Romanas Pertinentes* Vol. III (Paris, 1906) #1199, #1200.

5 *Marrinus*: *Inscriptions Grecques et Latines de la Syrie* (hereinafter *IGLS*) Vol. 7.4059, undated (indexed incorrectly as #4050); *Marinos*: IGLS 6.2750, Roman imperial period (appears as a patronymic). On other variations in Greek transliterations see H. Wüthnow, *Die Semitischen Menschannamen in Griechischen Inschriften und Papyri des Voderen Orients* (Leipzig, 1930) p. 73. Also worth noting is the use of "Marin" and "Marinos" as a personal name within the Jewish community in Cyrenaica; see P.M. Fraser and E. Matthews, *A Lexicon of Greek Personal Names Vol. I (Oxford, 1987) p. 298 s.v.*

6 *Oxford Classical Dictionary* (hereinafter *OCD*) (2nd ed.) p. 648 = *RE* 14.2 (1930) col. 1796 s.v. "Marinos (4)."

in that city. In the absence of additinal evidence we cannot be certain that Marinus of Tyre was a Phoenician by ancestry.

Bunbury[7] has argued that Ptolemy's remark "of our own time" (see the quotation above) can only mean that Marinus was a very close contemporary. This would suggest dates of *c*.75-*c*.140 for the Tyrian geographer. He produced at least three editions of a geographical commentary. These were accompanied by maps, though Ptolemy's comments about them are annoyingly vague regarding their method of construction. Marinus is certainly credited with map-making in later Arabic cartographic tradition.[8] His third edition, from which Ptolemy worked (and quoted), was not to be final

> "... because, as he [Marinus] says, he has not yet come to the last delineation of his maps in which, so he tells us, he would make the necessary corrections..." (*Geog*.1.17.1)

These corrections, according to Ptolemy, would be in the *klimata* (the zones or regions north and south of the equator) and the "hour divisions" (east or west of the "prime meridian").

It would seem that Marinus died before completing that revision. The scope of his commentary and even its formal name remain uncertain, though Thomson, Photinos and others have proposed that Ptolemy's use of the expression "Correction of the (World) Map" may be Marinus' own title.[9] Ptolemy specifically cites only Book 3, from which he gives us verbatim a comment by Marinus concerning the Zodiac. This is worth reproducing, as much for its tone as its content—though the latter was understandably of greater interest to Ptolemy. It allows us direct access to the mind of the man who exercised such a powerful influence on Ptolemy and, through him, the entire medieval concept of geography:

> "The Zodiac is considered to lie entirely above the torrid zone and therefore in that zone the shadows change, and all the fixed stars rise and set. Ursa Minor (the "Little Bear", our "Little Dipper") begins to be entirely above the horizon [500] stadia [about one hundred km] distant from the north shore of Ocelis. The parallel through Ocelis is elevated eleven and two-fifths degrees.
>
> We learn from Hipparchus [the astronomer, see below] that the star in Ursa Minor which is the most southerly or which marks the end of the [Bear's] tail, is distant from the [north] pole twelve and two-fifths degrees, and that in the course of the sun from the equinoctial to the summer solstice [i.e. from 21 March to 21 June], the north pole [star] continually rises above the horizon while the south pole [star] is correspondingly depressed, and that on the contrary in the course of the sun from the equinoctial to the winter solstice [21 September to 21 December] the south pole [star] rises above the horizon while the north pole [star] is depressed" (*Geog*. 1.7.4-5; Stevenson trans.).

7 *Ancient Geography* Vol. II pp. 519 and n.1. In spite of Bunbury's sensible assertion that Marinus wrote and published closer to c. 125-140 there is still a tendency to date his work in the first decade of the second century, e.g. Dilke, *Maps* p. 72; Honigmann, *RE* 14.2 (1930) col. 1768 (both "c. 110").

8 Dilke, *Maps* p. 177.

9 J.O. Thomson, *A History of Ancient Geoqraphy* (New York, 1965 [reprint of 1948 edition]) p. 334; cf. Dilke, *Maps* p. 72 and n.3; Photinos, *RE Supplementband* 12 (1970) cols. 795-797.

Of more than passing interest here is the emphasis on a known constellation, one of prime interest to geographers. The pattern of the heavens was of crucial importance in establishing the location of places on earth, in this case the exact position of Ocelis (at the southern entrance to the Red Sea). The rising and setting of certain stars at certain seasons was almost as important to "fixing" a site as was the angle of the sun at any given day. The *unity* of the "cosmos" was taken for granted by the ancients, a concept too easily forgotten today when we open an "atlas" or consult a gazetteer of place-names, or visit a planetarium.[10]

The mention of Hipparchus (c.195-c.125) is one indication that Marinus inherited (and in some instances revived) geographic techniques and traditions dating from the Hellenistic period. This included measurements made of the earth's circumference (its sphericity was taken for granted) and the mapping of that portion of the earth called in Greek the *oikoumenê*, i.e. the "inhabited" area. The Phoenician portion of the *oikoumenê* would have been of particular interest to Marinus, and we shall examine in some detail the ancient descriptions and maps of Phoenicia with that in mind. But it might be * worthwhile first to review briefly the extent of knowledge of the world in which Marinus lived since that will form the background against which any study of the Phoenicians must be placed.

2. Orient et Occident: Marinus' Concept of the World

Marinus' most distinguished predecessor was the Alexandrian geographer Eratosthenes (c.275-c.200), famous in his time for determining the earth's circumference (his estimate was slightly larger than ours) and for reckoning the length (from Gibraltar to the coast of Phoenicia) of the Mediterranean Sea (that estimate was also a bit exaggerated). Both distances were based on a fixed figure: one degree of latitude at the equator was equal to 700 stadia (=140 km.). Such was the the so-called "long degree" of Eratosthenes. None of these figures was sacrosanct since there were no fixed standards of measurement (e.g. the length of a stadion)[11], and the methodology of measurements varied.

A century and a half later Poseidonius of Apamea (a Syrian city just north of the Phoenician "border") recalculated the earth's circumference using a base figure of one degree equal to 500 stadia (=91 km.). Poseidonius' earth was thus considerably smaller than Eratosthenes'[12] and we may assume that his figure for the length of the Mediterranean Sea must have been correspondingly shorter. Ptolemy tells us that Marinus accepted Poseidonius' reduced figure for the earth's circumference, and onto that sphere projected Eratosthenes' longer Mediterranean. The result was a "stretched"

10 See the opening chapters of T. Ferris I Coming of Age in the Milky Way (New York, 1988). *

11 J. Skop, "The Stade of the Ancient Greeks," *Surveying and Mapping* 10 (1950) pp. 50-55.

12 I. Frischer, "Another Look at Eratosthenes' and Posidonius' Determinations of the Earth's Circumference," *Quarterly Journal of the Royal Astronomical Society* 16 (1975) pp. 152-167.

effect which even Ptolemy's recalculations could not rectify. It is evident that this seemingly arbitrary use of sources resulted in some basic errors.

We are not told what lay behind Marinus' choice of figures, but he was just as selective in his plotting of fixed points beyond the Mediterranean region. The northern limit of the "inhabited world" he set at Thule (Mainland, the southernmost and largest of the Shetland Islands)[13] rather than the North Polar Region theorized by Hipparchus. Marinus set the southern limit at Prasum Promontory south of his equator, probably, Cape Delgado on the northernmost coast of what is now Mozambique. To the west he discarded the prevailing opinion that the Sacred Promontory (Cape St. Vincent) on the Atlantic coast of Spain marked zero degrees longitude.[14] Marinus boldly fixed his "prime meridian" some two and a half degrees west of the European-African coastline, through the Fortunate Islands (Islas Canarias) west of Morocco. This new calculation (also slightly in error) caught the fancy of Ptolemy, who canonized it in the *Geography*. So seductive was this *idée fixe* that German cartographers set their prime meridian on Ferro, the westernmost island of the Canaries, well into the nineteenth century.[15]

Marinus set the easternmost limit of the *oikoumenê* at Sera (believed to be the capital of what we call China), some 225 degrees east of the Canaries and about two-thirds of the distance around the globe. This elongation of the inhabited world was noticed by Ptolemy, who made some attempt to reduce it. The exaggerated distances for Asia were matched by inflated figures for locations along the southeastern coast of Africa. In both cases Marinus relied upon traveler's reports, accurate (as Ptolemy notes) for distances between well-known points but inevitably enlarged regarding distances "that are great in extent, and rarely traveled, and not fully explored" (*Geog*. 1.10.3).

Marinus also accepted a revisionist tradition, in vogue after the time of Strabo, that the continents of Africa and Asia were joined by a land mass of indeterminate dimensions called *Terra Incognita*. It is easy to scoff at such credulity, especially in a man who might have given some serious thought to Herodotus' report (had he read or heard of it) about a Phoenician circumnavigation of Africa from east to west "around the Cape" some seven and a half centuries before his own time. But Herodotus hardly represented the majority opinion on the size or shape of Africa in his own time much less in Marinus' day. As the "Father of Lies" Herodotus was mercilessly pilloried in an essay by the moralist Plutarch, another contemporary of Marinus.

What prompted the tradition of an "Unknown Land?" There is every reason to believe that mariners of the first century A.D. who plied the southern Indian Ocean may have

13 We know this from Ptolemy's location of Thule. For other locations see (e.g.) *OCD* (2nd ed.) 1075 s.v. "Thule."

14 This belief (unfortunately erroneous) goes back at least to Eratosthenes; see Bunbury, *Ancient Geography* Vol. I p. 629.

15 H.F. Tozer, *A History of Ancient Geography* (2nd ed., Cambridge [U.K.], 1935) p. 342; cf. Bunbury, *Ancient Geography* Vol. II p. 567 and n.7, who observes that Ferro is 18 degrees 20 minutes west of the Greenwich meridian and 9 degrees west of Cape Vincent, so that Marinus (followed by Ptolemy) erred some seven degrees of longitude.

heard about, or even glimpsed from time to time, the northern coast of Australia. The view of that enormous stretch of land, seemingly desolate and extending some 2,500 km. in either direction (southeast or southwest) from its nearest proximity to the Asian mainland, might well have seemed a land-link between Africa south of Ethiopia and the Farthest East.

Ptolemy had no trouble accepting the idea of *Terra Incognita* and it became an established feature of his *Geography*. The psychological significance of this has also been noted:

> "Representing supposedly dangerous *terrae incognitae* in map form as an extension of familiar territory may have have served to lessen fear of the peripheral world."[16].

For many medieval Europeans that unknown land-link was a reality until Portuguese ships circumnavigated Africa from west to east at the end of the fifteenth century. *Terra Incognita* was one of several cartographic myths (perhaps inspired by mariners, tales) that Europeans took for granted until the advent of the Enlightenment.

3. Marinus, Ptolemy and the "Hippodamian Grid"

Hipparchus had laid down the principles of mathematical geography based on celestial observations. In theory the location of any point on the earth's surface could be precisely established, and its distance from any other fixed point determined, by accurate calculations of the solstitial day (for degrees of latitude) and comparative observation of eclipses (for degrees of longitude). One could thus establish a "grid-system" of such coordinates for plotting the location of every settlement (cities, towns, villages) and every prominent physical feature (mountains, rivers, bays, islands, capes and straits). Perhaps this idea came to Hipparchus by analogy with an architectural feature synonymous with the Hellenistic age: the "grid" or rectilinear system of city-planning popularized by Hippodamus of Miletus (fifth century B.C.).[17]

Whatever its origin such a system was ideally suited for mapping the Mediterranean, a region roughly rectangular and relatively well-known to Graeco-Roman cartographers. That same system of map-making would also work well for plotting the main features and settlements of the west-Asian region: Mesopotamia, Persia and Bactria. But distortions occurred if the grid was extended farther north or south than those central areas.[18] Hipparchus the mathematician must have recognized the difficulty of making a flat map of a spherical earth, but there is no indication that he addressed the problem. Nor is there any evidence that Marinus, following him, was concerned.

16 G.M. Lewis in J.B. Harley and D. Woodward (eds.), *The History of Cartography* (Chicago, 1987) Vol. I p. 53.

17 Hipparchus was born at Nicaea in Bithynia, the only Hellenistic city for which we have a written description (Strabo, *Geog*. 12.4.7-8) of its "Hippodamian" plan. Alexandria (Egypt), also described in detail by Strabo, was laid out in "Hippodomian style". Hipparchus spent his mature years in the city of Rhodos on the island of the same name.

18 O. Neugebauer, *The Exact Sciences in Antiquity* (2nd ed., Providence, 1957) p. 220.

The theory behind a system of coordinates was sound, but impractical given the limitations of Hipparchus' time. Latitudes were relatively simple to calculate as long as the sun could be seen clearly. Longitudes required a coordinated system of simultaneous observers at many points during a solar eclipse. In lieu of widespread scientific observations Marinus was forced to settle for a system of dead reckoning based on travel reports compiled by merchants and officials, and the publications of earlier geographers. This led him to fix positions and calculate distances in an approximate way for all regions beyond the Mediterranean. The farther removed the place from Marinus' own desk the greater was the risk of error. Ptolemy could do no better (though he claimed to) and in some very noticeable ways seems to have done worse.[19]

The central focus on any "grid-map" of the *oikoumenê* was the island of Rhodes, which Marinus and others believed lay conveniently on the parallel of latitude (36 degrees north) that passed between the Straits of Gibraltar, through the port of Issus (Alexandretta/Iskandarûn) on the coast of what is now south-east Turkey, and included the fabled city of Ecbatana in central Persia. Rhodes thus lay mid-way between the latitudes of Thule to the north and Ethiopia to the south. Those were the realistic limits; beyond them maps were drawn with more speculation than verifiable information.

Rhodes also lay at a longitude of fifty-eight degrees east, about halfway between the Canary Islands and the Punjab region of the upper Indus River. The latter was the easternmost point of Alexander's conquest and exploration and it represented the real limit of practical geographical knowledge of the Far East. Rhodes was therefore the *locus locorum* of classical geographers from the Hellenistic period until late antiquity. It may have seemed appropriate to Hipparchus that the city of Rhodos at the northern tip of the island was said to have been laid out on the ground (in 408 B.C.) in rectilinear fashion by Hippodamus.[20]

The inherent difficulty with a grid-system of mapping was failure to compensate for the curvature of the earth. This could be minimized by construction of a series of flat maps in sheets rather than attempting a representation of a mathematical sphere. That is probably what Marinus had rendered in the maps drawn to accompany his commentaries, and it would seem that his maps were far easier to consult than his written commentaries. Ptolemy specifically complains that a major flaw in those commentaries was that the latitude and longitude of any given place had to be sought in different sections. Perhaps in a later edition, Ptolemy hints, Marinus' revisions would have included the principles of true map "projections" and systematic tables of coordinates available for consultation by anyone without maps and from which accurate maps could

19 See (e.g.) his treatment of the British Isles (particularly the orientation of Scotland) and Italy as discussed by O.A.W. Dilke in Harley and Woodward, *History of Cartography* pp. 192-197.

20 We have the testimony of Strabo (*Geog*. 14.2.9) that the same architect who designed Athens' harbor of Piraeus also planned the city of Rhodes, namely Hippodamus. The standard argument that the architect's advanced age (he would have been about 90 by 408 B.C.) effectively disqualified him as the planner of Rhodes was successfully demolished by R.E. Wycherley, "Hippodamus and Rhodes," *Historia* 13 (1964) 135-139 (not noted in *OCD* (2nd ed.) p. 519 s.v. "Hippodamus").

be constructed. This was left for Ptolemy to do, a task he set about with a maximum of enthusiasm, a minimum of modesty and the resources of the Alexandrian library.

II

Strabo, Pliny, Ptolemy and the *Tabula Peutingeriana*: Cultural Geography and Early Maps of Phoenicia

INTRODUCTION: A REMINISCENCE OF AL GLOCK

In the late spring of 1979 I met Al Glock for the first time at the Albright Institute in Jerusalem. I had crossed into Israel from Jordan at the Allenby Bridge the previous day and, after a lengthy interlude at the border, took a "service" taxi to Ramallah where I stayed with old friends Hugh and Shirley Harcourt, former colleagues at the American University of Beirut. They and Al were on the faculty at Birzeit University, then closed for an indeterminate amount of time by the military governor of Ramallah. Hugh and Shirley had contacted Al on my behalf and were glad I could "service" into Jerusalem the following morning to meet him. That was not my only chance to make his acquaintance, but it is special to my memory because the topic of my contribution is directly related to it. It was also significant because Al was at that time "wearing two hats": one as head of the Albright Institute and the other as Professor of Archaeology at Birzeit University in the West Bank.

Al was waiting in the Director's Office and immediately made me feel welcome. He wanted to know if there had been any problems at the border, and whether the Old City had changed much since my last visit. I answered affirmatively to both questions. Al knew I had last been in east Jerusalem in 1966, fourteen months before the Israeli annexation during the "Six-Day War." He wanted me to fill him in on the situation in Lebanon, where the civil war was entering its fifth year. He asked me what my latest project was. I said "researching the geography of Lebanon." Al had a few maps of "The Holy Land" in his office and we made small-talk about them.

We had lunch at the Albright Institute and he drove me out to the new campus of Birzeit University. Bulldozers and scaffolding were the main features then, as the architect's plan began to take shape in the warm, white sunshine of a May afternoon. Al was enthusiastic as he conjured up images of the completed buildings that would house the classrooms and laboratories and storage area of his fondest dream, a new archaeological center. Later we drove the few kilometers to the old campus, within walking distance of where I was staying. A few administrators were there, but classes were suspended. The atmosphere was tense and uncertain.

Al was happy that I had read his recently published article "*Homo Faber*: The Pot and the Potter at Taanach" (*BASOR* 219 [1975]), a thought-provoking and articulate essay that explored aspects of what he termed his "philosophy of archaeology through ceramics." I mentioned that the Latin portion of the title (meaning "Creative Man") evoked the anthropological expression *Homo Habilis* ("Handy Man") given to an early branch of hominids who fashioned tools and weapons. He was pleased that I made the connection and we spent the remaining time together discussing the role of pottery in the evolution of archaeological techniques from the earliest typology sequences almost a century ago through the development of thermoluminescence, then still a sophisticated ceramic dating process in the experimental stages.

That led to the discovery that we both shared an interest in the relentless curiosity of Thomas Jefferson, who "excavated" an American Indian burial mound on his estate at Monticello. "Today it seems to be the American expatriates who know more than just the outlines of American history," he said. I suggested that it was no longer politically correct to dig into cemeteries whether they were in Virginia or in Israel. Al laughed. "In Jefferson's day no one understood that. He was interested in the *culture* of those who had lived on his property long before he settled there. His notebooks indicate that he had a rough idea of *stratification* within that mound. Not bad for the late eighteenth century, hmm?"

Al's digression on the Enlightenment's contribution to archaeology was, I learned subsequently, just one facet of his active mind. He expressed concern that his students at Birzeit develop a "Palestinian focus" for the fieldwork they did, realizing it was limited by the political situation that then obtained in the West Bank. I was also struck by his interest in the archaeology of the early Islamic period. He knew that Prof. Dimitri Baramki at the A.U.B. was one of few Palestinians who had turned to archaeology as a vocation during the British Mandate period. Baramki's 1940s excavations at the Umayyad-built "Palace of Hisham" (Khirbit al-Mafjar) had been "groundbreaking" in more than one sense.

In the late afternoon we said our goodbyes. Al had to drive back to Jerusalem and I would be departing the next day for the return trip to Amman. He asked, "what are you going to do with all those old maps of Lebanon?" I answered, "write up an article when I make sense of them." We shook hands and he slid behind the wheel of his car. "Don't forget," he added, "maps are more than just geography, more than just lines on a paper. They have some cultural information to convey as well. About the past as well as the present." I smiled. "Jefferson would've understood," I said.

That double emphasis on culture, I learned, was typical of Albert Ernest Glock. He had a highly developed sense of how the present might inform or instruct us in the way we understand the past, and how the past could teach us about the present. It was his legacy to his profession, to his students, to his colleagues, and to his friends and family. It is a worthy legacy of a good and gracious man.

This paper is dedicated to Al's respect for "the culture of archaeology" and "the culture of old maps." He himself, since that visit, has become part of the "cultural geography" of the Palestine he loved and, in a very real sense, to which he dedicated his life. As someone who had lived and worked a large portion of his adult life in the Near East, he understood that ancient Palestine and Phoenicia were not just contiguous regions.

They formed then a closely related cultural area; language was only one aspect of their symbiosis. Iron Age Phoenician and Biblical Hebrew were dialects of the older Canaanite lingusitic matrix. Language is simply a reflection of the culture from which it has come, and the Palestinian–Phoenician cultures of antiquity were almost indistinguishable at some levels. For that reason it seems appropriate to explore, in Al's honor, the topic of this essay.

THE PHOENICIAN HOMELAND

What the Phoenicians themselves thought and wrote about their "homeland" is almost totally unknown. Commentaries written by Marinus of Tyre (ca. AD 75–140), had they survived complete, might have offered some insights.[1] There is no reference to physical geography or topography in the fragments of Philo of Byblos' *Phoenician History* (published ca. AD 125). Perhaps the echo of a native voice praising the Phoenician countryside can be heard in some passages of the Old Testament (e.g. portions of Canticles, certain Psalms). This would be appropriate in light of the close cultural ties (fostered by economic and dynastic bonds) between Iron Age Phoenicia and Palestine. That material is best examined separately since it represents a "local" tradition and its context is poetic allusion rather than prose description.

From the Late Bronze Age through the end of classical antiquity there is mention of the Phoenicians (*Kinnaḥu, Chna, Phoinikês, Poeni, Chanani*) in written sources. Homer's "Sidonians" are evident in many pages of the *Iliad* and the *Odyssey* but nowhere is there a descriptive passage referring to their homeland. Herodotus (*Hist.* 2.44, see also 1.1; 7.89) related a visit to Tyre during a "tour" of the Levant (mid-fifth century BC), but it is not until the beginning of the Hellenistic Age (330–30 BC) that the first important *descriptive* accounts begin to appear in the aftermath of Alexander the Great's extended conquest.

Gradually we gain a fairly detailed picture of the Phoenician landscape, one that combines familiar characteristics with sometimes disconcerting images. For most minor sources, physical geography is incidental to some other purpose, e.g. descriptions of flora and fauna, the narrative of a military campaign, the production of purple or glass. Those noted here are representative, not exhaustive.

Three comprehensive accounts of Phoenician geography survive complete in portions of Strabo's *Geography*, Pliny the Elder's *Natural History* and Ptolemy's *Geography*. All three works are prefaced by statements of intent, the details and clarity of which vary. It will be worthwhile to outline here what all three had to say, so that the objectives of each can be compared and contrasted. This will also permit us to check the details of their descriptions against those stated intentions. It will also allow us to compare and contrast all three accounts against the evidence of an important, and probably independent source, the *Tabula Peutingeriana*. Though this document in its present form is a medieval copy of a map produced in late antiquity, portions of it may indicate that a prototype existed some centuries earlier.

Strabo held that the utilitarian aspects of geography should be of interest to "statesmen and governments, because they can conduct their affairs with greater satisfaction if they comprehend a country's size, its position and its unique features" (*Geog*. 1.1.1 with 1.1.16). Pliny's approach was equally pragmatic. He believed that the study of the natural world (*rerum natura*) would educate men of influence in the Roman state (*HN* Praef. 13).

Ptolemy's task was somewhat different, since his handbook (*hyphêgêsis*) was not a prose descriptive geography. Thus he first defines the term geography as "a representation (*mimêsis*) in pictures (i.e. maps) of the entire world and the phenomena therein" (*Geog*. 1.11) and then goes on to say that the geographer is obligated to portray his world accurately, to establish the boundaries of regions, to note the peoples, cities and physical features peculiar to each region, and to plot by longitude and latitude the location of each (*Geog*. 1.19).

These introductory comments do not touch upon what modern anthropologists would call the "social landscape" of a region: the relationship of geography to culture, the influence of a particular physical environment on the historical development of its human inhabitants. Such concerns are not modern, but they were never fully expressed in antiquity. Some pre-Socratics (e.g. Xenophanes) hinted at potential aspects of what we term "cultural anthropology." Perhaps no one in antiquity came closer to defining them than Herodotus, but even he stopped just short of exploring the link between environment and "national identity."

Herodotus had counted the Thracians potentially among "the greatest" of peoples (*Hist*. 5.3) of his day, but never speculated that the physical limitations imposed by their Balkan homeland could have thwarted the chances for unification and the development of a powerful nation-state.[2] In like manner he devoted all of Book 2 to Egypt, offering copious observations on Egyptian topography, ethnography, botany and climate. When he summarized this wealth of detail, his conclusion was that the changeless climate and "the gift of the river" (i.e. the Nile) produced the great differences between Egyptians and Greeks (*Hist.* 2.35; cf. 2.5; 2.77). But we must infer that it was those contrasting characteristics that made Egypt such a great nation for so long.

We look in vain for that kind of detail concerning Phoenicia. Precisely where we expect to find it there is only anecdote. That occurs when Herodotus breaks off his narrative of Egypt to tell us of a visit to Tyre. That visit (*Hist.* 2.44) produced one paragraph of information on the Phoenicians consisting of what he saw and heard in Tyre. Not a single word is devoted to the Phoenician landscape or national characteristics (apart from a sense of historical *tradition*) of the people. The latter comes, also in the form of anecdote, elsewhere in the *Histories*.

Even if he had apportioned as much space to Phoenicia as to Egypt or Persia, it is doubtful that any connection would have been drawn between the physical setting and the achievements of its people. Fortune and the Gods, he constantly reminds us, determine a person's and a nation's destiny, not Nature. Polybius might have been the one source from whom we could expect an analysis of geography's effect on history. Certainly he was concerned with the cause and effects of wars (*Hist.* 3.6–8) and had we all of Book 24 instead of the fragments gleaned from later writers (particularly Strabo and Pliny) that theme of cause and effect might have included geography and imperialism.

The caveat is clear: we should not ask more of our sources than they were meant to provide. Concomitantly no single source is consistently accurate, but the margin of error, be it the distance from seacoast to inland lake, or the location of a river's source, is sometimes astonishingly small. That can only be judged by comparison with the results of modern geographic surveys of the same region. For just such a purpose it would be prudent to begin a review of Phoenician geography in ancient sources with a brief account of the region as it appears on maps today, to review the important written evidence, and then to come full circle and examine last the land of Phoenicia as it appears in ancient maps.

EXCURSUS: A SKETCH OF LEBANESE GEOGRAPHY

The mountains of modern-day Lebanon (Arabic *Lubnân*, "White") are among the major features of middle eastern geography (fig. 1). The coastal range (Jebal Lubnân, Mt. Lebanon), parallel to its inland counterpart, extends some 175 km from north to south, with many of its western foothills reaching the Mediterranean. The loftiest tip (elev. 3,083 m) in this range is Qurnat Sawdâʾ (Black Nook) southeast of Tripoli. The inland range (Jebal Lubnân Sharqî, Mt. Lebanon East) is nearly equal in length with its highest point (elev. 2,814 m) at Mt. Hermôn (Holy Mountain), southeast of Tyre. This is the Jebal Shaykh ("Mt. Greybeard") of early Arabic geographers, so named as much for its imposing authority on the surrounding countryside as for its perpetual snow. The northern foothills of both ranges reach almost to Homs (ancient Emesa) in the Orontes valley. The Lebanon range presents a monolithic façade to the Mediterranean coast with no natural passes (other than difficult gorges) to the interior between Mt. Carmel in the south and the Eleutheros River valley to the north. Travel inland went over, not through; a day's journey in either direction consisted of a long, laborious ascent followed by a lengthy but somewhat less arduous descent.[3] *

In Graeco-Roman antiquity those parallel ranges were referred to simply as the Lebanon and Anti-Lebanon and the plain between them as the *Aulôn* (Valley) of Syria or *Koilê* Syria ("Hollow" Syria). Today that valley is called in Arabic *Biqâʿ* (the "hollow" or "depression"; Wild 1973, 290–91; cf. Joshua 11:17 [*Biqât ha-Libânôn* "Valley of Lebanon"]). It is roughly 17 km wide and 160 km in length, at an average elevation of 800 m. Two modest but lengthy rivers, the Nahr al-ʿAsi (ancient *Orontes*) and the Lîtanî (ancient *Litas*), flow north and south respectively from springs and a major watershed in the upper (northern) end of the Biqâʿ (Abel 1933). Two riverine systems flow from the Anti-Lebanon range, the Hasbâni/Jordan to the south (from Hermôn) and the Nahr Baradâ (Bardines, Chrysorhoas) to the east (from Jebal Shaykh Mansûr).

Numerous rivers, none navigable inland, are born on the western slopes of the Lebanon range. Many reach the Mediterranean through gorges of often spectacular beauty, e.g. the valley of the Nahr Qadîsha ("Holy" River) southeast of Tripoli. The ancient name (Graeco/Roman

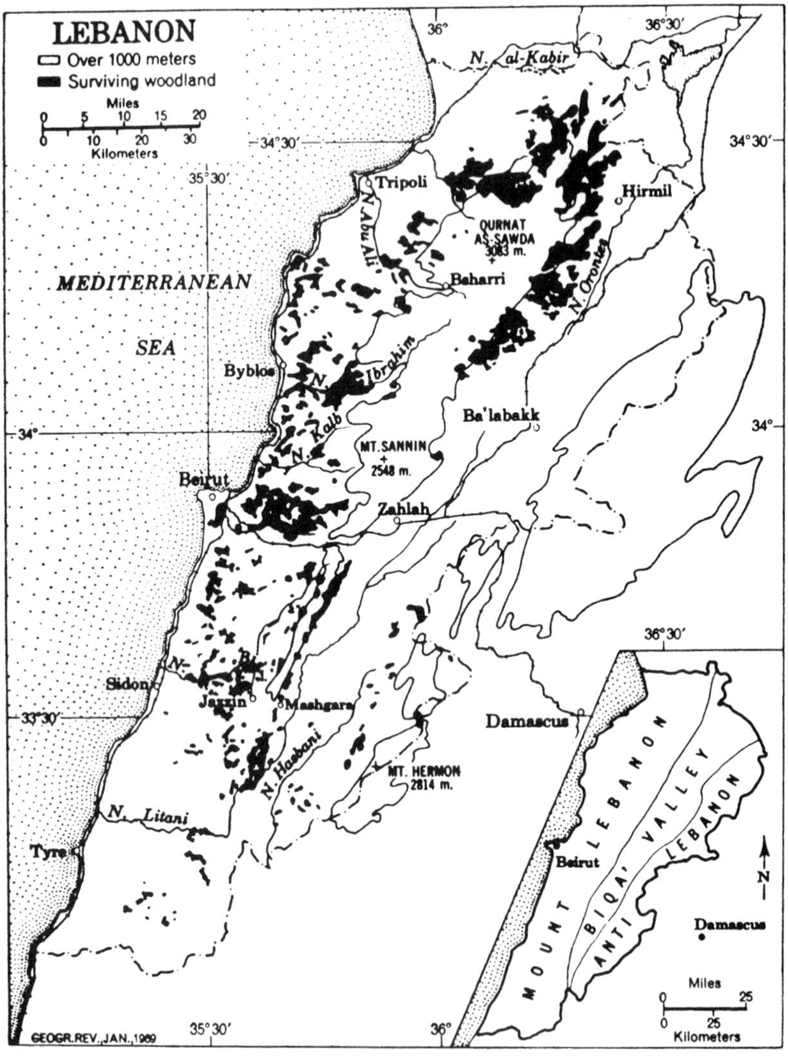

Fig. 1. Lebanon, generalized relief and surviving woodland. Reprinted with permission of *Geographical Review*.

or Semitic) of most is known. From north to south the principle rivers are the Nahr Kabîr (Eleutheros), Nahr Ibrâhîm (Adonis), Nahr Kalb (Lycus), Nahr Beirut (Magoras), Nahr Dâmûr (Damouras or Tamyras; also Leôn)[4] and Nahr Awwali (Bostrenus). The oldest stone bridges in Phoenicia are Roman, though it is possible that wooden bridges were constructed before then. Until bridges were built, a day's journey along the coast was nearly as difficult as taking the inland route. Even when men and animals did not have to ford the rivers and streams, they still had to tackle the narrow walkways or "ladders" (Greek *klimakês*; Latin *scala*) around the headlands (Arabic sing. *râs*) that protruded into the sea in half a dozen places. The *Scala Tyriorum* (Ladders of Tyre) at Râs Nâqûra was only the most famous of those. Sailing was a much faster and commercially much cheaper way to communicate along the coast. For a country bereft of any good natural harbors, it was a strong incentive to build both ships and ports. Before they developed an alphabet and were called Phoenicians, the inhabitants of the Canaanite littoral must have perfected a *lingua nautica*.

The Lebanese mountains were celebrated in antiquity as a place of beauty, a source of water and timber (fig. 2), a sanctuary for refugees, a base of operations for brigands and a home for the deities of Phoenicia. Quite understandably they became part of the folklore of the indigenous Canaanites and the neighboring peoples. For outsiders from lowlying and arid regions near or far, the first sight of such majestic mountains, especially in winter, must have been memorable. Some episodes of the Sumero-Babylonian *Epic of Gilgamesh* may be located in the Lebanese mountains[5] and the Old Testament abounds with references both historical and mythological.[6]

PHOENICIA IN THE HELLENISTIC PERIOD

Two of Aristotle's pupils had a firsthand acquaintance with Phoenicia and its fabulous geography. Alexander the Great was forced

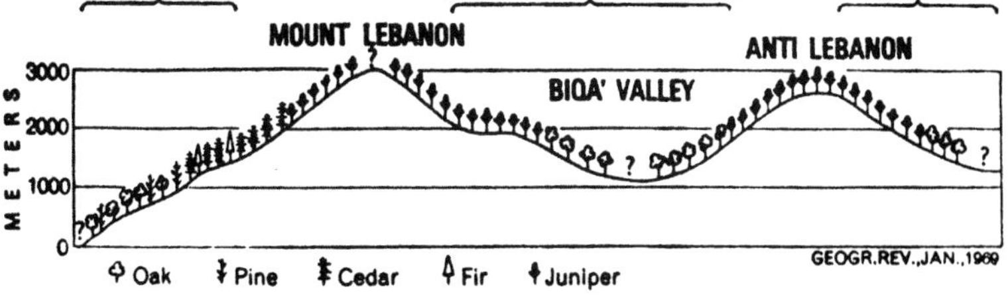

Fig. 2. Profile of primordial or potential forest cover. Reprinted with permission of *Geographical Review*.

to lead a punitive expedition into the mountains behind Tyre to counter "guerillas" who harassed his troops during the great seige of that city in the summer of 332 BC. All accounts[7] of this raid have Alexander and a "flying column" cross the Biqâʿ Valley as far as "Arabia" (i.e. the territory in the Anti-Lebanon range [and farther east] controlled by Arab tribesmen). The military objective may have been more than a display of force; one scholar has suggested that the raid was intended to open a much-needed supply line to the agricultural interior (Engels 1978, 56). Plutarch's biography of Alexander highlights this episode by inserting an account of hand-to-hand combat with Lebanese mountaineers, an incident Plutarch borrowed from the memoires of Alexander's chamberlain or Master of Ceremonies, Chares of Mytilene:

> In the middle of the seige [late April–early May, 332 BC] he made an expedition against the Arabs who lived near Antilibanus and he ran into danger because of Lysimachus his *paidogogos* (for Lysimachus accompanied him, saying he was as good as and no older than Phoenix). When Alexander reached the hill-country and, leaving his horse behind, advanced on foot, the others went a long way ahead; but when Lysimachus began to grow weary and faint, though evening was coming on and the enemy were near at hand, Alexander refused to leave him; and encouraging him and helping him along with a few companions he unexpectedly found himself cut off from the main body and obliged to spend the night in a wild spot in darkness and extreme cold. Then he saw, at a distance, a number of scattered fires of the enemy burning; and trusting to his own nimbleness and endurance, while himself continually encouraging the despairing Macedonians, he ran up to the nearest party that was burning a fire; with his dagger he struck at two barbarians who were sitting over the fire, and snatching up a firebrand returned with it to his companions; they built a large fire and immediately frightened some of the enemy into flight and turned back a party that attacked; and so they passed the night safely. This at least is the story Chares has told. (*Alex*. 24:6–8).[8]

Plutarch's editorial remark is worth noting. He may have doubted the veracity of the incident, but it was too colorful to pass over in silence. Certainly the ambiance is evocative of Lebanese mountain weather in mid-spring, balmy and invigorating during the day but still dangerously cold at night. Substantial pockets of snow remain in shaded ravines at the higher elevations until early summer. Though some details of this episode were undoubtedly embroidered, it has the aura of versimilitude if not verifiable authenticity.

Another Aristotelian protegé, Theophrastus, left a vivid description of aromatic plants that grew in the *Aulôn* ("the Valley") of Lebanon, i.e. the Biqâ'. So vivid is his presentation that one suspects we are reading the words of an observant traveler who described what he saw ca. 300 BC:

> Sweet-flag (*calamus*) and ginger-grass (*schoinus*) grow beyond the Libanus between that range and another small range, in the depression (*aulôniskos*) thus formed; and not, as some say, between Libanus and Antilibanus. For Antilibanus is a long way from Libanus, and between them is a wide, fair plain called "the Valley" (*Aulôn*). But, where the sweet-flag and ginger-grass grow, there is a large lake, and they grow near it in the dried-up marshes, covering an extent of more than thirty *stadia* (6 km) ... as you approach the spot, immediately a sweet smell strikes you. However it is not true, as some say, that the fragrance is wafted to ships approaching the country [i.e. Phoenicia]; for indeed this district is more than 150 *stadia* (30 km) from the sea. (*Inquiry into Plants* 9.7.1–3).[9]

The location within the Biqâ' of this *aulôniskos* (literally "little valley") and its fragrant lake has occasioned some debate.[10] The figure of "more than 30 km" from the sea given in Theophrastus' account may be explained as a straight line distance. If so, it is remarkably accurate. The modern road-distance from Beirut directly east to Shtoura, on the western edge of the Biqâ', is exactly 45 km. As the crow flies a figure of "more than 30 km" for that same distance is quite reasonable. Theophrastus' account is devoid of any village or town names and his "generic" designation for the central valley, *Aulôn*, may mean that the indigenous name for this segment of the Great Rift Valley was unknown to him or his source. Besides his botanical observations, Theophrastus also left us commentary on limestone and limeburning in Phoenicia, the forest-cover and royal "parks," the names of Phoenician winds, and Tyrian law.

Less than half a century later, a reference to the same valley under the name *Massyas* occurs in a papyrus document discovered in the discarded archives of the Finance Minister under King Ptolemy II of Greek-ruled Egypt. The document (*Papyrus Cairo Zenon* #59093 of 257 BC) records various legal and illegal transactions and customs-difficulties involving the purchase and transshipment of Phoenician and other goods (including slaves) from Phoenicia to Egypt. In passing, there is a reference to an expedition for the purpose of securing horses "in Massyas [Valley]." Whatever was purchased (or rustled) eventually found its way into the cargo of an Alexandria-bound merchant ship soon departing from Sidon or Tyre.[11]

Later still, Polybius relates a series of military campaigns during the Fourth Syrian War with Egypt (221–217 BC) in which Seleucid forces attempted to enter Ptolemaic Palestine either through the "Marsyas" (sic) Valley or along the Phoenician coast road. His description of the Lebanese Biqâʿ is dramatic and accurate:

> From this town [Laodiceia-under-Lebanon] the king [Antiochus III] took the offensive with his whole army and crossing the desert entered the defile (*aulôn)* known as Marsyas, which lies between the chains of Libanus and Antilibanus, and affords a narrow passage between the two. Just where it is narrowest it is broken by marshes and lakes from which the perfumed reed (*calamus* = sweet-flag) is cut, and here it is commanded on the one side by a place called *Brochoi* ("Springs") and on the other by *Gerrha*, the passage between being quite narrow. After marching through this defile for several days and reducing the towns in its neighborhood, Antiochus reached Gerrha" (*Hist.* 5.45.7–5.46.2).[12]

The Ptolemaic commander of Gerrha secured his position with ditch and stockade; a frontal assault by Seleucid forces failed to breach the defences. That signal failure, plus trouble in the northern portion of his kingdom, persuaded Antiochus to abandon the enterprise. In the spring of 219 BC he again attacked the garrisons at Brochoi and Gerrha (*Hist.* 5.61.5–10). Leaving a sizeable force to besiege them, Antiochus out-maneuvered the enemy by a coastal attack into Palestine. It took a third campaign the following year to occupy Palestine and Transjordan. But an attempt to invade Egypt itself in 217 BC resulted in a disastrous defeat at the battle of Raphia. The Biqâʿ and coastal Phoenicia south of the Eleutheros River remained in Ptolemaic hands.

Polybius leavened his central discussion of politics and matters military with an occasional excursus on descriptive geography. He knew, for instance, that the source of the Orontes River lay in Phoenician territory. His detailed account of Seleuceia (the port of Antioch) includes a note to that effect. Polybius states that the city lay at the mouth of the Orontes:

> [A river] which, rising in the neighborhood of Libanus and Antilibanus and traversing what is known as the plain of Amyce [in modern Syria that plain is still called *'Amq*], passes through Antioch carrying off all the sewage of that town by the force of its current and finally falls into the Cyprian Sea near Seleuceia. (*Hist.* 5.59.10–12 [Loeb trans.]).

While the Ptolemies controlled Phoenicia, the already ancient shrine of Baʿalbak was renamed Heliopolis. When Phoenicia eventually passed under Seleucid rule, one or more members of that Macedonian dynasty planned to develop the site as a major Hellenistic sanctuary.[13] The project was inherited, unfinished, by the Roman governors of Syria who took office after Pompey the Great (63 BC) brought much of the Near East within the imperial domains. On the foundation blocks of a shrine (presumably originally dedicated to Apollo Helios) begun by the Seleucid kings, the Emperor Augustus later caused to be raised a temple of awesome dimensions and spectacular appointments that was dedicated to Jupiter of Heliopolis.

It was there that Trajan (perhaps in the company of his architect Apollodorus of Damascus) came ca. AD 115 on the eve of his Parthian war to consult the Oracle (Macrobius, *Saturnalia* I.23.14–16). The remaining six columns of this colossal temple still dominate the skyline of the northeastern Biqâʿ Valley. Until the outbreak of the Lebanese civil war in 1975 these and other equally imposing ruins served as the setting for the international Baʿalbak Festival where, of a summer's evening, one could enjoy a concert by Ella Fitzgerald, a performance by the Bolshoi Ballet, or a play by Euripides.

PHOENICIA IN THE ROMAN PERIOD

In the twilight years of Seleucid rule the Ituraean Arabs[14] from east and south of the Anti-Lebanon established a capital at the site Polybius called Gerrha (modern ʿAnjar, perhaps the *Chalkis* ["Bronze"-town][15] of later writers) in the southern Biqâʿ Valley and a secondary stronghold in the ancient Bronze Age city of Arca (Tell ʿArqa) northeast of Tripoli. They proceeded to terrorize the coastal communities and the inland farms of Phoenicia until Roman forces under Pompey infiltrated the hill country, stormed the bandit headquarters and executed the ringleaders.[16]

Evidence that endemic banditry survived in the Phoenician mountains is given by a Latin inscription dating from the time of the famous "census of Quirinius" alluded to in Luke 2:1–5. A military prefect serving under Quirinius (consular governor of Syria 9–6 BC) attests that he carried out a census of Apamea in Syria and led an expedition "against the Ituraeans of Mt. Lebanon (*in Libano monte*) and captured a castle of theirs" (*Inscriptiones Latinae Selectae* #2683). Eventually the Romans suppressed these desperadoes. The Ituraean stronghold of Arca later achieved fame, under the romanized name of *Caesarea ad Libanum*, as the birthplace of the third century emperor Alexander Severus (AD 225–233; Starcky 1971/72).

The mountains of Phoenicia attracted the attention of the Roman historian Tacitus. In the early years of the second century AD he penned this brief but evocative description:

> Of the mountains, Lebanon rises to the greatest height, and is in fact a marvel, for in the midst of the excessive heat its summit is shaded by trees and covered with snow; it likewise is the source and supply of the river Jordan. (*Hist.* 5.6 [Loeb trans.]).

It would seem that Tacitus conflated descriptions of the higher peaks of the coastal mountains with Mt. Hermôn at the southern edge of the interior range. This makes sense in the context of his narrative point of view: his comments are part of a sketch of Judaea and adjacent regions. The beauty of the forest, the grandeur of its ambience, the magic of its summer snow, the gift of its waters to an arid land: all that is parenthetical background to his now-lost account of the Roman capture of

Jerusalem in AD 70. Turn the seasons around and one would expect to find somewhere in ancient sources a description of Phoenicia in winter. There is none. That was left to the Ministry of Tourism in the modern Republic of Lebanon: colorful posters advertising "sea and ski" in the same winter day, featuring lifts and lodges just a few hours' drive from sun-dappled Mediterranean beaches (and Beirut nightclubs in the evening).

But the great, green forests are now secluded groves, melancholy reminders that much has been lost. Defoliation is not a modern phenomenon; its effects in Phoenicia were noticeable not long after the time of Tacitus. The pragmatic Hadrian (AD 117–138), near the end of his reign, designated specific areas of the coastal mountains as an imperial forest, and delineated its extent with boundary-markers at intervals along the western and eastern flanks of the coastal range. The motivations were not purely ecological, but it was evident even then that some of the Mediterranean forests were in danger of extinction.

PHOENICIA IN THE BYZANTINE PERIOD

In the early Byzantine period, Eusebius of Caesarea (ca. 325) remarked in his *Chronicon* (trans. and commentary in Brown 1969, 82–84) that proof of the biblical Flood could be seen in fossilized sea-life in the Phoenician mountains. About a century later, St. Jerome affirmed that snow from Mt. Hermôn was welcomed as a summertime luxury by certain residents of Tyre.[17] A Graeco-Egyptian poet named Nonnus, a contemporary of Jerome, wrote the *Dionysiaca*, an epic describing the adventures of the god Dionysus in his travels to India and back. Part of the poem describes the seasonal pattern of life for "a farmer of Libanus."[18] A still-later Byzantine text notes that:

> Democritus records a natural signal, and advises the planting [of wheat and barley] at the setting of *Corona* [*Borealis*—the northern constellation]. Not only are abundant rains likely to fall then, but the earth has a natural receptive tendency to render fertile the seeds sown at that time. The setting of *Corona* in the regions of Phoenicia takes place roughly speaking on the 7th day before the *kalends* of December [November 25]." (trans. Brown 1969, 20 with commentary)

The tenth century AD compiler of this text cited a number of earlier sources, among them a *Collection of Farming Occupations* by Vindanius Anatolius of Beirut (fourth century AD?) from which this notation is probably taken. Perhaps it was belated recognition in the Byzantine age that the pagan, celestial deities still had some influence upon the activities of man, especially upon those who farmed the Phoenician littoral and the great inland valley. The Democritus of this text may or may not be the fifth century BC "pre-Socratic" credited with the "atomic" theory of matter and scolded by Pliny (*Natural History* 30.9) for popularizing "magical works" discovered in the tomb of "Dardanus the Phoenician." Strabo reported (*Geog.* 16.2.24) a tradition known to Poseidonius of Apamea that "the ancient doctrine concerning atoms is [that] of Mochus of Sidon, born before the time of the Trojans." There is a complex web of literary and "scientific" tradition involved in this that cannot be unraveled here and is best discussed in another context.

Even so brief a review of literary/historical references may serve to demonstrate the constant interest evoked by the physical geography of Phoenicia throughout antiquity. Two other sources must now be examined: comprehensive descriptions and pictorial representations (i.e. ancient maps). As will be shown, there are detailed but conflicting descriptions of Phoenicia in Strabo's *Geography* and Pliny the Elder's *Natural History* and a schematic account in the text of Ptolemy's *Geography* (see Appendices). The extant maps of Phoenicia are also a mixed blessing. We can study medieval copies of two Graeco-Roman maps that illustrate vividly how Phoenicia appeared to anyone in antiquity with access to such documents.[19] Here again the evidence is contradictory. Let us begin with the descriptive accounts.

STRABO AND PLINY ON PHOENICIA

Strabo probably set down what he knew about Phoenicia during a sojourn in Alexandria between 24 and 20 BC It was evident to him that the mountains were the most distinctive features of the country and, accordingly, they dominate his account (*Geog.* 16.2.15–34). His descriptive point of view is from the seacoast looking inland. Mt. Libanus, he says, *runs inland from the headland of Theouprosôpon* ("God's Face," modern *Râs Shakka*) just south of Tripoli. The Anti-

Libanus range *runs parallel to it from the coast near Sidon*. Both ranges terminate "above" (i.e. beyond) Damascus in the Syrian interior.

Between them lies a plain (part of "Hollow [*Coele*] Syria"), 200 *stadia* (40 km) wide and 400 *stadia* (80 km) long. This plain is well-watered by rivers, among them the Jordan, the Chrysorhoas ("Gold-Flowing", modern Wadi Baradâ) "rising (*arxámenos*) in the city and *territorium* of Damascus," and a third called the *Lycus* ("Wolf," modern Nahr Kalb), which empties into the Mediterranean. Strabo states that both the Lycus and the Jordan are navigable inland and are used for transport by ship, particularly merchant-vessels from the island-city of Aradus (now Ruʿad island within modern Syria).

His description becomes even more detailed when the single great plain between the mountains is shown to be composite. There are in reality two plains, the *Macra* or *Macras*-Plain near the seacoast and the *Massyas* inland. The latter in places is mountainous, with Chalkis as "the acropolis, so to speak, of the Massyas." Beyond Massyas is a "Royal Valley" about which we are told nothing, and farther yet is the city and territory of Damascus. But then he summarizes his discussion by saying,

> the entire country south of Seleuceia [the coastal district of Syria], as far as Egypt and Arabia, is called *Coele Syria*, but the part delimited by the Libanus and Anti-Libanus is given that name in a special sense. The remainder [of Coele Syria] from Orthosia [near Aradus] to Pelusium [in the eastern delta of Egypt] is called Phoenicia, a narrow corridor of land, some of which projects into the sea.

Pliny, writing no later than AD 77, is also aware of the Phoenician mountains. The Libanus range, he says, begins behind Sidon and extends to Zimyra (near Aradus), some 1,500 *stadia* (300 km) away. "Opposing [Libanus], with a valley between, is Antilibanus, once connected [to Libanus] by a wall" (*NH* 5.77). East of the Antilibanus range is the region of the Decapolis; south of Antilibanus is Palestine. The Orontes River, he notes, "rises (*natus*) between Libanus and Antilibanus next to Heliopolis" (*NH* 5.80). His list of coastal cities belonging to Phoenicia begins, as does Strabo's, with Aradus in the north but ends with Caesarea (Straton's Tower) in the south.

Pliny implies that he considers the great interior plain and the Antilebanon range as parts of Greater Syria, since he uses the term

Coele Syria to describe the Orontes Valley north of the Biqâʿ. It is evident that he read Theophrastus' account of the aromatic plants from the Aulôn since his own discussion of *calamus* notes that it is found in "a medium size valley ... about 150 stades from *Mare Nostrum* (the Mediterranean) between Libanus and another low mountain—not, as some think, Antilibanus" (*NH* 12.104). Pliny locates the river Jordan in Palestine, and knows that it flows south to the Dead Sea.

There is little hope of reconciling these two conflicting descriptions of Phoenicia. The garbled account of Strabo testifies to his own ignorance. Somehow he managed to travel to and from Egypt bypassing Phoenicia, since even in his detailed sketches of Aradus (16.2.13–14) and Tyre (16.2.23–24) his information is attributed not to a named historian or geographer but to an anonymous "(as) it is said." Throughout the *Geography* he credits Poseidonius and Polybius for specific geographical information, but his sources for Phoenicia remain unknown to us.

In the face of that, one is at a loss to explain such basic errors in Strabo as the east–west alignment of the mountain system, his estimate of the size of the intervening valley, and his comments on certain rivers. Strabo's Massyas plain is approximately twice the width and half the length of the Biqâʿ. Worse yet, the width of the valley should correspond to the distance between Theouprosôpon and Sidon (120 km), western terminal points (as Strabo tells us) of the Lebanon and Antilebanon ranges. Yet he gives the breadth of the valley as only one-third that figure.

Were it not for those fundamental mistakes, the details of his description would appear less bizarre than they do. There is today a large plain northeast of Tripoli, the *ʿAkkâr* ("Dark," perhaps from deposits of alluvial silt), which corresponds in name and location to Strabo's Macras.[20] The Royal Valley beyond the Massyas is recognizable as *Abilenê*, a tetrarchy (princedom) tucked in a fold of the eastern Antilebanon and known to Josephus (*Antiquities of the Jews* 19.5.1; *Jewish War* 2.11.5) and the author of the Gospel of Luke (3:1).[21]

Chalkis is identified as the key strategic site in the Biqâʿ. In an earlier passage (*Geog.* 16.2.10), Strabo correctly associates Chalkis and Heliopolis. Strabo's account of the Jordan River reaching the Mediterranean coast is difficult to understand unless one makes the desperate effort of emending the Greek text to read *Orontes* instead of

Iordanes.[22] But there is no semantic fig leaf that will hide the embarrassment of his observation that Damascus is the source, rather than the gift, of the Chrysorhoas River.

The source of Pliny's more accurate description is not noted in his text but it is obvious he did not consult Strabo or Strabo's source(s). Neither does it seem that he ever traveled to Phoenicia, in spite of attempts to restore his name in an honorary inscription from Aradus.[23] There are well-documented instances where Pliny utilized military records available to him (e.g. *NH* 6.14) or had access to maps prepared to accompany campaign accounts—especially the eastern campaigns of Cn. Domitius Corbulo and C. Licinius Mucianus (*NH* 6.40). It is very probable that he made use of such reports, some as recent as the Jewish War of AD 66–74 which Pliny knew of as a conflict in progress.

Pliny's note on the source of the Orontes at Heliopolis/Baʿalbek is accurate (and unique), but his estimation of the length of the mountain ranges is almost double what it should be. Remains of the "connecting wall" between the Lebanon and Antilebanon ranges have been traced on the ground (Ghadban 1981, 143–68, esp. 158–59).[24] There is no mention in Pliny of the fortress town of Gerrha.

Neither Strabo nor Pliny attempts to define the political situation obtaining at the time he wrote. Phoenicia was part of geographical Syria; for Pliny this includes the Massyas Valley (unnamed in his account). Strabo's belief that Phoenicia included coastal Palestine (*Philistia*) as far as Pelusium agrees with the statement in Josephus (*AJ* 15.5.1) that Antony gave Cleopatra the Phoenician cities (except Sidon and Tyre) "between the Eleutherus River and Egypt." That exaggerated view may mean that "Phoenicia" and "Coele Syria" (the latter in its broadest geographical context) were for them (or their sources) synonymous.

PTOLEMY OF ALEXANDRIA AND PHOENICIA

It would be useful now to compare the evidence of ancient maps with the testimony of Strabo and Pliny. Some caution must be expressed at once since our sources are very meagre and in every case the original map is no longer available for consultation. Indeed, a healthy dose of skepticism concerning the practical value of Graeco-Roman maps and itineraries has very recently been voiced (Bekker-Nielsen 1988). But even so, the evidence of maps cannot be ignored. Maps drawn to illustrate Ptolemy's *Geography* were probably produced in his lifetime. Many facsimile editions have appeared since the medieval period (with Latin or Greek notations),[25] but since all are based on the figures compiled in Ptolemy's handbook, the variations are minimal (fig. 3). Their value lies entirely in the visual image, the ability to render in a meaningful pattern the dry list of place-names and coordinates of the *Geography*.

Ptolemy's "Phoenicia" appears twice (as a district of Syria) under the heading *Phoinikê*. First is a list of twelve coastal cities (*Geog*. 5.14.3–4), from Simyra to Dora, and features of physical geography. The latter include four rivers (the Eleutheros, Adonis (modern Nahr Ibrahîm), Leôn and Chorseos), the promontory of Theouprosôpon near Tripoli, and Mt. Carmel. A supplementary list (*Geog*. 5.14.17) gives four "inland" towns. The source of the river Jordan is correctly located at Caesarea Panias (modern Banias in Upper Galilee), one of those "interior" towns. Aradus and Tyre are listed as "islands adjacent to Syria" in a separate entry (*Geog*. 5.14.21).

So far we appear to be on firm ground. But a close comparison of handbook and map reveals some disturbing discrepancies. Under the heading Laodicenê (*Geog*. 5.14.16) are the names of two towns, Laodiceia (further identified as *Scabiosa* [= "Rough"] by Ptolemy) and Paradisus (in the upper Orontes Valley) associated with Phoenicia. Another town, Iabruda, he places in the tetrarchy of Abilenê. The Chrysorhoas River inexplicably flows *northwest* (!) to Damascus from the distant interior of Syria. The town of Palaeobyblos is located inland between Botrys and Byblos instead of on the coast between Byblos and Beirut.

But these oddities, however disconcerting, are minor compared to the disposition of the Lebanon and Antilebanon mountains. These are not associated with "Phoenicia" but are named (and their coordinates given) in a separate entry (*Geog*. 5.14.6–7) listing "the notable mountains of Syria." When their coordinates are actually plotted, Ptolemy's map shows the "Libanos and Antilibanos" mountains parallel to each other *but at nearly right angles to the Mediterranean*. Their latitudes correspond to those of Theouprosôpon and Sidon respectively, but the twin ranges begin at a considerable distance inland and terminate east of Damascus. This rearrangement actually places the

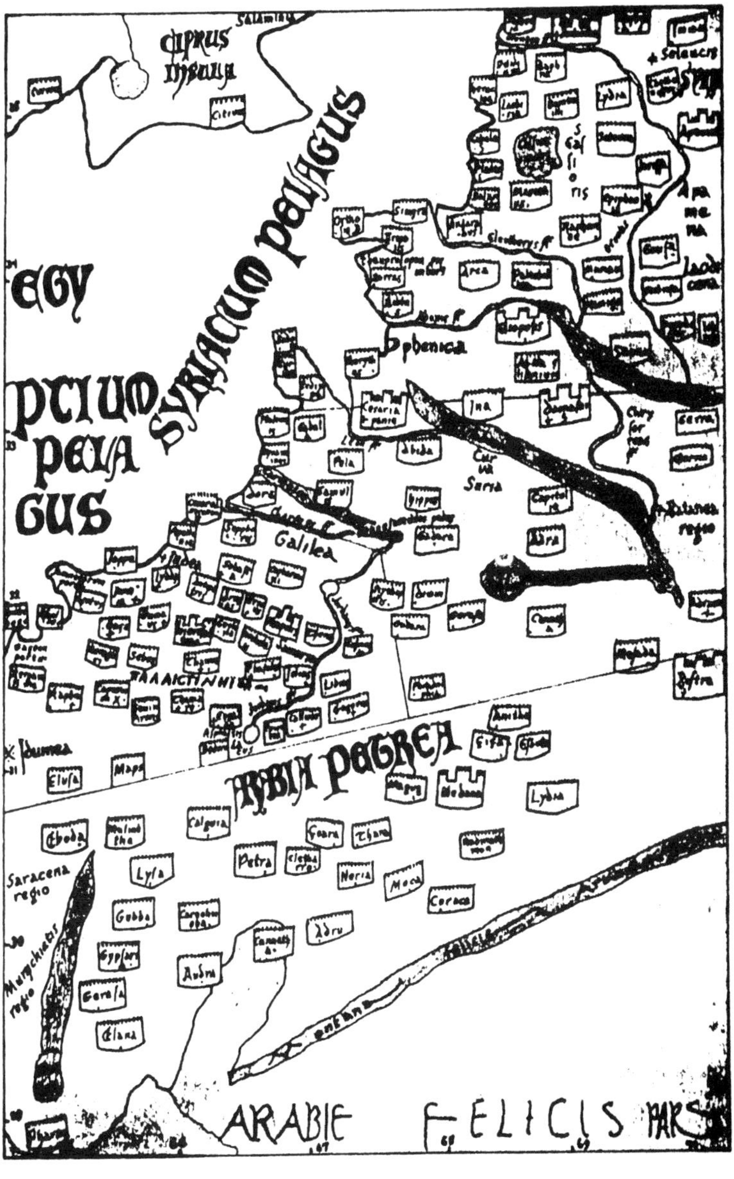

Fig. 3. A portion of the Ptolemaic map depicting the Near East based on the medieval copy of the Ptolemaic map in the *Vatican Urbinas Greek Codex* 82, ed. J. Fischer (Leiden: Brill, 1932). The physical features are copied from Fischer's pl. 19, but the Latin forms of most Greek names are taken from his pl. 46. Map enlarged from that given in R. North, *A History of Biblical Map-Making* (1979, 65 fig. 12). Reprinted with permission of L. Reichert Verlag.

mountains and their valley within *another* district of Syria called by Ptolemy "Coele Syria and the Decapolis." The latter entity (*Geog.* 5.14.18–19) includes eighteen cities, though it is not stated which belong to Coele Syria and which to the district or region called the Decapolis. Among the eighteen Ptolemy lists are Heliopolis, Abila (capital of Abilenê) and Damascus in west to east order between "Libanos and Antilibanos." Still farther east is another district named *Batanaea* (*Geog.* 5.14.20–21) in which a "Gerrha" is located. Such extraordinary disposition of topography, towns and territory associated with Phoenicia demands some explanation. Ptolemy has introduced an aspect of what might be called social or cultural geography.[26]

PHOENICIA IN THE *TABULA PEUTINGERIANA*

The eleven sheets comprising the *Tabula Peutingeriana* or Peutinger Maps are also of medieval vintage (fig. 4).[27] The map is a linear representation of the known world with the major emphasis on exact distances between towns and cities. The sheet on which northern Britain, the Iberian peninsula and the western half of North Africa were depicted is missing. The remaining portions of the map measure about 7 m in length by about one-third of a meter in width, an elongated rectangle (with inevitable distortions) showing the roads and major stopping-places between southern Britain and the Far East. Christian notations related to biblical place names clearly show that the Peutinger Map, or at least its Near Eastern segments, was in use from the fourth century AD Internal evidence demonstrates that the prototype of some segments (if not the entire map) dates from the first century AD. It is possible that the ultimate prototype was the famous *Orbis Terrarum* attributed to Marcus Agrippa (10 BC), which Pliny the Elder observed on the walls of the Agrippan Portico in Rome (NH 3.2.17).[28]

Fig. 4. (Opposite.) The *Peutinger Table*, enlarged segment showing Palestine, Lebanon, and Syria (K. Miller, *Die Peutingersche Tafel*, 2nd edition, 1929). Dark areas are the sea and light areas are land. Road distances and major stations are shown. The central portion of the lower third of the map shows two mountain ranges; the legend *PALESTINA* runs between them. Roman roads from Damascus (bottom, just right of center) run to Heliopolis (Baʿalbek) and thence to Berytus, or from Damascus via Caesarea Paneas through the costal range to Tyre. There is no indication of a Roman road *through* the Biqâʿ (i.e., from Heliopolis to Caesarea Paneas). Reprinted with permission.

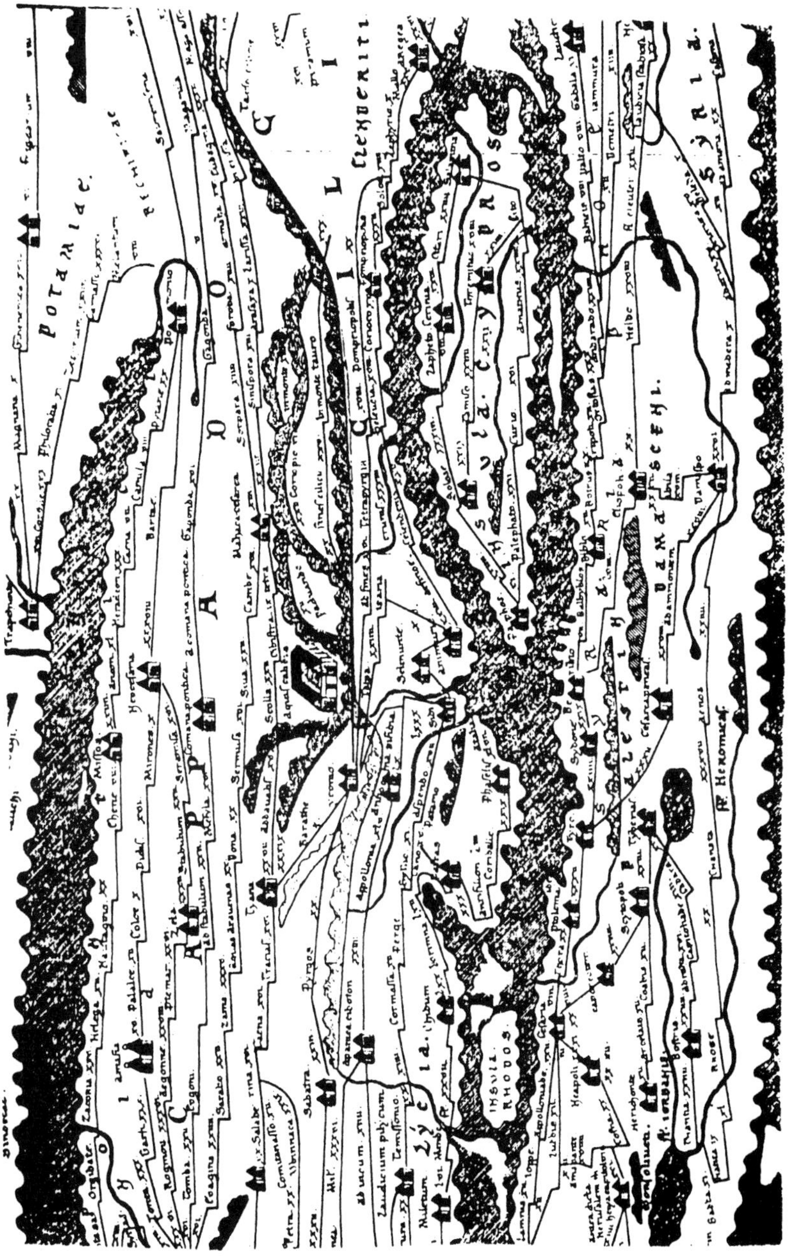

However that may be, the map as we have it dates from some centuries after Ptolemy. *Syria-Phoenici* is clearly labeled along the Mediterranean coast on Segment 10 of the map, extending as far north as the upper Orontes valley. The towns and cities of the Phoenician coast are shown as vignettes featuring the façade of a building. Parallel mountain ranges (unlabeled and not directly opposing each other) are shown inland, the outer (easternmost) running considerably farther north. The annotation *Palestina* obtrudes from the south into the valley between those mountains. Beyond the eastern range is *Damasceni*.

Two rivers are associated with Phoenicia: the Eleutheros with its mouth between Antarado(s) and Balneis (Balnea) on the northern coast and another, unnamed river, perhaps the Belus (*Nahr Naʿmân*),[29] debouching between Ptolemaide (Ptolemais) and Cesaria (Caesarea) on the southern coast. The coastal road is marked with appropriate stops and the mileage between each.

Two roads run inland from the coast, one from Tyre directly through the Lebanon range to Caesarea Paneas (the *Caesarea Philippi* of the New Testament), a distance of thirty-two Roman miles (47 km). The other runs from Berytus around the northern edge(?) of the Lebanon range to Eliopoli (Heliopolis). The distance shown is 108 Roman miles (158 km) with no stops indicated. That road bifurcates at Heliopolis, one branch going north to Laudicia (sic) Scabiosa and the other east to Abila and Damascus. The Jordan River, marked as such, flows directly from Lake Tiberias to the Dead Sea.

CONCLUSION

The descriptive geographies of Strabo and Pliny, and the Ptolemy and Peutinger Maps, represent four independent accounts of Phoenician geography. There are some superficial resemblances between texts and maps. This is most apparent when Strabo and Ptolemy err in the orientation of the Lebanon and Antilebanon or when Pliny and the Peutinger Map concur on the correct alignment of those mountains. But the discrepancies far outnumber the agreements. Strabo's Jordan reaches the coast, Ptolemy's flows to the Dead Sea. Pliny's Orontes and Jordan Rivers have their headwaters near Heliopolis and Caesarea Panias respectively. On the Peutinger Map the source of the Orontes is shown near Emesa and the Jordan is created by, instead of creating,

Lake Tiberias. In short there seems to be no reason, other than occasional coincidence of detail, to connect Strabo with Ptolemy, or Pliny with the Peutinger Map.

Where we might expect the descriptive accounts to draw some important parallels between the physical geography of Phoenicia, and the historical and cultural development of the Phoenicians, there is silence. That silence is all the more noticeable in light of the lofty intentions of both Strabo and Pliny set out in the prefaces to their respective works.[30] Pliny does at least manage in passing to note the contribution of the Phoenicians to Mediterranean culture when he states (*NH* 5.67) that "the Phoenician race has glorified itself by innovations in the alphabet, astronomy, navigation and the art of warfare."

Not a word there of how or why that came to pass. A few pages later (*NH* 5.76) we find this bittersweet remark for the city that founded Lepcis Magna, Utica, Gades and Carthage: "Now all of its glories reside in a mollusc and its purple." Such is his epitaph for Tyre. Strabo is also aware of Phoenician glories won and lost and notes (*Geog.* 16.2.23) that seamanship and dyemaking were the two skills in which "the Phoenicians excelled beyond all peoples." He is also careful to add (*Geog.* 16.2.24) that Greeks attribute to Phoenicians knowledge of astronomy and arithmetic "and many other philosophies from their cities."

PLINY, *NATURAL HISTORY* V, 15–17

A tergo eius Libanus mons orsus MD stadiis Zimyram usque porrigitur Coeles Syriae quae[2] cognominatur. huic par interveniente valle mons adversus Antilibanus obtenditur quondam muro coniunctus. post eum introrsus Decapolitana regio praedictaeque cum ea Tetrarchiae et Palaestines tota laxitas; in ora autem subiecta Libano fluvius Magoras, Berytus colonia quae Felix Iulia appellatur, Leontos Oppidum, flumen Lycos, Palaebyblos, flumen Adonis, oppida Byblos, Botrys, Gigarta, Trieris, Calamos, Tripolis quam Tyrii et Sidonii et Aradii optinent, Orthosia. Eleutheros flumen, oppida Zimyra, Marathos, contraque Arados septem stadiorum oppidum et insula ducentis passibus a continente distans; regio in qua supradicti desinunt montes: et interiacentibus campis Bargylus mons.

XVIII. Incipit hinc rursus Syria, desinente Phoenice. oppida Carne, Balanea, Paltos, Gabala, promunturium in quo Laodicea libera, Dipolis, Heraclea, Charadrus, Posidium. dein promunturium Syriae Antiochiae: intus ipsa Antiochia libera, Epi Daphnes cognominata, Oronte amne dividitur; in promunturio autem Seleucia libera Pieria appellata. super eam mons eodem quo alius nomine, Casius, cuius excelsa altitudo quarta vigilia orientem per tenebras solem aspicit, brevi circumactu corporis diem noctemque pariter ostendens. ambitus ad cacumen $\overline{XIX}$ p. est, altitudo per directum $\overline{IV}$. at in ora amnis Orontes natus inter Libanum et Antilibanum iuxta Heliopolim. oppida Rhosos—et a tergo Portae quae Syriae appellantur, intervallo Rhosiorum montium et Tauri,—in ora oppidum Myriandros, mons Amanus in quo oppidum Bomitae. ipse ab Syris Ciliciam separat.

Behind Sidon begins Mount Lebanon, a chain extending as far as Zimyra in the district called Hollow Syria, a distance of nearly 190 miles. Facing Lebanon, with a valley between, stretches the equally long range of Counter-Lebanon, which was formerly connected with Lebanon by a wall. Behind Counter-Lebanon inland is the region of the Ten Cities, and with it the tetrarchies already mentioned, and the whole of the wide expanse of Palestine; while on the coast, below Mount Lebanon, are the river Magoras, the colony of Beyrout called Julia Felix, Lion's Town, the river Lycus, Palaebyblos, the river Adonis, the towns of Jebeil, Batrun, Gazis, Trieris, Calamos; Tarablis, inhabited by people from Tyre, Sidon and Ruad; Ortosa, the river Eleutheros, the towns of Zimyra and Marathos; and facing them the seven-furlong town and island of Ruad, 330 yards from the mainland; the region in which the mountain ranges above mentioned terminate; and beyond some intervening plains Mount Bargylus.

XVIII. At this point Phoenicia ends and Syria begins again. There are the towns of Tartus, Banias, Bolde and Djebeleh; the cape on which the free town of Latakia is situated; and Dipolis, Heraclea, Charadrus and Posidium. Then the cape of Antiochian Syria, and inland the city of Antioch itself, which is a free town and is called 'Antioch Near Daphne,'[a] and which is separated from Daphne by the river Orontes; while on the cape is the free town of Seleukeh, called Pieria. Above Seleukeh is a mountain having the same name as the other one, Casius, which is so extremely lofty that in the fourth quarter of the night it commands a view of the sun rising through the darkness, so presenting to the observer if he merely turns round a view of day and night simultaneously. The winding route to the summit measures 19 miles, the perpendicular height of the mountain being 4 miles. On the coast is the river Orontes, which rises between Lebanon and Counter-Lebanon, near Baalbec. The towns are Rhosos,—and behind it the pass called the Gates of Syria, in between the Rhosos Mountains and Mount Taurus,—and on the coast the town of Myriandros, and Mount Alma-Dagh, on which is the town of Bomitae. This mountain separates Cilicia from Syria.

STRABO, *GEOGRAPHY* XVI, 15–18

15. Μετὰ δὲ Ὀρθωσίαν ἐστὶ καὶ τὸν Ἐλεύθερον Τρίπολις, ἀπὸ τοῦ συμβεβηκότος τὴν ἐπίκλησιν εἰληφυῖα· τριῶν γάρ ἐστι πόλεων κτίσμα, Τύρου, Σιδῶνος, Ἀράδου· τῇ δὲ Τριπόλει συνεχές ἐστι τὸ τοῦ Θεοῦ πρόσωπον, εἰς ὃ τελευτᾷ ὁ Λίβανος τὸ ὄρος· μεταξὺ δὲ Τριήρης, χωρίον τι.

16. Δύο δὲ ταῦτ᾿ ἐστὶν ὄρη τὰ ποιοῦντα τὴν Κοίλην καλουμένην Συρίαν,[1] ὡς ἂν παράλληλα, ὅ τε Λίβανος καὶ ὁ Ἀντιλίβανος, μικρὸν ὕπερθεν τῆς θαλάττης ἀρχόμενα ἄμφω· ὁ μὲν Λίβανος τῆς κατὰ Τρίπολιν, κατὰ τὸ τοῦ Θεοῦ μάλιστα πρόσωπον, ὁ δ᾿ Ἀντιλίβανος τῆς κατὰ Σιδόνα· τελευτῶσι δ᾿ ἐγγύς πως τῶν Ἀραβίων ὀρῶν τῶν ὑπὲρ τῆς Δαμασκηνῆς καὶ τῶν Τραχώνων[2] ἐκεῖ λεγομένων εἰς ἄλλα ὄρη γεώλοφα καὶ καλλίκαρπα. ἀπολείπουσι δὲ μεταξὺ πεδίον κοῖλον· πλάτος μὲν τὸ ἐπὶ τῇ θαλάττῃ διακοσίων σταδίων, μῆκος δὲ τὸ ἀπὸ τῆς θαλάττης εἰς τὴν μεσόγαιαν ὁμοῦ[3] τι διπλάσιον. διαρρεῖται δὲ ποταμοῖς ἄρδουσι χώραν εὐδαίμονα καὶ πάμφορον, μεγίστῳ δὲ τῷ Ἰορδάνῃ. ἔχει δὲ καὶ λίμνην, ἣ φέρει τὴν ἀρωματῖτιν σχοῖνον[4] καὶ κάλαμον, ὡς δ᾿ αὔτως καὶ ἕλη· καλεῖται δ᾿ ἡ λίμνη Γεννησαρῖτις. φέρει δὲ καὶ βάλσαμον. τῶν δὲ ποταμῶν ὁ μὲν Χρυσορρόας, ἀρξάμενος ἀπὸ τῆς Δαμασκηνῶν πόλεως καὶ χώρας, εἰς τὰς ὀχετείας ἀναλίσκεται σχεδόν τι· πολλὴν γὰρ ἐπάρδει καὶ βαθεῖαν σφόδρα·[5] τὸν δὲ Λύκον καὶ τὸν Ἰορδάνην ἀναπλέουσι φορτίοις, Ἀράδιοι δὲ μάλιστα.

17. Τῶν δὲ πεδίων τὸ μὲν πρῶτον, τὸ ἀπὸ τῆς θαλάττης, Μάκρας καλεῖται καὶ Μάκρα πεδίον· ἐν τούτῳ δὲ Ποσειδώνιος ἱστορεῖ τὸν δράκοντα πεπτωκότα ὁραθῆναι νεκρόν, μῆκος[6] σχεδόν τι καὶ πλεθριαῖον, πάχος δ᾿, ὥσθ᾿ ἱππέας ἑκατέρωθεν παραστάντας ἀλλήλους μὴ καθορᾶν, χάσμα δέ, ὥστ᾿ ἔφιππον δέξασθαι, τῆς δὲ φολίδος λεπίδα ἑκάστην ὑπεραίρουσαν θυρεοῦ.

18. Μετὰ δὲ τὸν Μάκραν ἐστὶν ὁ Μασσύας, ἔχων τινὰ καὶ ὀρεινά, ἐν οἷς ἡ Χαλκίς, ὥσπερ ἀκρόπολις τοῦ Μασσύου· ἀρχὴ δ᾿ αὐτοῦ Λαοδίκεια ἡ πρὸς Λιβάνῳ. τὰ μὲν οὖν ὀρεινὰ ἔχουσι πάντα Ἰτουραῖοί τε καὶ Ἄραβες, κακοῦργοι πάντες, οἱ δ᾿ ἐν τοῖς πεδίοις γεωργοί· κακούμενοι δ᾿ ὑπ᾿ ἐκείνων ἄλλοτε ἄλλης βοηθείας δέονται. ὁρμητηρίοις δ᾿ ἐρυμνοῖς χρῶνται, καθάπερ οἱ τὸν Λίβανον ἔχοντες ἄνω μὲν ἐν τῷ ὄρει Σινναν καὶ Βόρραμα καὶ ἄλλα τοιαῦτα ἔχουσι τείχη, κάτω δὲ Βότρυν καὶ Γίγαρτον καὶ τὰ ἐπὶ τῆς θαλάττης σπήλαια καὶ τὸ ἐπὶ τῷ Θεοῦ προσώπῳ φρούριον ἐπιτεθέν, ἃ κατέσπασε Πομπήιος, ἀφ᾿ ὧν τήν τε Βύβλον κατέτρεχον[1] καὶ τὴν ἐφεξῆς ταύτῃ Βηρυτόν, αἳ μεταξὺ κεῖνται Σιδόνος καὶ τοῦ Θεοῦ προσώπου.

15. After Orthosia and the Eleutherus River one comes to Tripolis,[1] which has taken its name from what is the fact in the case, for it is a foundation consisting of three cities, Tyre and Sidon and Aradus. Contiguous to Tripolis is Theuprosopon,[2] where Mt. Libanus terminates; and between the two lies Trieres, a kind of stronghold.

16. Here are two mountains, Libanus and Antilibanus, which form Coelê-Syria, as it is called, and are approximately parallel to each other. They both begin slightly above the sea—Libanus above the sea near Tripolis and nearest to Theuprosopon, and Antilibanus above the sea near Sidon; and somewhere in the neighbourhood of the Arabian mountains above Damascenê and the Trachones,[1] as they are called, the two mountains terminate in other mountains that are hilly and fruitful. They leave a hollow plain between them, the breadth of which, near the sea, is two hundred stadia, and the length, from the sea into the interior, is about twice that number. It is intersected by rivers, the Jordan being the largest, which water a country that is fertile and all-productive. It also contains a lake, which produces the aromatic rush[2] and reed; and likewise marshes. The lake is called Gennesaritis. The plain also produces balsam. Among the rivers is the Chrysorrhoas, which begins at the city and country of the Damasceni and is almost wholly used up in the conduits, for it irrigates a large territory that has a very deep soil; but the Lycus and the Jordan are navigated inland with vessels of burden, mostly by the Aradians.

17. As for the plains, the first, beginning at the sea, is called Macras, or Macra-Plain. Here, as reported by Poseidonius, was seen the fallen dragon, the corpse of which was about a plethrum[1] in length, and so bulky that horsemen standing by it on either side could not see one another; and its jaws were large enough to admit a man on horseback, and each flake of its horny scales exceeded an oblong shield in length.

18. After Macras one comes to the Massyas Plain, which contains also some mountainous parts, among which is Chalcis, the acropolis, as it were, of the Massyas. The beginning of this plain is the Laodiceia near Libanus. Now all the mountainous parts are held by Ituraeans and Arabians, all of whom are robbers, but the people in the plains are farmers; and when the latter are harassed by the robbers at different times they require different kinds of help. These robbers use strongholds as bases of operation; those, for example, who hold Libanus possess, high up on the mountain, Sinna and Borrama and other fortresses like them, and, down below, Botrys and Gigartus and the caves by the sea and the castle that was erected on Theuprosopon.[1] Pompey destroyed these places; and from them the robbers overran both Byblus and the city that comes next after Byblus, I mean the city Berytus,[2] which lie between Sidon and Theuprosopon.

NOTES

1. For Marinus' contribution see MacAdam (in press).
2. The tragic modern parallel is the present situation in what used to be known as Yugoslavia. There, the combination of cultural diversity and divisive physical geography is manifest. The closer we come to the beginning of the twenty-first century, the more the map of Europe begins to resemble the map of Europe precisely a century ago. In 1900 there was no Yugoslavia, no Soviet Union, and no Czechoslovakia; Germany was then (and is again) united.
3. A concise and colorful introduction to Lebanese geography can be found in Hitti (1967, 11–24). The best maps available are the series prepared during the French mandate and tabulated by Brown (1969, xxv). A useful bibliography of maps is given by Ghadban (1981, 143–45, n. 2). For the etymology of Lebanese (and some Syrian) place-names the standard work is now Wild (1973). It has not completely eclipsed its predecessor, Freyha (1972).
4. Wild (1973, 273), who overlooked Ptolemy's (*Geog*. 5.14.3) reference to the river of that name. Some modern writers (e.g. Hitti 1967; Jones 1971, map V opposite p. 226) have incorrectly identified the River Leôn ("Leontes") with the Litâni. Strabo (*Geog*. 16.2.22) and Pliny (*NH* 5.74) note a "Leontopolis" near the river Tamyras.
5. The relevant texts are in Pritchard (1969, 78–81). See also Brown (1969, 167) for commentary.
6. References are collected in Brown (1969, 164, 167, 172 [mythological]; 180–81, 201–203 [historical]).
7. Arrian, *Anabasis of Alexander* 2.20.4; Quintus Curtius, *History of Alexander* 4.3.1; Polyaenus, *Strategems* 4.3.4; Plutarch, *Alexander* 24.6.
8. Pearson (1960, 56). Chares (or Plutarch) seems to distinguish between the *Arabes* of the Antilebanon and the *barbaroi* ("non-Greeks") of the Lebanon. Curtius (4.3.1) refers to Alexander's antagonists more specifically as *Arabum agrestes* ("Arab peasants"). Both terms must refer to the Ituraeans of a later time (see n. 14 below and Brown [1969, 32 n. 15]).
9. Loeb translation. On the basis of this and other references to Phoenicia in Theophrastus, Brown (1969, 15) believes the botanist actually saw what he described, or at the very least drew upon an eyewitness account (verbal or written).
10. Rey-Coquais (1964, 296–301), plausibly situates it in the southern Biqâʿ.
11. For translation and commentary see Harper (1928, 28–29).
12. Loeb translation. For commentary see Walbank (1957, 577). Gerrha has long been identified with modern ʿAnjar; the identity of Brochoi is less

certain. On the latter especially see Rey-Coquais (1964, 289–96). Though *Brochoi* has a Greek meaning relevant to its location, it probably is a fortuitous transliteration of an indigenous place name (e.g. the nearby modern sites of Barûq and Baraka). ʿAnjar is probably elision for ʿAyn Gerrha (sing.) or ʿAyûn Gerrha (pl.), i.e. the Spring (or Springs) of Gerrha. It is just possible that "Brochoi Gerrha" may mean the same thing and that Brochoi is modern Majdal ʿAnjar and Gerrha is ʿAnjar proper.

13. See Ragette (1980, 28) with sketch. See also Rey-Coquais (1976), s.v. "Heliupolis."
14. On the Ituraeans see Schürer (1973, Appendix I); Schottroff (1982, 125–52).
15. The identification Gerrha/ʿAnjar is virtually certain: Wild 1973, 254 s.v. "ʿAnzar." Restoration of the place-name *Ain(garr)ia* in a Greek inscription (*Supplementum Epigraphicum Graecum* 1.545) found near ʿAnjar has more recently (*Inscriptions Grecques et Latines de la Syrie* 6.2986) been disproved. Gerrha must be the ancient place name *Garis* on the upper reaches of the River Litas (modern Nahr Litâni) where a battle was fought between Muslim forces in AD 743 (Theophanes, *Chronographia*, translation and commentary in Brown 1969, 70–71). The identification *Gerrha/Chalkis* is doubted by Rey-Coquais (1981, 171–72).
16. For Pompey's submission of the coastal cities see Strabo, *Geog.* 16.2.8. A parallel account in Flavius Josephus (*Antiquities of the Jews* 14.38–40) describes an inland campaign through the Biqâʿ.
17. Jerome's commentary on Eusebius, *Onomasticon* s.v. "Aermôn" (translation and commentary in Brown (1969, 55).
18. *Dionysiaca* 42.282–312 at line 282; translation and commentary in Brown (1969, 4–6).
19. Talbert (1989) has argued that a "uniform absence of map-consciousness" was characteristic of the Graeco-Roman world. That parallels the general belief that only a small percentage of the population in classical antiquity enjoyed literacy. The modern world may not be as "map conscious" as we suppose. Our advantage lies only in having accurate maps to consult, not in any enhanced awareness of their value.
20. *Macra* is Greek for "Big"; the modern name for the nearby Eleutheros River is Nahr Kabîr, "Big River." But Strabo's Macras (*Pedion* = "Plain") probably transliterates the original Semitic name of that coastal plain, of which ʿAkkâr is an echo (cf. Arabic *ʿakâra* = "sediment", *muʿakkar* = "muddy" and associated meanings in Freyha (1972, 117).
21. *Abilenê* (the valley of the upper *Wadi Baradâ*) seems the logical location (following R. Benzinger, *Realencyclopädie* 2.2 [1896] col. 2414) based on Strabo's "seacoast to interior" progression of valleys. Abilenê was

rejected by Dussaud (1927, 399), which proposes the southern Biqâʿ, and by Rey-Coquais (1964, 301–306 and Appendix 2) which argues for the upper Jordan valley (Nahr Hasbani).

22. As was done by Rey-Coquais (1965).
23. IGLS 7.4011—see especially Rey-Coquais' judicious commentary on this much-published inscription.
24. Ghadban proposes that the wall (at the northern entrance of the Biqâʿ; photos *planche* VIII), represented the political and physical border between Ptolemaic and Seleucid territory. This barrier is also mentioned by Strabo (*Geog*. 16.2.19), where it is called "the Egyptian Wall", i.e. the former frontier between Seleucid (northern) Syria and Ptolemaic (southern) Syria, the latter belonging administratively to Egypt.
25. A representative sample of maps produced from Ptolemy's text (or copied from other maps) can be seen in Fischer (1932) with other facsimiles in a supplementary volume. For purposes of easy consultation, and comparison with a modern physical map on the same page, see Müller (1901, 35–36 [Near East—one section of this is reproduced here]).
26. On two specific instances of how Ptolemy shows an awareness of cultural geography, see MacAdam (1989, 306–307, discussing Judaea [Palestine] and Nabataea [Arabia]).
27. See the facsimile edition in two volumes (Weber 1976). On the rationale of this and other ancient maps see Levi (1981).
28. Moynihan (1985, 153–56 and 162), has argued unconvincingly against this view. On the Agrippan map and Pliny's description of it see Bowersock (1983, 164–67).
29. The Belus is also called the *Pacida* (Pliny *NH* 5.75; 36.190; Josephus, *JW* 2.10.2). See also the comments by Rey-Coquais in *IGLS* 7 #5050 n. 3 (p. 79).
30. The intentions of each are discussed in MacAdam (1989, 295–97 [Strabo] and 290–91 [Pliny]).

REFERENCES

Abel, F.-M.

1933 Oronte et Litani. *Journal of the Palestine Oriental Society* 13: 147–58.

Bekker-Nielsen, T.

1988 *Terra Incognita: The Subjective Geography of the Roman Empire.* Pp. 148–61 in *Studies in Ancient History and Numismatics presented to Rudi Thomsen*, eds. A. Damsgaard-Madsen et al. Aarhus: Munksgaard.

Bowersock, G.
1983 *Roman Arabia.* Cambridge, MA: Harvard University.

Brown, J. P.
1969 *The Lebanon and Phoenicia, Vol. I: The Physical Setting and the Forest.* Beirut: American University of Beirut.

Dussaud, R.
1927 *Topographie historique de la Syrie antique et médievale.* Paris: Geuthner.

Engels, D.
1978 *Alexander the Great and the Logistics of the Macedonian Army.* Berkeley: University of California.

Fischer, J.
1932 *Claudii Ptolemaei Geographia Codex Urbinas 82: Pars altera, tabula geographicae LXXXIII, Graecae-Arabicae Latinae e Codicibus LIII selectae.* Leiden: Brill.

Freyha, A.
1972 *A Dictionary of the Names of Towns and Villages in Lebanon* (Arabic). Beirut: Librairie du Liban.

Ghadban, C.
1981 Les frontières du territoire d'Héliopolis-Baalbeck à la lumière de nouveaux documents. Pp. 143–68 in *La Géographie Administrative et Politique d'Alexandre à Mahomet*, ed. T. Fahd. Paris: Geuthner.

Harper, G., Jr.
1928 A Study in the Commercial Relations between Egypt and Syria in the Third Century Before Christ. *American Journal of Philology* 49: 1–35.

Hitti, P.
1967 *Lebanon in History* (3rd ed.). New York: Macmillan.

Jones, A. H. M.
1971 *Cities of the Eastern Roman Provinces*, 2nd ed. Oxford: Clarendon.

Levi, A., and Levi, M.
1981 Map Projection and the Peutinger Table. Pp. 139–48 in *Coins, Culture and History: Numismatic Studies in Honor of Bluma L. Trell*, eds. L. Casson and M. Price. Detroit: Wayne State University.

MacAdam, H.
1989 Strabo, Pliny the Elder and Ptolemy of Alexandria: Three Views of Ancient Arabia and its Peoples. Pp. 289–320 in *L'Arabie Préislamique et son Environnement Historique et Culturel*, ed. T. Fahd. Leiden: Brill.

in press Marinus of Tyre and Scientific Cartography: The Mediterranean, The Orient and Africa in Early Maps. *Graeco-Arabica* 7/8.

Moynihan, R.
1985 Geographical Mythology and Roman Imperial Ideology. *Archeologia Transatlantica* 5: 153–62.

Müller, C.
1901 *Claudii Ptolemaei Geographia (Vol. 3: Tabulae)*. Paris: Didot.

Pearson, L.
1960 *The Lost Histories of Alexander the Great.* New York: American Philological Association.

Pritchard, J. B., ed.
1969 *Ancient Near Eastern Texts Relating to the Old Testament* (3rd ed.). Princeton: Princeton University.

Ragette, F.
1980 *Baalbek*. London: Chatto & Windus.

Rey-Coquais, J.-P.
1964 Notes de Géographie syrienne (2): Le lac aux roseaux aromatiques de Théophraste et la Vallée Royale de Strabon. *Mélanges de la Université St. Joseph* 40: 296–306.
1965 La navigation fluviale des aradiens. *Mélanges de l'université Saint-Joseph* 41: 226–35.
1976 Heliupolis. Pp. 380–82 in *The Princeton Encyclopedia of Classical Sites*, ed. R. Stillwell. Princeton: Princeton University.
1981 Les Frontières d'Hélioupolis: Quelques Remarques. Pp. 171–72 in *La Géographie Administrative et Politique d'Alexandre à Mahomet*, ed. T. Fahd. Paris: Geuthner.

Schottroff, W.
1982 Die Ituräer. *Zeitschrift des Deutchen Palästina Vereins* 98: 125–52.

Schürer, E.
1973 *A History of the Jewish People in the Time of Jesus Christ Vol. I*, rev. and ed. F. Millar and G. Vermes. Edinburgh: T. & T. Clark.

Starcky, J.
1971/72 Arca du Liban. *Les Cahiers de l'Oronte* 10: 103–13

Talbert, R.
1989 Review of *A History of Cartography* Vol. I. *American Historical Review* 94: 407–408.

Walbank, F.
1957 *A Historical Commentary on Polybius* Vol. 1. Oxford: Oxford University.

Weber, E.
1976 *Tabula Peutingeriana, Codex Vindobonensis 324: Vollständige*

Faksimile-Ausgabe im Original format. Graz: Akademische Druck und Verlagsanstalt.

Wild, S.

1973 *Libanesische Ortsnamen: Typologie und Deuting.* Weisbaden: Steiner.

III

PTOLEMY'S *GEOGRAPHY* AND THE WADI SIRHAN

INTRODUCTION

The representation of the Wādī Sirḥān on modern physical maps is often misleading, as Nelson Glueck noted forty years ago (1). It occupies an area about 320 km in length and as much as 75 km in width of the territory in northwestern Saudi Arabia (2). The western approaches to it actually begin only 60 km east of ᶜAmmān and continue gradually for another 60 km east and south through the Azraq depression until the entrance to the Wādī itself at the Jordan-Saudi Arabia border.

The eastern approaches to the Wādī are through the expanses of the Nefud desert of inner Arabia, and through the al-Hamad wastelands. The major oases of Azraq and Dūmat al-Jandāl (al-Jawf) are at the northwestern and southeastern approaches to the Wādī, but as will be argued below they did not effectively control movement of men and animals into or out of the Wādī. The term wādī is itself misleading, and it would be more accurate to designate the entire 320 km length of it as *baṭn*, i.e. « depression » (3). Extensive wādī systems feed into this depression from hills on either side ; some of the hills are extinct volcanic peaks just over 1,000 m altitude. But there is no great gorge in the earth as one finds as a feature of the spectacular wādīs of al-Ḥesa and al-Mūjib in central Jordan. The ends of the Sirhān depression are somewhat more elevated than its central section, and there is subsequently a large, marshy area precisely there. (See the maps in figs. 1 and 2).

Travel through the Sirḥān can be rapid or painfully slow depending upon the sector traversed and the mode of transportation. Glueck (4) motored easily through the northern part, and described hunting teams chasing gazelles by car in the same area. By contrast the Czech scholar Alois Musil travelled extensively by camel with the Bedouin and said :

« Walking in the depression of Sirḥān is difficult for man or beast. The ground is overlain with a crust of salt one to five cm thick, beneath which there is often found a deposit of lime dust or sand ten to twenty cm deep. Both men and animals sink into it at every step and hence make slow progress (5) ».

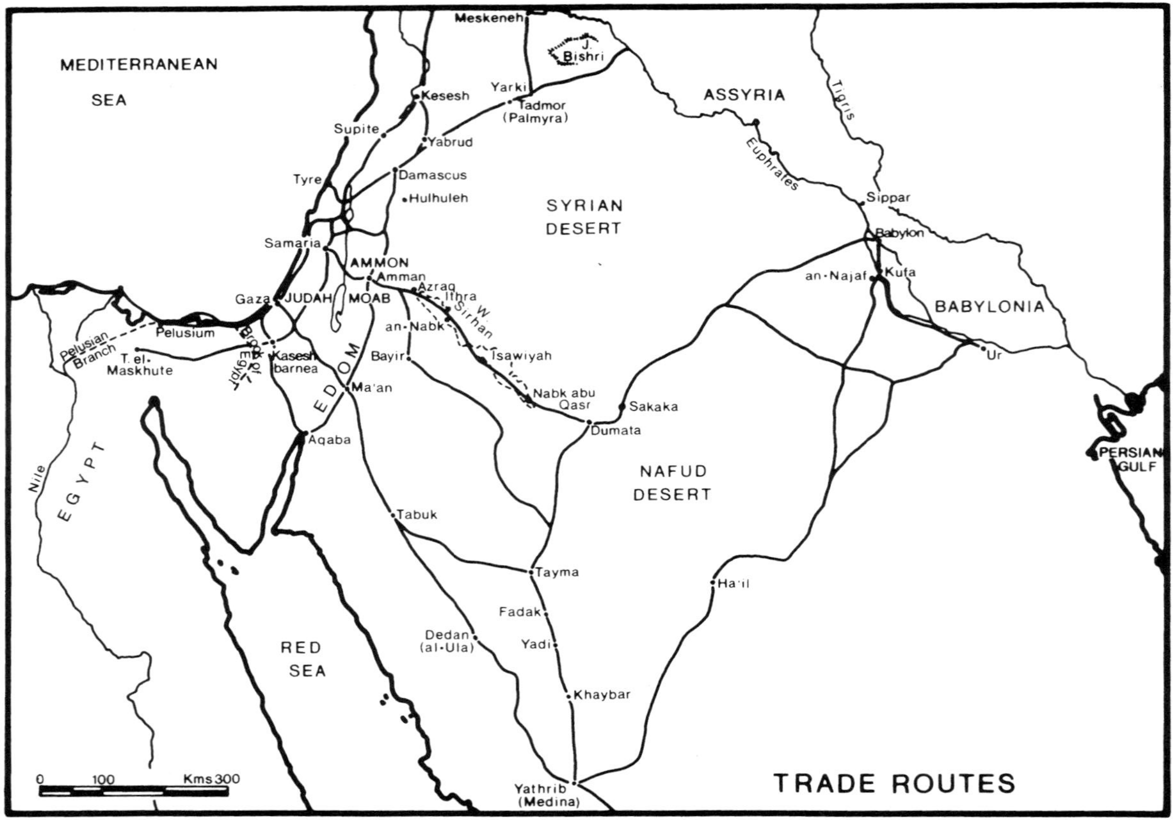

Fig. 1 : Trade routes of the Ancient East centred on Dumata and the Wādī Sirḥān. Adapted from I. Ephʿal, *The Ancient Arabs* (1982) 241, by Julie Kennedy, with permission from E.J. Brill.

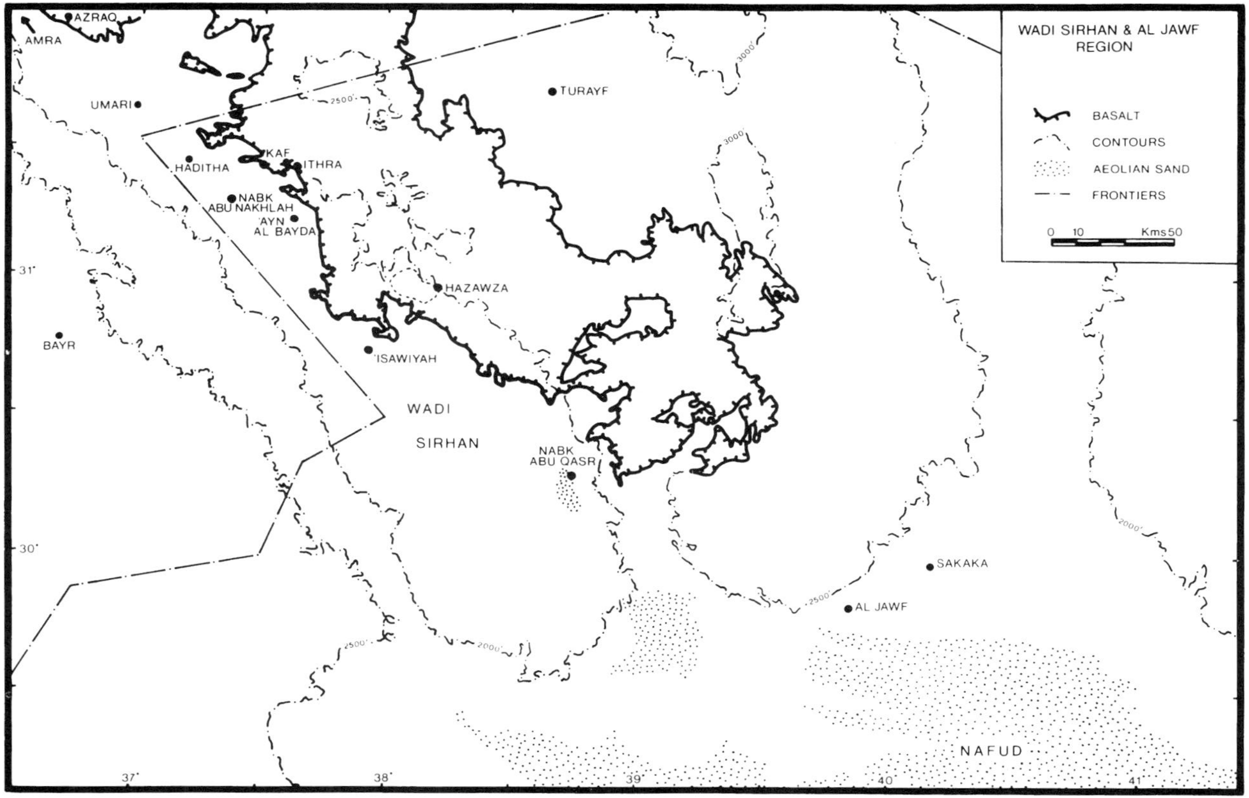

Fig. 2 : The Wādī Sirḥān and al-Jawf regions. Adapted from R.M. Adams et al., *Atlal* I (1977), by Julie Kennedy, with permission from the publisher.

The Wādī Sirḥān has served as a travel and invasion route from earliest times ; in the early 7th century B.C. the Assyrians captured the fortress of *Adummatu* (Jawf) in a major military campaign against the Arab rulers of the city (6). No systematic exploration of any area nor excavation of a site within the Sirḥān has yet been undertaken. But the picture is gradually emerging of the Wādī as a flourishing trade route from eastern and southern Arabia into the central and southern cities of Jordan and the southern cities of Syria. The decline of Petra in the first century A.D., and the destruction of Palmyra in the third, must have contributed much to the wealth of merchants who operated from Azraq and Jawf and their respective emporia : ᶜAmmān and Bostra in the north, Gerrha and Taymāᶜ in the south.

Thus when Ptolemy compiled that portion of his *Geography* devoted to Arabia Deserta (V, 18) he may have had some knowledge, albeit second-hand, of the territory which is today designated as the Wādī Sirḥān. It is the intention of this paper to demonstrate that certain place-names in the register of towns within Arabia Deserta, and on the maps produced to accompagny the *Geography*, conform with surprising accuracy to distances between, and locations of, sites within the Sirḥān depression. Most of the names known to Ptolemy no doubt represented only encampments for caravans.

TEXTUAL ANALYSIS

In most editions of the *Geography* the list of towns and villages in Arabia Deserta contains thirty-nine names. Ten of these are located on or near the Euphrates river, and three near the Persian Gulf. The remaining twenty-six Ptolemy designates as « inland » beginning with Barathena in the north-central sector and ending with Salma in the south-east corner. It has been customary to treat this list of inland towns as if it had been compiled at random. Musil is particularly guilty of this. He had little difficulty in finding a name from his own notes which was similar to the classical place-names. He at least had the sense to confine his identification of the names within the bounds of Arabia Deserta.

That there is some methodology involved in the arrangement of the names of the inland towns is evident from the coordinates given by Ptolemy. The list of twenty-six names divides itself almost exactly into thirds. One group contains eight names (Barathena to Erupa) ; with the exception of Rhegana far to the east, all the names form a loop in the west-central part of Deserta. A second group (7) of nine names, from Themme to Zagmais, forms a larger loop in the east-central sector. The final group of nine names (Arrade to Salma) stretches along the entire border between Deserta and Felix, with four towns to the west, and four to the east, of Dumaetha. This group is carefully arranged, and Dumaetha is a known site (8). See the Appendix to this article.

Something must be said here of the place-names as they appear in the various MSS of Ptolemy's *Geography* . Most are naturally transliterations into Greek of Semitic originals – especially those of the « interior towns ». Some remain patently Semitic, and are no doubt genuine, e.g. Salma, Sora, Aurana, Dumaetha, Obaera. Others are quite uncertain, e.g. Arrade, Odagana, Luma, Erupa. Others still bear some resemblance to Greek or Latin names, e.g. Zagmais, Tedium, Artemita. Precisely because of this uncertainty, the present study will make no attempt to correlate the names on Ptolemy's list with any place-name on a modern map – with the exception of Dumaetha/Dumāt al-Jandāl. Ptolemy was first and foremost a mathematicien, and he plotted the location of cities, towns and villages throughout the known world as carefully as he could (9). Even so there are major mistakes where we do not expect to find them : e.g. Scythopolis is located slightly east of Philadelphia, Canatha is far to the west of Bostra. Duplication of place-names is common, and here the error may be due as much to the ignorance of Ptolemy or his source as to the carelessness of the copyist. There are two Gerasas, two Adras, two Alatas, two Salmas. The duplications may not represent mistakes but the simple fact that place-names are repetitive. One must be cautious, and one must make allowances for errors. But one can also learn much from a careful, considerate study of Ptolemy (10).

EPIGRAPHY

Recently David Kennedy and I published our reading of a rediscovered Latin inscription from the Azraq fort (11). The opening lines of the text are missing, but the remaining portion would seem to be the record of work carried out by Roman military units at or near Azraq itself c. A.D. 300. Four place-names are noted. Two, Bostra and Basienisa, can be confidently identified with known places north-west of Azraq, and the mileage from each accords exactly with Azraq being the original locus of the inscription (See figs. 3 & 4).

The remaining two names, Dasianis and Bamata-Dumata, are more problematical to identify. The mileage given (208 MP = 305 km) from the latter to the former is one clue, and the element « Dumata » indicates in which direction to look. We reasoned that « Dasianis » (perhaps « Dasiana ») was the ancient name for Azraq, and the « Bamata » was to be sought at a distance of 305 km south-east, in the direction of Dumāt al-Jandāl, but not at the oasis itself which is some 450 km from Azraq. It is unfortunate that no other name is given between Dasianis and Bamata to indicate more specifically the route along which mileage measurements were made. The only identifiable ancient road in the Azraq vicinity is the cleared track north of the fort along which Kennedy discovered mile-stones (12). No traces of a built road appear until one reaches Umm al-Quṯṯayn in the Jordanian Ḥawrān (13).

Another clue to aid us was the similarity of the name « Banatha » in the *Geography*. Various MSS locate it due west or slightly north-west of Dumaetha. The modern track west of Jawf does intersect another coming south from al-ᶜIsāwaīyah within the Wādī Sirḥān. That crossroad (nameless on modern maps) is indeed about 208 MP southeast of the Azraq fort. In addition there is the attractive possibility of identifying another place-name, Obaera – located by Ptolemy north and west or Banatha – with the well-know site of Bāyir, north and west of the crossroad point (14). The reasons for rejecting these possible identifications for Banatha and Obaera will be given in more detail in the next section of this paper. For now it will be enough to state that the Azraq text implies clearly that the Roman authorities c.300 had assumed direct control of the major trade route between Azraq

Fig. 3 : The « Dasianis » Inscription from the Azraq Oasis.

Photographed by H.I. MacAdam, June, 1985.

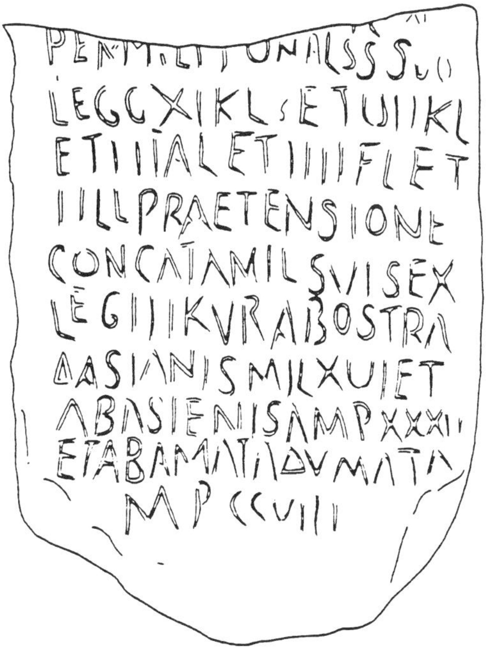

[unknown number of lines]

PEM (or N or R) [1 or 2]LỊỊỤ (or Ọ or Ṿ) NILSSSUOṢ
LEGG. XI KL. ËT VII KL.
ET I ITAL. ET IIII FL. ET
I ILL. PRAETENSIONE
CONCATA MIL. SUIS EX
LEG. III KVR. A BOSTRA
DASIANIS M.P. LXVI ET
A BASIENISA M.P. XXX
ET A BAMATA DUMATẠ
M.P. CCVIII

Fig. 4 : Facsimile drawing of the « Dasianis » Inscription from the Azraq Oasis. From D.L. Kennedy and H.I. MacAdam, *ZPE* 60 (1985) 100. Line 1 is a slight modification of our original reading. For a different reading of some lines, and a new interpretation, see now M.P. Speidel, *Historia* 36 (1987) 213-221.

and Jawf – i.e. the Wādī Sirḥān. Evidence for this had already been accumulating through a number of related epigraphical discoveries at the Azraq oasis itself, from sites within the Sirḥān depression, and from Jawf (15). The remains of a strong Roman presence in the Azraq area are still evident. The fort at Azraq Durūz, of Diocletianic date but on the site of an earlier (Severan ?) *castrum*, is only the most spectacular example. There is no comparable evidence from Jawf of Roman occupation and garrisons in that oasis. Nor need there have been. Control of the Sirḥān depression could best be effected by small military detachments, most probably auxiliary forces, placed at strategic locations (wells, springs, narrow defiles) *within* the Wadi itself. Musil noted one example of the way in which Bedouin raiders could easily bypass the fortress of Jawf and conduct campaigns in Jordan and Syria :

« We were going through the region of al-Bijāẓ, which is favored by [the tribe] Shammar when they travel to Syria. Watering their camels at Zelīb Ṣwēr, they circle al-Ǧowf to the north, drink at an-Nabk abu Ḳaṣr and then at al-Azrak, and finally may rob the settlers at Boṣra and on the western edges of the Ḥawrān (16) ».

It would therefore be more likely that the « Bamata » near Dumata be sought inside the southern entrance of the Sirḥān depression at a point as nearly as one can reckon to be 208 Roman miles from Azraq. That the Romans would ensure that they controlled this point will therefore come as no surprise. With the Sirḥān secure at both ends, a large Roman presence in Jawf itself would not be necessary and indeed was not likely to be effective. Caravans leaving Jawf for Jordan and Syria could be assured of safe passage, which meant the security of travelling a well-established route of the shortest mileage to the north.

A small outpost of dromedary auxiliaries could effectively control passage through the Wādī and guard the water. They may well have been posted at such a site as al-Nabk abu-Qaṣr. It is located at a point where the track through the Wādī curves, the Wādī narrows and, more importantly, it is the first source of abundant water after entering the southern mouth of the depression, and the last source of water for someone travelling to Jawf from the Azraq oasis. As I now hope to demonstrate, this site accords well not only with the Bamata of the Azraq text but the location of Ptolemy's Banatha.

CARTOGRAPHY

Medieval copies of maps which were produced to accompany Ptolemy' *Geography* have been collected and published in various editions. The most comprehensive and carefully edited collection is that produced by Joseph Fischer just over fifty years ago (17). The Next of the *Geography* still awaits a definitive edition, called for most recently by Neugebauer (18). But a comparison of the various fascimile maps which depict the Near East indicates that there is more agreement than disagreement on the location of sites plotted from Ptolemy's coordinates. There are, of course, variations in spellings, and in some cases names are omitted from the lists in certain MSS or do not appear on some maps. The representation of Arabia Deserta is especially important, since no other source from classical antiquity – descriptive geographies or maps – provides us with a comparable representation of the territory east of the *Via Nova Traiana* (19) (See fig. 5).

One thing is readily apparent from a glance at Ptolemy's maps, and that is their distortion or misrepresentation of some basic geographical features. The parallel ranges of the Lebanese mountains are shown running east-west rather than north-south. Mountain ranges appear between Arabia Deserta and Babylonia where none exists. There is also a tendency in the layout of the maps to stretch the land mass depicted longitudinally, so that overall distances (e.g. from the Mediterranean to the Persian Gulf) are exaggerated. This has resulted in some embarrassing blank spaces, the major one being the entire north-western sector of Arabia Deserta from the middle Euphrates to just east of Bostra, and a correspondingly large gap toward the eastern border.

But in spite of these obvious flaws there is a strong sense of purpose behind the maps : to represent as precisely as possible the location of all place-names, tribal names and regional names known to Ptolemy. To that end each site was fixed by means of longitude and latitude, measuring the former from the « base-line » of the Blessed Isles and the latter from the equator. Much of the Near East falls between his cordinates of 20°-40° north and 65°-80° east. Within that, the towns of Arabia Deserta lie between 29°30' and 35°05' north, 70°00' and 79°00' east.

Musil (20) and others have attempted to identify nearly *every* place-name of the 39 noted earlier. In reality only a few have been positively and satisfactorily matched with existing sites on the ground. As one moves westward into Arabia Petraea, Palestine, Phoenicia and the Decapolis there is a considerable increase in the number of identifiable place-names. The reasons for the obscurity of the place-names in Deserta are simple. Many were little more than caravan halts between the major emporia. There is also the factor that the territory depicted on Ptolemy's map of Deserta today embraces portions of five modern countries : Syria, Iraq, Jordan, Saudi Arabia and Kuwait. A sizeable proportion of that same territory still remains very remote and inaccessible.

Certain names plotted by Ptolemy were no doubt already located by earlier geographers through their own coordinates, and these figures he could check against his own calculations. But many communities would be known to him only by name, general location and distances to other places. This last factor is important, because it does provide a means of checking distances computed from Ptolemy' coordinates with distances calculated from modern maps.

Ptolemy's standard of measurement was the *stadion*, and in both the Introduction (I,2) and the Conclusion (VII, 5) of the *Geography* he states clearly his acceptance that 1° of longitude *at the equator* is equal to a distance of 500 stadia. This figure had earlier been proposed by Marinus of Tyre, of whom Ptolemy is generally critical (21). In modern terms this allows us to determine that 1° of longitude on Ptolemy's map *at the equator* equals 91 km (22). At the parallel of Rhodes (36° north) the longitudinal distance is reduced to 1°

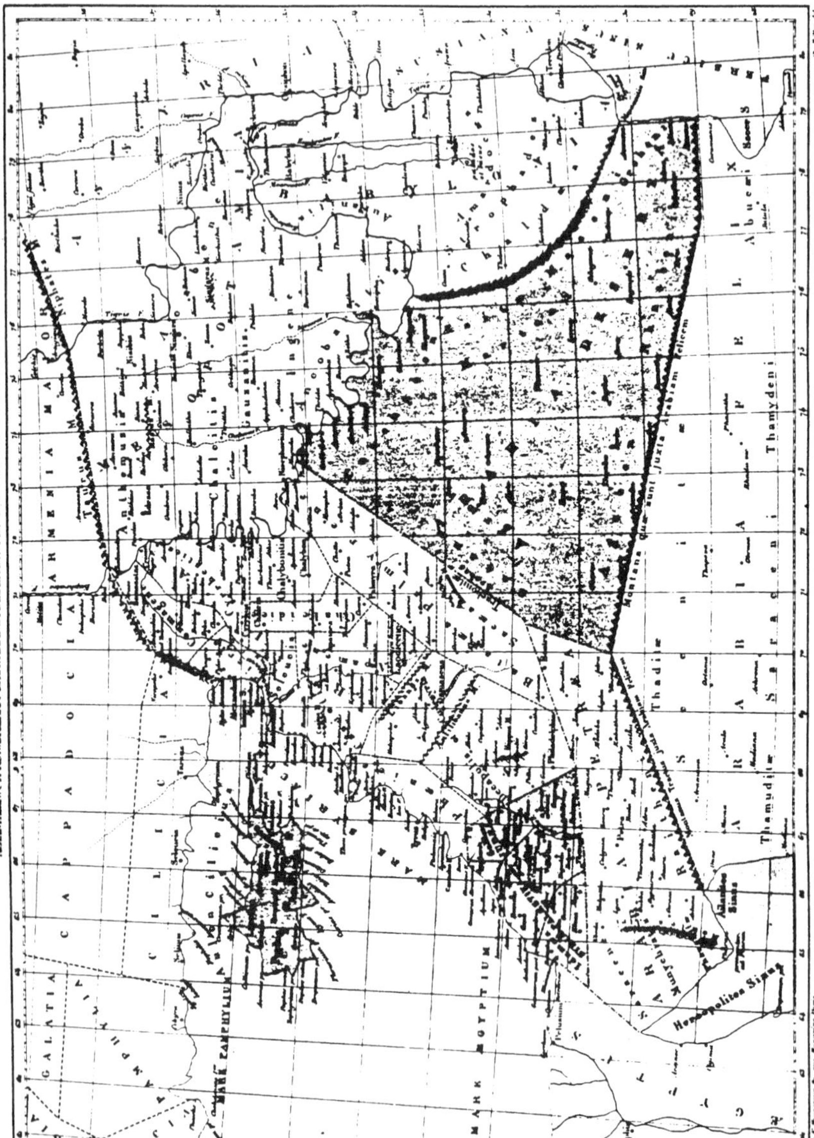

Fig. 5 : Arabia and the Near East based on various maps in editions of Ptolemy's *Geography*. C. Müller (ed.),

equals 400 stadia or 72.8 km. Since the portion of Arabia Deserta dealt with in this paper lies at approximately 30°, I shall use the round figure of 1° of longitude equals 80 km. That almost the same equivalence holds for meridians of latitude is most fortunate (23), since it allows us to plot geometrically the location of Ptolemy's sites and to compare the results with representations on the various facsimile maps (24) (See fig. 6).

One method of testing this is by comparing the relative distances of two known sites in the region. For instance, Ptolemy places Philadelphia (ᶜAmmān) at 68° east and Dumaetha at 75° east. The distance between them can thus be calculated as 7° or approximately 580 km. The straight-line distance on a modern map is 440 km, but the actual *ground distance* would be much closer to Ptolemy's figure. The latitudinal distance, however, does not accord. Ptolemy places Philadelphia only 1°40' north of Dumaetha, i.e. 150 km. The actual distance is 225 km. The mistake is one of interest, since latitude is normally much easier to reckon. At any rate the figure of 1° (longitude) = 80 km can be taken as reasonably accurate. This would probably represent the distance of two-day journey by sea or by land.

Any investigation of the Wādī Sirḥān based on ancient accounts or maps must begin with the site of Dumaetha/Jawf. Ptolemy located it at 75°00' east and 29°40' north. It is furthermore placed on his maps against the northern flank of the « mountains » which separate Deserta from Felix. It lies in approximately the same latitude as Alata, Bere, Calathua and Salma to the east, and Banatha to the west. I submit for consideration that these mountains shown on maps of Ptolemy's *Geography* are merely symbolical : they * represent in pictorial form the southern extent of Roman rule in Arabia (25).

Banatha, as noted above, is suspiciously similar to the Bamata of the Azraq inscription, but the similarity of names could be no more than coincidental (26). Fortunately we have the mileage distance and a direction for Bamata : 305 km toward Dumata/Jawf. If Banatha is but a variant spelling, its location should coincide closely if not exactly with the proposed location of Bamata. Banatha is plotted by Ptolemy at 1°45' west, 0°0' north, of Dumaetha, which would be 140 km. At such a distance directly west of Jawf there is the crossroad already mentioned. But at 140 km west and slightly *north* of Jawf is the site of Al-Nabk abu-Qaṣr (125 km straight-line distance but with an allowance for ground distance). This coincides nicely with the location posited for Bamata. Once again Ptolemy' longitudinal distance seems to be more accurate than the latitudinal distance, although here the difference is be attributable to a copyist's error (27). Thus there is reason to believe that epigraphy, cartography and textual analysis support each other and place the location of Bamata/Banatha within the southern entrance of the Sirḥān depression.

Musil reached almost the same conclusion. He knew that the other Nabk (abu-Nakhla), 170 km north-west of abu-Qaṣr and within the Sirḥān, was a well-known oasis stop in the early Islamic period and in his own day. He thus saw in the variant spelling « Banacha » simple metathesis for « Nabacha » and made the error compound (28). Ironically he had actually visited the site of abu-Qaṣr and reported that :

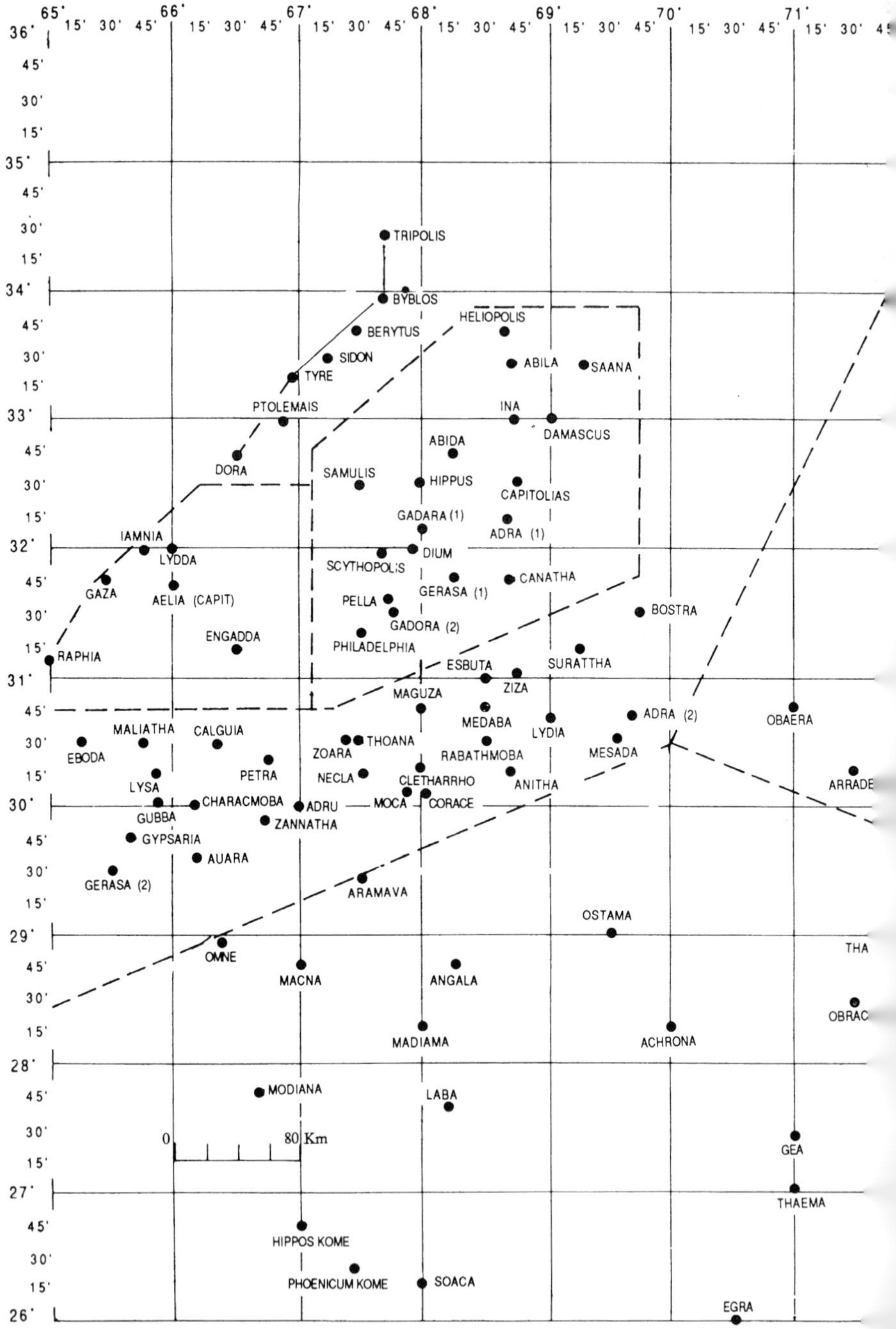

Fig. 6 : The towns and villages of Arabia Deserta (with some of those in Arabia Petraeca a[...] Arabia Felix) plotted by longitude and latitude based on the coordinates in Ptolem[...] *Geography*. (Prepared by the Draw division of C.R.A., C.N.R.S., Valbonne).

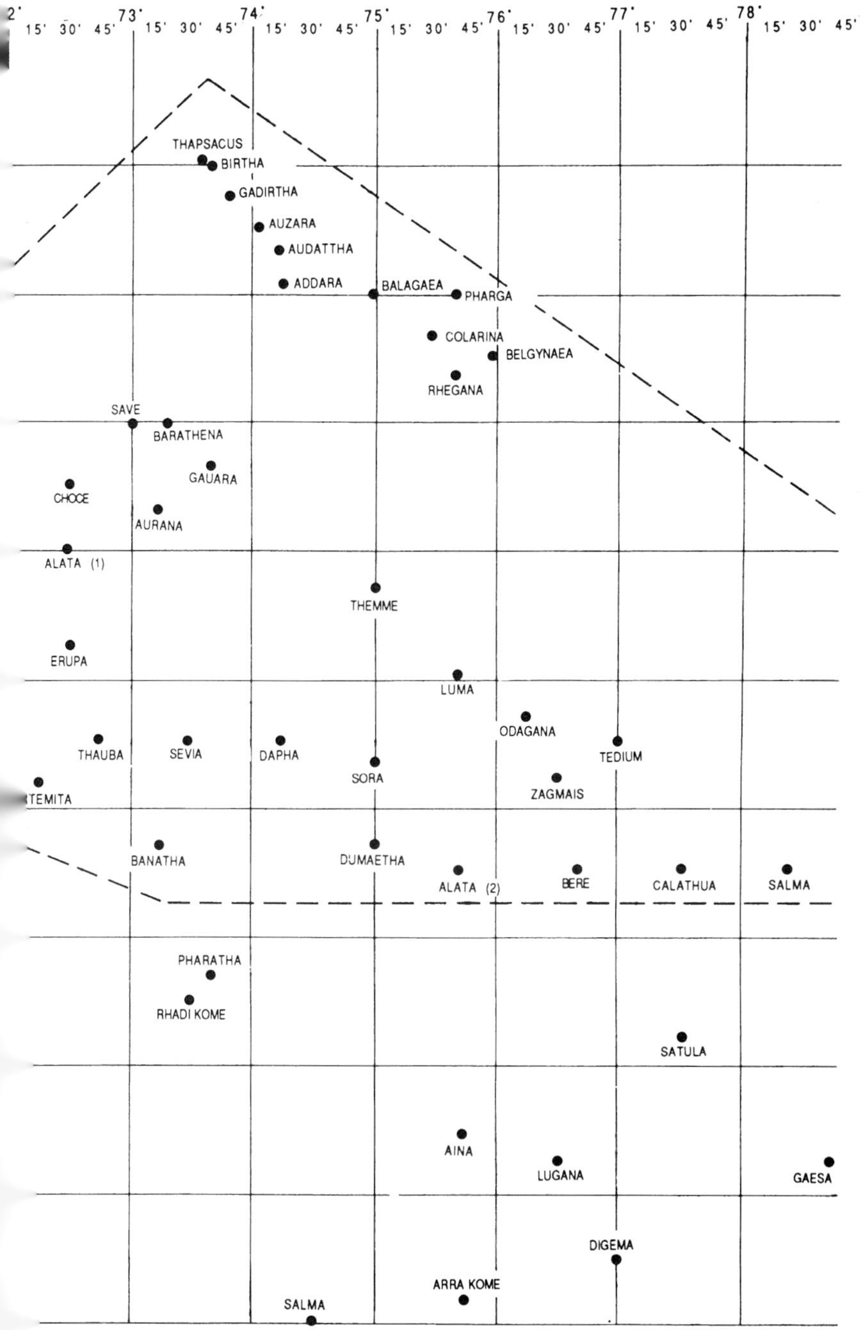

2°
15' 30' 45'
73°
15' 30' 45'
74°
15' 30' 45'
75°
15' 30' 45'
76°
15' 30' 45'
77°
15' 30' 45'
78°
15' 30' 45'
THAPSACUS
BIRTHA
GADIRTHA
AUZARA
AUDATTHA
ADDARA
BALAGAEA
PHARGA
COLARINA
BELGYNAEA
RHEGANA
SAVE
BARATHENA
GAUARA
CHOCE
AURANA
ALATA (1)
THEMME
ERUPA
LUMA
ODAGANA
THAUBA
SEVIA
DAPHA
SORA
TEDIUM
ZAGMAIS
TEMITA
BANATHA
DUMAETHA
ALATA (2)
BERE
CALATHUA
SALMA
PHARATHA
RHADI KOME
SATULA
AINA
LUGANA
GAESA
DIGEMA
ARRA KOME
SALMA

« ... we stopped almost due southwest of Abraḳ an-Nabč, a sandy hill at the base of which the small oasis of an-Nabč ash-Sherži is situated in the shade of several palm trees. This oasis is also called an-Nabk abu Ḳaṣr, since there is a little half-ruined stone farm (ḳaṣr) there (29). »

There is no need to insist that this site is the precise location of Bamata/Banatha, but there is reason to suspect that it lay near there. And if Ptolemy's Banatha can be located within the Sirḥān, what about the other place-names plotted farther north and west on his map ?

Three more names appear in the list : Artemita, Obaera and Arrade. Artemita is plotted by Ptolemy at 1°00' west and 0°30' north of Banatha. The co-ordinate distance is about 80 km, which would place it at or near the present site of al-ᶜĪsāwīyah (82.5 km on the modern map). The name Artemita or its slight variants may, as Musil suggested, preserve the plant-name *artam* or *ratam*, a very common feature of Bedouin place-names (30). On the other hand it may be one of a half-dozen Arabian place-names in Ptolemy that appear to be Greek.

Just fifteen kilometers east of al-ᶜĪsāwīyah is a very large depression labelled Ḥaẓawẓā on modern maps. It is in fact a water catchment area central to the entire Sirḥān into which a large number of wādīs feed during the rainy season to produce a marsh (Arabic *sabkhah*) area of more than 25 square km. Once again we have an eye-witness description by Musil :

« The Sabkha Ḥaẓawẓā is a salty swamp which after heavy rains becomes transformed into a single lake. Almost from the very center rises a black hill... No one can swim or wade across the swamp and whoever would ride into the Ḥaẓawẓā upon a camel would disappear with his mount before he could take ten steps (31) ».

Might it be that an extensive water-basin such as this, with some nearby springs (ᶜAyn al-Mābīyya (32)), could support a caravan stop and enough wildlife to warrant an evocative name such as Artemita ? Some investigation of the area might well reveal traces of a permanent settlement.

Next on the list of place-names is Obaera, located 1°15' and 0°35' north of Artemita (i.e. 120 km). But the name preceeding Obaera in many MSS, i.e. Arrade, is given coordinates of 71°39' west and 39°15' north. If these are accurate, Arrade should actually be placed between Artemita and Obaera in the list, at 0°45' west and 0°05' north of Artemita. The co-ordinate distance is thus about 60 km, which would be at or near the site of ᶜAyn al-Bayḏā. There is no mention of this small oasis by that name in Musil, but on one of his trips through the Sirḥān he stayed overnight at « ... the springs of ᶜUyūn (plural of ᶜayn) ᶜEḏwānāt... we encamped upon a sandy *firs*-covered height, which rose about two meters above a surrounding sandy marsh » (33). Musil's location of this site leads me to believe that it and ᶜAyn al-Bayḏā are one and the same place. The distance, the direction and the circumstances all indicate that the location would suit Ptolemy's Arrade (34).

We are left with the place-name Obaera which Ptolemy locates at 0°30' west and 0°30" north (about 60 km) of Arrade. On the modern map this would mean a site among the many Qurrayāt al-Milḥ or « Salt-Villages » at the north-western end of the Wādī Sirḥān and familiar to Arab geographers. There are today two dozen of these lying some ten to thirty kilometers east of the modern track between Nabk abu-Nakhlah and Ḥaditha, the latter of which is the Saudi frontier post monitoring traffic to and from Jordan.

Among these many villages are Kaf and Ithra, both displaying ancient ruins and both recently visited. Winnett and Reed observed near Ithra

« ... the foundation courses of an ancient structure, twenty by eighteen meters ... The floor-plan of the structure ... suggests that it may have been a Nabataean sanctuary. » (35)

That, plus surface pottery and inscriptions from the Nabataean-Roman period, led them to suggest strongly that the site should be excavated. Near Kaf they saw what are probably the remains of another Nabataean temple (36) and at Qarqar recorded a number of Thamudic graffiti and one Palmyrene funerary inscription that may date to A.D. 174 (37). Other finds suggest continuous habitation of the area throughout the Islamic period.

Obaera is the westernmost town in Arabia Deserta recorded by Ptolemy. Though it has been identified with the well-known site of Bāyir due to the obvious analogy of names, Obaera could designate *any* site boasting a well or wells. What is of primary importance is its location on the maps based on Ptolemy's coordinates. It is the last place-name plotted north-west from Dumaetha just east of Arabia Petraea and just north of Arabia Felix. It thus fits nicely with the proposed identification among the villages of Qurrayāt al-Milḥ on the north-western edge of the Sirḥān depression and – coincidentally – on the modern border between Saudi Arabia and Jordan.

Ptolemy himself was quite specific about borders in this very region. In book V Chapter 16 of the *Geography* he clearly states that the border point where Felix, Deserta and Petraea come together is precisely 70°00' east and 30°30' north. That point is just 1° west and a bit south of Obaera or, if my identification is correct, some 80 km west of the northern entrance to the Wādī Sirḥān. On a modern map such a distance would place sites such as Azraq, Qaṣr Karanah and Qaṣr Amra just inside the border of Arabia Petraea. That is precisely where one would look for the place-name *Dasianis* which I have argued is the ancient name for Azraq. But when all the sites in the extreme east of Arabia Petraea have been plotted on a graph there is no name among the unidentified - Surattha, Anitha, Lydia, Mesada, Adra – which clearly evokes the name. The distances also argue against any identification. Adra (a duplication of the name of the city associated with the Syrian Ḥawrān) is the closest to Obaera, but it lies 1°20' to the west, which is 105 km. It is interesting, but nothing more, that the Greek spelling of Adra (AΔPA) could easily be a corruption of AMPA. The spectacular hunting-baths of the Omayyad Qaṣr al-Amra lie just 105 km west of where I located Obaera (38).

The absence of a place-name identifiable as Dasianis is frustrating but understandable. At the time Ptolemy was preparing his *Geography* (c.150) he may have remained ignorant of the caravanserai which surely then stood on the site of Azraq. Fifty years later, perhaps even a bit earlier, a Roman *castrum* was constructed at Azraq Durūz which became the hub of a great network of military fortifications (Asaykhin, ᶜUwaynid, Ḥallabāt) and roadworks linking the Azraq area (and the Wādī Sirḥān) with the *Via Nova* and the provincial capital at Bostra. One may note as a parallel that the caravan-city of Palmyra is conspicuously absent from Strabo's description of Syria, revised no later than c. 23. Fifty years later Palmyra figures prominently in Pliny's account of the same area. The difference had to do with Roman intervention.

NOTES

(1) Glueck (1944) 12.

(2) Bramkamp (1977). The Wādi is located between 37°00' and 39°30' east and between 29°45' and 31°30' north.

(3) Musil (1978) 335 and *passim*.

(4) *Op*. cit. 12.

(5) *Op. cit.* 116. Both writers tended to generalize their impressions, although Musil travelled the entire length of the Sirḥān depression more than once and Glueck saw only the upper third under very different conditions. Even so, Musil's account is contradictory. He describes (*ibid*, 120) Bedouin scouts being sent on return reconnaissance missions of 300 km from Nabāj in the Sirḥān to Jawf. They were expected to cover this distance (by camel) in 48 *hours*. Yet Musil and his entourage took thirteen *days* to reach Jawf from Nabāj ! (*ibid*, 120-160).

(6) Ephaᶜal (1982) 118-123. There is to date no archaeological evidence, from the area of Jawf and Sakaka, of occupation « in the mid-1st millennium B.C. ». (Adams [1977] 38) ; cf. Parr (1978) 42.

(7) There are actually two sub-groups : Thauba, Sevia, Dapha and Sora constitute one, the remainder of the names the other. For this and all subsequent reference to the text I shall use Stevenson (1932) unless otherwise indicated.

(8) Vaglieri (1965). See Bramkamp (1976) for Jawf and sites north and east.

(9) « Arabian » place-names in Pliny and Strabo are almost exclusively limited to the Nabataean region and Arabia Felix. The exception is Pliny's Dumata (cf. *Nat. Hist.* 6, 32 - here distinguished from another homonymous place-name on the Euphrates. This distinction was not noticed by Musil [1978] 514-515). Strabo had nothing to report of interior Arabia east of the Nabataean Kingdom.

(10) Toomer (1975), Polaschek (1965) and Dilke (1985a) 72-86 and Appendix VII. A more popular assessment of Ptolemy's value is Dilke (1985b).

(11) Kennedy and MacAdam (1985) 100-104 and Tafel IId.

(12) Kennedy (1982) 169-177.

(13) Sections of this road, and a milestone, were discovered by members of the Southern Hawran Survey team in June, 1985. An announcement will appear in our preliminary report for *ADAJ* (1986) now in press.

(14) Musil (1978) 508 opted for this identification without hesitation. The site of Bāyir, which boasts some extensive Nabataean remains, was visited a number of times by Glueck (1944 : 17 and note 10). See also Field (1960) 99-101 and 158 for an earlier visit.

(15) This evidence is conveniently discussed in Sartre (1982) 18-22 and less comprehensively by Bowersock (1983) 154-159. Neither scholar takes account of the recent archaeological field-work done by the Saudi Arabian Department of Antiquities and Museums ; see Adams (1977) and Parr (1978).

(16) Musil (1978) 463.

(17) Fischer (1932). The influence of Ptolemy's maps on European cartography is best summarized by Fischer in Pt. I, 1, pp. 290-415, but see also Dilke (1985a) 154-166.

(18) (1975)) I, 935 : « Four centuries during which classical scholars kept talking about the cultural heritage from antiquity have not yet produced a reliable edition of the Greek text. » See also his note 7 on the same page.

(19) Weber (1976) Vol. 1 (Kommentar) ; 27-28. The *ar(i)ae fines Romanorum* in the margin of segment X need not refer only to the frontier with the Persian Empire, but could serve to delineate the *entire* eastern frontier shown on segments IX and X. See also Levi (1981) 139-140.

(20) (1978) 505-508. Those names which Musil had identified with sites in the Wādī Sirḥān are accepted by Sartre (1982) 40.

(21) Marinus had discarded the figure of 1° = 700 stadia proposed by Eratosthenes some four centuries earlier.

(22) On modern maps the figure is 1° = 111 km.

(23) 1° = 91 km. This remains a constant distance whatever the latitude.

(24) A representative selection is given in Fischer (1932).

(25) One need only look at other areas of the Roman Empire, e.g. north-west Africa, to observe the same phenomenon on other maps of the *Geography*.

(26) A variant spelling of BANAΘA is BANAXA, but this would still be close enough to warrant suspicion.

(27) Some MSS place Banatha 0°15' north of Dumaetha, e.g. Muller (1901) II 1016.

(28) NAXABA in the ed. pr. has no support.

(29) (1978) 121. Some months later he passed the same site and noted : « ... low, yellow hills in which is the abandoned settlement of an-Nakb abu Ḳaṣr ...»

(30) Musil (1978) 508. See the instructive article by Bailey (1984) for a discussion (p. 45) and list (p. 52-53) of common place-names derived from plants and trees.

(31) (1978) 313 combined with comments on 314 note 72.

(32) *Ibid.* 314. Ḥazawẓā is the lowest point of the Sirḥān depression.

(33) *Ibid.* 105 ; cf. 320.

(34) Bailey (1984) 53 notes the plant-name *ᶜarad* which appears in the place-name Wādī ᶜArada in Sinai.

(35) (1970) 59. Adams (1977) 37 and plate 10a and b notes a Qaṣr at Ithra and a « ruined building » at Dawqira (65 km to the east) which may be Ghassānid or Umayyad.

(36) *Ibid.* 62.

(37) *Ibid.* 64 ; 161-162.

(38) There is a small ruined site between Azraq and the Saudi Arabian border named al-ᶜUmarī and described (as ᶜAmrī) by Glueck (1944) 14-16, who reported « numerous Roman and Byzantine sherds » including *terra sigillata*. A kilometer to the south Glueck found the ruins of « a very large caravanserai, which stretched over an area almost a kilometer long ». He designated this site as « Khirbit ᶜAmrī ». To my knowledge it has not been revisited since. If the place-name Adra had been plotted 1° farther east and included among the list of towns in Arabia Deserta it would correspond very nicely to the location of al-ᶜUmari. For a comprehensive survey of all the recent archaeological work in this area, see Kennedy (1986). I wish to thank the author for allowing me to see the typescript of this article.

BIBLIOGRAPHY

ADAMS (R.) et al. 1977 – « Preliminary Report on the First Phase of the Comprehensive Archaeological Survey Programme ». *Atlal* 1. p. 21-40.

BAILEY (C.). 1984 – « Bedouin Place-Names in Sinai : Towards Understanding a Desert Map ». *PEQ* 116, p. 42-57.

BOWERSOCK (G.W.). 1983 – *Roman Arabia* (Harvard Univ. Press).

BRAMKAMP (R.A.) and RAMIREZ (L.F.). 1976 – *Geographic Map of the Jawf-Sakakah Quadrangle, Kingdom of Saudi Arabia* (Map GM 201 B), Directorate General of Mineral Resources.

DILKE, (O. A. W.). 1985a — *Greek and Roman Maps* (Thames & Hudson).

DILKE, (O. A. W.) and (M.S.). 1985b – « The Imprint of Ptolemy », *The Geographical Magazine* (Oct.). p. 544-549.

EPHᶜAL (I.). 1982 – *The Ancient Arabs : Nomads on the Borders of the Fertile Crescent, 9th-5th Centuries B.C.* (E.J. Brill).

FERGUSON (K.P.) Jr. et al. 1984 – *Geographic Map of the Arabian Peninsula*, Compiled by U.S. Geological Survey and ARAMCO for the Deputy Ministry for Mineral resources, Kingdom of Saudi Arabia.

FIELD (H.). 1960 – *North Arabian Desert Archaeological Survey, 1925-50* (Peabody Museum Papiers XLV No. 2)

FISCHER (J.). 1932 – *Claudii Ptolemaei Geographiae Codex Urbinas 82 : Pars altera, tabulae geographicae LXXXIII Graecae-Arabicae-Latinae e Codicibus LIII Selectae* (E.J. Brill and Harrassowitz).

GLUECK (N.). 1944 – « Wadi Sirhan in North Arabia ». *BASOR* 96, p. 7-17.

KENNEDY (D.L.). 1982 – *Archaeological Explorations on the Roman Frontier in North-East Jordan* (B.A.R.)

KENNEDY (D.L.). 1986 (forthcoming) – « North West Saudi Arabia : A.D. 100-600° », *Atlal* 10. In press.

KENNEDY (D.L.). and MACADAM (H.I.). 1985 – « Latin Inscriptions from the Azraq Oasis, Jordan ». *ZPE* 60. p. 97-107.

LEVI (A.) and (M.). 1981 – « Map Projection and the Peutinger Table » in L. Casson & M. Price (eds.). *Coins, Culture and History : Numismatic Studies in Honor of Bluma Trell* (Wayne State Univ. Press). p. 139-148.

MÜLLER (C.). 1901 – *Claudii Ptolemaei Geographia*. 3 vol. (Firmin-Didot).

MUSIL (A.). 1978 (reprint) – *Arabia Deserta* (American Geographic Society).

NEUGEBAUER (O.). 1975 – *A History of Ancient Mathematical Astronomy* . 3 vol. (Springer Verlag).

PARR (P.J.) et al. 1978 – « Preliminary Report on the Second Phase of the Northern Province Survey ». *Atlal* 2 : 29-50.

POLASCHEK (E.). 1965 – « Ptolemaios als Geograph ». *RE* Supplement 10 : col. 680-833.

SARTRE (M.). 1982 – *Trois Études sur l'Arabie Romaine et Byzantine* (Col. Lat. 178).

STEVENSON (E.L.). 1932 – *Geography of Claudius Ptolemy* (New York Public Library).

TOOMER (G.J.). 1975 – « Ptolemy » in the *Dictionary of Scientific Biography* 11 : 186-206.

VAGLIERI (L.C.). – « Dumat al-Djandal » in the *Encyclopedia of Islam*, 2nd ed. (E.J. Brill).

WEBER (E.). 1976 – *Tabula Peutingeriana, Codex Vindobonensis 324 : Vollstandige Faksimile-Ausgabe im Originalformat* (Akademische Verlagsenstalt, 2 vol.).

WINNETT (F.) and REED (W.L.). 1970 – *Ancient Records from North Arabia*. (University of Toronto Press).

APPENDIX

CHAPTER XVI : Location of Arabia Petraea (Fourth map of Asia)

ARABIA Petraea is terminated on the west by that part of Egypt to which we have referred ; on the north by Palestina or Judaea and the part of Syria along the line which we have indicated as its southern border ; on the south by the end of the Arabian bay and by the Heroopolites bay to the terminus as indicated on the confines of Egypt near the Pharan promontory, which is located in

65 28 30

and by the bay, which is the Elanite, to its turn which is in 66 29

the position of the village Pharan is

65 28 40

village Elana, which is located in the angle of a bay of this name, has this position

65 50 29 15

on the east its boundary is the line leading to the eastern terminus of Syria, as we have indicated, and very near Arabia Felix, to the part of this line which is in 70 30 30

along the Arabia Deserta and the remaining part of the line.

The mountains in this land called Melanes (Niger) extend from that angle of the bay which is near Pharan, toward Judaea.

From these mountains toward the west along Egypt is Saracene ; below this Munychiatis ; below which on the bay is the Pharanita region ; near the mountains of Arabia Felix are the *Raitheni.*

The towns and villages in the interior are :

Eboda	65 15	30 30
Maliattha	65 45	30 30
Calguia	66 20	30 30
Lysa	65 50	30 15
Gubba	65 50	30
Gypsaria	65 40	29 45
Gerasa	65 30	29 30
Petra	66 45	30 20
Characmoba	66 10	30
Auara	66 10	29 40
Zanaatha	66 45	29 50
Adru	67	29 55
Zoara	67 20	30 30
Thoana	67 30	30 30
Necla	67 30	30 15
Cletharrho	67 50	30 20
Moca	67 50	30 10
Esbuta	68 30	31
Ziza	68 45	31
Maguza	68	30 45
Medaba	68 30	30 45
Lydia	69	30 40
Rabathmoba	68 30	30 30
Anitha	68 40	30 15
Suratha	69 15	31 10
Bostra legion III Cyrenaica	69 45	31 30
Mesada	69 20	30 30
Adra	69 40	30 40
Corace	68	30 5

(From Stevenson, 1932)

CHAPTER XVIII : Location of Arabia Deserta (Fourth Map of Asia)

ARABIA Deserta is terminated on the north by that part of Mesopotamia which borders on the Euphrates river as we have noted ; on the west by a part of Syria and of Arabia Petraea ; on the east by Babylonia separated by those mountains which begin at the terminus as we have indicated, near the Euphrates river extending to the interior bend of the Persian gulf near the bay, the location of which terminus is in 79 30 10
and that part of the Persian gulf to a terminus, the location of which is 79 29
on the south moreover by Arabia Felix terminating in the confines of Arabia Petraea which we have indicated as being near the Persian gulf.

The *Cauchabeni* inhabit the parts of Arabia Deserta which are near the Euphrates river, the *Batanaei* the parts near Syria, the *Agubeni* the parts which are near Arabia Felix, next to these are the *Rhaabeni*, and the *Orcheni* on the shore of the Persian gulf ; the *Aesitae* inhabit the parts near Babylonia and the parts which are below the *Cauchabeni*, and above the *Rhaabeni* the Masani (inhabit) ; in the interior moreover are the *Agraei* near the *Batanaei*, and the *Marteni* near Babylonia.

The towns and villages in this land and in that near the Euphrates river are

Thapsacus	73 30	35 5
Birtha	73 40	35
Gadirtha	73 50	34 45
Auzara	74 5	34 30
Audattha	74 15	34 20
Addara	74 20	34 10
Balagaea	75	34
Pharga	75 40	34
Colarina	75 30	33 40
Belgynaea	76	33 30

In the parts near the Persian gulf are the towns:

Ammaca	79	30 10
Idicara	79	29 30
Iucara	79	29 15

The inland towns are :

Barathena	73 20	33
Save	73	33
Choce	72 30	32 30
Gauara	73 40	32 40
Aurana	73 15	32 20
Rhegana	75 40	33 20
Alata	72 30	32
Erupa	72 30	31 15
Themme	75	31 40
Luma	75 40	31
Thauba	72 45	30 30
Sevia	73 30	30 30
Dapha	74 15	30 30
Sora	75	30 20
Odagana	76 15	30 40
Tedium	77	30 30
Zagmais	76 30	30 10
Arrade	71 30	30 15
Obaera	71	30 45
Artemita	72 15	30 10
Banatha	73 15	29 40
Dumaetha	75	29 40
Alata	75 40	29 30
Bere	76 40	29 30
Calathua	77 30	29 30
Salma	78 20	29 30

(From Stevenson, 1932)

IV

Some Hellenistic Toponymns of Phoenicia

The toponomy of Phoenicia provides a number of dynastic names or names clearly associated with one or another of the rival Hellenistic kingdoms in Syria and Egypt. In every case the Greek name would appear to be honorific only, with no political significance other than a royal favor shown to a Phoenician town or city. Such benefaction might be a reward for loyalty or simply recognition of commercial value. Seleucid toponyms [80] are found in northern and central Phoenicia, coastal and inland. Ptolemaic toponyms are associated particularly with the Biqâ` Valley (the one area of Phoenicia which the Ptolemies held until 200 B. C.), and one or two sites on the coast. I shall begin with the latter.

There are three place-names which can be associated with Ptolemaic rule in Phoenicia. One is Heliopolis (Ba`albek), the ancient sacred area in the central Biqâ`. The time and circumstances of its naming are unknown, but there is obviously some correlation between the cultic aspect of the Phoenician site and Egyptian Heliopolis (ancient Om) in what is now Cairo. Polybius makes no mention of Heliopolis in his account of the campaigns made by Antiochus III through the Biqâ`. There is also no reference to the « Egyptian Wall » (noted above) across the northern entrance of the valley. Since the ancient shrine at the site of Heliopolis [81] apparently had no strategic value it may have been among the nameless « other towns of the region » captured (temporarily) by Seleucid forces during the Fourth Syrian War. The major Ptolemaic garrisons were placed precisely where the Biqâ` narrowed, i.e. at Gerrha (Anjarr ?) and Brochoi, both sites with indigenous names.

Another Ptolemaic place-name is Arsinoë. Stephanus of Byzantium's *Ethnica* lists an Arsinoë which is described as a « city of Syria, in the *Aulôn* ». This « Arsinoë of the Aulôn » (presumably named for Arsinoë II, *c.* 276-270)

---

80. It is particularly disappointing that GRAINGER, *Cities of Seleukid Syria* did not include the cities of Phoenicia south of the Eleutherus or south of Laodiceia *ad Libanum* in several places in the text where it would have been appropriate : « The Cities and the Villages » (Chap. 4) and Appendix I : « Concordance of City-Names ».

81. The indigenous (Aramaic) place-name for this site may be *Shamsimuruna* (« Shamash is our Lord ») ; see P. BORDREUIL, « A l'origine du nom d'Héliopolis-Baalbek ? » in Gatier, *Géographie Historique*, p. 309-10. Greek *Helioupolis* simply affirms the recognition of the sun-god as the predominant deity of the site.

was long ago identified as Damascus by Victor Tscherikower [82]. But Damascus does not lie in the « Valley of Syria » nor in a « Royal Valley » (Abilene ?) mentioned by Strabo. The Aulôn of Syria, as we know from the Zenon papyri and Polybius, is specifically the « Massyas » or « Marsyas » Valley between the Lebanon and Antilebanon ranges. Arsinoë would be an as yet unidentified site in the Biqâ`, as Père Abel suggested [83]. But it is more likely that the Ptolemaic toponym disguises a known site such as the fortress of Gerrha.

Equally difficult to locate is Stephanus' « Arsinoë of Coele Syria », identified with the preceding Arsinoë (and therefore with Damascus) by A.H.M. Jones [84]. Tscherikower [85] believed it was located in northern Palestine, a supposition strengthened by recent excavations at Tell Anafa in the north-eastern corner of the Huleh Valley in northern Israel [86]. The absence of both Arsinoës in extant Hellenistic sources means nothing.

The third name is « Heracleia in Phoenicia » mentioned in one letter of the Zenon correspondence (*PCZ* 59088.9-10) dated 258 B. C. [87]. It also appears among the thirty Heracleias registered in Stephanus' *Ethnica*. The two Phoenician Heracleias were identified with each other, and with the Heracleia of Strabo's *Geography* (Bk. 16.2.7-8) by Père Vincent [88]. The assumption that the two Heracleias « in Phoenicia » were the same town is probably correct, but Strabo's Heracleia is known to lie between Seleuceia (the port of Antioch) and Laodiceia *ad Mare* (modern Lâdhiqîyah) on the north Syrian coast. That would be near the heartland of the Seleucid kingdom and considerably beyond the limits of territory controlled by the Ptolemies. Furthermore no town or city that far north would be designated as « in Phoenicia ».

The identity of « Heracleia of Phoenicia » was discovered by that indefatigable topographer Ernst Honigmann [89]. He noticed that a list (in Greek) of bishops attending the synod of Antioch (A.D. 444) included an Epiphanius « of Heracleia ». The Latin translation of that list gave Epiphanius' bishopric as

---

82. « Die Hellenistische Städtegründungen von Alexander dem Grossen bis auf Die Römerzeit », *Philologus Supplementband*, 19.1 (1927), p. 65-67.

83. F.-M. Abel, *Géographie de la Palestine*. 2 vols. (Paris, 1967 [Reprint of 1938 edition]) Vol 2 : 131.

84. *Cities* 240 and note 20.

85. V. Tscherikower, *Hellenistic Civilization and the Jews* (Philadelphia, 1959), p. 106.

86. G. Fuks, « Tell Anata : A Proposed Identification », *SCI*, 5 (1979/80), p. 178-84.

87. An improved reading was published in T.C. Skeat (ed.), *Greek Papyri in the British Museum*, Vol. 7 : *The Zenon Papyri* # 1933 lines 9-10. « Heracleia » with no qualifier, but almost certainly the same town, is also mentioned in *PCZ* 59044.1-2 and 59093.9, both documents of approximately the same date.

88. L.H. Vincent, « La Palestine dans les papyrus ptolémaiques de Gerza », *RB*, 17 (1920), p. 161-202 at p. 178 note 2.

89. *Patristic Studies* (Rome, 1953), p. 123-4.

« Arca » (Tell `Arqa, near Tripoli). The curious survival of the Greek name for more than seven centuries solved the mystery. Why Arca would be designated « Heracleia » is now as obscure as when that change of name occurred. Apart from the widespread popularity of the name is the obvious association of Greek Heracles and Phoenician Melqart, e. g. at Tyre and distant Gades (Cadiz in Spain). There is as yet, however, no evidence for a cult of Melqart/Heracles at Arca. Heracles was honored, along with Dionysius, as a « dynastic deity » of the Ptolemies.

Several Seleucid dynastic names are associated with Phoenicia. Two Antiocheias are known. One is clearly identified by Stephanus as « Antiocheia of Pieria which the Syrians call Aradus » [90]. The renaming of Aradus can most probably be attributed to Antiochus II (261-246) following the Third Syrian War. Less certain is the identification of an « Antiocheia under Libanus » mentioned by the second century A.D. historian Appian (*Syriaca* 57). The context is a list of cities attributed to Seleucus I (312-281) and this name occurs between references to a « Laodiceia in Phoenicia » and « Apamea of Syria ». The attempt by Jones [91] to see some analogy between this name and the later *Caesaraea ad Libanum* (Arca) is pure guesswork. Appian's association of « Antiocheia under Libanus » with Seleucus I, if correct, would mean the site must have lain north of the Seleucid/Ptolemaic border at the Eleutherus River.

There are also two Laodiceias within Phoenician territory. One is identified with ancient Qadesh (mod. Tell Nebi Mend) on the western bank of the upper Orontes. This is the « Laodiceia of Lebanon » cited by Polybius (*Hist.* 5.45.1), the Laodiceia *sub Libano* of Pliny the Elder (*Nat. Hist.* 5. 82), and the Laodiceia *Scabiosa* (Rough ?) » of Ptolemy (*Geog.* 5. 14. 16) and the Peutinger Map [92]. The fact that it appears in Polybius in the context of the Third Syrian War means that its re-naming occurred at least as early as the reign of Antiochus II. If this is Appian's (*Syriaca* 57) « Laodiceia in Phoenicia » a foundation date as early as the reign of Seleucus I would be correct [93].

Beirut was re-named « Laodiceia of (or "in") Phoenicia », perhaps by Seleucus IV (187-175). Bilingual coins of the second century B. C. proclaim

90. *Pieria* refers to the old Macedonian town, and may be a nostalgic reflection of the earliest inhabitants of Antiocheia.

91. *Cities* 244 and note 44

92. *Scabiosa* is Ptolemy's transliteration into Greek of the Latin name, the implications of which are unclear. The nickname begs comparison with that of Laodiceia *Combusta* (« Burnt ») near mod. Konia in Turkey (Strabo, *Geog.* 14. 2. 29). That colorful name was probably due to the smelting-furnaces near the site ; see W.M. CALDER, « A Journey Round the Proseilemmene », *Klio*, 10 (1910), p. 232-42 at p. 242.

93. GRAINGER, *Cities of Seleukid Syria* does not include this site in his discussion (Chap. 3) of cities founded by Seleucus Nicator, nor does it appear on his map, « The Cities of Seleukos » p. 232. Archaeological work at the site has produced some Hellenistic material ; see the reports cited by Grainger, *ibid.* 208.

Beirut as « Laodiceia the *mêtrôpolis* of Phoenicia » (in Greek) and either « Laodiceia which is in Canaan » or « Laodiceia the mother of Canaan » (in Phoenician). Contemporary Greek inscriptions from Delos attest « Laodiceia in Phoenicia » [94]. But if this is to be identified with the « Laodiceia in Phoenicia » of Appian, as seems likely, his attribution of it to Seleucus I is an anachronism.

Modern sites confidently identified with Hellenistic toponyms share some common features. Many are located at strategic points and lend themselves to the garrisoning of military detachments. All but Beirut were on or near borders between Seleucid and Ptolemaic portions of Phoenicia. Only two, however, Antiocheia/Aradus and Laodiceia/Beirut, enjoyed the privilege of coining. The reason for the granting of such a coveted prestige remains unclear. Commercial preeminence was undoutedly a major consideration, and ranked those two cities with the other important coastal emporia of Tripolis, Byblos, Sidon and Tyre.

94. P. ROUSSEL, « Laodicée de Phénicie », *BCH*, 35 (1911), p. 433-41 ; *SEG* 3.676 ; P. BORDREUIL, « Les inscriptions monétaires phéniciennes de Laodicée de Kanaan », in Gatier, *Géographie Historique*, p. 304-08.

V

STRABO, PLINY THE ELDER AND PTOLEMY OF ALEXANDRIA : THREE VIEWS OF ANCIENT ARABIA AND ITS PEOPLES

(For Otto E. Neugebauer on his 90th birthday)

Introduction

The world of classical antiquity has bequeathed to us only three works of scholarship in which comprehensive accounts of the Arabian peninsula and the Near East survive complete. These are Strabo's *Geography* (written and revised between 25 B.C. and A.D. 23), Pliny the Elder's *Natural History* (A.D. 77) and Ptolemy's *Geography* (c. A.D. 150). The intention of each work is similar : to record from eyewitness observations and previous written evidence the *oikoumenē* from western Europe to India and from the Baltic Sea to the source of the Nile River. But the methodology of each was different, as we shall see, so that we have three very idiosyncratic views of this *oikoumenē*, aspects of which sometimes overlap but more often do not. What is striking about all three is that each account includes a preface in which the aim, scope and method is spelled out (in varying degrees of detail and clarity) for the interested reader. Thus we are allowed to compare these prefatory comments with the information in the pages that follow each to see whether intention and result bear any relationship. Moreover, we can then compare the introductory statements and accounts of one author with another. This paper will first examine the prefatory comments of Strabo, Pliny and Ptolemy, and then compare and contrast those comments with the description each gives of Arabia and its neighboring regions. We will be examining, in effect, a work of historical geography, a compendium or encyclopedia of natural history, and a handbook of mathematical geography. It is only Ptolemy who will provide visual evidence in the form of maps.

The Introduction to Pliny's *Natural History*

Rather than proceed chronologically to investigate the three works just mentioned, I will begin with Pliny, work back in time to Strabo and then forward to Ptolemy. There are a number of reasons why *this* order of inquiry suggests itself. The first is that the lifetime of Pliny just barely overlaps that of Strabo and (with less certainty) Ptolemy. The second is that Pliny's Latin and a bibliography "unique in its comprehensiveness" (*OCD*[2] 846) lie outside the tradition represented by Strabo and Ptolemy. The third is that the preface to Pliny's *Natural History* has only just come under recent scrutiny in an important article by Nicholas Howe (see *Latomus* 44 [1985] 561-576). This provides a handy springboard for similar analyses of Strabo and Ptolemy.

Howe's analysis of Pliny's methodology can be summarized briefly. The famous dedication of the *Natural History* to Titus (*nobis quidem qualis in castrensi contubernio – Praef.* 3) sets the tone for the entire introduction. The *NH* was intended to be "a didactic work necessary for the reformation of Rome" (Howe 1985 : 561) and is imbued with a dislike for poetic forms of expression. The literary models for Pliny were Cato, Varro and (to a lesser degree) Livy. The homespun virtues of integrity, simplicity, self-discipline and piety are praised throughout, and it is these qualities that "allowed Pliny to elevate the study of the natural world above the realm of mere curiosity to that of moral statement" (Howe 1985 : 564). It is the study of the natural world (*rerum natura – Praef.* 13) that Pliny hopes will set his work apart and will educate men of influence in the Roman state. As one who had risen through the ranks of the equestrian order via military commands, the study of law and a procuratorship in Spain, Pliny embraced the imperial spirit of his time with Stoic pragmatism. He had kept his political profile deliberately low during most of Nero's reign and was justifiably pleased when Vespasian and his sons emerged victorious in 69.

Howe's assertion that poetic works had squeezed didactic writers such as Pliny from the center of the literary stage is not convincing. He fails to perceive that the best of poets are themselves didactic. Pliny would have understood that. Virgil hardly rates a mention in the preface, but that was because Virgil chose poetry rather than prose as his medium of expression, not because Virgil had nothing to say. Howe also fails to note that Pliny's notorious use of circumlocutions in place of simple, declarative sentences all but obscures the fact that he does tell us what his overall intentions are in some detail. This occurs almost halfway through (*Praef.* 15) the preface and is presented as what I term Pliny's "Reflexive Beatitudes". Blessed am I (he seems to imply) for in my *Natural History* I have been able to give (1) novelty to what is old (*vetustis novitatem dare* – the verb is understood in the phrases that follow), (2) authority to what is new (*novis auctoritatem*), (3) brilliance to the commonplace (*obsoletis nitorem*), (4) light to the obscure (*obscuris lucem*), (5) glitter to the lackluster (*fastiditis gratiam*), (6) credibility to the doubtful (*dubiis fidem*), (7) a natural quality, indeed, to everything (*omnibus vero naturam*) and (8) all her qualities to nature (*et naturae sua omnia*). What Pliny meant by the last two is far from clear, but like those *other* eight beatitudes (*Matt.* 5 : 3-11) the attitude taken is positive and optimistic (contrast *Lk.* 6 : 20-27 for a study in opposites).

In order to fulfill the encyclopedic scope of his work Pliny tells us a few paragraphs later (*Praef.* 17) that he has extracted information from about 2,000 volumes, condensing that into 36 books containing no fewer than 20,000 interesting facts previously noted by 100 authors but including as well a great number of hitherto ignored or absolutely new facts. The Younger Pliny tells us (*Epist.* III. 5) about the rigorous regimen adhered to by his uncle in order to make the most of his waking hours. The results of this are what we must examine next.

Pliny's Arabia

There appear to be four distinct areas of the Near East to which Pliny gives the name Arabia. The first we encounter in Bk. V.12.65. This is the Arabia stretching eastward from Egyptian Pelusium to the Red Sea and contiguous there with a second Arabia which he calls "blessed" : *Ultra Pelusiacum Arabia est, ad Rubrum Mare pertinens et odiferam illam ac divitem et beatae cognomine inclutam.* A third Arabia, east of the Dead Sea, is given the name of "Arabia of the Nomads" (*ab oriente Arabia Nomadum* [V.15.72]). The fourth Arabia Pliny locates on one side of the upper Euphrates river : *Arabiam inde laeva, Orroeon dictam regionem, trischoena mensura dextraque Commagenen disterminat*... (V.20.85).

This rather complex scenario, as so often in Pliny's geographical essays, is somewhat misleading. The Arabia east of Pelusium is said by Pliny to be a barren land, claiming only one notable mountain peak (Casius), and inhabited by a number of named tribes. Among the latter are the *Scenitae* and *Nabataei.* Two major towns are also named : Aelana

(Ayla) on the Red Sea and Gaza *in nostro mari* (V.12.65). The frontier between this Arabia and Egypt is later noted (V.14.68) as lying 65 Roman miles (95 km) from (i.e. east of) Pelusium, and still later this Arabia is said to separate Judaea from Egypt (... *Arabia Iudaeam ab Aegypto disterminat* ... [XII.46.100]). It is only when Pliny begins to describe Arabia in generalities that we begin to realize that his "four" Arabias are in fact only two. Arabia, he says (VI.32.142) is inferior to no other country in size, extending from Osroene in the north to the Egyptian coast and including tribal territory *in media Syriae ad Libanum montem.* This "Greater Arabia" also includes *ipsa Arabia,* i.e. "a peninsula projecting between two seas, the Red and Persian ... in size and shape resembling Italy, with the very same orientation so that it shares the same fortunate situation (*in illo situ felix*). We have already discussed its inhabitants from the Mediterranean to the Palmyrene desert" (*a nostro mari usque ad Palmyrenas solitudines*) (VI.32.143). He then goes on to recount the peoples of this portion of Arabia, i.e. the Nomads, the Scenitae and the *Nabataei oppidam incolunt Petram nomine* (*ibid.* 144). These Petrans are at the junction of two important roads, one coming east from Gaza and the other going north-east to Palmyra. There are even Petrans, he says, who make the journey to the town of Forat, near Charax on the Persian Gulf, some 735 Roman miles (1073 km) from Petra and nearly twice that distance from Gaza (*ibid.* 145). At a later point Pliny estimates the circumference of Arabia "from Charax to Aelana/ʿAqaba" as 4665 Roman miles (6811 km) (*ibid.* 156).

But "Greater Arabia" for Pliny is now clearly the northern and western portions already described, and the remainder to the south and east which he has not yet described. A large portion of Bk. VI (32.147-162) is given over to precisely that description. The important town of Charax is for Pliny the border between northwestern and southeastern Arabia. As early as Bk. VI.31.138 he makes the explicit statement *Charax oppidum Persici sinus intimum, a quo Arabia Eudaemon cognominata excurrit,* and from there he goes on to describe the regions, tribes and settlements of Eudaemon from Tylos/Bahrain on the north-east coast to ᶜAqaba on the north-west coast. It is evident that an imaginary line from Charax to ᶜAqaba separated the two Arabias in Pliny's mind. Included in his description of Eudaemon is a remarkably censored account of the expedition of 26/25 B.C. led by Aelius Gallus. There is no hint in Pliny that this was indeed a disastrous undertaking ; indeed, Pliny's only contribution to the history of the Gallus expedition is to provide a list (omitted by earlier writers) of the towns destroyed by Roman military forces. To read only Pliny's rendition, one could readily believe that Gallus' invasion of Arabia was an anthropological journey punctuated occasionally by urban massacres :

> The other discoveries that he reported on his return are : that the Nomads live on milk and the flesh of wild animals ; that the rest of the tribes extract wine out of palm trees, as the natives do in India, and get oil from sesame ; that the Homeritae are the most numerous tribe ; that the Minaei have land that is fertile in palm groves and timber, and wealth in flocks ; that the Cerbani and Agraei, and especially the Chatramotitae, excel as warriors ; that the Carrei have the most extensive and most fertile agricultural land ; that the Sabaei are the most wealthy, owing to the fertility of their forests in producing scents, their gold mines, their irrigated agricultural land and their production of honey and wax : of their scents we shall speak in the volume dealing with that subject. The Arabs wear turbans or else go with their hair unshorn ; they shave their beards but wear a moustache – others however leave the beard also unshaven. And strange to say, of these innumerable tribes an equal part are engaged in trade or live by brigandage (*ibid.* 161-162, Loeb trans.).

All in all, says Pliny, the inhabitants of Arabia Eudaemon are among the wealthiest in the world. They sell what they produce "from sea and forest" to Romans and Parthians alike, yet they purchase nothing (*ibid.* 162). There is no clearer example in the *Natural History* that Pliny was as concerned with a trade imbalance as are some economic pundits today. It is also clear that he understood the significance of Gallus' failure, though he was obliged to underemphasize it for his imperial patrons. Pliny later (see below) notes another *expeditio Arabica* of c. A.D. 1 associated with Gaius Caesar. But his explicit statement (*ibid.* 160) that Gaius only "peeked at" (*prospexit*) Arabia indicates that this obscure campaign was ordered, rather than led in person, by Gaius. It is clear that Pliny could relax his moral Stoic stance when circumstances demanded that he do so ; his glowing report of the doomed Gallus campaign is a masterpiece of *trompe-l'œil.*

The *Natural History* abounds with references to Arabia as the source of a variety of natural products, but it is not my intention here to give an exhaustive accounting. Some examples will illustrate the mystique of Arabia for Pliny himself, and for the authors of the sources he plundered for information. Pliny notes that the treatise on Arabia by the Mauretanian king Juba II contained a reference to a man in Arabia restored to life (*revocatum ad vitam*) by means of an unnamed plant (XXV.5.14). Arabia shared with India a reputation for providing the world with "compounds and mysterious concoctions" (*compositiones et mixturae inexplicabiles*), and that "for even a small sore a medicine is imported from the Red Sea" (XXIV.1.5). Arabia ranked with Persia, Ethiopia and Egypt as the home of Magi consulted as gurus by inquisitive westerners such as Pythagoras and Democritus (XXXV.5.13). It is odd not to see India included in this list.

Specific treatments for particular ailments are associated with or come directly from Arabia. A tooth powder can be made by kiln-baking an Arabian stone (*Arabus lapis* = onyx marble ?), but "if mixed with lint or placed on a linen dressing applied locally" this same powder would cure hemorrhoids (XXXVI.41.153). According to Democritus, Pliny says, Magi who wish to summon deities (*deos evocare*) make use of a plant, the *aglaophotis* (perhaps the peony ?), which grows only in the marble quarries on the Persian (i.e. eastern) coast of Arabia (XXIV.102.160). Good quality *ladanum*, an antidote to diarrhea, can be found in Cyprus, but a better quality (*nobilius*) of this plant can be found in Arabia. In short, there is little in Pliny regarding Arabia that is not positive or useful – a notable exception being the tapeworm which he says infests not only that region but Egypt, Syria and Cilicia (XXVII.129.145). Peculiar to Arabia is an olive which produces a tear (*lacrima*) of fluid which is widely used as a styptic for the closure of cuts and open wounds (XII.37.78). But in the same passage Pliny notes (in contradiction to his observation on exports only in Bk. VI.32.160 above) that Arabia imports perfumes (*odores*) in spite of its reputation as a source of exotic scents.

But of all products from Arabia none, with the possible exception of myrrh, excited the imagination of Pliny and his sources as did frankincense. The *NH* devotes five and a half printed pages to the location, description and export of that most mysterious and expensive of woods (the account of myrrh takes only three printed pages). The discussion of frankincense actually elicited from Pliny an admission that he was postponing a report on cinnamon to catalogue "the wealth of Arabia and the reasons that gave it the nicknames of Fortunate and Blessed" (*Arabiae divitias indicari conveniret causasque quae cognomen illi felicis ac beatae dedere*) (XII.30.51). Yet when the summary of Arabian riches draws to a close and Pliny assesses just why this distant and enigmatic land so captivates the attention of the world, his tone becomes noticeably caustic. Arabia has no cinnamon or casia, he says, "yet even so it is called *Felix* ...

a deceptive and undeserved nickname" (XII.41.82). The reason for this ? "The luxury of man has made Arabia Blessed even in death" (*Beatam illam fecit hominum etiam in morte luxuria*) (*ibid.*). The frankincense and myrrh that daily are used in burials throughout the world far exceeds the little of each that is offered on altars to the gods. The gods, Pliny goes on, once accepted (in the Good Old Days) a bit of salt as an offering – but then the gods were more generous to man. And it is not only the *land* of Arabia that should be called Felix – the sea should also, for the pearls there are as much a luxury as spices. "By the minimal computations India, China and the Arabian peninsula drain 100 million sesterces from our Empire every year" (*ibid.*, 84). Cato, he implies, would have been shocked at such scandalous economic extravagance.

The Introduction to Strabo's *Geography*

The same emphasis on didactic pragmatism is a constant theme of Strabo's Introduction to his *Geography*. There is no dedication to an imperial patron, but he makes it clear throughout Bks. I and II that geography is a discipline worthy of the attentions of philosophers, and its utilitarian results should be of primary concern to statesmen and governments (*πρὸς τὰς πολιτικὰς καὶ τὰς ʿηγεμονικὰς*) (I.1.1 C2 ; see also I.1.16 C9). "For in this way", he goes on "they (i.e. men and states) can conduct their business more satisfactorily if they understand the size of a country, its position, and its own peculiarities" (I.1.16 C9). Strabo comprehended the Mediterranean of his own day as a unified empire under the benevolent rule of Augustus, just as Pliny accepted and supported the Flavian imperialism of a later age. In fact Strabo takes pains to ensure that his readers know exactly what he means by "the special term 'inhabited world'" (*ἰδίως καλοῦμεν οἰκουμένην*) (*ibid.*), but even if the "*oikoumenē* was of one rule and one state, it need not follow that all portions of it will be equally well known" (*ibid.*). Thus the crucial role of the geographer : to investigate, to consolidate, and to instruct.

Like Pliny, Strabo adhered to Stoic principles but is much more forthright about expressing them, especially when he distances himself *in attitude* from one of his major sources, Poseidonius, whom he criticizes as an Aristotelian (II.3.8 C104). Also like Pliny he had published an earlier work, totally lost, which was historical (I.1.22-23 C13 ; II.1.9 C70) ; this accounts for the great emphasis on political history in his *Geography*. This latter point is greatly expanded upon by François

Lasserre in a recent and useful study of Strabo's methodology (*ANRW* II.30.1 [1982] 867-896).

Strabo shares Pliny's enthusiasm for the "encyclopedic" (*πολυμαθία*) approach to the study of geography (I.1.12 C7). But for Strabo this mass of information is to be sifted and sorted, and only that material relevant to the geographical study at hand is to be retained. Thus what for Pliny would constitute a separate but equal aspect of his overall study would for Strabo be relegated to a footnote or a parenthetical expression. Strabo also shares with Pliny a reverence for an earlier epoch in the history of learning. Strabo, and many predecessors (he says) including Hipparchus himself, consider Homer to be "the founder of the science of geography" (*ἀρχηγέτην εἶναι τῆς γεωγραφικῆς ἐμπειρίας*) (I.1.2 C2). Here the echo of the heroic age is heard, and the contrast with Pliny could not be more striking : the *poet* as model for the practitioner of prose. But the tribute to Homer, however sincere, is verbose and tedious and hardly edifying. It occupies a disproportionate chunk of his Introduction (I.1.2-10 ; ten pages) and serves only (or so it would seem) to afford Strabo a chance to find fault with Poseidonius (I.1.7 C4). But the scope of his work is stated clearly enough, and its intent, if nothing else, would have pleased Pliny had the latter occasion to consult Strabo :

> ... to this encyclopedic knowledge let us add terrestrial history – that is, the history of animals and plants and everything useful or harmful that is produced by land or sea ... In fact all such studies are important as preliminary helps toward complete understanding. And to this knowledge of the nature of the land, and of the species of animals and plants, we must add a knowledge of all that pertains to the sea ; for in a sense we are amphibious, and belong no more to the land than to the sea. (I.1.16 C8 – Loeb trans.).

The shorter, formal part of Strabo's Introduction (which serves in effect as a Preface) ends at I.1.22-23 (C14), and even this is more than twice the length of Pliny's (twenty-four pages of printed text versus ten). The preface ends with the hope that his work (*τὸ σύγγραμμα*) will be acknowledged useful by those who read it – statesmen and the public – and the promise that its pages will not be burdened by "trifles and unworthy matters". A few lines later his *syngramma* is referred to as a *κολοσσουργία*, and the reader is asked to judge it as he would judge other colossal works, i.e. with attention to the whole and not its constituent parts. Such a remark serves as an unintentional warning to the reader, who shortly discovers that quantity far outweighs quality in what follows. The remainder of the Introduction ocupies the next 236 pages; fortunately, only a small portion of it merits a reference.

STRABO'S ARABIA

Strabo's description of the *oikoumenē* as a whole likens it in shape to a *chlamys* as it appears "in the geographical map" (*εἰς τὸν γεωγραφικὸν πίνακα*) (II.5.13 C118). Whether this *pinax* (also referred to as *ὁ χωρογραφικὸς πίναξ* at II.5.17 C120) is actually the *Orbis Terrarum* of Marcus Agrippa or not, for Strabo a large portion of it depicts countries of the Near East. "After Mesopotamia", he says, "are the lands this side (i.e. southwest) of the Euphrates. And these are the whole of Eudaemon Arabia, bounded by the entire Arabian and Persian Gulf, and all the land inhabited by the Skenitai and the Phylarchoi (extending to the Euphrates and Syria)" (II.5.32 C130). Across the Arabian Gulf (i.e. the Red Sea) are Ethiopians, Arabs and Egyptians (*ibid.*).

It is not until we reach the third chapter of Bk. XVI that we begin to get a full description of what Strabo again terms "Greater Arabia" (*Ἀραβία πᾶσα*). Here it becomes evident at once that Strabo is an arm-chair geographer, for most of what follows concerning Arabia and its peoples is extracted from the publications of others, notably Eratosthenes, Artemidorus and Poseidonius. The only originality involved is Strabo's detailed account of the Aelius Gallus expedition (thanks to his friendship with Gallus) and an eye-witness account of life at the Nabataean capital, Petra (thanks to his friendship with the philosopher Athenodorus).

The northernmost parts of "Greater" Arabia border on the Parthian Empire, and "the phylarchs of the Arabs" (*τῶν Ἀράβων οἱ φύλαρχοι*) are allies of the Romans in the border territory near the Euphrates (XVI.1.28 C748). Elsewhere, Strabo refers to the region of the "Phylarch Arabs" as Parapotamia (XVI.2.11 C753). The other Arab group, the Skenitai nomads (*Σκηνῖται όι νομάδες*) of the same region are more apt to be allies of the Parthians (C748) and are related to the "Skenitai clan" (*ἀνδρῶν Σκηνιτῶν*) who inhabit the region south of Apamene (C753). These "Arabs and Skenitai", he goes on, are politically less developed than the Syrians, who have organized princedoms such as Arethusa under Sampsiceramus (*ibid.*) Strabo's distinction of "Arabs" and "Skenitai" can only mean, as Irfan Shahid pointed out, that the former were considered sedentary and the latter nomads (*Rome and the Arabs* [1984] 55, n. 19). Strabo emphasizes this dichotomy by noting later that the Skenitai group themselves "in a tiny band in wretched, waterless territories, farming little or none, but herding various animals, particularly camels" (XVI.3.1 C765). He describes the region beyond (i.e. south and east of) Skenitai territory as a "vast desert" (*ἐρημός πολλή*), and south of *that* is Eudaemon Arabia. It appears that Strabo's "Greater" Arabia is composed of Eudaemon in the south and Phylarch-Skenitai in the north. Just where the division was is not stated. There is also, as often observed, no mention of the Arabs who by Strabo's time must have settled at the great oasis in Palmyra, precisely in the desert territory between Apamene and the Euphrates frontier. Certainly a settlement of some kind existed in the late 40's B.C., since Appian (*BC* V.9) relates that it was the object of a futile raid led by Mark Antony. It would seem that even when he revised the *Geography* early in the reign of Tiberius, Strabo was unaware that Rome had brought that caravan-city within imperial domains. Arabia east of Damascus is *terra incognita* for Strabo, as it probably was for the prototype of the famous Peutinger Table. It would have been no problem for a cartographer of the late Empire to sketch in the road from Damascus to Dura via Palmyra depicted on the medieval copy we now possess. That Strabo and the PT may reflect a common source (i.e. Agrippa's map of 10 B.C.) is an intriguing possibility and one worth exploring.

Just as Pliny does, Strabo begins his description of the interior of Arabia Felix by first noting the features of the Persian Gulf coast. The great emporium of Gerrha/Thāj (see D. T. Potts, *Proceedings of the Seminar for Arabian Studies* 14 [1984] 87-91), the islands of Tylos/Bahrain and Arados/Muharraq, and other aspects of the coast and its hinterland are discussed. Most of Strabo's description comes from his major source, Eratosthenes (XVI.3.3-6 C766-767). It is clear that Strabo agrees with Eratosthenes' bi-partite division of Arabia since he reproduces it when he records the names of the larger tribes. The Nabataeans, Chaulotaeans and Agraeans are all, according to Eratosthenes, to be located in the northern or desert portion of Arabia (XVI.4.2. C768). "Beyond those (tribes) is Eudaemon [Arabia], extending 12,000 stadia (2,400 km) to the south, as far as the Atlantic [sic] Ocean" (*ibid.*).

The picture of Eudaemon is one of large tribal settlements (the Minaeans and Sabaeans are prominent), farms where the soil and water are adequate, pastoralism where they are not, and the abundance (as in Pliny) of aromatics so sought after in the Mediterranean. There are also notes on architecture, dynastic succession and anthropological customs (male sexual mutilation is among the most spectacular) completely lacking in Pliny (XVI.4.2-20 C768-779 *passim*). But when Strabo returns to a discussion of the Nabateans and their capital, Petra, he introduces an element of confusion into our understanding of his (or Eratosthenes') perception of which Arabia to associate with them : "The first people above (i.e. south of) Syria who *inhabit Eudaemon Arabia* are the Nabataeans and the Sabaeans ..." (*πρῶτοι δ' ὑπὲρ τῆς Συρίας Ναβαταῖοι καὶ Σαβαῖοι τὴν Εὐδαίμονα Ἀραβίαν νέμονται ...*) (XVI.4.21 C779). This at first seems a contradictory statement, for we saw already that Strabo accepted the Nabataeans as inhabitants of desert Arabia, where Eratosthenes had placed them. The confusion, I think, lies not with Strabo or his source, but in the fact that the Nabataean kingdom embraced portions of Arabia Deserta (the Negev region of Israel, most of Jordan, and southernmost Syria) as well as the northwestern part of Arabia Felix (the Ḥijāz of Saudi Arabia – certainly Qurayya and Hegra/Madā'in Ṣāliḥ, and probably Dedan/al-ᶜUlā – see G. W. Bowersock, *Roman Arabia* [1983] 57 ; 95).

Confirmation of Nabataean control of the Ḥijāz in Strabo's day is indeed found in his own account of the Gallus expedition (XVI.4.22-24 C780-782). In one explicit statement Strabo notes that the expedition arrived "at Leukē Kōmē in Nabataean territory" (*εἰς Λευκὴν Κώμην τῆς Ναβαταίων γῆς*) (XVI.4.23 C780). The site of Leukē Kōmē, long disputed, now seems to be satisfactorily identified with the site of ᶜAynūnah, directly east of the mouth of the Gulf of ᶜAqaba (see M. L. Ingraham *et al.*, Atlal 5 [1981] 76-78 ; L. I. Kirwan, *Stud. Hist. of Arabia* II [1984] 55-61 and maps 5 & 5a). This portion of the Ḥijāz may well be the "Nabataea" referred to by Strabo in descriptions of coastal regions and settlements on either side of the Red Sea. At one place he refers to a promontory on which is "the Rock (Petra) of the Nabataean Arabs" and shortly thereafter discusses (in the context of the Gulf of ᶜAqaba) :

> ... Nabataea, a country with a large population and well-supplied with pasturage. They also dwell on islands situated off the coast nearby. These Nabataeans formerly lived a peaceful life, but later, by means of rafts, went to plundering the vessels of people sailing from Egypt. But they paid the penalty when a fleet went over and sacked their country. (XVI.4.18 C777 – Loeb trans.).

This piratical behaviour, followed by severe reprimand, was also known to the historian Diodorus of Sicily (III.43.5) who, like Strabo, relied on an earlier source (on both accounts, see Bowersock, *RA* [1983] 20-21). Thus Strabo and/or his sources correctly comprehend that the

Nabataea of the late first century B.C. included parts of both Arabias. This does not mean that Eratosthenes wrongly ascribed them to just Arabia Deserta, for in *his* day, two centuries earlier, their "kingdom" may have embraced no more than the territory around Petra. That Strabo gives so much attention to the Nabataeans is worthy of comment. Surely this has much to do with the fact that a personal friend lived among them at their capital city for a period of time. And it indicates as well that they were the most important Arabian people of the Augustan age. How important can be gauged not just by what Strabo has to say about them, but, by contrast, what he has to say about their fellow Arabs in the peninsula.

Petra is discussed in glowing terms – secure, prosperous, law-abiding, sophisticated. It is described as a place where a philosopher could feel welcome, and where one could expect to rub shoulders with "numerous Romans and many other foreigners" (XVI.4.21 C779). The Nabataeans are characteristically prudent, acquisitive, sociable and live under wise and moderate rulers. They are related to the Idumaeans, but the latter were banished from among them long ago and became Jews (XVI.2.34 C760). The Nabataeans worship a solar deity. Their kingdom is fruitful (except for the olive) and boasts abundant livestock (except for horses). Strabo's statement that the Nabataeans treat their dead like "dung" (XVI.4.26 C784) has long seemed incongruous given the positive portrait he is painting. This remark on Nabataean burial customs (perhaps a custom for only a tiny proportion of the population) has recently been shown to be a misunderstanding by G. R. H. Wright (*PEQ* 101 [1969] 113-116 ; see also A. Negev, *Nab. Archae. Today* [1986] 69-72).

The peninsular Arabians are less well-known to Strabo, and perhaps because of that of considerably less interest. They are poor soldiers and worse sailors, more fond of buying and selling than fighting (XVI.4.23 C780). Arabia Felix is a patchwork of five kingdoms in which social castes are ironclad and natural products (frankincense and myrrh predominate) are the basis of wealth. Strabo describes a society in which a woman can be shared by many men, and in which sexual intercourse between a man and his mother is permissible. Conviction for adultery is death, but in such a milieu, Strabo implies, it is difficult to be adulterous.

Arabia, Strabo concludes, is Fortunate indeed. For proof of that he reminds the reader (XVI.4.27 C785) that Alexander had planned a military invasion of Arabia following his return from India (see P. Högemann, *Alex. der Grosse und Arabien* [1985] esp. 120ff.). The motivation for that was Arabia's refusal to send ambassadors to Alexander either before or after his Indian campaign, a story Strabo related in some detail earlier (XVI.1.11-12 C741). But the sudden death of Alexander ended the planned expedition. Thus Arabia, or more particularly Eudaemon Arabia, retained its independence, its remoteness, its mystique and its fabulous wealth. The failed expedition of Gallus, which Strabo (in contrast to Pliny) narrates in painful detail, did not really "add much to our knowledge of those places, but nevertheless something small was gained" (XVI.4.24 C782). The blame for the failure Strabo puts squarely on the shoulder of Syllaeus the Nabataean *epitropos* (XVI.4.23 C780), though no specific motive for Syllaeus' duplicity is given. Thus Arabia was twice saved from conquest, once by an unexpected death and once by unforseen treachery. This is a remarkably sober assessment of the situation in his day, especially so from one so sympathetic to Roman intervention abroad. It stands in stark contrast to Pliny's heroic attempt to gloss over Roman failure to subdue the Arabian peninsula. This is no more clearly stated by Pliny than in the remarkably optimistic passage at *HN* XII.30.55 :

> We have carried on operations in Arabia, and the arms of Rome have penetrated into a large part (*in magnam partem*) of it ; indeed, Gaius Caesar, son of Augustus, won great renown from the country (*inde gloriam petiit*). (Loeb trans.).

Remarkable indeed. No mention there of Gallus. And the statement is tucked away in the midst of a discussion of the incense-tree.

The Introduction to Ptolemy's *Geography*

The fundamental study of Ptolemy's Introduction appeared a half-century ago in Hans v. Mžik's *Des Klaudios Ptolemaios Einführung in die darstellende Erdkunde* (*Klotho* 5 [1938]), a German translation and commentary on Bks. I-II.1.9. Mžik clearly understood that in a book written by a mathematician one could expect the prose Introduction to be precisely formulated. Ptolemy's table of contents concisely notes what the twenty-four chapters of the Introduction will discuss, ranging from a distinction between Geography and Chorography through a carefully measured critique of the methodology of Marinus of Tyre, through the step-by-step procedure for creating spherical and linear representations of the earth on paper. It is a work by a man about whom we know almost nothing. He carefully entitled it *Γεωγραφικὴ Ὑφήγησις*, i.e. Geographical

Manual (or Handbook). It was not intended to be a prose descriptive geography, as its opening clearly states :

> Geography is a representation (μίμησις) in picture of the whole known world together with the phenomena which are contained therein ... It is the prerogative of geography to show the known habitable earth as a unit in itself, how it is situated and what is its nature ; and it deals with those features likely to be mentioned in a general description of the earth, such as the larger gulfs and great cities, as well as the peoples and the principle rivers. Besides these it treats only of features worthy of special note on account of their beauty. (I.1.1-2 Stevenson trans. with corrections).

Throughout this portion of the Introduction Ptolemy compares and contrasts geography with chorography (*χωρογραφία*), which he says (I.1.2) concentrates on particulars (harbors, farms, villages) and does not utilize mathematics (I.1.5). Through mathematics, he goes on, "the most sublime and most beautiful" of theories are revealed to human intelligence (I.2.7). This is a constant theme throughout the Introduction. Even so, Ptolemy realizes that as much as mathematical theory can help us comprehend the world around us, the theory must be tested against something substantial and, indeed, practical. That something is nothing less than travel history (*ἱστορία περιοδικὴ*), i.e. "the body of knowledge gleaned from the reports of those who have carefully investigated particular regions" (I.2.2). This "on the ground" information cannot alone determine the precise distances between places, because no one, Ptolemy maintains, travels with mathematical precision. But traveler's itineraries, especially those of merchants who utilize established routes, can be a guide toward establishing correct coordinates on a map. This is as true of sea routes as it is of those over land (I.2.4).

Man's knowledge of the world, he continues, has improved with time, and every generation has the obligation to improve the records of earlier periods (I.5). Thus Ptolemy sees it as *his* responsibility to review carefully and correct errors in the geographical works of his older contemporary Marinus of Tyre (I.6-20 *passim*). It is through his criticisms of Marinus that we see his own methodology at work but here there is need only to summarize what is discussed. Marinus is said to have consulted all important works of earlier scholars, introduced corrections where necessary, and even corrected errors in earlier editions of his (Marinus') work. The creation of maps to accompany the commentaries is found worthy of praise by Ptolemy. But some imperfections remain. Marinus' known world (on a map) projects too far toward the east and south. Ptolemy accepts the by-then standard of computation of 1° of latitude (at the equator) as equal to 500 stadia (i.e. 92 km). This figure is approximately the same for longitude at the equator (I.7.1). The itineraries of recent voyages on land (those of Septimius Flaccus and Julius Maternus from Libya to Ethiopia) and on sea (that of Diogenes from Aromata [the Spice Islands/Indonesia ?] to Rhapsus [Dar es-Salaam, Tanzania ?]) were erroneously accepted by Marinus as representing the accurate distances (I.8-9) to places so far apart :

> Just as one should have doubts with regard to distances that are great in extent, and rarely traveled, and not fully explored, so in regard to those that are not great and not rarely but frequently gone over, it seems right to give credit to the reports of the voyagers (I.10.3 – Stev. trans.).

This statement directly contradicts the attitude of Marinus, who (according to Ptolemy) distrusted the distances related by travelling merchants (I.11.7). In one chapter heading (I.16) Ptolemy takes Marinus to task for miscalculating "the boundaries of provinces" (*τοὺς τῶν ἐπαρχιῶν περιορισμοῦς*). The use of the term *eparchia* seems at first noteworthy, since in its specific, political sense it denotes an administrative unit. This would mean that Marinus – and Ptolemy – represented the Roman portion of the *oikoumenē* on maps by delineating provincial boundaries. This may have been the case for Marinus. But it is clear from the remainder of his Introduction that Ptolemy conceptualized the Roman world in terms of geographic regions only, and it is in those terms that we must accept a broader meaning for *eparchia* : country or region rather than province. This aspect of the *Geography* was not discussed in a short study of Ptolemy's "provinces" (A. Diller, *CP* 34 [1939] 228-238). In the cases of Judaea, the Decapolis and Arabia, as we shall see, Ptolemy also thought in terms of ethnic or cultural identity as well.

Something should be said here about the geographic region which elicits special comments from Ptolemy. This is the Indian subcontinent. In chaps. 13 and 14, and particularly 17, he has much to say of calculating correct distances and locations "because we have learned many more details concerning India, especially of its divisions into *eparchiai* and ... its interior" (I.17.4). Such a statement must reflect the excitement in his own day that India and the East were re-open to serious geographic and cartographic investigation. This was the direct result of the calculated exploitation of the monsoon winds and the subsequent appearance of such navigation handbooks as the anonymous *Periplus of the Erythrean Sea*

c. A.D. 60 (this will appear with a new English translation and commentary by Lionel Casson in a year or two). By the time Ptolemy wrote, increasing knowledge of India meant that geographical works such as that of Marinus were in need of constant revision, no matter how recently they appeared.

Now that we have seen something of the scope and method of Ptolemy, it remains to examine his aim. Ptolemy's ultimate purpose in compiling the register that is his *Geography* is to permit anyone with a reasonable knowledge of mathematics to create an accurate set of maps (I.18). Furthermore

> ... we have given special attention to a better method in fixing the boundaries of all countries (*ἐπὶ πασῶν τῶν ἐπαρχιῶν*) ; we have given their particular position both in longitude and in latitude. After that we have recorded noteworthy information concerning the peoples (*ἐθνῶν*) and their relations one to another. We have noted the chief cities, rivers, gulfs and mountains, and all other things which in the map itself might show distances where they are worth knowing ... we are able therefore to know at once the exact position of any particular place, and the position of the countries themselves (*τῶν ἐπαρχιῶν αυτῶν*), how they are situated in regard to one another (and) how situated as regards the whole *oikoumenē* (I.19 – Stev. trans. with corrections).

The remainder of the Introduction (I.21-24) is a technical discussion of how both spherical and linear representations of the earth may be constructed, which need not detain us. It is worth noting, however, that Ptolemy accepts (I.21) (as did Marinus and *his* major source) the island of Rhodes as the *locus locorum* of cartography. The island's position placed it at the exact center of the *oikoumenē*, equidistant between the Fortunate Isles (Islas Canarias) in the west and the Indus River in the east, and equally distant from Thule (Shetland Islands) in the north and the Prasum Promontory (southeast Ethiopia) in the south. Rhodes was, in effect, the *omphalos* of cartographers throughout all of classical antiquity, until its secular centricity was displaced by the sacred *loci* of Christian Jerusalem and Muslim Mecca.

One may note that Mžik's study of the Introduction included Bk. II.1-9 (*op. cit.* 76-78). Ptolemy gave the title of *Prologos* to this section of the *Geography*. It intruduces his description of the three continents (Europe, Africa and Asia) known to him, and newly discovered portions of those three whose longitudes and latitudes can be "computed from their proximity to regions already known" (II.1.3). Beyond that he notes only that the proper orientation for a map is with north at the top, and east to the right, of the viewer (II.1.4). For someone living and working in Alexandria, that is logical. Ptolemy then devotes the next five books (II.10-VII.3) to a discussion of what he terms the *σατραπεῖαι ἢ ἐπαρχίαι* (II.1.7).

PTOLEMY'S ARABIA

In an instructive article published in the *Proceedings* of a recent conference (*Géographie historique au proche-orient* [CNRS] ed. by P.-L. Gatier, 1988 : 47-53), G. W. Bowersock drew attention to the fact that Ptolemy's representation of Arabia was remarkably different from the bipartite division exemplified by Strabo and Pliny and paralleled in non-geographical works of the first and second centuries (Josephus, Dioscurides, Appian). There are in Ptolemy's *Geography* three distinct Arabias : the traditional two (Deserta and Felix) and a unique entity, Arabia Petraea. Ptolemy's Felix corresponds exactly with the area described by Strabo and Pliny, namely the entire peninsula. But Ptolemy has subdivided what was traditional Deserta in order to delineate his third Arabia. Deserta is now only the territory facing on the Euphrates and the Persian Gulf. Arabia Petraea corresponds to the central and westernmost portions of traditional Deserta, from the Syrian lava-lands south of Damascus to the eastern Delta of Egypt. That geographical region had been until A.D. 106 the kingdom of the Nabataean Arabs, but was at the time Ptolemy wrote the Roman province of Arabia. Bowersock goes on to note that Ptolemy's unparalleled Arabia Petraea gained acceptance only in later writers (pseudo-Agathemerus and Marcianus) who blatantly plagiarized the *Geography.* "Petraea" was ignored by all others (Cassius Dio, Ammianus, the extant fragments of Glaucus and Uranius, the epitome of Stephanus' *Ethnica*) in favor of the traditional two Arabias.

Remarkable as is the designation Arabia Petraea, even more noteworthy is the omission of the Nabataeans among the tribes (Pharanitai, Rhaithēnoi) or tribal placenames (Sarakēnē, Mounchiatis) within the borders of Petraea. For Bowersock this total absence of any reference to Nabataeans or Nabataea "must be seen as a contemporary reflection of second-century discourse in and concerning the Roman Near East" (*ibid.* 51). The Nabataeans, he goes on to say, are also absent in the fragments of Glaucus which deal with portions of their defunct kingdom. Since Glaucus was roughly contemporary with Ptolemy, the silence regarding the Nabataeans must be deliberate, an "unofficial *damnatio* accorded to a defunct dynasty" (*ibid.* 52).

Petraea without Nabataeans is but one interesting aspect of Ptolemy's third Arabia. The territorial disposition of some towns and cities is also worthy of note. Petraea is manifestly *not* superimposed upon the political borders of *provincia* Arabia. Bowersock observes that the cities of Gerasa and Philadelphia, incorporated into the province in 106, are assigned by Ptolemy to his list of cities for that enigmatic entity "Coele Syria and the Decapolis" (V.14.18). These two cities were never part of the Nabataean kingdom. But two towns that had been – Elusa and Mampsis in the Negev desert – Ptolemy assigns to Idumaea (V.15.7). Both towns were in reality within the Roman province of Arabia. Thus it seems that Ptolemy chose to ignore the political situation of his own day regarding Rome's disposition of what had been the Nabataean kingdom and the equally defunct Decapolis (whatever that latter term meant). "Coele-Syria and the Decapolis" in the *Geography* reflects the attempt by some cities to maintain the fiction that they were an independent or at least a separately governed entity within the eastern provincial system. This attitude is more graphically expressed in contemporary coin-legends and epigraphy (on this see H. I. MacAdam, *Studies in the History of the Roman Province of Arabia*, B.A.R. Inter. Series # 295 [1986] 68-79). Neither "Coele-Syria and the Decapolis", nor the intrusion of Idumaea into Roman Arabia, nor Arabia "Petraea" itself, represents the *Realpolitik* of the mid-second century in the Near East.

The Nabataeans were only one of two prominent Near Eastern peoples suppressed by Roman arms in Ptolemy's lifetime. Hadrian had even more recently (A.D. 135) crushed the Bar Kokhba revolt, and it is worth noting how Ptolemy treats the disposition of Jewish territory as well. What had been Roman Judaea since A.D. 6 (except for the short reign of Agrippa I) was incorporated into Roman *Palaestina* at the conclusion of the second Jewish revolt. This is duly acknowledged by Ptolemy under his heading *Παλαιστίνη* (V.15.1), the administrative designation which Hadrian himself undoubtedly chose. But the chapter heading and the introductory statement carefully add the qualifying expression *ἢ Ἰουδαία Συρία*, and one complete section of the chapter (V.15.5) is given over to "Judaea" as one of six constituent districts of Palestine. Ptolemy's treatment of the re-named Jewish capital city is almost identical – "Jerusalem which is now called Aelia Capitolina" (V.15.5). The Jews are explicitly acknowledged whereas the Nabataeans are recalled (obliquely) only by association with their former capital. This contrast must reflect to some degree the presence of a large Jewish community in Ptolemy's Alexandria, and the relative absence of Nabataeans from among the ethnic groupings resident there.

For both the Jews and the Nabataeans the official, provincial name for their formerly independent territories reflects a conscious attempt by the Romans to neutralize the political map of the Near East. Trajan gave the annexed Nabataean kingdom the most dilute of ethnic designations which could still be considered accurate : Arabia. For the twice-defeated Judaea Hadrian revived a toponym unused since the time of Herodotus (*Hist.* I.105), a name which recalled the Philistines, traditional enemies of the Jews in a bygone time. *Palaestina* or *Syria Palaestina* was a deliberate affront to Jewish identity in the *oikoumenē* (M. Avi-Yonah, *The Holy Land* [1966] 114 ; cf. *idem* RE Supp. XIII [1973] col. 405), an insult which Prolemy managed to redress somewhat by equating "Palestine" with his own term "Judaean Syria". Thus in both cases Ptolemy made an effort to qualify the colorless character of the provincial name by appending a term or an adjective which evoked the culture and identity of the ancient peoples whose descendents in his own day inhabited Roman Arabia and Roman Palestine. One may note that no such effort was needed regarding Dacia (III.8-9), incorporated as a province (after two monumental military campaigns) at the very same time that Nabataea was annexed. Ptolemy's manner in the chapter he devotes to Dacia is absolutely meticulous and clinical – and devoid of any sentiment.

In the case of Arabia Petraea Ptolemy's fictional name is a remarkably clever appellation. To refer to the former kingdom as Arabia Nabataea would have been anachronistic and unacceptably nationalistic. Arabia Romana would be nonsensical. Arabia with no qualifying adjective would indicate acceptance of the political reality imposed by Rome. Arabia Petraea evoked the Nabataean kingdom through its famous and magnificent capital of Petra, designated a *metropolis* by Trajan and later honored with the imperial epithet *Hadrianē*. Perhaps we have a hint here that Ptolemy read Strabo's account of life at Petra (see above), or perhaps the enduring fame of the city was known through merchants of Alexandria who traded with Petra via Pelusium. Whatever the case, Ptolemy's careful choice of "Petraea" was both imaginative and expressive. That it did not endure as an acceptable designation for that portion of Arabia is not surprising, since imagination and expressiveness are hardly qualities one associates with the geographic tradition of late antiquity. The Madaba Map is a stunning exception. There is something of a humanist in Ptolemy the mathematician, the cold and calculating scholar who left such an imprint on Arab and European scientific thought (O. A. W. & M. Dilke, *The Geog. Mag.* 57 [1985] 544-549). It is rewarding to catch a glimpse of it in the *Geography.*

The three Arabias described by Ptolemy are not grouped into one segment of the *Geography.* Instead they are presented in turn as one moves south and east of Palestine, north to Mesopotamia, southeast into Babylonia, along the Persian Gulf and eventually to the Arabian peninsula. His description of Petraea and Deserta is brief and schematic, and each component requires only the barest of summaries here. Felix is the exception, as we shall see.

Petraea is introduced (V.16) imediately following his description of Idumaea. The borders are delineated carefully : Egypt to the west, Sinai and the Gulf of ᶜAqaba to the south, Felix farther yet south, and Deserta to the north and east. Ptolemy goes so far as to pinpoint by longitude and latitude the place where the borders of all three Arabias meet : at precisely 70° East and 30°30′ North (V.16.1 – see map following the appendix). Petraea does not include the Ḥijāz, which as we saw was considered by Strabo to be a part of the Nabataean kingdom. But Ptolemy's *eparchiai,* as already noted, present geographic or regional concepts rather than political units. The omission of the Ḥijāz from Ptolemy's Petraea cannot be construed as evidence that the region was never part of Nabataea. Conversely, it cannot be taken as proof that Roman Arabia did not incorporate the Ḥijāz since Petraea also does not correspond accurately to the limits of the Trajanic province. That the Ḥijāz was *not* incorporated into provincial Arabia has been recently and forcefully argued by David Graf (*Géog. hist. du proche-orient* [1988] 171-211). If the region-name Sarakēnē is derived from the tribe Sarakēnoi (*Geog.* VI.7.21 – located precisely in the Ḥijāz), it is the only tribe of Arabia Petraea apparently known from later sources. But the *Saraceni* of the Byzantine period is a generic term the etymology of which is far from certain (contra D. F. Graf & M. O'Connor, *Byzantine Studies* 4 [1977] 52-66). Its association with Ptolemy's Sarakēnoi may be simply coincidental.

In all Ptolemy lists twenty-eight towns and cities in Petraea, in geographical order from the southwest to the northeast. Bostra the capital is correctly associated with its garrison legion, *III Cyrenaica,* formerly one of two garrison legions stationed near Alexandria. This is one of several instances where Ptolemy associates place-names with the Roman army (see, e.g., his notations on certain British towns : Bk. II.3.8, 10, 11, 13). Only four of the twenty-eight place-names of Petraea cannot be identified with certainty : Maguza, Surattha, Mesada and Adra. The identifications proposed for Maguza (RE 14.1 [1928] col. 521) and Mesada (RE 15.1 [1931] col. 1071) are pure guesswork. Adra was long ago identified with the oasis-site of Azraq by Aloys Sprenger, *Die alte Geographie Arabiens* (1875 : par. 221), but a recently published Latin inscription from the fort at Azraq indicates that the ancient name for that site was Dasianis (D. L. Kennedy & H. I. MacAdam, *ZPE* 60 [1985] 101-102) or Basianis (M. P. Speidel, *Historia* 36 [1987] 217-218). Adra may simply duplicate the Adra in "Coele-Syria and the Decapolis" (V.14.18) and both of those may be imaginative clones of the Adrama (mod. Derᶜa) in Batanaea (V.14.20 – see MacAdam, *Studies* [1986] 4-6). I have suggested that Surattha may be modern Umm al-Jimāl in the Jordanian Ḥawrān (*ibid.* 16-17).

Ptolemy's Arabia Deserta (V.18-19) borders on Mesopotamia to the north (including the Euphrates), Babylonia to the north-east, Syria and Arabia Petraea to the west, and Arabia Felix to the south. Two ranges of non-existant mountains traverse the northern and southern borders. As elsewhere in the *Geography* (e.g. central North Africa) such mountains are simply included as conventional designations of the extent of Roman rule or Roman knowledge of the region. There is no mention under the rubric of Deserta, as in Strabo and Pliny, of the offshore islands near the coastal border with the Persian Gulf. Ptolemy includes these in his discussion of Arabia Felix (see below). Eight Arab tribes are noted, of which six are otherwise unknown. The tribe Kauchabēnoi is known by a variant spelling (*Χαυχαβηνοὶ*) in Greek inscriptions from southeastern Syria (MacAdam, *Studies* [1986] 130 # 21). The tribe named Agraeoi must correspond to the tribe of similar name in Strabo (XVI.4.2) and Pliny (VI.32.159).

The names of thirty-nine towns are listed in geographical order from the very north to the far south. Of these, only two can be identified with certainty : Thapsacus on the Euphrates and Dumaetha (Dumāt al-Jandāl/Jawf) in the Nafūd Desert of Saudi Arabia. Recently I have suggested that four other place-names (Obaera, Arrade, Artemita and Banatha) are to be located along the Wadī Sirḥān in northwestern Saudi Arabia between the Azraq Oasis and Dumaetha (MacAdam, *Géog. hist. au proche-orient* [1988] 55-75). But even if these are added to the two certain identifications, we are still at a loss regarding the remaining thirty-three place names. Both Kurt Fischer in Müller's unfinished edition of Ptolemy's *Geography* (Vol. 1.2 [1901] 1011-1017) and Alois Musil in his ground survey of that region (*Arabia Deserta* [1927] *passim*) were able to find modern place-names to match many in Ptolemy's register. Neither Fischer nor Musil paid any attention to the map coordinates given by Ptolemy, but merely equated a name from the *Geography* with a homophonic modern name. Sometimes the guess was reasonable, e.g. Ptolemy's *Aurana* is likely to be the Wadī Ḥawrān in north-east Jordan. But this is hardly the way to proceed. It ignores one of the basic tenets of Ptolemy's methodology set out in his Introduction : every place on earth can be precisely plotted by coordinates based on given distances and fixed points of reference.

It is therefore important to take Ptolemy seriously. He learned of these from familiarity with other sources, most probably Marinus. Strabo and Pliny display as profound an ignorance of easternmost Arabia Deserta as does the famous Peutinger Table. Another source Ptolemy mentions in the Introduction are the reports of travelers and merchants. The fact that his thirty-nine names fall into three clusters of towns when plotted on a graph demonstrates clearly enough that there was no randomness involved in Ptolemy's calculations. Variant spellings in the manuscript tradition are inevitable, and only a definitive edition of the *Geography* will provide the reliable readings needed. There is every reason to hope that many of the nearly three dozen unidentified towns in Arabia Deserta can eventually be pinpointed, or at the very least their modern regional location can be determined.

When we turn to Ptolemy's description of Arabia Felix (VI.6-7) we immediately encounter problems less evident in the discussions of Deserta and Petraea. Foremost of these is text. Müller's unfinished edition (not noticed as such by Max Carey in his additional notes to H. F. Tozer's *A History of Ancient Geography*[2] [1935] xxxii) of the *Geography* ends with Bk. V. For texts of Bk. VI, including Arabia Felix, we must rely on the far less acceptable editions – now approaching their sesquicentenary – of Nobbe and Wilberg/Grashof. Some recent interest in other portions of Bk. VI and some parts of Bk. VII is an encouraging sign ; on this entire matter of a new text see the Appendix.

Ptolemy's chapter on Arabia Felix is sandwiched between discussions of Carmania Deserta and Carmania, just as his chapters on Petraea and Deserta were separated by Mesopotamia. It is evident at once that Ptolemy had at hand a huge mass of data regarding peninsular Arabia, far more than he did for the other components. This at once begs the question of his sources, for as Nigel Groom has pointed out quite recently (*Proceed. Sem. for Arab. Studies* 16 [1986] 65-75) Ptolemy's text is a palimpsest of geographical material, some of it as old as the early Hellenistic period. The question of sources cannot be dealt with here, but it should be stressed that Ptolemy's depiction of Arabia Felix is far more detailed than his treatment of any other portion of Arabia.

Arabia Felix is introduced by a description of its coastal regions (there are five), its interior portions (no subdivisions) and lastly the islands in the Arabian Gulf (i.e. mod. Red Sea) and the Persian Gulf. Both groups of islands are as hopelessly confused as they are in Pliny's *Natural History*; on the latter see S. B. Miles, *JRAS* ns 10 [1878] 157-172) and H. von Wissmann, *Osterr. Akad. d. Wissen., phil.-hist. Kl., Sitzungsberichte* 324 [1977] 40, n. 60 – I owe these references to Daniel Potts). These groups of names are but a small percentage of the lengthy register of proper names catalogued for Arabia Felix. A qualifying term is appended to many names, except for what must have been insignificant settlements. Geographical notations include bays, harbors, rivers (i.e. wadis), gulfs, promontories, coasts, islands and mountains. There are even, says Ptolemy (VI.7.20) four "nameless (*ἀνώνυμα*) mountains", for which he diligently gives coordinates.

The register of settlements totals 151. Many are described as villages (*κῶμαι*), fewer as towns (*πόλεις*) and fewer still as market-towns (*εμπορία*). Six of the interior towns are qualified as *μητρόπολεις*. It seems likely that this distinction was due to their size and economic importance, which is why some, if not all, were administrative centers, i.e. "district capitals". Five have long been identified satisfactorily: Mara (Mārib), Nagara (Najrān), Sabbatha (Shabwa), Maepha (Mayfa'ah) and Sapphar (Ẓafār). For the sixth, Maocosmos, Groom (*ibid.* 68-69) has proposed Qaryat al-Faw. Three of the coastal communities are distinguished as *βασίλεια*: Ravana, Carman and Sava. What Ptolemy means by *basileion* is unclear ; such places may once have been royal treasuries. The town of Neogilla (in the frankincense region, on the east-central coast – see the map) is said (VI.7.11) to be an *ἐπίνειον* (naval base). Its omission in the anonymous *Periplus* (see above) is problematical (on its location see RE XVI.2 [1935] col. 2401). The port of "Arabia" (mod. Aden) on the south-west coast is noted (VI.7.9) as an *emporion.* This is the "Eudaemon Arabia" of the *Periplus* (para. 26), which "not long before" the time of its author was said to have been attacked or destroyed (*κατεστρέψατο*) by some "Caesar". Mommsen long ago (*Römische Geschichte*[4] V [1885] 611-612 and esp. note 2) suggested that the attack on this port was carried out by Gaius Caesar in A.D. 1. That very same argument was vigorously propounded by M. P. Charlesworth (*CQ* 22 [1928] 94-100) who, astonishingly, does not mention Mommsen (the latter is also absent in the discussion of Eudaemon Arabia in RE VI.1 [1907] cols. 890-891). Mommsen's view was totally ignored by W. A. Schoff, *The Periplus of the Erythrean Sea* (1912) 115-116, and K. Wellesley's dismissal of the attack on Aden as a "fable" (*Par. del Passato* 9 [1954] 401-405) is not convincing. The matter remains unsettled, but whether or not a "Caesar" ordered or led the attack, the port of Eudaemon Arabia was sacked, otherwise (as Mommsen astutely noted) is would not be described in the *Periplus* as a *polis* which had become a *kōmē*. There is also no need to assume, with J. O. Thomsen (*History of Ancient Geography* [1948] 296), that Ptolemy's mention of the port as an *emporion* indicates that by the mid-second century it had revived. We simply do not know the source of Ptolemy's information, though it was certainly not the *Periplus*!

Almost as numerous as the communities are the tribes and peoples of Arabia Felix. The register of these totals fifty-six, almost five times the number of tribes in Deserta and Petraea combined. They are not only named, but located. One group of five inhabit the northern region of the Arabian Gulf, and another group of three the territory near the Persian Gulf. The remaining forty-eight tribes are scattered throughout the interior of the peninsula, from the very north (the Scenitai, Sarakēnoi and Thamudēnoi) through the central sector (the Minaei, Sabaei and Omanitai) to the far south (the Sappharitai and Ascitai). The Sarakēnoi are linked with the Thamūd (of enduring fame in Islamic sources) in a region that, as noted above, must be the Ḥijāz. This may indicate that Ptolemy was aware, as an Alexandrian, that the western Sinai region he calls Sarakēnē may have taken its name from the tribe that subsequently moved southeastward to Arabia Felix.

There have been numerous attempts to identify the multiplicity of tribe and place-names in Ptolemy's Arabia Felix. Perhaps no one undertook such an endeavor with more enthusiasm and fewer qualifications than Charles Forster, *A Historical Geography of Arabia* II (1844 : 209-276). The result remains a monument to the incredible optimism of early Victorian clerical scholarship but it hardly ranks with such serious studies as Sprenger's magisterial *Die alte Geographie Arabiens* (1875), a work which has not yet outlived its usefulness. That latter work is still the basis for the identity of most Arabian place-names in the *Realencyclopädie*. Some progress in the process of identification was achieved recently with the publication of the first volume (letters A-E) of the *Gazetteer of Arabia :*

A Geographical and Tribal History of the Arabian Peninsula (1979) edited by S. A. Scoville. On earlier Arabian gazetteers, see her Introduction to that volume ; for her own assessment of its value and history of compilation, see *PSAS* 12 (1982 : 73-78).

Accurate modern maps are essential and it is encouraging to note that a new cartographic series (1 : 500,000) is now being produced by the Saudi Arabian Ministry of Petroleum and Mineral Resources, Directorate General of Mineral Resources. Since 1972 five sheets have appeared ; at least a dozen more are planned for publication. The maps are based on satellite photographs coordinated with corresponding ground surveys and the series will supersede all others. The combination of maps and the Saudi *Gazetteer* should eventually offer great assistance to those who ponder the maps and text of Ptolemy. The third essential, a reliable text of the *Geography*, is still awaited.

Conclusion

Of the three accounts of ancient Arabia discussed here only one – that of Ptolemy – presents us with what we might term a conclusion and/or epilogue. The straightforward presentation in the *Geography* of "satrapies and regions" ends with an account of Taprobane (mod. Sri Lanka) in Bk. VII.4.13. Thereafter follows a summation (VII.4.14) of what has been achieved, a descriptive account (VII.5.1-16) of a world map, a descriptive account (VII.6.1-7) of a spherical representation of the earth and ultimately a step-by-step account (all of Bk. VIII) of the maps to be produced for each of the three habitable regions of the earth. It has long been suspected that the second half of Bk. VII and all of Bk. VIII are not the work of Ptolemy himself (see e.g. A. Diller, *TAPA* 67 [1936] 238).

There remains to assess, however briefly, the impressions left by these three differing views of ancient Arabia and its peoples. It must be noted at once that all three accounts were produced by men who had never (as far as we know) set foot in any portion of Arabia.

Strabo's description of Arabia was influenced (as we saw) by the eye-witness descriptions of Nabataean Petra and the military expedition to Arabia Felix. Both accounts derive from people known personally to the author. The Hellenized Nabataeans, clients of Rome, are contrasted favorably with the traditional, tribal, independent Arabs of the peninsula. Rome's incursion into Arabia, ostensibly to strike at the centers of trade in the far south, failed only because of treachery. On the motives and chronology of that campaign see S. E. Sidebotham, *Latomus* 45 (1986 : 590-602). There is no evidence that Strabo revised his section on Arabia, which must have been written no later than 2 B.C. If he knew of a second expedition (by sea or land) against "Eudaemon Arabia" he did not include it when he revised other parts of the *Geography* c. A.D. 17-23.

Pliny's account of Arabia is very idiosyncratic and strikingly ambivalent. His division of Arabia into "Deserta" and "Felix" maintains a tradition established in the Hellenistic era and accepted by Strabo. Arabia is described as a naturalist would view it, but here and there in the "scientific" narrative intrudes a tone of bitterness and frustration. The Gallus expedition's failure still looms large in the thoughts of Pliny, who at the time of writing was himself the holder of a military command. Rather than shift the blame for failure from Gallus to his Nabataean "ally" (as does Strabo), Pliny ignores the defeat. In compensation he inserts throughout the segments on Arabia allusions to military success scored by Gaius Caesar during the latter's eastern campaign (on this see F. E. Romer, *TAPA* 109 [1979] 199-214). The Nabataeans are mentioned only as one of several tribal groups and there is no attempt to compare and contrast them with other Arabs in peninsular Arabia. Indeed, Pliny shows greater interest in the Palmyrene Arabs (V.88-89) who were in his day far more valuable allies on the turbulent eastern frontier.

Lastly there is Ptolemy's schematic account of Arabia, complete with maps. The Nabataeans, who were presented as an orderly kingdom and exemplary society by Strabo, and who were at least acknowledged by Pliny, are relegated to the adjective "Petraea". Arabia Petraea appears to be as much a fictional creation as Pontus Cappadocicus (V.6.5, 10 – see A. H. M. Jones, *CERP*[2] [1971] 428 n. 45). The register of tribes and place-names, particularly for Arabia Felix, is more extensive than Strabo and Pliny combined.

There is no indication that Ptolemy used either Pliny or Strabo as a source of information about Arabia. Pliny surely would have consulted Srabo, but the latter's absence in Pliny's extensive bibliography can only mean that Strabo's *Geography* was unknown to him. Thus we have, in effect, three independent accounts of Arabia spanning a century and a half. This is important, inasmuch as these accounts offer a three-dimensional panorama which we might otherwise lack.

We do not again get such a comprehensive picture of Arabia until the Islamic middle ages. The geographical dictionary produced by Yāqūt

(c. 1180-1229) became the standard work of the medieval period. But it was the cartographers such as Balkhī (c. 850-934), Istakhrī (10th cent.) and Idrīsī (12th cent.) who left the most graphic record. Balkī's major work, now lost, was a world map in twenty sheets with explanatory notes. What direct influence there may have been from classical antiquity is uncertain. It is known that Balkī's teacher, Kindī, had commissioned a translation into Arabic of Ptolemy's *Geography* (see EI^2 I [1960] 1003).

Istakhrī also produced a world map with commentary, a work which overlapped (and continued) the "atlas of Islam" begun by Balkhī. Istakhrī's map survives and it is evident that he made no attempt to render accurate distances, geographical features or political boundaries. There is also no indication that Istakhrī was influenced by either the methodology or the maps of the Greco-Roman era (see EI^2 IV [1978] 222-223).

Much different is the text and world map, including its much-copied segment on the Near East, by Idrīsī. The map was commissioned on the orders of the Norman king of Sicily, Roger II, and completed in 1154. In conrast to Istakhrī, Idrīsī was especially fond of topographical features (especially mountains). Love of color and great detail also figure strongly in his depiction of the Mediterranean world and especially Arabia. But once again there is no evidence that Idrīsī knew or utilized any earlier non-Arab tradition in cartography (see EI^2 III [1971] 1032-1033).

It was not until the European Renaissance that interest revived in the works of Strabo, Pliny and Ptolemy. But by then it was Ptolemy alone, through the influence of the Roman Catholic Church, who dominated European scientific thinking, particularly cartography. His *Geography*, especially the maps, became the standard by which medieval maps of the Near East were judged. It was nearly the nineteenth century before any really innovative geographical work was undertaken.

APPENDIX

Ptolemy's *Geography* Bks. VI-VIII

> Regardless of its merits as a scientific treatise, Ptolemy's *Geography* has been one of the most celebrated works on the subject and has probably exerted more influence than any other geographical work. Because of its apparent scientific character and because it covers such a vast portion of the earth's surface (thirty-two provinces in Europe, eight in Africa, and forty-four in Asia, including over 8,000 designations of places, rivers, mountains, etc.), it has attracted the attention of scholars and scientists of widely differing fields of interest and training from all over the world.
>
> W. H. Stahl, *Ptolemy's Geography: A Select Bibliography* (1953) 5.

Without any attempt at being definitive, Stahl easily amassed a register of 1500 books and articles (some repetition of titles was inevitable) on aspects of the *Geography* published since the eighteenth century. It is extraordinary that so many generations of scholars have had to work with a text of which only slightly more than half has been accorded a rigorous, critical edition.

When Karl Müller (see note at end) died in 1894 he left unfinished his major edition of the *Geography*. Books I-III had been published in 1883 ; Books IV-VIII were planned for another two volumes. There would be a complementary volume of maps. At the time of his death Müller had reached Bk. V.15. His friend and colleague Kurt Fischer completed Bk. V.16-20 but at that point abandoned the enterprise (see Fischer's Preface to Müller's *Claudii Ptolemaei Geographia*, Vol. I Pars 2 [1901] i-ii). That volume, and a correspondingly abbreviated volume of maps, appeared the same year.

Müller's edition was meant to supersede those of F. G. Wilberg/C. H. F. Grashof, *Claud. Ptol. Geog.* (1838-45, incomplete in six fascicles including Bks. I-VI) and C. F. A. Nobbe (1833-45 ; sec. ed. reprinted 1903). The latter was (and still is) the only complete edition in print. By later standards neither of these could be considered critical editions, and Wilberg/Grashof's has proved to be especially difficult of access. Müller's enormous energy and careful scholarship (the *FHG* and *GGM* are among his best works) led him to examine forty MSS (some quite fragmentary) of the *Geography*, "but the oldest of all, the [Codex] Urbinas [Graecus 82], which is the archetype of a large part of the others, he was unable to use because it was mislaid in the Vatican Library" (A. Diller, *CP* 34 [1939] 228). Anyone who has ever been told by a librarian that a rare book is "missing" will appreciate the full impact of that statement.

It was not until after WWI that interest in the Indian sub-continent prompted a new study of Ptolemy's text, L. Renou's *La géographie de Ptolémée : L'Inde*

(VII.1-4) published in 1925. This was a newly-edited text, with apparatus and a French translation. Less than a decade later Joseph Fischer's monumental study of Ptolemy's maps appeared in four volumes : *Claudii Ptolemaei Geographicae* (1932). This included (Vol. 2 Pt. 1) photographs of the entire text of the Codex Urbinas Graecus 82. That same year an English translation of the complete *Geography* was published in a sumptuous but flawed volume by E. L. Stevenson, *The Geography of Claudius Ptolemy* (including reproduction of maps from the c. 1460 Ebner Manuscript). The translation was based on "Greek and Latin MSS and important late fifteenth and early sixteenth century printed editions" (title page). None of these MSS was reproduced and there was no critical apparatus. The reception of Stevenson's volume was very mixed indeed ; contrast the blistering review by Aubrey Diller (*Isis* 22 [1934/35] 533-539) with that of W. W. Hyde (*AJP* 54 [1933] 293-295). It was another seven years before the appearance of the first comprehensive attempt, exhaustive for its time, to sort out the MS difficulties. This was Paul Schnabel's *Text und Karten des Ptolemäus* (1939).

Not until quite recently has any portion of the text of Book VI been re-examined since Wilberg/Grashof and Nobbe. This is I. Ronca's *Ptolemaios Geographie 6.9-21* (*Ostiran und Zentralasien*) published in 1971. Ronca contributes a newly-edited Greek text with apparatus and German/English translations. Unfortunately he does not acknowledge the latest comprehensive study of the *Geography*, Erich Polaschek's "Ptolemaios als Geograph", RE Supplementband X (1965) cols. 680-833.

Fifty-five years ago W. W. Hyde (*AHR* 38 [1932/33] 727) expressed hope that the then-forthcoming third volume of the Teubner Ptolemy would be devoted to the *Geography*. Alas, when Vol. III did appear (1940) it was devoted instead to Ptolemy's essays on astrology (III.1 – the *Tetrabiblos*) and philosophy (III.2 – on epistemology). Ironically, the Teubner edition of the *Tetrabiblos* was duplicated that very same year by the Loeb edition and translation.

The *Geography* still awaits a definitive edition, called for most recently by Otto Neugebauer : "Four centuries during which classical scholars kept talking about the cultural heritage from antiquity have not yet produced a reliable edition of the Greek text" (*A History of Ancient Mathematical Astronomy* [1975] Vol. I, Pt. 2 : 935). Perhaps by the end of this century that call will be answered. At the very least a critical edition of the text of Arabia Felix alone (VI.6-7) would make a useful doctoral dissertation and a valuable contribution to the study of the ancient Near East.

Additional Note

Karl (also Carl or Charles) Müller (1813-1894) remains an obscure figure among the historians and philologists of the nineteenth century. A piecemeal sketch of his career through the late 1870's appears in C. Bursian's *Geschichte der classischen Philologie in Deutschland* II (1883) 865 ; 868-869 n. 3 ; 898-899 (with mention there of his younger brother Theodor [1816-1881], also a scholar). Müller is mentioned only in passing in later histories of classical scholarship (e.g. Sandys, Wilamowitz-Moellendorff) by reference to Bursian. This is difficult to understand considering his achievements, but I am not the first to realize it : "I have not found an article on Carl Müller in any biographical source" (A. Diller, *The Tradition of the Minor Greek Geographers* [1952] 81 n. 24). Müller's dates and reference to correspondence of his on file in the Archives Firmin-Didot (Paris) are the only new data on his career in P. Petitmengin, "Deux têtes de pont de la philologie allemande en France" in M. Bollock *et al.* (eds.), *Philologie und Hermeneutik im 19. Jahrhundert* II (1983) 76-98 *passim.* I owe this reference to Edward Champlin.

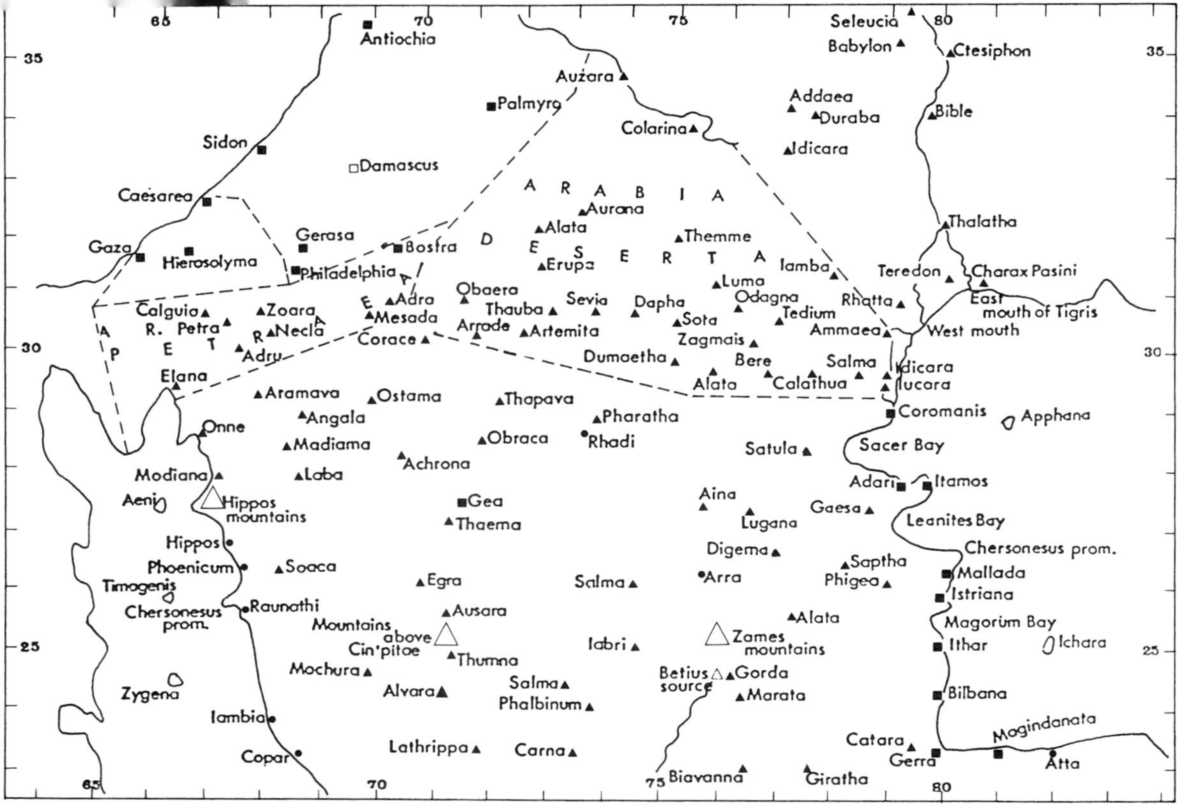

This map of Arabia Petraea, Arabia Deserta and the northermost portions of Arabia Felix, is reproduced with permission from N. Groom, "Eastern Arabia in Ptolemy's Map", *Proceedings of the Seminar for Arabian Studies* 16 (1986), p. 73. The map which follows, of southern Arabia Felix, is from the same source, p. 74.

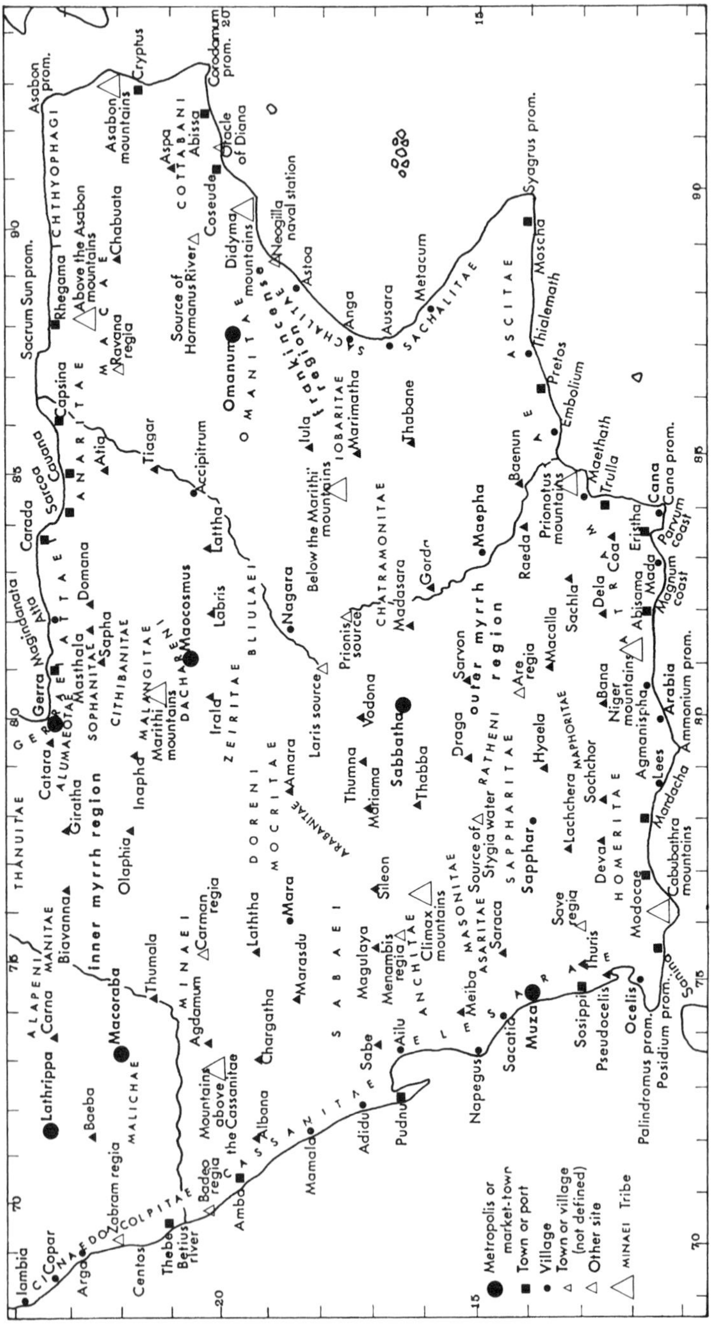
Metropolis or market-town
Town or port
Village
Town or village (not defined)
Other site
MINAEI Tribe
Asabon prom.
Sacrum Sun prom.
Cryptus
Corodamum prom.
Asabon mountains
ICHTHYOPHAGI
Rhegama
Above the Asabon mountains
Chabuata
MACAE
Ravana regia
Aspa
COTTABANI
Abissa
Oracle of Diana
Coseude
Source of Hormanus River
Didyma mountains
Neogilla naval station
Astoa
Omanum
OMANITAE
frankincense region
CHATRAMOTITAE
Anga
Ausara
Metacum
SACHALITAE
Syagrus prom.
Moscha
Thialemath
Pretos
Embolium
ASCITAE
Capsina
ANARITAE
Atia
Tiagar
Accipitrum
Iula
IOBARITAE
Marimatha
Thabane
Baenun
Prionotus mountains
Maethath
Trulla
Cana
Cana prom.
Parvum coast
Carada
Sarcoa
Cauana
Gerra
Magindanata
Atta
GERRAEI
ATTAEI
Domana
Masthala
Sapha
SOPHANITAE
CITHIBANITAE
MALANGITAE
Marithi mountains
DACHARENI
Maocosmus
Lattha
Labris
BLIULAEI
Nagara
Below the Marithi mountains
CHATRAMONITAE
Madasara
Gorda
Maepha
Raeda
Sachla
Dela
Coa
Eristha
Mada
Magnum coast
Abisama
Prionis source
Laris source
ZEIRITAE
Irala
outer myrrh region
Sarvon
Are regia
Macalla
Bana
Niger mountains
Agmanispha
Arabia
Ammonium prom.
Catara
ALUMAEOTAE
Giratha
inner myrrh region
Olaphia
Inapha
Amara
DORENI
MOCRITAE
Thumna
Vodona
Sabbatha
Thabba
Draga
RATHENI
Hyaela
MAPHORITAE
Sochchor
Lees
Mardacha
THANUITAE
Biavanna
MANITAE
Carman regia
Laththa
Mara
Mariama
ARABANITAE
Sileon
Climax mountains
Source of Stygia water
SAPPHARITAE
Sapphar
Lachchera
HOMERITAE
Cabubathra mountains
Deva
Modocae
ALAPENI
Carna
Macoraba
Thumala
MINAEI
Agdamum
Marasdu
Magulaya
Menambis regia
MASONITAE
ASARITAE
Saraca
Save regia
Thuris
Lathrippa
Baeba
MALICHAE
Mountains above the Cassanitae
Chargatha
SABAEI
Sabe
Ailu
ELISARI
Meiba
Sacatia
Muza
Sosippi
Pseudocelis
Ocelis
Posidium prom.
Palindromus prom.
Napegus
Pudnu
Adidu
Mamala
Albana
CASSANITAE
Badeo regia
Ambe
Zabram regia
COLPITAE
Thebe
Betius river
Centos
Arga
Copar
Iambia
NABATAEI

VI

Philadelphia ('Ammān, Jordan) in the Classical Period

Alexander and After: The Hellenistic Age

Alexander's expedition to and from Egypt in 332–331 BC held to the coastal road and ignored the inland portions of Syria-Palestine. Rabbath-Ammon and its imposing acropolis were of no strategic importance for the conquest of Persia, and accordingly played no role in that campaign. Syria (in its broadest geographical sense) was administered from Damascus as a satrapy until Alexander's premature death in 323 BC.[1] Immediately thereafter Rabbath-Ammon and all of Transjordania fell within the bounds of the Greek kingdom (centred on Egypt) that had been carved from Alexander's empire by his resourceful marshal Ptolemy (Sōtēr). The Near Eastern segments of Ptolemy's domain were immediately contested by several other of Alexander's 'Successors', foremost among them Seleucus (Nicatōr). It would be another generation, concluding with the Battle of Ipsus in 301, before the frontiers between the Seleucid and Ptolemaic kingdoms solidified.

1. Ptolemaic Ammanitis

Ptolemaic Syria included all of Phoenicia and Palestine, and the territory east of the River Jordan from Damascus to the Red Sea. Ptolemy I Sotēr (d.283) consolidated his hold on that territory, but there is no evidence of close administrative control during his reign. Rabbath-Ammon was one of the larger settlements within Ptolemaic territory east of the Jordan. Like Bostra to the northeast and Pella to the northwest it could boast of a history stretching back to the Bronze Age and perhaps beyond. An

[1] Bosworth (1974).

ethnographical work of late antiquity informs us that the city was 'first [called] Ammana, then Astartē, then Philadelphia.'[2] The same source goes on to say that the official dynastic name Philadelphia ('Brother/Sister-Loving') derives from Ptolemy II Philadelphus (283–246 BC), who thus honored either himself or his sister/wife Arsinoë II. St Jerome's commentary on *Ezekiel* also notes that the city's name was associated with Ptolemy II: 'Rabbath, which today is named Philadelphia, from the king of Egypt, Ptolemy (called) Philadelphus'.[3]

Had Rabbath-Ammon been refounded as a Ptolemaic colony it would have received a sizeable Greek population, a Greek constitution, and perhaps the privilege of coining. There is no evidence for any of this during the Hellenistic age, though the city did attain the status of *polis* in the Roman era (see below). The change of name seems to have been purely propagandistic symbolism, and was perhaps made simply to advertise Ptolemaic possession of a strategic site. Third and second century sources ignore 'Philadelphia' and use instead the pre-Ptolemaic name 'Rabbatammana'.[4] Much the same was undoubtedly true for other towns such as the port of Aela/'Aqaba (which received the name Berenice) and the Phoenician religious centre at Ba'albek (renamed Heliopolis). Only cities which had already enjoyed autonomy would have maintained any special civic status, i.e. Akko (renamed Ptolemais), Pella (Berenice) and Bethshan (Scythopolis).[5] The date at which Rabbatammana became

[2] Stephanus of Byzantium, *Ethnica* s.v. 'Philadelphia (3)'. On the significance of the name *Astartē* see Tscherikower (1961), p.100 and notes 79, 80; his use of the term *polis* regarding *Hellenistic* Philadelphia is anachronistic.

[3] *Rabbath, quae hodie a rege Aegupti Ptolemaeo cognomento Philadelpho ... Philadelphia nuncupata est* (*St Jerome*, in *Hiezech*. 25). On various forms of the name see Thomsen (1907), p.113, and especially Abel (1933/8), pp.424–5). In the sixth century AD account of the martyrdom of Saints Zenōn and Zenas (see main text below) the city is described as 'Philadelphia of Arabia ... which in the Law (i.e. the O.T.) is called *Emman* [sic].' Text: *AcS* Iun. vol.V, Ch.1.2, p.406; commentary: Milik (1960), p.162 n.32.

[4] *PSI* 616.27 (of *c*.258) and Polybius, *Histories* 5.71.4, where the historian *c*.150 is utilizing a third-century source. Polybius likewise ignores the dynastic name 'Berenice' when he makes a contemporary reference to Pella (*Hist.* 5.70.12).

[5] For concise accounts of these three cities see Schürer (1979), pp.121–7 [Ptolemais]; 145–8 [Pella]; 142–5 [Scythopolis]. It should be noted that the

Philadelphia remains uncertain. Akko received its dynastic name no later than 261 BC,[6] and it may be that all such honorary benefactions (except perhaps the two Berenices), date to the 260s.[7] But there is indirect evidence that Philadelphia was not known as such until as late as the end of the Second Syrian War (255 BC).

Professor A.H.M. Jones observed that traces of the administrative system in the Ptolemaic Near East are evident in some of the district names attested in Hellenistic and later sources.[8] Such names end in *-ites* or *-itis*, common topographical suffixes used by Greeks in Egypt. Most of those names are regional, e.g. *Samareitis* in Palestine, or *Trachonitis*, *Auranitis* and *Gaulanitis* in the south of modern Syria, or *Gabalitis* and *Moabitis* in south-central Jordan. But a few are named for cities. That distinction may indicate their importance to the Ptolemies. *Esbonitis* refers to Ḥisbān and its vicinity, and *Ammanitis* designates the region of Rabbatammana. Ammanitis is in fact the oldest attested of these terms, occurring in several papyrus documents of the mid-third century BC (see below).[9] Certainly all the major towns would have been under Ptolemaic authority, either directly through royal garrisons or less directly through local chieftains commanding resident Greek or Macedonian veterans. Philadelphia would have been no exception.[10]

The Ptolemies were content to administer their portion of Syria in much the same fashion as they governed Egypt, through a centralized bureaucracy responsible to the crown. The official name for the entire region was 'Syria and Phoenicia', but unofficially the name remained simply 'Syria'. Ptolemaic Syria's

---

two Berenices may have been so named as early as the reign of Ptolemy I or as late as the reign of Ptolemy III.

6 *BMC*, 'Phoenicia', p.lxxviii.

7 Will (1985, p.239, n.14) argues that since 'Philadelphia' does not occur in the Zenōn documents the change of name occurred *after* 259.

8 Jones (1971), pp.239–40.

9 E.g. *PCZ* 59003.13 of 259 BC (see the discussion below) and *PSI* 406.13 (undated, but probably of the same year). Hellenistic and later Greek sources use *Ammōn* and *Ammanitis* interchangeably. In the fourth century AD Eusebius (*Onom.* 24.1–2) drew a distinction between the two spellings. 'Ammanitis' is used throughout this paper.

10 Tscherikower (1937), pp.36–8.

financial affairs are known to have been overseen by a *dioiketēs* ('treasurer'), not, as in the other Ptolemaic possessions, by an *oikonomos* ('manager'). But the pattern of administration in other regions under Ptolemaic control (e.g. Lycia, Cyprus, Cyrenaica) suggests that Syria would also require a *stratēgos* (military commandant) as overall 'governor'.[11] There is some support for this from the fact that once Ptolemaic Syria passed to the Seleucids an inscription attests a named '*stratēgos* and *archiereus* (high priest) of Coele Syria and Phoenicia'.[12] Therefore it is likely, though as yet unattested, that Ammanitis and the other 'districts' of Ptolemaic Syria were governed collectively by a *stratēgos* with full civil, and perhaps some religious, authority. This would be fully consonant with the region's 'frontier' position vis à vis the Seleucids.

The smallest administrative unit in Ptolemaic Syria, as in Egypt, was the village (*kōmē*). At village level the official in charge was the *kōmarchos* (headman or *shaykh*).[13] The unit of intermediate size was called a *hyparchia*, not (as Jones supposed) a *nomos* or *toparchia*.[14] We may assume, in the absence of formal proof, that Ammanitis was one such *hyparchia*. The official in charge of this administrative unit is nowhere named in contemporary sources, but we know that each *hyparchia* had at the head of its financial affairs an *oikonomos*. Each of those, in turn, was responsible to the provincial *dioiketēs* who then reported to the king's finance minister.

2. *Ammanitis in the Zenōn Archive*

The unique structure of the administrative system in Ptolemaic Syria indicates that the region was particularly important to the crown. Not only was Syria the largest of the provinces, it

---

[11] Bagnall (1976), pp.213–20, esp. p.219.

[12] *OGIS* 230 (of shortly after 200 BC).

[13] Bagnall (1976), pp.18–21.

[14] The term *hyparchia* appears in *SB* 8008 (*c*.261 BC) which was published in 1936. Tcherikover (1961, pp.61–2), correctly incorporated the term, but Jones (1971, p.239) failed to mention it in the text of both his editions (it is acknowledged in n. 19 of that chapter). See more recently Bagnall (1976), pp.14, 18 and n.35.

was among the wealthiest. Agriculturally rich areas such as the Massyas (Biqā) Valley in eastern Phoenicia, and the Esdraelon Valley in northern Palestine, must have commanded the utmost attention from Egypt. The export of wine, grain and oil was a standard feature of commerce between those two regions and Alexandria. The commercial wealth of the Phoenician city-states was also a major factor in the close attention paid to the internal affairs of Ptolemaic Syria. But it is less easy to discern the economic importance of Ammanitis and the other territories east of the Jordan, where pastoralism was prevalent outside the few urban settlements. A recent archaeological survey of western Ammanitis reported that the number of inhabited sites dropped from 145 in the Iron Age to only 35 in the Persian-Hellenistic period.[15]

Some aspects of social and economic life may be found in the remarkable corpus of papyrus business documents known as the Zenōn Correspondence or the Zenōn Archive. This was among the earliest of the papyrological collections discovered in the Fayyūm district of Egypt, but it has been published in a scattered and piecemeal fashion over the last 75 years. The archive consists of letters, sale contracts, expense accounts, customs payments and the like. One of these recorded the sale of a young slave-girl to Zenōn, the business agent of Egypt's Finance Minister under Ptolemy II. The bright light this document casts on the internal affairs of Ammanitis at this time (259 BC) makes it worth quoting at length:

> In the twenty-seventh year of Ptolemy [II] son of Ptolemy [I] ... in the month Xandicus [April-May], at Birta of Ammanitis. Nicanor son of Xenocles, Cnidian, in the service of Tobias, has sold to Zenōn son of Agreophon, Caunian, in the service of Apollonius the *dioiketēs*, a [Sid]onian (?) girl named Sphragis, about seven years of age, for fifty drachmae. Guarantor: ... son of Ananias, Persian, *kleruchos*, of the horsemen of Tobias. Witnesses: ... (a judge) the son of Agathon, Persian, and Polemon son of Straton,

[15] Villeneuve (1988), p.274. The statement of Mazar (1957, p.142) that 'The land [of Ammanitis] was rich in water and fertile soil, which could be cultivated intensively' is exaggerated. Only the Baq'a plain, some 24 sq. km. in area, might fit that description. It lies 20 km north of 'Ammān, just south of the Wādī Zarqā (biblical Jabbok). See Gatier (1986), p.13.

Macedonian, *kleroucho*i, [both] among the horsemen of Tobias; Timopolis son of Botes, Milesian; Heraclitus son of Philippus, Athenian, Zenōn son of Timarchus, Colophonian, Demostratus son of Dionysius, Aspendian, all four in the service of Apollonius the *dioiketēs*. [Verso] Sale of a female slave.[16]

'Birta' transcribes Aramaic *bīrtā*, itself a loan-word from Akkadian *bīrtu*, the primary meaning of which is 'fortress' or 'citadel'.[17] Since Père Vincent identified it with 'Araq al-Amīr, 17 km southwest of modern 'Ammān, Birta has become what Claude Orrieux calls a *mot magique* for archaeologists, historians and philologists.[18] The ruins of large and splendidly-built structures at 'Araq al-Amīr caught the imagination of all early visitors. The physical remains and the archaeological dating accord well with Josephus' (*AJ* 12.4.11) and chronology of the construction he attributes to the Tobiad prince Hyrcanus (187–175 BC). Josephus calls the site Tyros (not Birta), which presumably transliterates an older Canaanite place-name Sōr (Phoenician Sōr: Gk. Tyros). 'Sōr' is preserved in the modern name of Wādī Sīr, the watercourse which flows past the site.[19] Josephus mentions in particular the *baris* ('palace', not 'fortress') constructed of white marble.[20]

Excavations in the 1960s established that the major structures did indeed date from the first quarter of the second century BC. Since 1976 joint French-Jordanian excavations have confirmed this mid-Hellenistic date.[21] The only earlier evidence for permanent occupation at 'Araq al-Amīr dates from the 11th century BC. That conclusion would seem to undermine the

16 *PCZ* 59003 = *CPJ* 1. The ethnic identity of Sphragis is uncertain; the editors of *CPJ* 1 (see esp. p.120) restored '[Si]donian' in preference to '[Baby]lonian'. Other restorations are possible. Her name is Greek.

17 See the prescient discussion of the term by Enno Littmann (Littman et al., 1921, p.6) who wrote eight years *before* this document was unearthed. More recently, see Mazar (1957, p.140), who assumed that Birta superseded an older place-name (Sōr) in the Persian period.

18 Vincent (1920), p.198; Orrieux (1979), p.323.

19 On this, see Mittmann (1970b), pp.202–3, and Mazar (1957), p.141.

20 On this meaning for *baris* see Will (1987), esp. pp.253–4.

21 For earlier archaeological work at the site see Mittmann (1970b), pp.203–4, n.21; the account by P. Lapp in *EAEHL* II (1976), pp.527–31; and the extensive bibliography in Villeneuve (1988), p.285 n.1.

identification of Birta, a place-name (cf. Birtha on the Euphrates)[22] evoking a military stronghold, with a site yielding no evidence of fortifications or permanent habitation at the time Zenōn purchased the slave-girl.

Siegfried Mittmann saw this difficulty and suggested instead that ʻAraq al-Amīr would better be identified with another place-name,[23] perhaps ʻSōrabittaʼ (also ʻSourabittaʼ), known from related documents in the Zenōn archive.[24] Such an identification had been proposed earlier, but that resulted in three distinct place-names being equated with ʻAraq al-Amīr.[25] Mittmann eliminated one by proposing that the phrase ʻBirta of Ammanitisʼ should be understood as the ʻZitadelle von ʻAmmānʼ, and that the transaction described in the document quoted above actually took place within the military stronghold of the district capital.

That conjecture has more recently been accepted by a noted papyrologist and several of the French team excavating at ʻAraq al-Amīr.[26] ʻBirta of Ammanitisʼ would thus specify the Ptolemaic sector of Rabbatammana, in particular the fortress on the acropolis. That same distinction seems to have obtained in an earlier period, when the ʻroyal cityʼ (the acropolis) and ʻthe city of watersʼ (the settlement around the Wādī ʻAmmān?) are noted separately in the Israelite capture of Rabbath-Ammon (2 Sam. 12:26–8). ʻRabbatammanaʼ would include both the acropolis and the residential area below. Some comments on the social background of this document will demonstrate that Mittmann's supposition is sound.

By the time of this slave-sale the name ʻTōbīahʼ had already been associated with Ammanitis for several centuries. Descendants of the same family (the son and grandson of our Tobias) were prominent in the political affairs of Palestine in

---

22 Ptolemy, *Geog.* 5.18.

23 Mittmann (1970b), pp.201–6.

24 *PCZ* 59004.6; *P. Lond.* 1930.175.

25 ʻThere can be no doubt that this [*Sōrabitta*] refers to the Tyrus ... of the Tobiads mentioned by Josephus. The Hebrew name of the place was therefore *Sōr* and its Aramaic name *Bīrthā*; it was the fortress of the land of Tobiahʼ (Mazar 1957, p.140).

26 Orrieux (1979), pp.324–5; Will (1987), p.254; Villeneuve (1988), pp.263, 278.

the late third and early second century.[27] Tobias in 259 BC was an important element in the Ptolemaic administrative system in Ammanitis. His ancestral home at ʻAraq al-Amīr /Tyros was unquestionably a showpiece; indeed the name *TWBYH* (*Tōbīah*) appears twice carved above cave-entrances at the site.[28] Thus it may well have served Tobias and his entourage as a Persian-style *paradeisos*, a place where royal officials such as Zenōn could be entertained and impressed.[29]

The three cavalrymen in the service of Tobias were military settlers, each with his *kleros* or allotted homestead. The two designated as 'Persians' may have been Persian-*born*, but are clearly not ethnic Persians. The patronymic (Hananiah) of the 'guarantor' is Hebrew. The other (the judge) is almost certainly Greek or Macedonian. He may well have had jurisdiction within the Greek community of Ammanitis. The man from whom the slave is purchased would seem to be a civilian in Tobias' employ. These are not local villagers related by birth or marriage to a *kōmarchos*. They are resident foreigners 'in the service of' a local man of considerable authority. Tobias himself is given no title in this or any other document in the Zenōn archive, so his exact status and the geographical extent of his authority (i.e. 'the [land] of Tobias'[30]) are conjectural.

How much prestige he enjoyed is evident from another document in the Zenōn collection. In a letter written to Apollonius in 257 BC, Tobias appended a note to Ptolemy II regarding a gift of animals. Though the note was relayed to the king by the finance minister, it is nevertheless significant that Tobias wrote in the certain expectation that the king himself would read it. Considerable imagination has been expended in assigning an appropriate title to Tobias: 'Ammonite (or Transjordanian) *shaykh* (or *chef*)', *judische Scheikh*, *seigneur*

[27] Good summaries of the Tobiad dynasty are given by Vincent (1920), pp.189–202) and Mazar (1957).

[28] The date of this epigraphy has been much disputed, ranging from late sixth to early third century BC; see Villeneuve (1988), p.261, n.8.

[29] Dentzer et al. (1982, p.207) have suggested that the site was an 'animal breeding centre' from which Tobias shipped prize specialities to Egypt.

[30] That phrase, perhaps equivalent to 'Ammanitis', appears in *CPJ* 2d (259 BC); see also I Macc. 5:13.

féodal or *Feudalherr*,[31] 'local prince' or 'Jewish aristocrat'[32] and even military ranks such as *stratēgos*, *Reiteroberst* or *Reitergeneral*.[33]

With military control went administrative duties. The military and administrative centre of Tobias' dominions cannot have been at 'Araq al-Amīr at the time of this document. The district 'capital' of Ammanitis was Rabbatammana/Philadelphia. It is there that we can expect Tobias to have transacted business involving a deputy of Egypt's minister of finance, and there that the requisite witnesses and guarantors would be found. In spite of its seeming awkwardness, the phrase 'Birta of Ammanitis' must represent what in the Old Testament was 'Rabbat of the Ammōnites'[34] and is today the 'Qal'a of 'Ammān'. Support for this comes very recently from a thorough study of the term *bīrtā* by Lemaire and Lozachmeur (1987). They argue convincingly that from the Persian period on the term has not only a military sense, but also an important administrative aspect as well. At the time of this contract Birta would refer not only to the Ptolemaic fortress on the acropolis at Philadelphia, but by extension to the administrative authority which emanated from it.[35]

Though the slave-girl is presumably a Near Easterner, her name is Greek. The low sale price indicates that she is untrained. Zenōn expected a substantially increased resale value in Egypt once she acquired skills. Ammanitis and neighboring regions

---

[31] Orrieux (1979), p.326, n.11.

[32] Tcherikower (1972), pp.97–8.

[33] Mittmann (1970b), p.207 and notes 41–2.

[34] The full descriptive name *Rbt bny 'mwn* (lit. 'Rabbat [i.e. principal city] of the sons of 'Ammōn') occurs as such only twice, in Deut. 3:11 and Ezek. 21:20. On the usage and meaning of the phrase *bny 'mwn*, see Block (1984).

[35] Since the document concerned is an official record of a transaction, the fact that 'Philadelphia' is not used almost certainly means that the dynastic name had not yet been bestowed. Portions of a massive walled structure, perhaps the 'Birta' itself, have recently been found on the Lower Terrace of the Citadel. The excavators date its initial construction to the Late Iron II period, and suggest some renovations in the Early Hellenistic Era. Silver and bronze coins of Ptolemy II Philadelphus (285–246 BC), the first of that king found in 'Ammān, were discovered in associated structures. See Zayadine et al. (1989, pp.362–3), and for a narrative account and detailed discussion of the entire siege episode see Zayadine (1990).

were themselves the source of slaves. A Minaean inscription of early Hellenistic date from Maʿīn in South Arabia attests a number of foreign women, probably brought there for service as temple-slaves. From among the dozens of names and places of origin are ʿAdanat from Ammon' (*'DNT bn 'MN*) and 'Ya'Ya from Moāb (*Y'Y bn M'B*).[36] The Zenōn Archive also abounds with references to slaves. One of these (*PSI* 406.13, *c*.258 BC) records a nameless slave-girl whom 'they [i.e. agents of Zenōn] took away from [the land of] Ammōn; they sold her in Ptolemais (Acco).'[37] This, then, is probably the single most important aspect of Egyptian interest in Trans-Jordania.[38] Of secondary but still considerable concern was livestock. There are indications elsewhere in the Zenōn papyri that horses and related species were a regular regional export, with Philadelphia perhaps the central market.[39] More exotic animals, also probably trans-shipped through Philadelphia, were sold or given as diplomatic gifts to the royal zoo at Alexandria.[40]

For the next half-century we know nothing of Philadelphia's history. During the same year in which this slave-sale was recorded, Seleucid and Ptolemaic forces clashed in what became the Second Syrian War (259–255 BC). The outcome of that struggle was far from decisive. An uneasy peace between the rival kingdoms was formalized by inter-dynastic marriage. Philadelphia seems to have played no part in that struggle, but we may assume that its military garrison was maintained and that fortifications on the acropolis were built or rebuilt. The civilian settlement which must have flourished in the area of the later Roman forum is known only through its pottery.[41]

---

[36] Mlaker (1943), p.39 [the 'Ammonite']; p.36 [the 'Moabite']. See also Graf (1983), pp.564–5, and *IDB* I.113.

[37] For numerous other examples see the 'General Index' under several rubrics for 'slave' (e.g. *sōma*, *sōmation*, *paidion*, *paidiskē*, etc.) in Pestman (1981).

[38] Tscherikower (1937), pp.16–20.

[39] Rostovtzeff (1922), pp.167–8. For a discussion of the types of animals (horses, asses, etc.) bred for racing or domestic use see Hauben (1984).

[40] Harper (1928), pp.13–16.

[41] Hadidi (1970b). No contemporary architectural remains have been found.

3. *Seleucid Ammanitis*

Our next glimpse of the city is during the Seleucid campaign into Trans-Jordan in the penultimate year of the Third Syrian War (221–217 BC). Antiochus III swept through Palestine in 218, capturing major Ptolemaic cities such as Philoteria and Scythopolis. The fortified towns beyond the Jordan had to be taken before an invasion of Egypt could be launched. Antiochus' forces were aided by Arab tribes in the vicinity. Polybius (*Hist.* 5.71–2) tells us that Gadara (Umm Qays) on its high bluff overlooking the confluence of the Yarmūk and Jordan Rivers 'was reckoned the strongest [town] in that region.' That estimation proved to be false; the city fell after a short siege. Learning that a major contingent of Ptolemaic forces was operating from 'Rabbatammana in Arabia' the king made its capture a priority.

The Seleucid army encamped below the citadel and reconnoitered the city's defences. Battering rams were brought forward and set to work at two sections of wall deemed vulnerable.[42] But even though the outer defenses were breached, the number and determination of the defenders held the acropolis during successive attacks 'by night and by day'. The city fell only through treachery. A captured prisoner revealed the location of an underground passageway by which the defenders of Philadelphia reached a hidden water source. Sappers broke into the tunnel and blocked it with 'wood, stones and other such material'. The thirsty defenders, confronted with a typically rainless summer, surrendered. A Seleucid garrison was installed and the king withdrew to Ptolemais on the coast, awaiting the spring and the planned invasion of Egypt.

The mention of Arabs as allies of the Seleucids, reference to Philadelphia as 'Rabbatammana', and the identification of that city as 'in Arabia', are interesting features of whatever source or sources Polybius utilized. The Nabataean Arabs of Petra had by this time established themselves as a growing power in the Jordanian plateau. They had foiled several attacks (motivation

---

[42] See Chapter 5 for a discussion of which sections of wall might have been vulnerable.

unknown) by Macedonian forces in 312 BC.[43] A half-century later slave-dealers in the employ of Zenōn had encountered Nabataeans in the Syrian Ḥawrān.[44] Nabataean inscriptions of Hellenistic date from that same area are still awaiting publication.[45] The 'Arab' allies of the Seleucids may or may not have been Nabataeans. In either event, ultimately the Seleucids would be obliged to confront the Nabataeans. The Third Syrian War ended with a Seleucid defeat at Raphia in 217 BC. Control of Ammanitis undoubtedly passed again to the Ptolemies, who would not have left such an important district in Seleucid control.

4. Nabataean Ammanitis

All of this changed when Ptolemaic Syria fell to the Seleucids at the end of the Fourth Syrian War in 200 BC. It is possible that Philadelphia was then given over to Nabataean control as reward for military assistance against the Ptolemies. Soon thereafter western Ammanitis was neither Seleucid nor Nabataean. A descendant of the Tobiad family, Hyrcanus, re-established hegemony in 'Araq al-Amīr and its vicinity *c.*187 BC, and did not relinquish control until his suicide *c.*175 BC. Josephus offers many details of the massive building program initiated by Hyrcanus, remains of which can still be seen.[46]

A late Hellenistic document clearly reveals that Philadelphia was not under direct Seleucid control during the reign of Antiochus IV (175–164 BC). About 172 BC the Hellenizing Jewish High Priest, Jason, was deposed and 'forced to flee into the region of Ammanitis' (2 Macc. 4:26–27). Some years later Jason led a failed uprising against Seleucid forces in Jerusalem. He was again forced to take refuge in Ammanitis (2 Macc. 5:7–8). But then, we are told, his luck ran out. Accusations brought him before 'Aretas, tyrant of the Arabs'. Jason fled yet again, this time to Egypt (2 Macc. 5:8–9). Aretas the *tyrannos* can only

[43] Diodorus Siculus 19.94.1 ff.

[44] *PSI* 406.21–22.

[45] On these see Starcky (1985), pp.167–8 (provenance unknown; Damascus museum, 3rd century BC], and Starcky (1966), p.930 (from Bostra, 2nd century BC).

[46] *AJ* 12.4.11. Doubts about that identification are noted in *IDB* I, p.113.

mean Aretas I, the earliest attested Nabataean king.[47] The implications are clear. Jason had fled to Nabataean-controlled territory. Seleucid displeasure at a rebel finding refuge in the territory of a client-kingdom led to the tribunal before Aretas and the subsequent exile of the Hasmonaean prince.[48]

This was not the last time that the Nabataeans would become involved in the political affairs of Palestine. Within a few years of Jason's ignominious departure, Ammanitis was attacked by forces under Judas Maccabaeus (*c.*165–160 BC). The motive appears to be territorial aggrandizement. When Judas had subdued areas of Palestine:

> ...he moved against the Ammanites, finding there strong forces and a sizeable population, under the command of Timotheus. [Judas] fought against them many times...[eventually] he captured Jazer and its villages, and turned back to Judaea (I Macc. 5:6–8).

A parallel account of this campaign (2 Macc. 12:17–19) has Judas besiege and destroy the stronghold of Charax and 'the garrison that Timotheus had left within [it]', in the region of 'the Tobiad Jews' (i.e. near 'Araq al-Amīr). The identity of Timotheus remains a mystery. He may have been a Greek or Macedonian mercenary, perhaps the *stratēgos* of Ammanitis in the pay of the Nabataean king.[49] Timotheus ultimately launched a reprisal against Judas, and was slain (1 Macc. 5:34–44). Jazer (Yazer, Gazara) is also known from the Old Testament (e.g. Num. 32:1). It has been identified with Khirbat Sār, 15 km west of 'Ammān.[50] Charax may be the newly discovered Hellenistic/Herodian fortress at Sūr (see below).

Such is the literary evidence for Nabataean rule in Ammanitis early in the Seleucid period. We may assume Ammanitis was

---

[47] For Jason's previous refuge in Ammanitis see 2 Macc. 4:26–7.

[48] See the comments in Habicht (1976, p.225, n.8b), and the account in Kasher (1988, pp.21–4).

[49] See the discussion in Goldstein (1976, pp.296–7), and the detailed account in Bar-Kochva (1989, pp.508–15). There is no evidence to support the latter's assertion (p.515) that Timotheus was 'the Seleucid *stratēgos* in Galaaditis'. The debate about the identity and role of Timotheus was best summarized more than fifty years ago by Johannes Regner (*RE* VI AII [1937] cols 1330–1).

[50] Also Butler (1907), pl.1, p.33, n.1, and Goldstein (1983), pp.393–4). Avi Yonah (1966, p.179) is less certain.

administered as part of the Nabataean realm centered on Petra. During the next century of Seleucid decline Nabataean influence expanded northward to Damascus and westward into the Negev Desert, while the Hasmonaean dynasty consolidated its control of central Palestine. Philadelphia stood at the crossroads of the lucrative trade with inner Arabia, some of which may have come westward through the Wādī Sirhān and the Azraq Oasis. The bulk of it came northward through Petra from the Ḥijāz and the Ḥismā. Philadelphian merchants transshipped those goods northwest through Gerasa to Pella and Scythopolis and then on to the Palestinian coast.[51]

It would have been essential to the Nabataeans to control such an important emporium, either directly through a *stratēgos* appointed by the king, or indirectly through a local *shaykh*. In the late second century (*c.*135 BC) we hear of a Zenōn Cotylas and his son Theodorus who were 'tyrants' of Philadelphia.[52] Zenōn may or may not be a Semitic name.[53] His Greek nickname of Cotylas ('drinking-cup') would be appropriate in the context of Nabataean banqueting.[54] Theodorus might be a rough translation of some Semitic name, e.g. 'Abdallah. The ethnic identity of Zenōn and Theodorus remains ambiguous, but Nabataean military commanders with Hellenized names are well-attested.[55] Elsewhere Josephus informs us that Gerasa,

[51] Strabo notes (*Geog.* 16.2.20) that South Arabian *merchants* (not just their *merchandise*) were at the mercy of bandits who raided the Ḥawrān from their strongholds in Trachonitis. That situation obtained until direct Roman intervention in 64/63 BC. This is interesting for a number of reasons. It indicates clearly that the Nabataeans did not control the area, and implies that such trade by-passed Philadelphia. Moreover, as Isaac (1989, p.242) points out, Strabo is our only witness for a direct commercial link between Arabia Felix and the Ḥawrān in the late Hellenistic period.

[52] Josephus, *BJ* 1.60; *AJ* 13.235.

[53] Zenōn is a common enough Greek name, but Clermont-Ganneau (*RAO* I: 5) demonstrated that Greek names beginning with *Zēn-* or *Dio-* could be used to render Semitic *Ba'al* (or Zeus). Cf. also Wüthnow (1930, p.50) and Sourdel (1952, p.20–21).

[54] Robert (1960), p.489, n.2; *LSJ* s.v. *kotylea.*

[55] *CIS* II 214 (AD 39/40) is the tomb inscription (Nabataean) of 'Matiyū the '*strtg*' (*stratēgos*), son of '*WPRNS* (*Euphronus*) the *hyprk*' (*eparchos*). In this case father and son are clearly associated with the military. See also *CIS* II 201 (AD 8/9), which attests a *klyrk'* (*chiliarchos*) with dual names, Nabataean

Gadara and Amathus were also controlled by Theodorus.[56] Gerasa later fell to the Hasmonaeans. The Nabataean hold on Philadelphia was strong enough to withstand sustained attacks on the city by Alexander Jannaeus (103–76 BC).[57] Perhaps the Hellenistic fortification walls on the lower terrace, dated to the second century BC by Zayadine, were instrumental in the city's successful defense.

Proof that Philadelphia was still Nabataean on the eve of the Roman conquest of Syria lies in a careful reading of Josephus' account of the Nabataean involvement in Hasmonaean affairs in 65 BC. Pompey's lieutenant, M. Aemilius Scaurus, was sent to Jerusalem in that year to relieve the Nabataean siege of the city. The Nabataean king, Aretas III, had intervened in the dynastic struggle between Jannaeus' sons Aristobulus and Hyrcanus. Scaurus threatened a Roman invasion of Nabataea unless the Nabataean forces withdrew. 'Aretas', says Josephus, 'terrified, fled from Judaea to Philadelphia.'[58] Clearly the city was an integral part of Aretas' dominions east of the Jordan. There is every reason to believe that Philadelphia was Nabataean from the very beginning of the second century and remained so until the end of Seleucid rule in Syria.[59]

The territory of early Hellenistic Philadelphia must have been enormous. It included all the villages and land within the city's effective control, but its exact dimensions remain unknown. Gerasa/Gerasenē to the north and Esbus/Esbonitis to the south were the nearest cities possessing territories of their own. Presumably the territories of all three cities were larger before the period of Hasmonaean expansion into the area east of the Jordan (the Peraea) in the late second century BC. Jones has pointed out that both Ammanitis and Esbonitis lost some western

---

(Hunaynu) and Greek (*HPSTYWN* = *Hephaistion*). Starcky (1971, especially p.157) gives several examples from epigraphy of Nabataean military officers whose fathers have Greek names transliterated into Nabataean, e.g. *CIS* II 234 (*DMSPS* = *Damasippus*).

[56] Gerasa: *BJ* 1.4.8; Gadara and Amathus: *AJ* 13.13.3; *BJ* 1.4.2.

[57] Josephus, *AJ* 13.13; *BJ* 1.4.

[58] *BJ* 1.128–9. Josephus' use of 'Philadelphia' here is consistent with his preference for that term rather than 'Rabbatammana'.

[59] *BJ* 1.128–9.

territory when Alexander Jannaeus annexed the Peraea.[60] The Hasmonaeans retained possession of the Peraea (including a portion of western Gerasenē and parts of Moabitis as well) throughout the period of Nabataean hegemony in Ammanitis. The Peraea included the towns of Amathus west of Gerasa, Gadara (Tell Jadūr, near Salṭ) west of Philadelphia, Julias/ Livias west of Ḥisbān, and Abila west of Mādabā.[61] Those four towns were the centres of the region's four toparchies.

Evidence for Nabataean influence in Philadelphia and Gerasa (and elsewhere in the region) has recently been reviewed by David Graf and Pierre-Louis Gatier.[62] Gatier concentrates exclusively on the literary sources, whereas Graf includes a brief account of the steadily increasing archaeological data. In the case of Philadelphia, it should be noted that no Nabataean material – ceramic or numismatic – from an archaeological context can be safely dated any earlier than the first century AD.[63] Nabataean epigraphy is so far completely absent. One may also add that the *amount* of material so far discovered is limited. But given the witness of Maccabees and Josephus, discussed above, there is no reason to doubt that physical evidence for the late Hellenistic period will yet be found.[64] For the rest of Ammanitis there is little reason to hope for important discoveries. The French survey of the region centered on 'Araq al-Amīr reported that neither pottery nor coins are plentiful enough to demonstrate occupancy between *c.*150–50 BC.[65] The chaotic political and economic conditions of that century may have been responsible for a decline in population.

---

[60] Jones (1971, p.455, n.39; p.462, n.64) with reference to Josephus and Syncellus.

[61] Neither Gadara nor Abila of the Peraea is to be confused with cities of the same name belonging to the Decapolis. Gadara has long been identified with Tell Jadūr near modern Salṭ. The location of Abila is still disputed in spite of Avi-Yonah's (1966, p.96) identification of it with Khirbat Kifrayn.

[62] Graf (1986); Gatier (1988).

[63] Hadidi (1974, p.85) notes the 'discovery of Nabataean sherds and coins of the first century AD' in the forum area.

[64] 'Hellenistic' pottery and coins were found mixed with Iron Age sherds beneath the Roman level of the forum. The coins were exclusively Seleucid. See Hadidi (1974), p.85.

[65] Villeneuve (1988), p.279. Results are based on surface surveys only.

Those circumstances were rectified only by direct Roman intervention.

Pompey and After: The Early Roman Period

Pompey's restructuring of Eastern affairs in 64/63 BC profoundly affected the subsequent history of Philadelphia. We have only the barest outlines of the internal affairs of Roman Syria at this time. As the political heirs of the Seleucids the Romans found themselves in direct control of northern Syria and in nominal control of the southern portion. In south Syria they encountered three native kingdoms, the Ituraeans in Phoenicia and the lava-lands south of Damascus, the Hasmonaeans in Palestine, and the Nabataeans. Phoenician Ituraea was reduced in size to just the territory of 'Arqa and its mountainous hinterland near Tripolis. The Ituraeans in Trachonitis were likewise left under the rule of a native prince. Both areas eventually became part of the Herodian kingdom.

The history of hostility between the Hasmonaeans and the Nabataeans during the century preceding Roman intervention presented Pompey with a dilemma. Outright annexation of either kingdom would have meant an additional burden on the provincial administrative system. Complete autonomy would encourage them to encroach on each other's territory. Pompey and his lieutenants Scaurus and Gabinius were content to accept the native dynasties in Jerusalem and Petra as clients once Roman hegemony was established. In one instance Pompey ordered Roman forces across the Jordan against 'the bandit strongholds and the treasuries of the *tyrannoi* ... [one of which was located at] Lysias, and those near Philadelphia.'[66] Lysias is perhaps to be identified with the modern site of Sūr, 4 km south-west of 'Araq al-Amīr.[67] The fortifications there will be discussed below.

---

[66] Strabo, *Geography* 16.2.40.
[67] Villeneuve (1988), pp.280–2.

1. The Territory of Roman Philadelphia

Roman Philadelphia was a more circumscribed entity than its early Hellenistic predecessor. The southern and eastern boundaries are the most problematic. Esbus/Ḥisbān is only 20 km southwest of Philadelphia. The border between their territories may have lain along the Wādī Kifrayn or its tributary, the Wādī Ḥisbān. Neither watercourse presents a well-defined, natural line of demarcation. The eastern limits of Philadelphia's territory would have lain no further than the line of habitation before the edge of the Jordanian steppe-land. Zarqā to the northeast, Quwaysma and Rajīb to the southeast, are modern villages that yield epigraphy of the Roman/Byzantine period.[68] There can be no doubt, because of their proximity, that they belonged to Philadelphia.[69]

There is less uncertainty about the northern and western limits of Philadelphia's territory. The Wādī Zarqā is a major landmark that would have presented a natural boundary between the territories of Philadelphia and Gerasa. The Wādī 'Ammān, an important tributary of the Wādī Zarqā, flows northeast from 'Ammān and describes a huge loop out into the steppe near the village of Zarqā, before turning northwest and joining the larger Wādī Zarqā, which then runs directly west as a tributary of the Jordan. The great bulk of Philadelphia's territory, therefore, lay to the north of the city. The early Church historian, Eusebius, noted (*Onom.* 144.4–6) that the town of Ramōth (Khirbat Jal'ad), 23 km northwest of 'Ammān, belonged to Philadelphia.

To the west Philadelphia adjoined the region of the Peraea. Gadara/Jadūr was the capital of the Peraea and central town of its own toparchy. How extensive its territory was may be gauged by noting Josephus' statement that the less important toparchy

[68] Gatier (1986) includes the epigraphy from Quwaysma and Rajīb; that from Zarqā will appear in *IJ*, vol. 5.

[69] Avi Yonah (1966, p.177) tried to establish the eastern border of Philadelphia's territory on the basis of milestone distances computed from Philadelphia or Bostra along the Roman road. Road distances were calculated north to south until AD 181, thereafter south to north. Milestone distances to or from any city have nothing to do with territorial limits.

of Julias/Livias further south incorporated 14 villages. At some point between ʿAmmān and Salṭ the territory of Roman Philadelphia and the region of the Peraea had a common border. This can be fixed at one point with some precision. Josephus (*AJ* 20.1.2–4) related that the Judaean procurator Cuspius Fadus (AD 44–45) had to settle a dispute between the Jewish residents of the Peraea and the city of Philadelphia 'concerning the boundaries of the village called Zia'. Zia is modern Zay, just a few kilometres northwest of Jadūr/Gadara.[70]

2. *Philadelphia and the Decapolis*

Certain cities belonging to the Hasmonaean and Nabataean kingdoms were designated as members of a Decapolis. Those cities and their territories were attached to the province of Syria.[71] One of the initial 'Ten Cities' was Philadelphia, whose calendrical system reckoned its foundation-year in 64/63 BC precisely.[72] Just what membership in the Decapolis actually meant can only be surmised. Philadelphia was the southernmost of nine cities east of the Jordan. Gerasa and Gadara were its nearest neighbors to the north. Scythopolis, alone out of the Palestinian towns, was a charter member. Canatha, once under Ituraean rule, was also given membership. If the territories of all ten original members were contiguous, the Decapolis 'region' stretched from Damascus in the north to Philadelphia in the south, and from Scythopolis in the west to Canatha in the east. The standard view since the 19th century has been that the Decapolis was created as an 'anti-Semitic blockade' against Jewish and Arab cultural influence in Hellenized districts. In that sense it was taken to be a 'League' or 'Confederation'.[73]

Parker has argued against that well-entrenched belief, observing that Strabo, who wrote at length about the Lycian League, had nothing to say about the Decapolis. Parker thus

---

[70] On the formation of the Peraea and the location of Zia see de Vaux (1941), pp.39–44.

[71] Josephus, *AJ* 14.4.4.

[72] Schürer (1979), p.156, n.381.

[73] Thus the view of Rey-Coquais (1982), p.7.

concluded that 'Decapolis' was a geographic expression.[74] But Isaac reproduced epigraphic evidence demonstrating that the Decapolis was an administrative district of Syria in the late first century AD.[75] Graf contends that the Decapolis was created to keep its ten member cities out of Hasmonaean control.[76] Gatier, without knowledge of Graf's study, took the issue a step further. He argues that the Decapolis was created expressly to preclude either Hasmonaean or Nabataean political control of those cities by placing them within the administrative authority of the Syrian governor.[77] The Romans thereby gained control of the northern half of the 'King's Highway' – the main trade artery between Petra and Damascus.[78]

None of the new studies ascribes any ethnic or cultural motive to the creation of the Decapolis. That signals a significant challenge to prevailing opinion, and requires some comment. At the moment of Roman intervention the degree of Hellenization in most of the Ten Cities, especially ones which had fallen to the Hasmonaeans, must have been minimal. Gadara is the only city for which there is sufficient evidence (albeit exclusively literary) for advanced Hellenization prior to Roman intervention. Both Will and Rey-Coquais have recently drawn attention to this.[79] In the two centuries from *c.*250 BC–*c.*50 BC. Gadara produced thoroughly Hellenized poets, teachers, philosophers and orators (e.g. Meleager, Philodemus, Menippus and Theodorus, respectively), and its native sons brought fame to the city well into the third century AD. Extensive excavations of the site have revealed only monuments and epigraphy of the Roman/Byzantine/Islamic city. There are as yet no traces of Meleager's 'Syrian Attica' of the pre-Roman period, which is perhaps some indication of the devastation that befell the city under Alexander Jannaeus.[80]

---

[74] Parker (1975).

[75] Isaac (1981), republishing *IGR* I:824.

[76] Graf (1986), pp.789–90.

[77] Gatier (1988), pp.161–3.

[78] Will (1985), p.238.

[79] Will (1985), p.240; Rey-Coquais (1982), p.9.

[80] The most recent comprehensive account of Gadara is Weber (1989). No structure or inscription earlier than the late first century AD has so far been

The earliest evidence for civic institutions in any of the Decapolis cities is of Neronian date. There are no coins or inscriptions of Hellenistic date from any of 'The Ten', including what Josephus called 'the greatest' city, Scythopolis.[81] The earliest dated inscription, found at Gerasa, is Tiberian.[82] Eventually all the cities of the Decapolis issued coins, but so far only those of Gadara date to the time of Pompey, i.e. to 'The Year One of Rome' (64/63 BC).[83] Those earliest Gadarene coins show immediate Greco-Roman influence in religious motifs.[84] But there are as yet no clear indications that the Hellenization process had made much headway elsewhere in the region, prior to Roman intervention.[85] Accordingly there is no need to suggest, as has often been done, that preservation of the Hellenized element in those cities was uppermost in Pompey's mind at the time the Decapolis was created.[86]

Just how the region was administered in that early period is unknown. The only evidence for any internal supervision dates from a century and a half later. This is a Greek inscription of *c.*AD 90 in which an equestrian official is attested as having

---

found. One may note that a native of Gadara named 'Diodorus the son of Heliodorus' was buried somewhere in Italy in the mid-second century AD. His tombstone (see *SEG* 30, 1980, no.1801) proclaims his city as 'Gadara of the Syrian Decapolis' a half-century *after* that institution ceased to exist. See, most recently, Gatier (1990), pp.204–5, no.1.

[81] *BJ* 3.9.7. A new Greek inscription from Scythopolis (*SEG* 37 (1987) no.1531), of Severan date, proclaims that city to be 'among the Greek *poleis* of Coele-Syria', the latter term presumably a substitute for 'Decapolis'. See Gatier (1990), pp.205–6, no. 2.

[82] Gatier (1982), p.10 and box A, p.11. The date is AD 22/23.

[83] Spijkerman (1978), pp.128–9.

[84] Spijkerman (1978), pp.128–9. Herakles and Athena are depicted on coins of 64/63.

[85] Braemer (1987, especially p.529) notes an occupational gap at Jarash between the 7th–2nd centuries BC. Either an early Hellenistic foundation lay elsewhere than the *tell*, or a settlement of that date did not exist. A preliminary study of Roman sculpture from the Decapolis cities has been published by Thomas Weber (1990).

[86] See, for example, Bietenhard (1977), p.232. Again the exception is Gadara, which had been destroyed by the Hasmonaeans. Pompey rebuilt the city for his Gadarene freedman, Demetrius. The Hellenization process in early Roman Palestine has been surveyed recently by Martin Hengel (1989).

jurisdiction in 'the Decapolis in Syria'.[87] How long that arrangement had obtained is conjectural. Isaac has theorized that the occasion of Herod's death (4 BC) and the reorganization of Judaean territory may have provided the right moment to place the region of the Decapolis under the direct supervision of an official responsible to the Syrian governor.[88] But Pliny the Elder, whose *Natural History* (5.74) does devote some notes to the Decapolis, employs the geographical term *regio* rather than a precise administrative expression. Pliny, however, is notorious for using archaic sources. The *Gospel of Mark* (7:31), perhaps contemporary with the *Natural History*, uses the expression 'boundaries (*horia*) of the Decapolis', which is hardly more precise. Josephus refers to just 'the Decapolis' (e.g. *BJ* 3.9.7). The overall impression is vague indeed. If the Decapolis was an administrative district prior to AD 90, there is not the slightest hint of that from the available sources.

Pliny indicates that the number of cities remained constant at ten. But the implication is that the names of the ten might vary. This can only mean that certain cities had 'lost' membership and others 'gained' it in their place. Ptolemy of Alexandria (*c.*150 AD) registers *eighteen* cities under the combined heading 'Coele Syria and the Decapolis' in his *Geography* (5.14.22). Presumably that list includes cities which became part of the Decapolis when one or more original members lost that status. Our sources give only two instances when that occurred. In the settlement following the Battle of Actium (31 BC), Augustus ceded to Herod the Great certain towns and territories on both sides of the Jordan. Among those were Gadara and Hippos.[89] Both towns are thought to be foundation members of the Decapolis. At Herod's death Gadara and Hippos (along

---

[87] Isaac (1981).

[88] Isaac (1981), pp.71–2. A parallel arrangement involving the administration of Trachonitis and Auranitis may be noted. Numerous epigraphic references (of the later Antonine period) attest centurions, acting as military attachés under the aegis of the Syrian governor, overseeing projects or honored by villagers. See MacAdam (1986, pp.54–7). The enhanced status of the Decapolis would have required a higher-ranking official, such as the equestrian attested.

[89] Josephus, *AJ* 15.7.3; *BJ* 1.20.3.

with Gaza) were separated from Judaea and made an appendage (*prosthēkē*) of Syria.[90] Early in the reign of Nero a town called Abila was added to the territory of King Agrippa II. That was probably Abila of the Decapolis.[91] In none of these accounts of territorial disposition is there mention of the Decapolis, nor is there any implication that the cities involved belonged to an association. It would therefore seem that no case can be made for the Decapolis, by that name, being a political unit before the time of Domitian.

3. *Philadelphia from Augustus to Trajan*

The historical outlines of this period are unfortunately very vague. Philadelphia remained on the periphery of larger political events unfolding across the Jordan. Pompey's punitive expedition into bandit territory on the western border of Ammanitis was an isolated event. Relations between the Hasmonaeans and Nabataeans were cordial until the last years of the struggle between opposing forces in the Roman civil war. Josephus relates that Cleopatra persuaded Mark Antony to pressure Herod the Great into war with Malichus I. The pretext was default of payments on the part of the Nabataean king; the underlying motive was the destruction of both monarchies. Herod's first campaign resulted in an ignominious defeat at Canatha in the Ḥawrān. The severe earthquake in the spring of 31 BC led to a Nabataean plundering of Herodian territory. That gave Herod the excuse he needed to launch a reprisal campaign, one which ended with a decisive victory on the borders of Ammanitis. 'Having encamped at Philadelphia ... [Herod] fought for possession of a fort captured by the Nabataeans' (*BJ* 1.19.5–6). It fell, and Herod's triumph was complete.

The fort in question may well be that recently surveyed by the French at Sūr, a site near 'Araq al-Amīr.[92] It is shaped somewhat like a spearhead, some 400m at its longest and about

---

[90] *AJ* 17.11.4.

[91] Josephus, *BJ* 2.13.2. Concerning the problem of which Abila is meant, see Schürer (1979), p.137, n.265.

[92] Villeneuve (1988), pp.280–2.

250m at its widest, overlooking the Peraea and the Jordan Valley to the west and the route to the interior of Ammanitis to the east. A rectangular structure, approximately 25 × 30m (the 'citadel' of the fortress?), was constructed at the northern end. In the absence of excavation the fort cannot be dated precisely. The survey team believe it can be no earlier than the second century BC, and no later than the end of the first century AD. It may well have been in use, and modified, within those three centuries. It occupies a strategic point on the western border of Ammanitis. As such it was either intended to guard an entrance to the Peraea from the east (as Villeneuve thinks), or defended the western approaches to Ammanitis. Its identification with Strabo's Lysias is conjectural; it may instead be the camp called Charax, captured by Judas Maccabaeus in his campaign against Timotheus (2 Macc. 12.17). It may, indeed, be *both* unidentified strongholds.

The sources are silent concerning Philadelphia and Ammanitis between the time of Herod the Great and the outbreak of the first Jewish revolt. It was during that latter event that the ancient animosity between the Jews of Palestine and the Hellenized communities of western Transjordania (many of which now belonged to the Decapolis) surfaced with particular violence. Again our witness is Josephus. He relates that the massacre of Jews by the gentile population of Caesaraea Maritima prompted severe reprisals by their enraged countrymen. Mobs of Jewish insurgents moved across the Jordan, where they attacked 'Syrian villages (*kōmai*) and the nearby cities (*poleis*)' (*BJ* 2.18.1–2). Philadelphia heads the list of cities (most belonging to the Decapolis) thus assaulted.

This would appear to be exaggeration on the part of Josephus. It is unlikely that groups of untrained dissidents could either seriously or lastingly disrupt the activities of any large city. But we may certainly accept that villages within Ammanitis were harassed, if not damaged. Whatever the specific details, the Jewish incursions led in time to counter-reprisals against the Jewish inhabitants of the Decapolis. Entire families were slaughtered, property was confiscated or destroyed. Some residents escaped. Others stayed and survived, only to be expelled later. Philadelphia is not explicitly named among the communities exacting vengeance on its Jewish inhabitants, but neither is it noted as one of the few cities which (Josephus says) exercised restraint. We simply do not know the level or extent of Philadelphia's response in the midst of these appalling circumstances.

There is nothing to indicate that Philadelphia was directly or actively involved in the Jewish War (AD 66–73) which followed. Apparently only one minor campaign was conducted east of the Jordan. The sole reference to it is a laconic statement in Josephus (*BJ* 4.8.1–2) about the meeting in Jericho (in June of AD 68) between Vespasian and his general Traianus (father of the future Emperor). Traianus had with him 'the (military) force he brought from Peraea, (the region) beyond the Jordan already having been pacified.' Nevertheless, the protracted Judaean War seems to have affected the status of Philadelphia's population, and perhaps that of other cities of the Decapolis.

The evidence for this is the tombstones of two soldiers, both of whom were natives of Philadelphia. A Latin epitaph from the faraway province of Pannonia Superior in central Europe attests a certain 'Proculus the son of Rabilus, of (the tribe) *Collina*, (from) Philadel(phia)'. Proculus had served with the Roman army in Syria as an *optio* in the *cohors II Italica civium Romanorum*. He was transferred, as part of a special archery unit, to the military base at Carnuntum, near what is now Vienna, where he died age twenty-six. He had served seven years in the military. The epitaph, which is undated, was set up by his brother Apuleius who presumably served with him in the same unit.[93]

The second epitaph (also Latin) is from Bostra, northeast of 'Ammān. The soldier, 'Titus Flavius Marcianus, the son of Marcus, of (the tribe) *Collina*, home(town) Philad(elphia)', had served as *optio* of the third-ranking centurion of the *Legio VI Ferrata*, and was remembered by his mother Luculla and his sister, Flavia Ialla. Again there is no date (*IGLS* 13.9179).

Proculus was from Syrian Philadelphia, either the city itself or a village in its territory. His name, and that of his brother,

---

[93] *CIL* 3.13483a (= *ILS* 9168).

tell us nothing about their ethnic background, but the patronymic *Rabilus* (*Rab'el*) is a well-attested Nabataean name, both for royalty and for commoners.[94] Proculus and his family were Arabs. But in the case of Marcianus, whose father has a Latin name, the ethnic identity is unknown. It is also less certain that he is from Philadelphia of the Decapolis. The Latin tribal affiliation, Collina, is not specific enough, as it could be associated with Philadelphia/'Ammān, or with Lydian Philadelphia in western Asia Minor. The circumstantial evidence regarding Marcianus points to the former. He had served with a Syrian legion (eventually transferred to Palestine), and was buried in a neighbouring province. Thus in both cases we are dealing with 'locals' recruited into the Roman army.

Proculus' epitaph cannot be dated with certainty. But as earlier editors have noted, his service on the Danube could be connected with the movement of units from Syria (against Vitellius) by the consular governor, Licinius Mucianus, toward the end of AD 69.[95] That date is attractive since it would mean that Proculus joined the Roman army at about the time of the first phase of the Jewish War, i.e. in the years AD 66–69. His tribal identification would then be significant, providing a Flavian date for the bestowal of citizenship rights on Philadelphia. Vespasian very probably had conferred citizenship throughout the Decapolis in return for support in the war. Nevertheless, the transfer of Proculus' unit from Syria may have occurred as late as Trajan's Dacian Wars (AD 101–106).

The date of Marcianus' funerary inscription is equally uncertain. His presence at Bostra is probably connected with the annexation of the Nabataean kingdom in the early second century. His *praenomen* Titus, and the *nomen* Flavius/Flavia in his family, point to either Vespasian or Titus for the privilege of citizenship and enrolment in the same tribe as Proculus. This would have occurred during the Jewish War. The initial recipient of this benefaction would have been the father or even grandfather of Marcianus.

---

[94] Wüthnow (1930), p.96, s.v. Rabbēlos, Rabēlos; cf. the onomastic index in Sartre (1985), pp.230–1, s.v. Rabibēlos.

[95] Tacitus, *Histories*, 2.83.

G.W. Bowersock has shown that the development of Syria's commercial and cultural potential was a Flavian priority in the immediate aftermath of the Judaean War.[96] Responsibility for that policy devolved upon the province's consular governors. The first of these was the elder Trajan, whose long tenure (AD 73/74–78/79) saw the securing of the Euphrates frontier and the active promotion of urban and commercial enterprises. Bowersock's study singled out the Syrian cities of Palmyra and Gerasa as *foci* of imperial and provincial attention, and Nabataean Bostra as a parallel case within the domains of that client-kingdom. Gerasa is of particular interest, since any developments there were bound to influence its sister-cities in the Decapolis. During the decade between AD 70 and 80, its urban layout was reoriented and an orthogonal street plan implemented. The city's fortification walls, once also thought to date to Flavian times, would appear to be some two centuries later.[97] But the northwest gate, dated epigraphically to AD 78/81, is articulated with the new street plan. Unless it was a free-standing monument there must have been earlier walls. With or without Flavian fortifications, Gerasa became a 'showcase' of urban renewal.

For Philadelphia only the barest outlines of any important transformations are discernable. The grant of citizenship to the city may have occurred, as argued above, *c.*AD 66–69. The earliest coinage we know of appears with the date '143' of the Pompeian era (that is, AD 80/81) on the reverse. This is discussed below. The appointment of an equestrian official with jurisdiction within Philadelphia and other of the Ten Cities may have been roughly contemporary with the documented developments elsewhere in Syria. We know for certain of only one such official, the nameless individual noted above who served the governor of Syria in some capacity c. AD 90. No known structure of the upper or lower cities dates to the Flavian era. The city walls were

---

[96] Bowersock (1973).

[97] This information was communicated by J. Seigne, 'Jarash romaine et byzantine: développement urbain d'une ville provinciale', read at the Fourth Conference on the History and Archaeology of Jordan, Lyons, France, May–June 1989.

undoubtedly rebuilt in Roman times. Some progress has been made in determining which portions of the present walls belong to the Roman period. A date in the second century seems probable. The earliest securely datable inscription is AD 150 (*IJ* 2.17).

4. Roman Philadelphia: Constitution, Calendar, and Coins

Along with an extensive territory, Philadelphia also enjoyed several other privileges of a constitutional *polis*. Among them were the prestige of civic institutions, a calendrical era and the privilege of minting. It is probable that all three were implemented at the time of Pompey, though the evidence for each is considerably later.

The City (*Polis*), its Council (*Boulē*) and the People (*Dēmos*) of Philadelphia are attested in several Greek inscriptions. In one dedication (*IJ* 2.23), found when excavating the forum area, 'The City of Philadelphia ... built a triple portico (*tristoön*) in the year 252 (that is, AD 189/90)'. In another, of uncertain date, the city honored an emperor (*IJ* 2.24). In each of these instances, the term *polis* collectively signifies the city's constituent government. We find the latter attested in the restoration of a damaged and undated Greek dedication (*IJ* 2. 29) in which 'The Council and the People, as a token of esteem', honor one Martas, son of Diogenēs. During the reign of Alexander Severus (AD 222–235) the Council and the People 'by decree' allowed a centurion to honor his dead daughter, perhaps with a statue (*IJ* 2.30). Less certain is the restoration of 'Council and People' in a badly-damaged and undated Greek inscription honouring Titus Flavius Longinus (*IJ* 2.28).

There is also an epigraphic attestation of individual members of the council and the specific magistracies they held. Martas, noted above, was 'Councillor and *Proedros*'. The latter term designates the 'President' or 'Chairman' of the city's Council. His father once held the office of *Gymnasiarchos*, normally a one-year appointment. The inscription is damaged where a second position, apparently held 'for life', was noted. Such distinctions are all the more remarkable since only at Gerasa and Canatha, among the cities of the Decapolis, are there parallels for these or other municipal offices.[98] Also worthy of mention is the mixture of Graeco-Roman and Semitic personal names in these civic inscriptions, a characteristic feature of urban onomastica throughout the Hellenized East. One may add that 'Philadelphus' as a personal name appears in several Greek inscriptions from nearby areas.[99]

Philadelphia and the villages within its territory utilized four different calendar-systems throughout the classical period. Most common were those based on the era of the Seleucids (dated from 312/11 BC) and on the Pompeian era (64/63 BC). Less frequent are examples of dating by regnal years of an emperor, and calculations according to the era of the province of Arabia (the latter only from AD 106). What little evidence there is indicates that Macedonian month-names were used.[100] The Pompeian era continued to be used in Ammanitis well into the Umayyad period. A Greek mosaic inscription (see below) from the floor of a church in the village of Quwaysma, six kilometres south of 'Ammān, is dated to 'the year 780' (that is, AD 717/718.[101]

Philadelphia issued coins from 80/81 in the reign of Titus until Elagabalus (218–222).[102] Two eras appear to be used for the dated varieties. Examples such as Spijkerman nos 1–3 and nos 7–10 are dated by the Pompeian era to 80/81. Spijkerman nos 4–5, dated by him to 441/442, cannot be based on that era, but would instead be of the Seleucid era (equating to 130/

[98] Gatier (1986, p.53) notes only the parallels from Gerasa. For municipal offices at Canatha, see *Wadd.* 2216; 2339 (councillors), *Wadd.* 2341 (*proedros*) and *Wadd.* 2330 (*agoranomos*).

[99] *IJ* 2.60, 2.61 from Ḥisbān; *IJ* 2.74 from a ruined monastery near Mt Nebo. All are Christian.

[100] A good summary and specific examples are given by Gatier (1986, p.24). The calculation of the Pompeian Era is reviewed by Rey-Coquais (1981, pp.25–7).

[101] *IJ* 2.53. The inscription commemorates the rebuilding of the church, presumably following the great earthquake of AD 717. That eliminates all but the Pompeian era in calculating the date.

[102] The fundamental study of the city's (and the region's) coinage is Spijkerman (1978, see esp. pp.242–57). Fr Spijkerman's division of Philadelphia's coinage into the now archaic classifications of 'quasi-autonomous' and 'colonial' is misleading.

131).[103] The iconography of most 'quasi-autonomous' coins features pastoral motifs: woven baskets, laurel wreaths and corn-clusters appear on the reverse, and representations of Demeter on the obverse. The 'colonial' imagery draws heavily on Philadelphia's identification with Herakles and his mother Asteria. More 'neutral' are depictions of the city's Tychē,[104] the goddess Athena, and the divine twins (*Dioscuri*) Castor and Pollux. One 'quasi-autonomous' issue of 80/81 surrounds the date on the reverse with a laurel wreath; another (of smaller module) has as motif a palm tree and fruit. The obverse of the first displays a bust of Athena, and the second a bust of Nikē. Each bears the legend *Philadelpheōn*. On larger denominations of the same date the obverse features the head either of Titus or Domitian (as Caesar) with an inscription naming each, and the reverse displays a bust of Herakles or Tychē, respectively.[105]

On both types of coins, and in the city's epigraphy, the phrase 'Philadelphia of Coele Syria' is prominent. It appears in coin legends as early as Hadrian's reign, and in a dated inscription of the late second century.[106] Much has been written about the meaning of 'Coele Syria' in the historical geography of the classical Near East. At the simplest level the qualifying expression 'of Coele Syria' distinguishes *this* Philadelphia from several others, notably Philadelphia (Neocaesaraea) in western Asia Minor. Beyond that, the city's identification with 'Coele Syria' is specifically propagandistic. It evokes the political geography of the Hellenistic era, especially the Seleucid period when Philadelphia was nominally part of 'Coele Syria and Phoenicia'. If Rey-Coquais' analysis is correct, Philadelphia's

---

[103] See, for example, Spijkerman (1978), pp.244–5, nos 4 ('year 441') and 5 ('year 442'). Spijkerman offered no comment except a question mark before each year-number. Both readings are impossible. In no.5 the unit number is more probably a *sigma* (6) than a *beta* (2). The possibility exists that both nos 4 and 5 were tooled, so that their dates should read 146 of the Pompeian era, i.e. AD 83/84. The same year, but a variant reading, was suggested by Hill, *BMC Arabia* no.37.1.

[104] Gatier (1986, p.53) draws attention to the marble head of Philadelphia's Tychē found during construction of the Archaeological Museum on the Citadel.

[105] Spijkerman (1978), pp.244–5, no.2; pp.246–7 nos 7, 9, 10.

[106] Coins: Spijkerman (1978), e.g. pp.246–7, nos. 11, 12; inscriptions: *IJ* 2.23 (AD 189/90); see also *IJ* 2.24, undated but probably mid-second century.

explicit association with 'Coele Syria' also signals a conscious effort to reject the Nabataean element in the city's history and culture.[107] The identity with 'Coele Syria' also provided a way by which Philadelphia might proclaim its 'autonomy' when the Decapolis was dissolved and the city was assigned to the Roman province of Arabia in AD 106. Lastly 'Coele Syria' proclaimed membership in a new association (*koinon*) of Hellenized cities which participated in the imperial cult established by Augustus and revived by Hadrian.[108]

Trajan and After: The Later Roman Period

By the end of the first century AD it became evident that Rome's long tradition of client-kingship in the Near East was drawing to a close. The kingdom of Commagene had been re-annexed by Rome in AD 72. The last remnants of the Herodian kingdom reverted to Rome upon the death of Agrippa II *c*.94; the various portions were attached to Syria or Judaea. In AD 105/106, upon the death of King Rabbel II, the same fate befell the Nabataean kingdom. In that case the annexation involved military forces entering from Syria and Egypt. The disposition of Nabataean territory was also handled differently; the bulk of it became the Roman province of Arabia.[109]

A secondary aspect of this new dispensation was the dissolution of the Decapolis. The distribution of its various cities and their territories was dictated purely by their geographical location. The northernmost cities were attached to Syria, and the westernmost to Palestine. The southernmost two, Gerasa and Philadelphia, were assigned to the new province of Arabia.[110] The sources are absolutely silent regarding Philadelphia in the early decades of the second century. There is a break in coinage

---

[107] Rey-Coquais (1981), pp.27–31.

[108] Rey-Coquais (1981), pp.27–31. That view is accepted by Bowersock (1988, pp.51–2) and rejected by Gatier (1986, p.48).

[109] Bowersock (1983, pp.79–89) summarizes the circumstances of the creation of Provincia Arabia.

[110] Bowersock (1983), pp.90–2.

during the reigns of Nerva and Trajan, and a resumption beginning with Hadrian. That issue, as noted above, proclaims the city as 'Philadelphia of Coele Syria'. The same inscription appears on coins until minting ceased during the reign of Elagabalus.[111] By that time a Roman province with the official name of Coele Syria (the northern half of the old province of Syria) had already existed for several decades. What began as a conscious anachronism ended in a confusion of terminology. 'Philadelphia of Coele Syria' was the city's way of clinging to the aura of respectability it once had as a member of the Decapolis, a privilege enjoyed since the time of Pompey the Great.

1. Philadelphia and the Via Nova Traiana

One immediately visible sign of a Roman presence was the new highway between the ancient port of Aela/'Aqaba on the Red Sea and the provincial capital at Bostra. Construction of that *via nova Traiana* began immediately after the annexation of Nabataea. Newly discovered milestones at 'Aqaba indicate that the southern portion of the road (to Petra) was completed in AD 111/112.[112] This confirms the dating of other milestones on sections of the road north from 'Aqaba. Philadelphia was incorporated into the *via nova*. This is clear from milestones found just north of the city, and traces of an ancient road entering Philadelphia from the south. The section of road between Bostra and Philadelphia is better known because it was better preserved, and therefore was surveyed several times at the beginning of this century.

The traveller moving south along that road would enter the territory of Philadelphia at what is now the site of Qal'at Zarqā, just beyond the forty-first milestone. When the Princeton Expedition surveyed that section of road in the spring of 1909, it appeared that the *via nova* forked at the forty-eighth milestone. The main road ran due south toward Mādabā and Petra, but a

---

[111] Spijkerman (1978), pp.256–7, nos 44–7.

[112] I am grateful to Dr Donald S. Whitcomb, Oriental Institute, University of Chicago, for this information.

branch road entered Philadelphia. It was also clear from dates on several milestones that the Bostra-Philadelphia segment was not completed until AD 114. Other milestones indicate road repairs north and south of Philadelphia undertaken during the reigns of Hadrian, Marcus Aurelius, Commodus, Pertinax, Septimius Severus, Caracalla, Elagabalus, Severus Alexander, Maximinus, Philip the Arab, Aurelian and Diocletian.[113] Milestone distances along the *via nova* were initially counted north from Petra to Bostra. Beginning with the reign of Commodus (the reason is not yet clear) distances were calculated from Bostra toward the south. This inevitably created some confusion regarding the mileage figures on certain stones.[114]

Philadelphia is also quite prominent on a famous road map of the early Roman empire, the Peutinger Map. The present map is a medieval copy, incorporating features associated with the Christian Roman Empire of late antiquity. But other features are dateable to the first century AD, and the map's ultimate prototype may be as early as the reign of Augustus.[115] What is relevant here is that Philadelphia is depicted as an important stop for traffic moving north or south along the *via nova*. The distinction is made by the cartographer's vignette of the city: twin towered structures of some sort. The same stylized drawing is attached to other prominent cities in the region, e.g. Petra, Bostra and Damascus. The significance of the vignette has variously been interpreted as indicating a stop on the imperial post route, or perhaps the presence of a military detachment.[116]

Butler's observation that Philadelphia was connected to the main highway by a branch road which swung in a loop through the city is not refuted by the Peutinger Map. The latter was designed for the edification of the traveller, and as such indicates

---

[113] Butler (1910), p.xiv; Bauzou (1988), p.294.

[114] Bauzou (1988), p.294. Low mileage figures (e.g. II) on milestones found just north of Philadelphia may refer to this branch road only. They are not, as Avi Yonah (1966, p.177) maintained, connected with Philadelphia's territorial limits.

[115] Bowersock (1983, p.167, n.10) discusses the various editions of the Peutinger Map, including the facsimile edition published in 1976. Segments 9 and 10 of the map show the road from 'Aqaba to Bostra and beyond.

[116] Bowersock (1983), p.174.

the regular stops along the major roads, with distances (in Roman miles) clearly specified between each. Alternative routes and 'by-passes' would not be shown. Also not indicated on the Peutinger Map is a second road north from Philadelphia, to Gerasa and then on to Adraa (modern Dar'ā), west of Bostra. Milestones from north and south of Gerasa have yielded Hadrianic dates for its initial construction.[117] The absence of the Philadelphia-Gerasa road on the Peutinger Map strengthens the argument that its archetype is far earlier than the Byzantine date once taken for granted.

2. *Philadelphia and the Roman Army in Arabia*

There is no clear indication of Philadelphia's role in the provincial garrison. Arabia was a one-legion province, with the governor in command, for the first two centuries of its existence. The legionary headquarters, and the governor's official residence, were at Bostra. Legio III Cyrenaica, brought from Egypt at the time of annexation, was the province's garrison force. The bulk of that legion was headquartered at Bostra, but units were outstationed where needed. There is a possibility, noted below, that Philadelphia served as the permanent base for a unit of that legion, and perhaps as a temporary home for a detachment of a legion based in neighboring Palestine.

Only a handful of the Greek and Latin inscriptions from Philadelphia are military in character. Three are dedications. The earliest, already touched upon above, dates to the reign of Alexander Severus (222–35). The Greek text notes that 'Herennius Moschus, centurion of the *Legio X Fretensis Severiana*, honors Herennia Eistha, his daughter prematurely dead, by decree of the Council and the People' (*IJ* 2.30). A veteran of that same legion, Aurelius Victor, is honoured in a damaged Greek inscription (*IJ* 2.26). The legion's imperial epithet is now *Gordiana*, dating the text to 238–44. The home base of the *Legio X Fretensis* was Jerusalem until *c.*300, when it was moved to Aela/'Aqaba. It has been conjectured that a detachment of the legion was stationed

[117] MacAdam (1986), p.29, 33 (see map, fig. 6).

at Philadelphia in the early third century as part of larger military movements on the eastern frontier.[118]

The third inscription is a well-preserved Latin dedication:

> To the most holy gods, Health and Asclepius, Terentius Heraclitus, *beneficiarius* of (the governor) Claudius Capitolinus, for the preservation of the imperial household and of his governor, and by the oracle of the god Jupiter, has completed his vow (*IJ* 2.13).

Capitolinus is attested elsewhere as legate of Arabia *c*.245. Heraclitus had been excused from normal military duties to assist the governor in some capacity.

An undated Latin tombstone (*IJ* 2.34) attests Tiberius Claudius Antoninus, a soldier of the *legio III Cyrenaica*, who had seventeen years of service. His burial at Philadelphia may suggest that a unit of the legion was on duty there. A badly damaged Greek funerary text (*IJ* 2.48) yields part of a man's name ([Theod]orus?) and his title, *cornicularius*. The title may refer to either military or civilian duties, the former as adjutant to a senior officer, the latter as administrative assistant or secretary to some official.

However distasteful the relegation to provincial status might have been to her citizenry, Philadelphia prospered under Roman rule. A strong military presence in the lava-lands to the north, where banditry had been endemic, ensured the regular flow of commercial traffic between Philadelphia and Damascus. The city's greatest internal development coincided with the Antonine period. The evidence for this is primarily the remains of major structures built during the period, and the epigraphic witness to known and unknown buildings of that era.

3. Philadelphia and Traditional Culture

Philadelphia celebrated and advertised its Hellenistic heritage with its dynastic name, its constitution and coins, and such structures as a theatre, an odeon, a gymnasium (as yet undiscovered), and a propylaeon. Its sense of Roman identity was linked to the forum, the baths, the temple complex on the

---

118 Gatier (1986), p.55.

citadel, the colonnaded streets, bridges, a splendidly engineered conduit, a military presence, dedications to emperors and governors, and the highways that ran through and near the city. The temples, nymphaeum and coin motifs were also evocative of Graeco-Roman culture. But in the midst of that it is well to keep in mind that the indigenous element, Arab and even pre-Arab, was a constant feature of life in late Roman Philadelphia. Two bits of evidence remind us of that.

One is an epigraphic discovery made at the site of Ziza (modern Jīza or Zizia), 27 km to the southeast of Philadelphia. From that site early this century came an undated bilingual (Nabataean-Greek) inscription of considerable interest.[119] Both texts are damaged, but one supplements the other nicely. Together they attest a certain Dēmas, son of Hellēl (?) and grandson of Dēmas, 'from 'Ammān' (*'MWN*), who built a temple dedicated to 'Zeus who is in Beelphegōr', and consecrated a shrine to another deity (*IJ* 2.154). The 'Zeus' for whom Dēmas built the temple is no doubt Ba'al Shamīn, localized near Mt. Nebo as 'Ba'al of (Mt.) Fogor'. The latter is familiar from the Old Testament.[120] A cube-shaped altar with sculpted reliefs, purportedly from 'Ammān, has recently been published. It is specifically attributed to worship of Zeus-Ba'alshamīn, and dated to the first or second century AD.[121] Dēmas, his father, and grandfather, are presumably Nabataean. The palaeography of both texts suggests a date in the second-century AD. It is striking that the older form of the city's name prevails in the Nabataean version.

Though the Nabataean element in Philadelphia and its territory was no doubt still strong, descendants of the pre-Arab people are also attested. This is apparent from our second piece of evidence. In the mid-second century the Christian apologist Justin Martyr, born in Neapolis (Nablus) in Palestine, remarked

---

119 Jaussen and Savignac (1909).

120 Gatier (1986), p.181.

121 Olávarri (1980). Independent publications announced the recent discovery of a Greek metrical inscription from an underground tomb complex at Rajīb, six kilometres south-east of 'Ammān. It attests for the first time the cult of Zeus-Demeter east of the Jordan. Associated evidence dates the inscription to the mid-second centuryAD. See Campagano (1988), Gatier and Vérilhac (1989).

that 'there are now [i.e. at the time he wrote] a great number of Ammonites (Gk. *Amanitai* [sic])'.[122] The context of that statement is a discussion of Near Eastern ethnic groups or 'nationalities', among which are 'Arabians'. It is therefore clear that Justin distinguished between 'Ammonites' and the Arab/Nabataean element in the Transjordanian population of his own time. That a similar distinction was not made by Stephanus of Byzantium (who calls on the testimony of Josephus) some centuries later is of no concern.[123] What matters is that such evidence fits together nicely with the indigenous names of other Philadelphians such as Martas (noted above), Kaioumus (*IJ* 2.46) and Obaidus (*IJ* 2.49), and names such as Tzobeus and Abbibus (*IJ* 2.53) from a site close to 'Ammān. Eventually we can glimpse, however indistinctly, the continuity of local culture within the Hellenistic/ Roman milieu.

Diocletian and After: The Byzantine Period

Our knowledge of the final phase of Philadelphia's pre-Islamic history is lamentably inadequate. The literary evidence is exceedingly sketchy, more so than for any earlier portion of the classical era. The reasons are clear enough. Byzantine Philadelphia was a prosperous and peaceful city. It was neither a political capital nor a 'centre' of church activity. There is no evidence that Philadelphia contributed to the philosophical or theological movements of late antiquity. Neither is there scandal or controversy associated with the name of the city. Like most of its sister cities in the once-famous and prestigious Decapolis, Philadelphia paid the price of obscurity for its modest success throughout the fourth, fifth, sixth and seventh centuries. To some extent we can fill in the shadows with the aid of epigraphy and archaeology, but even that evidence is limited and conspicuously centred on the church and church affairs.

---

[122] *Dialogue with Trypho* 119 (*PG* 6.752).
[123] *Ethnica* s.v. 'Amanon'.

1. Byzantine Arabia: Borders and Defenses (fig.10)

The reigns of Diocletian and Constantine saw major transformations in the Roman Empire. A second Rome was established, first at Nicomedia and later at Constantinople. Diocletian's reorganization of the provincial system *c*.300 had a dramatic effect on the province of Arabia, which had been created by Trajan and later enlarged by Septimius Severus. The entire southern two-thirds of Roman Arabia was administratively detached and transferred to the authority of the governors of Palestine. For two centuries the border lay along the line of the Wādī Ḥasā, and thereafter was redrawn along the Wādī Mūjib farther north. Arabia received a second legion, the *IV Martia*, which was installed in the newly constructed *castrum* called Betthoro, at modern Lejjūn (east of Karak). Philadelphia remained within the shrunken territory of what we may call Byzantine Arabia.[124] When Eusebius compiled his *Onomasticon* in the early fourth century he noted Philadelphia as a 'distinguished (*episēmos*) city of Arabia'.[125]

The introduction of a second legion reflected a massive increase of troop strength throughout the eastern provinces. A military road, officially styled the *Strata Diocletiana*, followed the edge of the desert, south from the Euphrates to the *castellum* and its subsidiary fortifications at the oasis of Azraq, 100 km directly east of Philadelphia.[126] The *Notitia Dignitatum* (compiled *c*.400), a 'directory' of civil and military posts throughout the empire, sets out the disposition of Byzantine forces province by province for the West (*Occidens*) and East (*Oriens*). Under the list of troops commanded by the *Dux Arabiae* there is no entry for a unit stationed at Philadelphia, nor for any big city of the province except Bostra.

But the *Notitia* (*Oriens* 37.20) does register a unit at a place it calls Gadda. Luckily the same name appears on the Peutinger Map, where it is located thirteen Roman miles along the *via nova* north of Philadelphia. Gadda is probably to be identified with

---

124 Bowersock (1983), pp.142–7.
125 *Onom*. s.v. 'Amman' and 'Ammōn'.
126 Dunand (1931).

modern Ḥadīd or Qal'at Zarqā. Both are the proper distance northeast of 'Ammān and are near the line of the ancient road. Gadda was the post of the *equites sagittarii indigenae*, a unit of mounted archers recruited locally. Gadda may have lain within or just beyond the *territorium* of Philadelphia; it obviously guarded the main approaches to that city from the north and east.[127]

2. *Byzantine Ammanitis*

The limited evidence that exists for economic growth and settlement patterns in Byzantine Arabia is primarily archaeological. Because of that, the published results are limited to certain sites or areas, and therefore fall short of creating a truly comprehensive cross-section of the province. The evidence from one region or site may contradict that from another. This is particularly true in the case of Ammanitis. Thus, it may be best to begin with some recent regional surveys of central Jordan, and then compare those results with similar studies undertaken in 'Ammān and elsewhere in Ammanitis.

Father Piccirillo has conveniently assessed the work done in various areas of Jordan during the past sixty years.[128] A comprehensive and detailed multi-volume study of excavations and other fieldwork in Jordan has been published.[129] From that rich harvest we may select some material relevant to the topic at hand. A survey of northern Ammanitis by Glueck, and of central Peraea by de Vaux and Benoit, were completed between the two World Wars. Most of those sites examined showed evidence of Byzantine occupation.

Within the past two decades three areas of the central plateau of Jordan have been extensively surveyed. Single-season surveys were conducted by a Belgian team in 1977, and by an American team from Emory University in the following year. The Belgians worked in the area between Ḥisbān and Karak, the Americans investigated between the Wādī Mūjib and Karak.[130] Teams from

[127] Parker (1986), pp.32–4.
[128] Piccirillo (1985).
[129] Homès-Fredericq & Hennessy (1986) and (1989).
[130] Homès-Fredericq (1986); Miller (1979).

Andrews University Seminary concentrated on sites in the region of Ḥisbān, and in the vicinity of Tell ‘Umayri to the north, both of which lie in the Mādabā Plain. Their multi-season survey also included sites to the west of Ḥisbān, where the wadi systems drain toward the Jordan Valley.[131] As noted above, for more than a decade the French have been conducting a survey in the region of western Ammanitis, centered on the site of ‘Araq al-Amīr.[132]

The results of the Belgian survey showed that of 30 sites investigated, only 16 yielded Byzantine material. But 21 of the 30 produced finds from the Roman period. This implied a twenty per cent decrease in settlement within that region during the Byzantine era. Emory University examined more than 30 sites, but the report does not include a complete list of places, nor a chronological breakdown of surface finds. The Andrews University team investigated 155 sites in five campaigns between 1968 and 1976. Most (125) of these lay within a ten kilometre radius of Tell Ḥisbān. But in 1976 they surveyed 30 different sites between Ḥisbān and ‘Ammān, a number of which lay within the territory of Philadelphia. When the results of the entire survey were tabulated, the Byzantine period was found to be represented at 133 of the 155 sites. Only 99 sites showed signs of habitation in the Roman period.[133]

In 1984 Andrews University began a separate survey of Tell ‘Umayrī and the surrounding area, on the very edge of the Mādabā plain where the territories of Ammanitis and Esbonitis meet.[134] Of interest here is the discovery that the settlement pattern at the tell and satellite sites ‘reached its peak in the Byzantine era’.[135] The French survey found that about sixty per cent (83 of 145) of the sites they surveyed near ‘Araq al-Amīr

---

[131] The result of five campaigns between 1968–76 were summarized in Boraas & Geraty (1978).

[132] The best summary of the work done is Villeneuve (1988). For a description of the area surveyed see Villeneuve (1988), pp.264–74.

[133] Ibach (1978), p.212 and Table 1.

[134] Younker et al. (1990) summarize the 1989 season. The 1984 season was reported in *AUSS* 23 (1985, pp.85–110) and that of 1987 in Geraty et al. (1988).

[135] Geraty et al. (1988), p.229.

were inhabited in the Roman/Byzantine period.[136] Roman and Byzantine occupation patterns cannot be compared since the figure given is composite.

Though the results of the Belgian and French surveys would appear to conflict, the number of sites and the area surveyed by each are vastly different. Moreover, the majority of sites investigated by the Belgians lay well outside the orbit of urban centres. Overall, the pattern shows expanded settlement in the Byzantine age, an aspect of late antiquity reflected in the results of surveys in other areas of Jordan.[137]

Hugh Kennedy (1985) has argued for a general decline in the economic and social life of (geographical) Syria in the last century (540–640) before the Islamic conquest. He does not single out one factor as responsible, but suggests that the combined effects of imperial mismanagement, a devastating series of earthquakes and plagues, and other less perceptible causes were to blame. For Ammanitis itself we may adduce a relative decline in prosperity compared with the pronounced urban development in the Antonine era. What wealth there was had never been based on a vast agricultural hinterland (in contrast to Bostra, to the northeast). Trade and commerce must have been the mainstay of the economy.

We may observe that during the Byzantine period in Philadelphia no new fortifications were constructed on the acropolis, that many of the churches so far discovered were badly built, and that intensified agricultural expansion eventually eroded what soil-cover existed on the surrounding hillsides. Suffice it to note that this progressive decline was one of several elements underlying the relative ease with which Islam supplanted Byzantine rule in Philadelphia and throughout the eastern provinces. It remains to be seen whether future fieldwork in Jordan and elsewhere will confirm or contradict Kennedy's thesis.

There are several epigraphic indications that pockets of prosperity did exist within the territory of Philadelphia. At Quwaysma, which is today on the southern edge of greater

---

[136] Villeneuve (1988), p.282.

[137] E.g. for southern Edom (Wādī Ḥasā area) see MacDonald (1981); for the Jordanian Ḥawrān and adjacent areas see King (1982, 1983).

'Ammān, a splendid Roman mausoleum shares pride of place at the site with the remains of two Byzantine churches. Three Greek inscriptions (all undated) appear within the sumptuous mosaics of Church B. One indicates clearly that a local benefactor is honored:

> For the health, the peace and the long life of our master, Stephanus the tribune, and for his servant Matrona and her children. Bless them, Lord God, with a spiritual benediction in the heavenly prayers of holy Kērykos. Amen. Lord, give assistance to your servant Magnus and his wife (*IJ* 2.54b).

Stephanus was very much a *patronus* of this church, and probably of his community as well. The woman Matrona may have been his wife or sister. It is probable that 'the holy structure' referred to in a nearby inscription (54c) is the church itself, for the construction of which this grand seigneur was almost certainly responsible. In a similar church dedication (*IJ* 2.43) from central 'Ammān the phrase 'for the health and longevity of our masters' undoubtedly refers to wealthy Philadelphians who underwrote the construction costs. There are no dated Greek or Latin inscriptions from Philadelphia or its territory later than the Umayyad period. But new discoveries at Umm al-Raṣāṣ to the south (see below) reveal a Christian community constructing churches and creating mosaics with consummate skill in the late eighth century. That argues for continuity (at least for the community at Umm al- Raṣāṣ) through the onset of the Abbasid era. Whether Umm al- Raṣāṣ was an isolated phenomenon, or represents conditions obtaining elsewhere, is presently unknown.[138]

3. Christianity in Philadelphia

The story of Paul's conversion at Damascus (Acts 9:1–26) would indicate that Christian belief had reached the area of the Decapolis at a very early date. Hans Bietenhard has even postulated that Paul's later sojourn 'in Arabia' (Gal. 1:17)[139]

---

[138] On the transitional period in Jordan see most recently Schick (1987, 1988).

[139] Bietenhard (1977), pp.255–6.

was spent not in the 'Arabian desert' but in one or more of the Decapolis cities south of Damascus, and F. F. Bruce has argued that Paul's preaching in the synagogues of Damascus was paralleled by similar activity within Nabataean-controlled territory:

> Had he gone to Arabia to commune with God at Mt. Horeb, like Moses and Elijah in earlier days, it is unlikely that he would have attracted the hostile attention of the Arabian authorities. Some activity of a more public nature is implied, and the tenor of his argument in Gal. 1:15–17 suggests that this public activity took the form of Gospel preaching.[140]

Christian communities such as that represented by Ananius at Damascus existed east of the Jordan a generation before the famous flight of the Jerusalem Christians to Pella at the onset of the First Jewish War (*HE* 3.5.3–4). But the evidence for early Christianity (i.e. during the first and second centuries) in Philadelphia is totally lacking. Nor do we hear of Philadelphia in the troubled third century, when churches in nearby cities such as Bostra were embroiled in doctrinal controversies (*HE* 6.33; 37) just prior to the outbreak of organized persecutions (*HE* 6.39).

Only at the onset of the fourth century is there any hint of a Christian community at Philadelphia. The evidence for that community is somewhat ambiguous and late, and falls within the genre of Byzantine literature known as 'hagiography' or, more accurately, 'martyrology'. (Of course, this raises the question of the historical value of such sources – a query not yet satisfactorily answered).[141] Those martyrs noted here are numbered among the 'many holy martyrs' of Provincia Arabia who were later commemorated by the Church. Those of Philadelphia, in particular, were remembered by a *synodus martyrum*.[142]

---

[140] Bruce (1975), p.23.

[141] The interested reader may review the standard theories on the topic via a superb short essay entitled 'Tradition and Form in the Acts of the Christian Martyrs' in Musurillo (1972, pp.l–lvii).

[142] *In Arabia acommemoratio plurimorum sanctorum martyrum qui sub Galerio Maximiano imperatore saevissime caesi sunt* (Propylaeum ad Acta Sanctorum [Decembris], p.72); on the *synodus* see *AcS* Nov. vol. II, pp.408, 410.

One tale, a 'Passion' narrative,[143] involves six friends, all Christian, who met privately for worship in an as yet unidentified town in Roman Arabia.[144] Sometime after the outbreak of the Diocletianic persecution in 303 they were betrayed, taken prisoner by the Roman authorities, and eventually transported to Philadelphia. There they stood trial before Maximus, the governor (*hēgemōn*) of Arabia, and were executed on 5 August.

The names of the six fall neatly into two categories. Theodorus, Julian and Eubulus represent the 'Hellenized' Christian community, Malcamon, Mocimus and Salamones the 'Semitic'. Their sufferings were shared by two among the Philadelphian Christians, Moses and Silvanus. The story has all the standard elements of a 'martyr's epic', which the editor of the document is quick to point out.[145] Yet there are details of geography and bureaucratic terminology that argue for a core of historical truth within the layers of pious embroidery. Other examples will demonstrate this.

A parallel narrative, the 'Passion of Saints Zenōn and Zenas', attests the deaths of two more martyrs at Philadelphia. Their martyrdom is dated to 'the year one of the Emperor Maximianus'.[146] Zenas was the slave/companion of Zenōn. Both were said to be, in the Latin rendition, *oriundi ex Philadelphia Arabiae*, i.e. native-born Philadelphians.[147] They too were brought to trial before Maximus, who must have held assizes regularly in the major cities of Arabia.[148] Their refusal to sacrifice resulted in their torture and a further review before Bogus (or Bonus), the military prefect (*dux*) of Arabia. This second

---

[143] Peeters (1926). The Georgian text is presented with a Latin translation and notes on pp.88–101.

[144] Peeters (1926, pp.86–7) has identified the town, called *Pede* in the Georgian text, as Pella. Pella was never part of Roman or Byzantine Arabia, and therefore outside the jurisdiction of that province's governor. Milik's (1960, p.165, n.42) conjecture that Pede transliterates Greek *pedion* ('plain') is implausible.

[145] Peeters (1926), p.84.

[146] *AcS* Iun. vol.v, pp.405–11, on p.406; Peeters (1926), p.84, n.2.

[147] *AcS* Iun. vol.v., ch.1; cf. Moore (1964), p.3. The excerpt is from the preface (*Commentarius Praevius*), p.405.

[148] Milik (1960, pp.162–3, and n.39) has identified a specific military term in this document that argues for its authenticity.

interrogation took place in the *Hippicus*, perhaps a reference to a hippodrome, or the horse-market, of Philadelphia.[149] Zenōn and Zenas were sentenced to beheading in June 304. Of several others we know only the names and the fact that they were put to death most probably during that same great persecution. Such are 'the holy martyrs of Philadelphia in Arabia: Cyril, Aquila, Peter, Domitian, Rufus and Menander.'[150]

St Elianus has only recently become prominent among the known martyrs of Philadelphia, thanks to several Georgian manuscripts published (without translation) in 1946, and a translation and commentary based on additional manuscripts published seventeen years later.[151] Elianus is said to have had a shop (*taberna*) near the Gerasa gate of Roman Philadelphia 'not far from the church that was [later] built there'.[152] During a visit to the city by the provincial governor (Maximus), a group of Christians were arrested and jailed after an outbreak of violence. Elianus visited them in prison, and was himself taken captive. The inevitable public interrogation followed, said to have taken place 'in a large, circular paved area, where a bronze statue of Kronus stood upon a bronze pillar'.[153] Elianus' refusal to sacrifice to the pagan gods (particularly Kronus) led to his torture and eventual martyr's death (by fire) 'near the Mādabā gate' of Philadelphia.[154]

Christian Philadelphia is otherwise known through the churches, chapels or tombs so far discovered, the evidence of epigraphy associated with those buildings or in other ways

---

[149] *AcS* Iun. Vol.v, ch.14. Milik (1960, p.162, n.33) believes the reference (*hippikon* in the Greek text) is to 'la place forte de la caserne de cavalerie'.

[150] Moore (1964), pp.4, 25.

[151] The initial publication was inevitably limited to those scholars reading Georgian. Milik (1960, pp.166–70) made no attempt to summarize the narrative. Garitte (1961), with introduction, résumé, Georgian text and Latin translation, plus commentary, is now the definitive publication.

[152] Garitte (1961), p.429. The name of St Elianus was later associated with a small, columned basilica in Philadelphia, identified as such by the Survey of Eastern Palestine in 1881. See Conder (1889), p.56, with Bagatti (1973), pp.271–2.

[153] Garitte (1961), pp.418, 421, 430. The description fits the 'oval forum' at Gerasa better than any known feature of Roman Philadelphia.

[154] Garitte (1961), p.442.

identifiably Christian, and the various accounts of Philadelphia's church leaders at ecclesiastical councils.

Some half-dozen buildings within the urban area of Byzantine Philadelphia have been identified as churches. One is located at or near the far end of the *cardo* (the northwest-southeast colonnaded street), on its northeastern side. It was long ago identified as such by Conder, and later by Butler. The second is the 'apsidal structure' just southwest of the nymphaeum, identified as a cathedral by Conder (fig.19; pl.76). Butler believed it was a church which had incorporated part or all of an earlier building. Subsequent opinion supports this, and the structure is generally accepted as the seat of Philadelphia's bishops. A nearby structure may have been a church. Neither of those poorly-preserved churches, understandably, received a mention in Butler's posthumous *Early Churches in Syria* (1929). Remains of a sixth-century church were identified in the 1930s by Italian excavators on the citadel's upper terrace, just northeast of the Archaeological Museum.[155] Conder identified a 'chapel', just south-west of the citadel.

Outside the ancient city limits a number of other churches are known. At Swafiyya, near the Sixth Circle on Jabal 'Ammān, portions of a sixth-century church have been uncovered.[156] The church floor was paved with an inscribed mosaic (9.5 × 5m) which was laid on an earlier mosaic floor. At Khuraybat al-Sūq, six kilometres south of the city centre, a late Roman temple of moderate size was converted into a church (with mosaic floor).[157] At Quwaysma, now a southeastern suburb of greater 'Ammān, two churches are known.[158] Church A, near the mausoleum at the site, has a mosaic floor inscribed in Greek and Aramaic. The Greek inscription (*IJ* 2.53) records repair work presumably associated with the great earthquake of January 717, which did considerable damage throughout Jordan and Palestine. Church B, which seems to date to the second half of the sixth century, also has an inscribed mosaic floor. At Jubayḥa, eight kilometres

155 Khouri (1988), p.16.
156 Khouri (1988), pp.37–8.
157 Khouri (1988), pp.31–2.
158 Khouri (1988), pp.33–5.

northwest of the city centre and near the University of Jordan campus, the remains of a Byzantine church with a mosaic floor were uncovered in 1976.[159] A similar church-floor mosaic from Yadūda, ten kilometres south of 'Ammān, records the installation of the mosaic 'in the year ?565' (AD ?502).[160]

Three other structures are worth noting: chapels, tombs and monasteries. At Jabal Akhḍar in the southern part of 'Ammān is what may have been a private chapel. There a small (1.42 × 0.5m) inscribed mosaic floor was found within a group of domestic structures that surrounds the 'Ammonite tower' at the site.[161] An undated Christian tomb was found at Jabal Jawfa in the southern part of 'Ammān in 1981.[162] Two painted scenes, now badly preserved, depict miraculous events from the New Testament. One is the raising of Lazarus, the other the healing of the blind. Two-word captions (*IJ* 2.47) identify each. The monastic life is represented by a complex of buildings from the village of Zia (Zay) near Salṭ.[163] Whether Zia lay within the territory or diocese of Gadara/Salṭ (as the excavators believe), or belonged to Philadelphia, is uncertain. No monastery has yet been identified at Quwaysma, though several scholars have postulated that one may have been associated with one or both of the churches at that site.[164]

Apart from the above buildings, there are certain inscriptions, explicitly or implicitly Christian, to consider. Many of these are entirely formulaic, but some are less so. At Jubayḥa a broken inscription (*IJ* 2.6) invokes 'The Lord to protect the entrance and the exit of this holy place' and to accept the offering made. Within the 'chapel' at Jabal Akhḍar was another inscribed invocation:

> 'Lord our God, King for Eternity, come to the aid of your servants Epiphanius, with his children and wife, and Kaioumus the deacon, by provision of [the latter]' (*IJ* 2.46).

---

[159] Mhaisen (1976).
[160] *IJ* 2.56. The numeral indicating hundreds is missing.
[161] Khouri (1988), p.26.
[162] Zayadine (1982b).
[163] Piccirillo (1982).
[164] Gatier (1986), pp.66–7.

The construction of a church was commemorated on a white marble plaque (*IJ* 2.43) found at Jabal Luwaybda ('Ammān) early this century:

> By the will of God, and the consent of A.mon... (?), priest of (the church of) St George, for the health and longevity of our masters, thanks to their generosity, this church has been built under (the aegis of) the holy bishop Polyeucte, through the zeal of Thalassamachias, a... (?).

The date of this inscription is much disputed, and the letters at the end of line one quite problematic. Gatier has restored there the Greek words for 'most holy monk', i.e. *ha[g(iotatos) mon[achos*]. However, a personal name would be more usual, followed by the person's office (in this case 'priest of St George's'). The status of Thalassamachias is unclear; Gatier suggests 'archiprêtre'. The 'masters' (*despotai*), like the *tribunus* Stephanus above, must be local gentry of some substance. The mention of a bishop is noteworthy: Polyeucte is not attested elsewhere. Two more names of otherwise unknown bishops appear in the epigraphy of Philadelphia and vicinity: 'the most holy' Thomas at Swafiyya (*IJ* 2.7), and 'the most pious and holy' Theodosius at Yadūda (*IJ* 2.56). The conciliar lists of the fourth and fifth centuries provide the names of two others. Cyrion attended both the Council of Nicaea in 325 and the Council of Antioch in 341; Eulogius represented Philadelphia at the Council of Chalcedon in 451.[165] Almost two centuries later Pope Martin I sent letters to a number of eastern dioceses, including one (AD 649) to 'Bishop John of Philadelphia'.[166]

4. Itineraries, Pilgrimages and Maps

Philadelphia would not have ranked among the most prominent sites in the topography of the 'Holy Land', but its Old Testament associations must have attracted some of the pious Christian travellers who, from the fourth century on, made their way to Jerusalem. Unfortunately we have no clear record of that. Michele Piccirillo has recently reviewed the literary and

---

165 Gatier (1986), Appendix following p.201.

166 Gatier (1986), Appendix [= *PL* 87.153–64].

archaeological evidence for the pilgrim route between Palestine and Transjordania.[167] From Jerusalem the standard itinerary led pilgrims to the River Jordan via Jericho, then on to some point where the Jordan was crossed. The two major attractions on the East Bank were Mt Nebo and the hot springs at Baaru (mod. Ḥammāmāt Ma'īn), which presumably offered spiritual and physical renewal, respectively. For many pilgrims Mt Nebo was the end of the journey. Such was the attitude of Egeria in the late fourth century, who turned back to Jerusalem. For the aged Peter the Iberian, a century later, Mt Nebo was an incidental pause on the way to Baaru via Mādabā.

The accounts of such pilgrims have been the focus of two recent studies.[168] But among the dozens of reports there is only one oblique reference to Philadelphia. Theodosius, an archdeacon and (probably) pilgrim of the early sixth century, produced a rather disorganized and much re-edited work, *De Situ Terrae Sanctae* (*On the Topography of the Holy Land*), which includes a list of places and routes, and occasional commentary on biblical passages. It has recently been argued by Yoram Tsafrir (1986) that much of Theodosius' topographical information was based on a map or maps used by contemporary tour-guides who conducted pilgrims from Palestine to sites in Transjordania, and that the Mādabā map (see below) used the same source or sources. Theodosius may have inserted information gained from his own travels, or by interviewing others who had made the trip. In chapter 24 of *De Situ*, thirteen cities of (Provincia) Arabia are noted, among them 'Filadelphia'. But there is not the slightest hint that Theodosius ever travelled to Philadelphia, or knew of any prior account of such a trip. The roll-call of martyrs, noted above, was not enough to put the city 'on the map' of tourist sites. Philadelphia was hardly alone in being ignored by the pious pilgrims who left a record of their journeys. Of the cities once belonging to the Decapolis, only Damascus and Scythopolis were regular stops on the pilgrimage itineraries.[169] Even Pella is absent

---

[167] Piccirillo (1987b).

[168] Wilkinson (1977) and Hunt (1982).

[169] One may consult with profit Wilkinson's (1977, pp.148–78) 'Gazetteer' of the biblical sites.

from the travel reports, an omission difficult to understand. Pella had been a refuge for Palestinian Christians in the first century and still flourished in the Byzantine age. It would appear that Christian interest east of the Jordan centred on the Old Testament, and in particular on the burial-place of Moses.

The famous mosaic map discovered at Mādabā at the end of the last century is the only visual representation we have of portions of the Near East from late antiquity.[170] The map was created sometime in the second half of the sixth century, and its *raison d'être* must be closely linked to Mādabā's fortuitous location near Mt Nebo. In its original state it displayed in colorful vignettes and cartouches all the names of towns and tribes, cities, rivers, mountains and deserts associated with the Old and New Testaments. In geographic extent it would have represented the Near East from Tyre and Damascus in the north to the Red Sea and the Nile Delta to the south, and from the Palestinian coast in the west to the Decapolis in the east. Unfortunately Philadelphia and virtually all the territory north of the River Arnon (Wādī Mūjib) and east of the Jordan is missing. The lacunae include, ironically, Mādabā itself.

How Philadelphia was depicted in very late antiquity may be inferred from a newly discovered eighth-century mosaic on the floor of the church of St Stephen at Umm al-Raṣāṣ, 30 km southeast of Mādabā.[171] This is not a mosaic map *per se*, but a geographical motif was used with great skill by the mosaicist. Two dedicatory Greek inscriptions give dates of AD 756 and 785. The church and its mosaics are technically from the early Abbasid

---

[170] A full bibliography of the map's publications can be found in Gatier (1986, pp.148–9). Handy facsimiles of the map, with Greek and English captions respectively, are presented in Wilkinson (1977) as endpieces. For a recent critique of the map and its significance see Donceel-Voûte (1988), who prefers a date in the early 7th century. Her argument (which is not convincing) focuses on the religious turmoil subsequent to the creation of the patriarchate of Jerusalem (mid-fifth century) and the prominence of Transjordanian bishoprics on the map itself.

[171] Piccirillo and Attiyah (1986) with black and white photos only (plates LXX–LXXVII). Almost the entire volume of *Biblical Archaeology* 51 (1988) is devoted to aspects of the new mosaics, accompanied by splendid color photographs. On its religious, social and artistic significance, see in particular Schick (1988), Piccirillo (1988) and Wilkin (1988).

era, but the tradition they represent is Byzantine Christian. Around the rectangular central panel (damaged sometime after AD 785) is an outer border consisting of eighteen city plans, all but one with the toponym spelled out beneath it. Eight are cities west of the Jordan, and ten (including Philadelphia) lie east of that river. An inner border of the central panel is a scenario from Egyptian geography: the Nile Delta region with ten of its cities and villages presented with captions.

Philadelphia, labelled as such, appears in the upper right-hand corner of the outer mosaic border. Above it is a depiction of a place labelled 'Castron Mefaa', which is now known to be the ancient name of Umm al-Raṣāṣ.[172] Below it is a representation of 'Midaba' (Mādabā). The panel in which Philadelphia appears measures about one metre in length and a half metre in width. The city is presented as one might view it from a nearby hillside, looking toward a city gate. The gate is flanked by towers, and a section of city wall is shown to the left and right of the towers. A number of buildings are shown within the city, in perspective, angled to the left and the right of the viewer, one behind the other. Behind the innermost building another section of wall is shown, with what appear to be the tops of two buttresses or towers above it. To either side of that building are two larger towers, with windows or arrow slits showing. It is difficult to know if those towers stand within the city, or are part of the outer defenses.

The depiction of Philadelphia is strikingly different from that of the larger town plan of 'Castron Mefaa' above it. It is, however, similar to that of 'Midaba', both in size and layout, though there are enough details of difference to convince the viewer that the mosaicist was not simply reproducing a stereotype of a city plan. Indeed, the plans of the other fifteen cities are rendered with some attempt at individuality. Where the topography of a city is known from other representations or descriptions (e.g. Jerusalem and Neapolis), its depiction in the Umm al-Raṣāṣ mosaic is reasonably accurate. This is the only detailed representation we have of Philadelphia. The buildings shown, each with a tile roof,

---

[172] For a dissenting opinion on this identification, see Elitzur (1989).

may be churches. The walls and gates are standard features of many, but not all, of the cities in the mosaic. This sketch may be more accurate than the stylized rendering of the walled citadel on the crown of the marble *Tychē* of Philadelphia, found in 1961.[173] Since we know that the physical appearance of Philadelphia (especially the citadel area) was transformed after the Islamic conquest, we may assume that the features shown at Umm al-Raṣāṣ are characteristic of the pre-Islamic period and are what travellers or pilgrims would have encountered before the Umayyad age.

5. *Philadelphia's Byzantine Historian*

Philadelphia produced one historian of 'international' stature in the early Byzantine period. This was Malchus (less certainly Malichus), who flourished in the late fifth and early sixth centuries.[174] It is worth noting that he was known by his native name only; Malchus transliterates either the Semitic word *malik (mlk)*, meaning 'king', or the well-known Arab name 'Mālik'.[175] His city of origin was said to be 'Philadelphia', which can only mean 'Ammān (not Philadelphia/Neocaesaraea in Lydia) in view of his name.[176] He apparently resided in Constantinople, where about the year 500 he compiled a Byzantine *History* (*Byzantiaká*; the exact title is uncertain). It survives only in fragments quoted by later sources, particularly the *Excerpta de Legationibus Romanorum* (10th century AD). Malchus' *History* was of unknown length, but it is likely that it covered events in the years 473–*c*.500. Its scope was nominally the entire Byzantine Empire, West and East, and the surviving fragments bear this out.[177]

---

173 There is a good photograph of this Tychē in Moore (1964, opposite p.16).

174 The most recent discussion of Malchus is that of Shahid (1989, pp.59–113, *passim*); this does not supersede the masterly article by Baldwin (1977). See also Blockley (1981, pp.71–85; 124–7; 1983, pp.402–62), and the additional bibliography given in Shahid (1989, p.59, nn.2, 3). The entry in *PLRE* II (p.73) is quite inadequate.

175 Shahid (1989), pp.61–2.

176 Baldwin (1977, p.92) placed Philadelphia in 'Palestine'. Even if he meant the Byzantine province of Palaestina (Tertia), it did not include central Jordan.

177 Baldwin (1977), p.104.

Malchus was much praised by later commentators for his clarity, simplicity and orderly style of writing. That acclaim may be due in part to his 'classical' training as a sophist and 'rhetor'.[178] Among his models for composition were Herodotus and Thucydides,[179] and therefore lengthy speeches must have been woven into his narrative at regular intervals. There has been some scholarly debate regarding Malchus' religious background, with rival claims put forward for either his Christianity or his paganism.[180] The fragmentary nature of his *History* indicates only that he held a 'secular position in his narrative and in rendering his historical judgements'.[181] The historical sources used by Malchus can only be conjectured. His approach to historiography was annalistic.

The closest we get to an account of a contemporary event affecting the Byzantine Near East is Malchus' description (Frag. 1)[182] of the seizure of the island of Iotabe (mod. Ṭīrān), at the entrance to the Gulf of 'Aqaba, by an Arab chieftain, Amorkesos, in 472–3.[183] Amorkesos then petitioned Constantinople for recognition as 'phylarch of (Arabia) Petraea', a concession which he was granted upon his conversion to Christianity.[184] The Byzantine Emperor Leo is strongly criticized by Malchus, not for awarding federated status to Amorkesos and his tribe, but for inviting him to Constantinople and seating him among the

---

178 The meanings of 'sophist' and 'rhetor' underwent modification from the classical period through Byzantine times. When applied to Malchus, they might mean 'teacher' and 'lawyer', respectively. See the discussion in Baldwin (1977), pp.91–2, n.4a.

179 Blockley (1981), p.90.

180 Baldwin (1977, pp.94–6) summarizes the issue.

181 Blockley (1981), p.77.

182 *FHG* IV, pp.112–13; *Excerpta Historica issu imp. Constantini Porphyrogeniti Confecta* (whence *Excerpta de Legationibus*) vol.I.1, pp.568–9). Shahid (1989, pp.112–13) has reproduced the Greek text of the latter. Frag. 1 is also reproduced in Greek, with an English translation and commentary, in Blockley (1983, pp.404–7).

183 'Amorkesos' in Greek has been taken to transliterate the Arabic *Imru' al-Qays*, but Shahid (1989, pp.61–3) suggests that 'A*mr ibn Kays* is also possible. His decision to use the Greek spelling throughout his discussion is judicious indeed. Baldwin (1977, pp.101, 103) refers to Amorkesos as a 'Persian'.

184 This incident is summarized well by Sartre (1982, pp.154–5).

Byzantine aristocracy. What the fragment reveals of Malchus' treatment of but one small incident in the history of his time makes the loss of his work especially regretful. Whether his native city of Philadelphia played any role in his *Byzantine History* is unknown. What is not doubtful is the high regard in which the *History* is held by several modern historians.[185]

Acknowledgements

I am indebted to Alastair Northedge for advice and encouragement during the preparation of this contribution. Grateful acknowledgement is also made to Dr Martin Price of the British Museum, and Dr Lawrence Keppie of the Hunterian Museum, for acute and helpful comments on numismatics and epigraphy, respectively. Professor Doron Mendels of the Hebrew University kindly brought to my attention several useful works concerning the Hellenistic period in Palestine/Trans-Jordan.

[185] E.g. '... its loss is to be deplored both as an invaluable source and as a superior work of historiography' (Blockley, 1981, p.85); 'All in all, Malchus was a readable and effective stylist ... The surviving fragments make one wish for more. That cannot be said of all late Greek historians' (Baldwin, 1977, p.107).

Abbreviations

AB	*Analecta Bollandiana*
AcS	*Acta Sanctorum*
ADAJ	*Annual of the Department of Antiquities of Jordan*
AE	*Année Epigraphique*
AfO	*Archiv für Orientforschung*
AJ	*Antiquities of the Jews*
AJP	*American Journal of Philology*
ANRW	*Aufstieg und Niedergang der Römischen Welt*
AS	*Ancient Society*
AUSS	*Andrews University Seminary Studies*
BA	*Biblical Archaeologist*
BAR	British Archaeological Reports
BASOR	*Bulletin of the American Schools of Oriental Research*
BF	*Byzantinisches Forschungen*
BJ	*Bellum Judaicum*
BMC	*British Museum Catalogue (of Coins)*
CIL	*Corpus Inscriptionum Latinarum*
CIS	*Corpus Inscriptionum Semiticarum*
CNRS	Centre National de la Recherche Scientifique
CPJ	*Corpus Papyrorum Judaicarum*
CQ	*Classical Quarterly*
DOP	*Dumbarton Oaks Papers*
EAEHL	*Encyclopedia of Archaeological Excavations in the Holy Land*
FHG	*Fragmenta Historicorum Graecorum* (ed. C. Müller)
HE	*Historia Ecclesiastica (Eusebius of Caesarea)*
IDB	*Interpreter's Dictionary of the Bible*
IEJ	*Israel Exploration Journal*
IGLS	*Inscriptions Grecques et Latines de la Syrie*
IGR	*Inscriptiones Graecae ad Res Romanas Pertinentes*
IJ	*Inscriptions de la Jordanie*
ILS	*Inscriptiones Latines Selectae*
JBL	*Journal of Biblical Literature*
JRS	*Journal of Roman Studies*
LA	*Liber Annuus*
LSJ	Liddell, Scott & Jones (*Greek-English Lexicon*)
MB	*Monde de la Bible*
MHA	*Memoria de Historia Antigua*
OGIS	*Orientis Graeci Inscriptiones Selectae*

Onom.	*Das Onomastikon der Biblischen Ortsnamen (ed. E. Klostermann)*
PCZ	*Papyrus Cairo Zenon*
PE	*Praeparatio Evangelica*
PG	*Patrologia Graeca* (ed. Migne)
PL	*Patrologia Latina* (ed. Migne)
PLRE	*Prosopography of the Later Roman Empire*
P Lond	*Papyrus London*
PPUAES	*Publications of the Princeton University Archaeological Expeditions to Syria*
PSI	*Publicazioni della Società Italiana*
RAO	*Recueil d'Archéologie Orientale*
RB	*Revue Biblique*
RE	*Realencyclopädie* (Pauly-Wissova)
RES	*Répertoire d'Epigraphie Sémitique*
SB	*Sammelbuch (Griechische Urkunden aus Agypten)*
SDB	*Supplement au Dictionnaire de la Bible*
SEG	*Supplementum Epigraphicum Graecum*
SH	*Studia Hierosolymitana*
SHAJ	*Studies in the History and Archaeology of Jordan*
Wadd.	W.H. Waddington, *Inscriptions Grecques et Latines de la Syrie*
ZDPV	*Zeitschrift des Deutschen Palästina-Vereins*
ZPE	*Zeitschrift für Papyrologie und Epigraphik*

Bibliography

Abel, F.-M. (1933; 1938), *Géographie de la Palestine*, 2 vols. (Paris, Librairie Lecoffre).

Almagro, A. (1980), 'The Photogrammetric Survey of the Citadel of Amman and other Archaeological Sites in Jordan', *ADAJ* 24: 111–19.

— (1983), 'The Survey of the Roman Monuments of Amman by the Italian Mission in 1930', *ADAJ* 27: 609–39.

Avi-Yonah, M. (1966), *The Holy Land: A Historical Geography* (Grand Rapids, Baker Book House).

Bagatti, B. (1973), 'Le antiche chiese di Filadelphia-'Amman (Transgiordania)', *LA* 23: 261–85.

Bagnall, R. S. (1976), *The Administration of the Ptolemaic Possessions Outside Egypt* (Leiden, E.J. Brill).

Baldwin, B. (1977), 'Malchus of Philadelphia', *DOP* 13: 91–107.

Bar-Kochva, B. (1989), *Judas Maccabaeus: The Jewish Struggle Against the Seleucids* (Cambridge and New York).

Bauzou, T. (1988), 'Les voies romaines entre Damas et Amman', in P.-L. Gatier et al. (eds.), *Géographie Historique au Proche-Orient* (Paris, CNRS) 293–300.

Bietenhard, H. (1977), 'Die syrische Dekapolis von Pompeius bis Traian', *ANRW* II.8: 220–61 (cf. *ZDPV* 79 [1963] 24–58).

Block, D. I. (1984), '*Bny 'mwn*: The Sons of Ammon', *AUSS* 22: 197–212.

Blockley, R. C. (1981), *The Fragmentary Classicizing Historians of the Later Roman Empire: Eunapius, Olympiodorus, Priscus and Malchus*, vol. I (Liverpool).

Blockley, R. C. (1983), *The Fragmentary Classicizing Historians of the Later Roman Empire: Eunapius, Olympiodorus, Priscus and Malchus*, Vol. II (Liverpool).

Boraas, R. S. & Gerarty, L. T., eds. (1978), *Heshban 1976* (Berrien Springs, Andrews University Press).

Bosworth, A. B. (1974), 'The Government of Syria under Alexander the Great', *CQ* 24: 44–64.

Bowersock, G. W., (1973), 'Syria Under Vespasian', *JRS* 63: 133–40.

— (1983), *Roman Arabia* (Cambridge, Harvard University Press).

— (1988), 'The Three Arabias in Ptolemy's Geography' in P.-L. Gatier et al. (eds.), *Géographie Historique au Proche-Orient* (Paris, CNRS), 47–53.

Braemer, F. (1987), 'Two Campaigns of Excavations on the Ancient Tell of Jerash', *ADAJ* 31: 525–9.

Bruce, F. F. (1975), 'Further Thoughts on Paul's Autobiography: Galatians 1:11–2:14', in E. Ellis & E. Grasser (1975) 21–29.

Butler, H. C. (1910), 'Trajan's Road from Bosra to the Red Sea: The Section between Bosra and 'Ammān', in *PPUAS* Division III (Greek & Latin Inscriptions in Syria) Section A Part 2 (Appendix) vii–xvi.

— (1907), 'Ammonitis', in *PPUAES* Division II (Ancient Architecture in Syria) Section A Part I (Leiden, E.J. Brill) 1–62.

Campagano, L. S. (1988), 'L'inscrizione metrica greca di Khirbet er-Rajîb', *LA* 38: 253–65.

Conder, C. R. (1889), *The Survey of Eastern Palestine* (London, The Committee of the Palestine Exploration Fund).

Dentzer, J.-M. et al. (1982), 'Iraq el Amir: Excavations at the Monumental Gateway', in A. Hadidi (ed.), *SHAJ* I: 201–7.

Donceel-Voûte, P. (1988), 'La carte de Madaba: cosmographie, anachronisme et propagande', *RB* 95: 519–42.

Dunand, M. (1931), 'La Strata Diocletiana', *RB* 40: 227–48.

Elitzur, Y. (1989), 'The Identification of Mefa'at in View of the Discoveries at Khirbet Umm er-Resas', *IEJ* 39: 267–77.

Ellis, E. & Grasser, E., eds. (1975), *Jesus und Paulus: Festschrift für Werner Georg Kümmel* (Göttingen, Vanden Loeth & Puprecht).

Frézouls, E. (1961), 'Recherches sur les théatres de l'Orient Syrien II', *Syria* 38: 54–86.

Garitte, G. (1961), 'La Passion de S. Elien de Philadelphie ('Amman)', *AB* 79: 412–446.

Gatier, P.-L. (1982), 'Inscriptions grecques et latines en Jordanie', *MB* 22: 10–11.

— (1986), *Inscriptions de la Jordanie* Vol. 2 (Paris, Paul Geuthner).

— (1988), 'Philadelphie et Gerasa du royaume Nabatéen à la province d'Arabie', in P.L. Gatier et al. (eds.), *Géographie Historique au Proche-Orient* (Paris, CNRS) 159–70.

— (1990), 'Décapole et Coelé Syrie: Deux Inscriptions Nouvelles', *Syria* 67: 204–6.

— and Vérilhac, A-M. (1989), 'Les columbes de Déméter à Philadelphie-Amman', *Syria* 66: 337–48.

Gavin, C. (1985), 'Jordan's Environment in Early Photographs', in A. Hadidi (ed.), *SHAJ* II: 279–85.

Geraty, L. T. et al. (1988), 'The Joint Madaba Plains Project: A Preliminary Report on the Second Season at Tell el-'Umeiri and Vicinity', *AUSS* 26: 217–52.

Goldstein, J. A. (1976), *I Maccabees: A New Translation with Notes and Commentary* (Anchor Bible Series Vol. 41.1), (New York, Doubleday & Co.).

— (1983), *II Maccabees: A New Translation with Notes and Commentary* (Anchor Bible Series Vol. 41.2), (New York, Doubleday & Co.).

Graf, D. F. (1983), 'Dedanite and Minaean (South Arabian) Inscriptions from the Hisma', *ADAJ* 27: 555–69.

— (1986), 'The Nabataeans and the Decapolis', in P. Freeman & D. Kennedy (eds.), *The Defence of the Roman and Byzantine East* (Oxford, B.A.R.) Vol. 2: 785–96.

Habicht, C. (1976), '*2. Makkabäerbuch*' in G. Kümmel (ed.), *Jüdische Schriften aus hellenistisch-römischer Zeit I: Historische und legendarische Erzählungen* (Güttersloh, Gerd Mohn).

Hadidi, A. (1970a), 'The Pottery of the Roman Forum at Amman', *ADAJ* 15: 11–15.

— (1970b), *The Roman Forum at Amman*, unpub. Ph.D. thesis, University of Missouri, Columbia.

— (1974), 'The Excavation of the Roman Forum at Amman (Philadelphia)', *ADAJ* 19: 71–91.

Harper, G. M. (1928), 'A Study in the Commercial Relations between Egypt and Syria in the Third Century before Christ', *AJP* 49: l–35.

Hauben, H. (1984), '"Onagres et hémionagres" en Transjordanie au IIIe siècle avant J.-C.', *AS* 15: 89–11l.

Hengel, M. (1989), *The 'Hellenization' of Judaea in the First Century After Christ* (Philadelphia).

Homès-Fredericq, D. (1986), 'Prospections archéologiques en Moab', in A. Théodoridès et al. (eds.), *Archéologie et Philologie dans l'Etude des Civilisations Orientales* (Leuven, Peeters) 81–100.

Homès-Fredericq, D. & Hennessy, J. B., eds. (1986), *Archaeology of Jordan* I: *Bibliography* (Leuven, Peeters).

— (1989), *Archaeology of Jordan II.1–2, Field Surveys and Sites, A–K, L–Z* (Leuven).

Hunt, E. D. (1982), *Holy Land Pilgrimages in the Later Roman Empire: A.D. 312–460* (Oxford, the Clarendon Press).

Ibach, R. (1978), 'Expanded Archaeological Survey of the Hesban Region', in Boraas & Gerarty (1978) 201–13 (= *AUSS* 16 [1978: 201-13]).

Isaac, B. (1981), 'The Decapolis in Syria: A Neglected Inscription', *ZPE* 44: 67–74.

— (1989), 'Trade Routes to Arabia and the Roman Presence in the Desert', in T. Fahd (ed.), *L'Arabie Préislamique et son Environnement Historique et Culturel* (Leiden, E.J. Brill) 241–56.

Jaussen, A. & Savignac, R. (1909), 'Inscription grèco-nabatéen de Zizeh', *RB* 6: 587–92.

Jones, A. H. M. (1971), *The Cities of the Eastern Roman Provinces*[2] (Oxford, The Clarendon Press).

Kasher, A. (1988), *Jews, Idumaeans and Ancient Arabs* (Tübingen).

Kennedy, D. L. (1982), 'The Contribution of Aerial Photography to Archaeology in Jordan: with Special Reference to the Roman Period', in A. Hadidi (ed.), *SHAJ* I: 29–36.

Kennedy, H. (1985), 'The Last Century of Byzantine Syria', *BF* 10: 141–83.

King, G. R. D. (1982), 'Preliminary Report on a Survey of Byzantine and Islamic Sites in Jordan (1980)', *ADAJ* 26: 85–95.

King, G. R. D. et al. (1983), 'Survey of Byzantine and Islamic Sites in Jordan: Second Season Report (1981)', *ADAJ* 27: 385–436.

Khouri, R. G. (1988), *Amman: A Brief Guide to the Antiquities* (Amman, Al Kutba Publishers).

Lemaire, A. & Lozachmeur, H. (1987), '*Bīrāh/birtā*' en araméen', *Syria* 64: 261–6.

Littmann, E. et al. (1921), 'Ammonitis' in *PPUAES* Division III (Greek and Latin Inscriptions in Syria) Section A Part I (Leiden, E.J. Brill) 1–20.

MacAdam, H. I. (1986), *Studies in the History of the Roman Province of Arabia* (Oxford, BAR Int. Ser. 297).

MacDonald, B. (1981), 'Wadi al-Hesa Survey', *BA* 44: 60–1.

Mazar, B. (1957), 'The Tobiads', *IEJ* 7: 137–45; 229–38.

Mhaisen, M. (1976), 'Jbeyha Church: 1976', *ADAJ* 21: 8–22 (in Arabic).

Milik, J. T. (1960), 'Notes d'épigraphie et de topographie jordaniennes', *LA* 10: 147–84.

Miller, J. M. (1979), 'Archaeological Survey of Central Moab (1978)', *BASOR* 234: 43–52.

Mittman, S. (1970a), *Beiträge zur Siedlungs und Territorial-geschichte des Nordlichen Ostjordanlandes* (Wiesbaden).

— (1970b), 'Zenon im Ostjordanland', in A. Kuschke & E. Kuschke (eds.), *Archäologie und Altes Testament: Festschrift für Kurt Galling* (Tübingen, J.C.B. Mohr) 201–10.

Mlaker, K. (1943), *Die Hierodulenlisten von Maʿīn* (Leipzig, Otto Harrassowitz).

Moore, E. A. (1964), *Some Soldier Martyrs of the Early Christian Church in East Jordan and Syria* (Beirut, Khayats).

Musurillo, H. ed.(1972), *The Acts of the Christian Martyrs* (Oxford, the Clarendon Press).

Olavarri, E. (1980), 'Altar de Zeus-Baʿalshamin (procedente de Amman)', *MHA* 4: 197–202.

Orrieux, C. (1979), 'Les papyrus de Zénon et la préhistoire du mouvement Maccabéen', in A. Caquot et al. (eds.), *Hellenica et Judaica: Hommage à Valentin Nikiprowetzky* (Leuven & Paris, Editions Peeters) 321–33.

Parker, S. T. (1975), 'The Decapolis Reviewed', *JBL* 94: 437–41.

— (1986), *Romans and Saracens: A History of the Arabian Frontier* (Winona Lake, Eisenbrauns).

Peeters, P. (1926), 'La Passion géorgienne des SS. Théodore, Julien, Eubulus, Malcamon, Mocimus et Salamones', *AB* 44: 70–101.

Pestman, P. J. ed. (1981), *A Guide to the Zenon Archive* (Leiden, E.J. Brill).

Piccirillo, M. (1982), 'Il complesso monastico di Zay el- Gharbi e la dicesi di Gadara della Perea', *SH* 3: 358–78.

— (1985), 'Rural Settlements in Byzantine Jordan', in A. Hadidi (ed.), *SHAJ* II: 257–61.

— (1987), 'The Jerusalem-Esbus Road and its Sanctuaries in Transjordan', in A. Hadidi (ed.), *SHAJ* 3: 165–72.
— (1988), 'The Mosaics of Um er-Resas in Jordan', *BA* 51: 208–13; 222–31.
Piccirillo, M. & Attiyah, T. (1986), 'The Complex of Saint Stephen at Umm er-Rasas-Kastron Mafaa: First Campaign (August, 1986)', *ADAJ* 30: 341–51.
Rey-Coquais, J.-P., (1981), 'Philadelphie de Coelé-Syria', *ADAJ* 25: 27–31.
— (1982), 'Décapole et Province d'Arabie', *MB* 22: 7–9.
Robert, L. (1960), *Hellenica XI–XII* (Paris, Adrien-Maisonneuve).
Rostovtzeff, M. (1922), *A Large Estate in Egypt in the Third Century B.C.* (Madison, Univ. of Wisconsin).
Sartre, M. (1982), *Trois études sur l'Arabie romaine et byzantine.* Collection Latomus 178 (Brussels).
— (1985), *Bostra: des origines à l'Islam* (Paris, Paul Geuthner).
Schick, R. (1987), *The Fate of the Christians in Palestine during the Byzantine-Umayyad Transition*, Unpub. Ph.D. dissertation, University of Chicago.
— (1988), 'Christian Life in Palestine during the Early Islamic Period', *BA* 51: 218–21; 239–40.
Schürer, E. (1979), *The History of the Jewish People in the Age of Jesus Christ (175 B.C.–A.D. 135)* Vol. 2 (revised and edited by G. Vermes et al.) (Edinburgh, T. & T. Clark).
Segal, A. (1988), *Town Planning and Architecture in Provincia Arabia* (Oxford, BAR Int. Ser. 419).
Shahid, I. (1989), *Byzantium and the Arabs in the Fifth Century* (Washington, DC).
Sourdel, D. (1952), *Les Cults du Hauran à l'Epoque Romaine* (Paris, Paul Geuthner).
Spijkerman, A. (1978), *The Coins of the Decapolis and Provincia Arabia* (Jerusalem, Franciscan Printing Press).
Starcky, J. (1966), 'Petra et la Nabatène', *SDB* 7: cols. 886–1017.
— (1971), 'Une inscription nabatéenne de l'an 18 d'Arétas IV', in A. Caquot & M. Philonenko (eds.) *Hommages à André Dupont-Sommer* (Paris, Librairie d'Amérique et d'Orient), 151–9.
— (1985), 'Les inscriptions nabatéennes et l'histoire de la Syrie méridionale et du nord de la Jordanie', in J.-M. Dentzer (ed.), *Hauran I: Recherches archéologiques sur la Syrie du sud à l'époque hellénistique et romaine* Pt. 1 (Paris, P. Geuthner) 167–81.
Tcherikover, V. (1961), *Hellenistic Civilization and the Jews* (Philadelphia, The Jewish Publication Society of America).

— (1972), 'Social Conditions', in A. Schalit (ed.), *The Hellenistic Age: Political History of Jewish Palestine from 332 B.C.E. to 67 B.C.E.* (The World History of the Jewish People, Vol. 6), (New Brunswick, Rutgers Univ. Press) 87–114.

Tscherikower, V. (1937), 'Palestine under the Ptolemies (A Contribution to the Study of the Zenon Papyri)', *Mizraim* 4/5: 9–90.

Thomsen, P. (1907), *Loca Sancta* (Halle, Rudolf Haupt).

deVaux, R. (1941), 'Notes d'histoire et de topographie trans-jordaniennes', *Vivre et Penser* l: 16–47 (= *Bible et Orient* [Paris, Les Editions du Cerf] 115–49).

Villeneuve, F. (1984), 'Iraq al-Amir', in F. Villeneuve (ed.), *Contribution Française à l'Archéologie Jordanienne* (Paris, I.F.A.P.O.) 12–19.

— (1988), 'Prospection archéologique et géographie historique: la région d'Iraq al-Amir (Jordanie)', in P.-L. Gatier et al. (eds.), *Géographie Historique au Proche-Orient* (Paris, CNRS), 257–88.

Vincent, L. H. (1920), 'La Palestine dans les papyrus ptolémaïques de Gerza', *RB* 29: 161–202.

Weber, T. (1989), *Umm Qais: Gadara of the Decapolis* (Amman, Al Kutba Publishers).

— (1990), 'A Survey of Roman Sculpture in the Decapolis: A Preliminary Report', *ADAJ* 34: 351–5.

Wilkin, R. L. (1988), 'Byzantine Palestine: A Christian Holy Land', *BA* 51: 214–7; 233–7.

Wilkinson, J. (1977), *Jerusalem Pilgrims before the Crusades* (Warminster, Aris and Phillips).

Will, E. (1985), 'L'urbanisation de la Jordanie aux époques héllenistique et romaine: conditions géographiques et ethniques', in A. Hadidi (ed.), *SHAJ* II: 237–41.

— (1987), 'Qu'est-ce qu'une *baris*?', *Syria* 64: 253–9.

Wüthnow, H. (1930), *Die semitischen Menschennamen in griechischen Inschriften und Papyri des voderen Orients* (Leipzig, Dieterich'sche Verlags).

Younker, R. W. et al. (1990), 'The Joint Madaba Plains Project: A Preliminary Report of the 1989 Season', *AUSS* 28: 5–52.

Zayadine, F. (1982a), 'Amman-Philadelphie', *MB* 22: 20–27.

— (1982b), 'A Byzantine Painted Tomb at Jebel el-Jofeh, Amman', *ADAJ* 26: 10–12 (in Arabic).

— (1990), 'La campagne d'Antiochos III le grand en 219–217 et le siège de Rabbatamana', *RB* 97: 68–84.

VII

BOSTRA GLORIOSA*

The two volumes reviewed here, and a third entitled *Trois Études sur l'Arabie romaine et byzantine,*[1] are the published results of the author's thèse de doctorat d'État at Lyons, begun in 1969 under the supervision of Jean Pouilloux and completed in May, 1978. The three volumes went to press simultaneously; the narrative history of Bostra was unduly delayed. *Trois Études* investigated aspects of the history of *provincia Arabia* in general terms: the provincial borders, the *fasti* of governors, and Roman contact with their client-kings, ethnarchs, phylarchs and the federated tribes within and without imperial domains. It thus stands apart from the epigraphic and narrative histories of the provincial capital represented by the two volumes under review. The inscriptions and the history of Bostra naturally form an integrated unit — in the words of the editor/author, "ces deux volumes sont indissolublement liés et ont été conçus comme un tout." Hence the inclusion of both in this review, "Ins." referring to pages in the volume of inscriptions, # to a specific inscription, and "Nar." to the historical synthesis.

The IGLS Series

In a communication to an archaeological congress on 9 April 1926 René Mouterde offered a summary of the work then done on the corpus of Greek and Latin inscriptions from French-mandate Syria.[2] The IGLS was the brainchild of Louis Jalabert, who announced it to a similar congress in 1905. Jalabert had enlisted the aid of Rudolph Brünnow in the initial stages of the project, and indeed it was Brünnow who pulled the laboring oar up to the moment of his premature death in 1917.[3] Mouterde secured

* Review article of Maurice Sartre, *Inscriptions Grecques et Latines de la Syrie,* Vol. XIII Pt. I: Bostra (IFAPO, BAH Tome CXIII), Paris, Librairie Orientaliste Paul Geuthner, 1982. 437 pp., 80 plates; Maurice Sartre, *Bostra: Des origines à l'Islam* (IFAPO, BAH Tome CXVII), Paris, Geuthner, 1985. 279 pp., 60 plates. No prices advertised.

[1] Sartre (1982b).

[2] Mouterde (1926).

[3] *Ibid.* 177-178; cf. Bowersock (1985: 139-141) expanding on Sartre's brief account, Ins. 27-29. The pathetically short introduction to IGLS I (1929) 1-3 presupposes too much. Brünnow's personal library, papers and photograph collection became the property of Princeton University, where he had taught until his death.

Brünnow's epigraphic *fichier* after World War I, and stepped into the role of collaborator with Jalabert. The latter seems to have maintained his own position as silent partner in the IGLS enterprise.

The corpus envisioned by Mouterde in 1926 embraced only six volumes.[4] The first, then well along in preparation, would include the epigraphy of the northernmost regions of Syria, and successive volumes would include regions farther south. Since the initial plan and the actual outcome of the series differ markedly, it may be useful to set out in column form the idea and the reality:

IGLS as proposed in 1926	*IGLS as published/planned today*
I Commagene & Cyrrhestice	I (1929) Commagene & Cyrrhestice
	II (1939) Chalcidice & Antiochene
	III/1 (1950) The Region of Amanus and the City of Antioch
II Aleppo, Antioch, Hama	III/2 (1953) Antioch, Antiochene
	IV (1955) Laodicaea, Apamea
	V (1959) Emesene
	VI (1967) Baalbek & the Biqa^{c}
III Ḥomṣ, the Orontes, Baalbek, the Biqa^{c} Valley	VII (1970) Arados & Possessions
	VIII/1 (forth.) Abila (Lysaniae) & Abilene
	VIII/2 (forth.) Damascus & Damascene
	VIII/3 (1980) Hadrianic Forestry Inscriptions of Mt. Lebanon
IV Beirut & the Phoenician Cities	IX (forth.) Palmyra
	X (forth.) Palmyrene
	XI (forth.) Middle Euphrates
	XII (forth.) The Phoenician Coast
V Palmyra, Dura & the Euphrates	XIII/1 (1982) Bostra
	XIII/2 (forth.) Batanaea
	XIII/3 (forth.) Trachonitis
	XIII/4 (forth.) Auranitis
VI Damascus & the Ḥawrān	XIII/5 (forth.) Gaulanitis

Mouterde believed that the IGLS would constitute but one part of the eventual corpus that would include the provinces of Arabia and Syria-Palestine and ultimately result in a collection of "épigraphie gréco-romaine du Sinaï au Taurus."[5] Jalabert died in 1943 and his place as co-editor was taken by Claude Mondésert. Mouterde and Mondésert produced Vols. III, IV and V within the space of nine years; an announcement in the introduction to Vol. V indicated that the next volume would contain the inscriptions from Arados, Damascus, Heliopolis and the .Hermon region. This proved to be somewhat premature. Mouterde died in 1961 and Mondésert asked Jean-Paul Rey-Coquais to assume the editorship of the series. Within five years Vol. VI appeared, limited only to the inscriptions from eastern Lebanon. But the format of that volume indicated clearly that some major editorial initiatives, long overdue, had been undertaken.[6] With the publication of IGLS VII (1970), also edited by Rey-Coquais, the IGLS series came under the aegis of the Institut Fernand-Courby in Lyons. The

[4] Mouterde (1926: 181-182).

[5] *Ibid.* 178.

[6] Bowersock (1985: 139) notes that "lemmata, transcriptions in minuscule, apparatus, and commentary, together with introductory material on geography and history (not neglecting the reports of early travelers) were supplemented by excellent plates, indexes, and maps."

continuous numeration of inscriptions in the series was broken with Vol. VII, and this initial gap was matched by others created by the subsequent appearance of IGLS VIII/3 and XIII/1. The intermediary volumes still to appear are outlined in a retrospective article by W. Van Rengen[7] which, however, fails to mention Breton's Hadrianic texts or Sartre's Bostran inscriptions then in preparation.[8]

Plans to extend the IGLS series have resulted in a collaborative effort between the Institut Fernand-Courby and the Jordanian Department of Antiquities. Five volumes of IGL de Jordanie are planned: vols. 1 and 2 (central and northwest Jordan) will be edited by P.-L. Gatier; vol. 3 (Moab) by F. Zayadine; vol. 4 (the south) by M. Sartre; vol. 5 (the eastern desert) by J. Marceilet-Jaubert.[9] Whether the series will eventually include Palestine remains to be seen.

Contents and Sources

The volume of inscriptions has a tripartite division. Chapter I sets out the record of archaeological and epigraphic exploration of the Ḥawrān from the initial journeys of Seetzen and Burckhardt in the opening decade of the nineteenth century through the Princeton expeditions a century later to the present work by the IGLS team and its associates. The last section of this background chapter documents the emergence of the IGLS series over the past eighty years (see the preceding section of this article). Bibliography for this entire volume is relegated to the footnotes. Chapter II details the styles of writing and the linguistic particularities in the Greek and Latin inscriptions of Bostra, and there is a summary of the various monuments upon which the inscriptions have been found. Together these two chapters will serve as a solid introduction to *all* the epigraphy from the lava-lands, including that from the Jordanian Ḥawrān. Notable among Sartre's comments is the skepticism expressed (Ins. 31 n. 1) about the epigraphic dating method developed a half-century ago by C.B. Welles for the Greek inscriptions from Jerash. Sartre's view (Ins. 35) that Latin epigraphy at Bostra terminated c. 370/380 can be substantiated by the evidence from other sites in the Ḥawrān (e.g. the *burgus*-inscription at Umm al-Jimāl is 371 precisely) and throughout the province (see now Parker [1986] passim). One may add that there are no milestone inscriptions from Arabia later than the reign of Julian (361-363).

Tomb-inscriptions supply the bulk of Bostran epigraphy, and Sartre's presentation of this material is worthy of careful reading. The ten terms denoting tombs which he discusses (Ins. 38-40) do not include, interestingly, τάφος. Also remarkable is the paucity of specifically Greek warnings against tomb violations, since this sort of text is so prevalent (Ins. 41) in Nabataean and Safaitic epigraphy. The simplicity of funerary architecture is paralleled by the simplicity and brevity of epigraphic eulogies (Ins. 45). Notification is given (Ins. 58 n. 1) of a recently-discovered necropolis located southwest of the theater/fortress which will be published eventually by J.-M. and J. Dentzer. Perhaps most important of Sartre's observations is that the funerary art of the Ḥawrān retained its own integrity throughout the Roman and Byzantine periods, with no identifiable influence from Jerash to the south or Palmyra to the north. Lacking, however, is any discussion by Sartre of the reverse process: where, and in what period,

[7] Van Rengen (1977), esp. 46-53.

[8] The introduction by Breton to IGLS VIII/3 is also silent regarding forthcoming volumes in the series.

[9] Gatier (1982a); (1983); (1983/84). Milestones and *instrumentum domesticum* will be published separately.

Bostran artisans may have influenced the style of funerary monuments elsewhere in the region — notably at Umm al-Jimāl.

Chapter III is devoted to the corpus of inscriptions and as expected occupies the lion's share (some seventy-five percent) of this volume. These are discussed in categories: pagan and Christian dedications; civic, provincial and imperial dedications; milestones; building construction texts; funerary inscriptions; and others of diverse nature. The presentation of each inscription adheres to the strict rules applied by Rey-Coquais to IGLS Vols. VI and VII (see note 6 above). Individual inscriptions will be discussed separately below.

The remainder of the volume contains the various tables and indices, some sixty pages in all and consistently excellent. Photographs of 340 of the 472 texts, all but a few taken by Sartre, conclude the work.

The bibliography for the narrative volume is set out in the first part of *Bostra.* The long delay in publication has meant that many recent works are, inevitably, missing — in spite of the list added under "note additionnelle" (Nar. 32-33). Essential now are the two volumes comprising *Hauran I* edited by J.-M. Dentzer (1985; 1986); Sartre had access to these in press. Also of interest are H. Seeden's reports on her *sondages* at the tell in western Bostra,[10] the second volume in the series of *Studies* in Jordanian history and archaeology,[11] and a short study of the urbanization of Bostra by D.S. Miller.[12] All of this and more (for the Syrian *and* Jordanian Ḥawrān) has been summarized recently.[13] But there are also a few slips and oversights not due to the time in press. Buhl's haphazard article on Bostra appeared in the *first* edition of the *Encyclopedia of Islam*; the entry by A. Abel in *EI*² (1960) is far superior. Among other thumbnail sketches of Bostra not noted but still useful: W.H. Waddington's commentary to Wadd. # 1907 (1870) and C. Colpe's entry under "Bostra" in the first volume of *Der Kleine Pauly* (1964). The latter demonstrates the need to replace the *RE* 3.1 (1897) entry in a forthcoming Supplementband of the *Realencyclopädie*. Rey-Coquais' summary of archaeological work at Bostra for the *Princeton Encyclopedia of Classical Sites* (1976) was written on the eve of the latest excavations. The entries under G.E. Kirk should have included his article on the Diocletianic era in *JPOS* (1937). There are also no references to articles by F.E. Peters in *JNES* (1978) and *AAAS* (1981/82), and the single entry under H.-J. Wolff does not account for his more recent work on the Babatha archive in *RIDA* (1976) and *ANRW* (1980). There is no reference at all to Eugen Wirth's *Syrien: Eine geographische Landeskunde* (1971), to Trimingham (1979) or Mercati (1895).

The Bostra volume is divided into a straightforward history of the city (part one) and an onomastic index with full commentary (part two). The historical section begins with a geographical sketch of the lava-lands of Syria, and then traces the history of the city from the Bronze Age through the Arab conquest in 635 (Chapters I-III). This is followed by a chapter on the ethnic composition of the city, with notes on occupations, religion and culture.

The Early History of Bostra

Sartre presents the little information available for the early history of Bostra in three segments: the origins of the city, its Nabataean identity, and the monumental architecture of the city before the Roman annexation of Nabataea in 106. For the latter segment Sartre

[10] Seeden (1983, 1984); Seeden & Kadour (1983).

[11] Hadidi (1985).

[12] Miller (1983).

[13] MacAdam (1986: 10-19).

has chosen to adopt the inclusive term *pré-provincial* because "il serait abusif de faire de l'annexion de 106 une ligne de partage entre une période préromaine et une ère romaine alors qu'elle ne fait que transformer un royaume en province" (Nar. 57 n. 108). The effect of using this term, occurring as it does in a chapter entitled "Buṣrā Préromaine", is somewhat confusing — the more so since using "pre-provincial" as a designation only for the architecture obscures the broader meaning of the term originally employed by Dentzer for the entire Ḥawrān.[14]

The Bronze Age history of Bostra is represented by Sartre only from the few references to the city in Egyptian Middle Kingdom and New Kingdom sources. That Bostra in the Ḥawrān actually existed at that early time was only recently demonstrated by Helga Seeden's excavations on the tell. The earliest excavation reports are acknowledged by Sartre in the addenda to the bibliography, but the information could not be assimilated into the text. Ceramic analysis establishes a settlement at the site in the Bronze Age (*see above*, pp. 5-76), and continuous habitation until the end of the second millennium B.C. There is then a prolonged break in occupation until the early Roman period, at least in the area of the tell excavated. The lack of Iron Age, Persian or Hellenistic material at the tell may simply mean that re-settlement occurred elsewhere, perhaps east of the principal spring (al-Jahīr) or at the unexamined tell near the West Gate of the city. A recent surface survey conducted by IFAPO[15] has produced no Iron Age ceramics in the eastern Ḥawrān, and it may be that Bostra lay abandoned until the Nabataean settlement attested in the last two centuries B.C. in the easternmost part of the modern site. No inscriptions from the site can be dated earlier than the second century B.C., and the date of *that* still-unpublished Nabataean text[16] is uncertain. Sartre is careful to note that a Nabataean presence in the Ḥawrān is attested as early as 259 B.C. (Nar. 47 and n. 36) but that these 'Αναβαταίοι (PSI 406) «sont alors des nomades, hostiles aux sédentaires araméens» (Nar. 47).[17] The absence of Bostra in the Zenon correspondence is no more remarkable than the absence of Canatha or Adraa. The city is attested as a stronghold a century later when it is said to have been sacked by Judas Maccabeus (164/163). But from then until the Roman occupation of Nabataea the city again goes unmentioned. The "Bostran" in a letter of Cicero is demonstrably a phantom;[18] there is no reference to the city in Strabo or Pliny. But Ptolemy's *Geography* (V.16.4) locates the city at 69° 45′ E and 31° 30′ N, identified as the headquarters of the *legio III Cyrenaica*.

Sartre's discussion of the occurrence of the name Bostra, and its etymology, is succinct (Nar. 46-49) but there are a few omissions worthy of note here. In his discussion of the "t" common to the Graeco-Latin spelling, he might have profitably drawn attention to the same process at work in other renderings of Semitic names with "ṣ", e.g. Phoenician Ṣur becomes Tyr(os)/Tyr(us).[19] There is no mention of the garbled reference to Bostra in a passage of Zonaras;[20] Waddington's comments on this are still apt (Wadd. # 2072). The confusion between place-names variously spelled as Bostra, Bosora, Bosor is noted, but no credit is given to Eusebius[21] for a heroic attempt at sorting it out. There is no

[14] Dentzer (1986: 388), acknowledged by Sartre.

[15] Braemer (1984).

[16] Starcky (1966: 930).

[17] J.T. Milik has found a Nabataean inscription of uncertain provenance (now in the Damascus Museum) which he dates to the third century B.C. Notice of this is given in Starcky (1985: 167-168).

[18] MacAdam and Munday (1983).

[19] On this phenomenon see Wild (1973: 243, 278-283 and the parallel examples quoted there).

[20] I. Zonaras, *Annalium* XII.19 (= CSHB Vol. 30, 584).

[21] *Onomasticon* (ed. E. Klostermann, p. 46) s.v. "Βοσόρ".

mention that Bostra is attested twice in a letter (P. Mich. 466) of A.D. 107 in the orthographical form that became standard.

Sartre's discussion of the Nabataeans in the Ḥawrān is full and informative and obviously owes much to his earlier study[22] of the political background of the late first century B.C. A Nabataean presence in Trachōnitis is strengthened by the announcement (Nar. 52 n. 84) of a then-unpublished Nabataean inscription (from the village of Ṣur) dated to the ninth year of Claudius (49/50).[23] It thus falls into the decade 44-54 when Herodian territory in Trachōnitis and Auranitis was held in obeyance by Rome and nominally administered from Syria. Might it be that Nabataean settlement in those regions was monitored less strictly by Roman than Agrippan authority? This also raises the question of the status of Canatha and its territory in the midst of Rome's fluctuating political arrangements with its clients in Judaea and Nabataea. But this may better be examined in a discussion of the annexation below.

Bostra in Roman and Byzantine Times

Sartre devotes more than a third of his chapter on Roman Bostra to the annexation of the Nabataean kingdom and the subsequent choice of a capital for the *provincia Arabia* created by Trajan. This is quite justified in the light of much recent discussion of these two issues, summarized well in Bowersock's *Roman Arabia.*[24] Of particular interest to Sartre is the role of Bostra in the latter years of Rabbel II (71-106), whose death actually triggered the military invasion of his kingdom by Roman forces from Egypt and Syria. The evidence continues to accumulate that this monarch undertook to transfer the political capital of Nabataea from Petra to Bostra. The majority of inscriptions attesting Rabbel II have been found in and near the Ḥawrān. The residence of the king at Bostra is implied by a Nabataean inscription of A.D. 93.[25] The shift in trade routes from inner Arabia through the Wadi Sirḥān to Bostra and Damascus may have had something to do with this move. But it is also worthwhile noting that Rabbel's presence at Bostra, and the massive building program there that he seems to have initiated, are coincident with the death of Agrippa II. Sartre rightly sees Agrippa's demise and the subsequent annexation of his kingdom by Rome as one major part of an orchestrated plan to phase out the last client-kings in the region. But there may well have been concern that Rabbel himself had designs upon the territory of Agrippa in the lava-lands. Between the Agrippan and Nabataean kingdoms in that region lay another block of territory, that of the city of Canatha. Its place in the scheme of annexation has never been discussed, primarily because so little is known about that city-state or its neighbor to the west, Adraa. Canatha was probably a foundation-member of the Decapolis, since its coinage consistently uses the Pompeian era. As a member of the Decapolis it would have been administered as a district of Syria, in light of the Domitianic inscription recently re-published by Isaac.[26] If that same status obtained for Canatha throughout the rest of the first century, the city and its territory were under the direct supervision of provincial authorities responsible to the Syrian governor. This would mean, in effect, that a strip of Roman territory lay between the Agrippan kingdom in Trachōnitis and northern Auranitis, and that part of

[22] Sartre (1979).

[23] This has now been published by Starcky (1985: 180) with a photograph on p. 177 (fig. 2).

[24] Bowersock (1983: 72-109).

[25] Cantineau II (1932: 21-23 = *Rec. Épig. Sem.* 83). A newly-discovered Nabataean inscription from Umm al-Rummān in the eastern Ḥawrān, dated in "the year 31 of Rabbel the King" (A.D. 100/101) has just been published by Starcky (1985: 180-181).

[26] Isaac (1981).

southeastern Batanaea (including Bostra) which was recognized as Nabataean. This problematic scenario, if true, meant that Canatha and its extensive territory[27] were actually a buffer-zone between the two client-kingdoms. Some hint that Canatha fulfilled a special function vis-à-vis Rome is the fact that it contributed a military unit, the *cohors prima Flavia Canathenorum,* as early as Vespasian.[28]

Sartre has judiciously reviewed the evidence favoring either Petra or Bostra as the provincial capital in the decades following annexation. His conclusion, that Bostra was the more reasonable choice, and that Petra received the title of metropolis as "une compensation honorifique" (Nar. 74) is quite reasonable. I would suggest that this choice may not have been made by the provincial authorities until the public announcement (on coins and milestones) of the acquisition of Arabia c. 114. That is precisely the date of the Trajanic inscription from the Petra forum (AE [1982] 904) which first attests that city as "metropolis". But surprisingly, Sartre avoids any discussion of what territory was assigned to Bostra. The only systematic discussion of that issue was an article published thirty-five years ago by Albrecht Alt.[29] Alt gave no independent thought to the extent of Bostran territory to the north. Instead he accepted A.H.M. Jones' erroneous conclusion that all of eastern Batanaea (the modern Nuqra) was given to Bostra. Alt also mistakenly assumed that territorial limits to the south could be fixed according to mileage distances from Bostra along the Trajanic highway to Philadelphia (ᶜAmmān). Sartre's own study of the *territorium* of Canatha convincingly demonstrates that the Nuqra belonged to that city. The northern limits of Bostra's territory were, most probably, fixed by the Wadi Zaydī, a tributary of the Yarmūk (Hieromax) River, which flows in a westerly direction only six km north of Bostra. An extension of the line of that wadi to the eastern foothills of the Jebel Drūz would delimit the *territorium* in that direction. The limits of the city's territory elsewhere would involve a detailed discussion, which I hope to deal with elsewhere.

The tribal organization of the city council had already been dealt with by Sartre in an earlier study.[30] There is now a thorough discussion of the Bostran constitution. The municipal functioning of the city and its magistrates are given the attention they deserve, the latter being identified in detailed registers (Nar. 84-87). To the list of city councillors one may add the names Aurelius Julianus Maximus and ..?.. Molianus, attested as such in a papyrus document of A.D. 265 (P. Oxyrh. 3054).

The major monuments of Bostra, with the exception of the theater/citadelle, have not received much attention since the time of Brünnow/Domaszewski and the Princeton University expeditions. Sulayman Moughdad, former Curator of Antiquities to whom the volume is dedicated, conducted numerous *sondages* in and around the city. One such dig revealed a tower-base at the southwest corner of the city walls (Nar. fig. 7). The colonnaded street was as distinct a feature of Bostra as it was of Jerash or Palmyra. The street leading from the theater to the central arch must have been particularly striking. Clearance and reconstruction demonstrate that the architect deliberately alternated columns of pale limestone and black basalt along either side, a feature which Sartre notes as "un aménagement plus originel" (Nar. 91). Sartre also notes that the street-pattern of the Nabataean (eastern) sector of Bostra closely parallels the plan of "Nabataean" Damascus produced long ago by Sauvaget.[31] The overall alignment of streets and gates between Roman and Nabataean sectors of Bostra is imperfect, but the Roman planners

[27] Sartre (1981).
[28] CIL VII 2394 & 2395; AE (1969/70) 435.
[29] Alt (1951). This is listed in Sartre's bibliography.
[30] Sartre (1982a: 77-80).
[31] Sauvaget (1949: 344-345).

obscured this where they could. F.E. Peters[32] has recently called attention to the tiny oval "forum" just inside the western gate which disguises the fact that gate and street are 7° out of alignment. Peters has also suggested that this street, the so-called *decumanus,* should instead be understood as a *via sacra* leading eastward to the *temenos* of the Nabataean city. The parallel for that is to be found at Petra.[33] These observations appeared too late in print to be discussed by Sartre. Among other monuments the "Palace of Trajan", in Sartre's view, should be classified as Nabataean — perhaps the royal residence of Rabbel II. The theater, that architectural jewel of the city, has recently been dated to the second quarter of the second century by the Dentzers (Nar. 96). The hippodrome south of the theater remains to be excavated. It receives no more than a mention from Sartre, and hardly more than that from a recent empire-wide study of such structures.[34] The location of the camp wherein the *legio III Cyrenaica* was garrisoned has been fixed since about 1960 outside the northern wall of the city, but within its own defensive perimeter of which there are a few vestiges (see figs. 1-2). Although none of the interior features of a formal *castrum* are visible on the ground or in aerial photographs, I found a half-dozen legionary tile-stamps in a surface survey of the large (400 m^2) area now surrounded by modern fence walls. All of my specimens are broken, but Raymond Brulet has just published a number of more complete examples in a preceding volume of *Berytus.*[35] The military tiles should remove any doubt that the legionary headquarters was here. The supposition of Peters[36] that the area of Bostra just north of the city walls was a *caravanserai* has to be abandoned. A stamped hypocaust brick reading *LEG III CYR* found by Seeden[37] in the late Roman level at the tell must have come from the camp as well. It is probable that the North Baths described by Butler[38] were actually located within the camp area and were used by the military. The Jahīr spring in the western part of the city is located not far from the camp area, and may have been tapped for the camp's water supply. I take this opportunity to present the results of surface sherding done by me in the presumed site of the Roman *castrum* in June 1980 (ceramic analysis by James Sauer, then Director, ACOR, Amman).

Time Period	*Approx. Date*	*No. of Sherds**	*% of Total*
Nabataean	100 B.C.-A.D. 100	1	3
Early Roman	63 B.C.-A.D. 135	1	3
Late Roman	A.D. 135-324	3	10
Early Byzan.	A.D. 324-491	14	45
Late Byzan.	A.D. 491-640	9	30
Omayyad	A.D. 640-750	2	6
Ayyubid	12th-13th cent.	1	3
	Total	31	100

* *Not counting the 22 sherds of indeterminate date, most of which probably fall between Late Roman and Late Byzantine — i.e. into the same time period as the majority of the dateable sherds.*

Bostra's Christian community is attested as early as the second decade of the third century, and the synod held there c. 240 indicates that city's growing importance as a

[32] Peters (1983: 274), unaware of S. Cerulli, *Fel Rav* 115 (1978:79-120; 133-176 [esp. 150 fig. 8])

[33] *Ibid.*

[34] Humphrey (1985: 492-495 and fig. 245a).

[35] Brulet (1984).

[36] Peters (1983: 275).

[37] Seeden and Kadour (1983: 92 and Tafel 18c). See also Wilson in *Berytus* 32, pl. 9: 17.

[38] Butler (1919: 264-265 and Illustrations 232 & 233).

Fig. 1: Remains of a tower base (?) projecting from beneath the line of a modern field-wall on the western side of the Roman Camp area, Bostra. Two other sub-structures of roughly the same dimensions were noted on the western side, and one on the northern side, of the camp area.

Fig. 2: Remains of the North Gate of the Roman Camp area, Bostra. Some clearance work near the base of the gate had been done by S. Moughdad. The wall directly behind the gate is modern, but many of the stones built into it are re-used, dressed basalt blocks.

(Photos June, 1980. Permission to publish was kindly granted by Dr. Adnan Bounni of the Directorate-General of Antiquities and Museums, Syrian Arab Republic).

center of the new faith. On the vexed question of Philip the Arab's identity as a Christian, Sartre is quite circumspect. The two points of view on this subject are best summarized in recent discussions by Bowersock[39] and Shahīd.[40] The episcopal list for Bostra before 325 contains only three or four names, and even then it takes a tortuous discussion (Nar. 102-103) to establish the identity of Hippolytus c. 260. Even the post-Nicene list (through the end of the fifth century) has only eight names. One of them is problematical: a certain Ἰοάννος is attested as ἱερ(εύς) in a previously unpublished inscription (Ins. # 9439) of 352/353. This title, as Sartre suggests, may refer to a pagan priest and not a Christian bishop, but here the name itself may be the clue. The Agapius attested as bishop in a Greek inscription from Jābir (copied years ago by Siegfried Mittmann) may be a Bostran prelate, but this is doubted by Sartre (Nar. 110-111). Sartre also argues convincingly that the "Bassora" of an anti-Julianist tract relative to the late sixth century is Arabian Bostra rather than Abbāsid Basrah in lower Mesopotamia. This parallels a recent re-identification of Bostra (and not Gaza) in a passage of Libanius (*Orat.* 50) by Gatier.[41] Attention is given (Nar. 117) to an inscription found in 1978 by Italian excavators in the Cathedral (SEG 29 [1979] 1602). This attests a "Jacob, archbishop of Bostra", and was dated (on palaeographic grounds) by its discoverers to the sixth century. Sartre has rightly taken issue with that, arguing that it could date from any time between the fifth and eighth centuries and that the impoverished character of the text would support the later date. There are few recognizable Christian buildings from the pre-Justinian period simply because later building programs eradicated so many earlier structures. The walls of Bostra, remarked upon by Ammianus Marcellinus (14.8.13) in the late fourth century, must have been torn down to supply building materials for the Ayyubid fortress now encapsulating the theater.

39 Bowersock (1983: 123-127).

40 Shahīd (1984a: 65-93). Cf. Trimingham (1979: 58-60) for a parallel but less eloquent argument.

41 Gatier (1982b).

For the remaining parts of that chapter, it may be worthwhile to comment on a few items:

p. 120: The date of the Tetrapylon near the central arch. As Sartre himself notes earlier (Nar. 91 and n. 221) this is to be identified with the same structure described in the *Expositio Totius Mundi* (XXXVIII); the date of that work (c. 350) therefore provides a terminus ante for the existing structure.

p. 121: Howard Crosby Butler's dating of Syrian and Arabian churches has recently been examined by John Wilkinson in an article[42] that one hopes will enjoy wide circulation.

p. 123: The brief discussion of the "*praetorium*" at Masmayah in the Lejā fails to note the most recent study of that enigmatic monument.[43]

p. 124: Sartre expresses agreement with Kleinbauer and Lassus that the model for the Cathedral at Bostra was the patriarchal cathedral at Antioch (later destroyed). There is no discussion of various suggestions[44] that the Bostran Cathedral was itself a model for the Dome of the Rock at Jerusalem.

pp. 135-136: We might have expected here some discussion of the Arab conquest of the city beyond the bare mention of it. Even the laconic statement on the fall of Bostra by Georgius Cedrinus would have been welcome:

> τῷ κδ′ ἔτει [i. e. 635] . . . [Οὔμαρος] . . . παρέλαβε Βόστραν
> τὴν πόλιν καὶ ἄλλας πολλάς, καὶ ἦλθε μέχρι τοῦ Γαβιθᾶ[45].
>
> "In the year 24 (of the Emperor Heraclius)... (the Caliph) [ʿUmar]
> ...captured the city Bostra and many other (cities), even as far as Gabitha."

Ethnography, Culture and Onomastics

The Greek and Latin epigraphy of Bostra has yielded some 250 personal names. Of these, 140 are identifiably Semitic, 100 Graeco-Roman, and ten "foreign". There are no specifically "Aramaean" names attested at Bostra. They may be, as Sartre guesses (Nar. 149), disguised within the "common Semitic" names. Among the "foreigners" attested: four Persians, a Goth, a Mantuan, a Carthaginian and, doubtfully, a Briton. As would be expected, Nabataean names are most common among the Semitic group, and of those the most striking are compound names including a royal element: *Abdoobdas, Abdomalikhos* and *Abdorabbēlos* are all attested (Nar. 146). Lacking so far is *Abdoaretas.* This is perhaps attested in a damaged Greek inscription from the Ḥawrān published eighty years ago by Savignac and Abel[46] and recently discussed again.[47] The patronymic is often the only clue to ethnic identity. The Archilaus and Iuli(u)s who made dedications to "Zeus of Ṣafā" are the grandson and son of *Masechus,* a name which "rappelle l'origine indigène des dédicants" (Nar. 148). A Nabataean-Greek bi-lingual is yet to be attested at Bostra (in spite of Sartre's Ins. # 9412 being included in the corpus; see below). Surely this is chance. So little of the city has been uncovered in any systematic, scientific fashion. The hundred or so Nabataean texts from the city published to date are mostly funerary. It is reasonable to think that when the commercial area of the city is thoroughly excavated some important bi-linguals will come to light. For a brief summary of the corpus of Nabataean inscriptions from Bostra, see Starcky (1985: 176).

Various occupations are attested; as expected, priests and soldiers seem to predominate. But we also know of a mosaic-worker, a mime, silver-, copper-, and goldsmiths, and a leather-worker. If slavery was an "occupation" then evidence for it is remarkably lacking at Bostra. Sartre's discussion of this topic (Nar. 154) would have

[42] Wilkinson (1984).

[43] Hill (1975).

[44] Creswell (1924); Grabar (1959: esp. 46 n. 77); *contra* this idea: Golding (1948).

[45] *Hist. Comp.* (ed. Bekker, CSHB 22 Part 1, p. 745).

[46] Sauvaget and Abel (1905: 95 # 7).

[47] MacAdam (1986: 196-197 # 19).

benefited from a reference to P. Oxyrh. 3054, a slave-registration in Egypt. The registrant is a Bostran lady, Aurelia daughter of Simon. We learn from the document (of A.D. 265) that the slave she is registering apparently had belonged to her father, who himself was the third owner. The slave, Procopton, was born as such into the household of another Bostran lady, Septimia the daughter of Septimius Severus, and thereafter sold in succession to two members of the city's council. The document is a very precious witness to an aspect of the city's social history otherwise unknown from the epigraphy and literature.

The deities of Bostra were as many and diverse as the ethnic background of the inhabitants. Dedications to Dushara, Allat and ʿUzzā are most common. Regional deities such as Qôs from Edom, Zeus of Baalbek, Damascus and Libya, and the commercial god Mercury were honored. Among the newly-published inscriptions (# 9143) is a fragment of architrave attesting the cult of Roma and Augustus (Nar. 156). Sartre's discussion of the *Dusaria Actia* (Nar. 156-158) is somewhat problematic. This religious/athletic festival, for which the city was honored as far away as Ostia (ILS 5233), is best attested on the coinage. But the only coin legend adduced for the games being introduced before the reign of Philip the Arab is the specimen re-published more than a century ago by de Saulcy.[48] Sartre presents this (Nar. 156 n. 14) without noting that de Saulcy himself expressed great misgivings about the **ΔΟΥCΑΡ. ΑΚ. ΝΕ** earlier editors had read. Every other attestation of the *Actia Dusaria* on Bostran coinage is from the time of Philip or later, and it is quite probable that the games were initiated by that Arab emperor (who presided over Rome's millennial celebrations in 248). Some hesitation should also be expressed about Sartre's acceptance of P. Herm. 74 as a reference to the *Actia Dusaria*. Both the type of event and its location are far from certain in that document.[49]

The last third of the book is an onomastic index with commentary (Nar. 165-245) and represents an enormous output of tedious work. The results are worth the effort and they will continue to serve as the standard reference for onomastic studies in this region for many years. On the following entries I offer some observations; unless it is necessary to reproduce the original, transliterations will suffice:

Agrippa(s): Sartre's comments on the frequency of this name in the Ḥawrān, particularly in areas under Herodian domination, are expanded upon in a separate article.[50]

Aineias: The spelling of this name at Bostra is very consistent. It could of course be the Latin Aeneas, but this would be more likely if the bearer of the name was in the Roman army. Here it is likely to be Semitic, i.e. Arabic Ḥny (Ḥanī).[51] But see also the spelling *Annios* in a Greek inscription from nearby Mashqūq.[52] There is probably a variant spelling in P.S.I. 771 (A.D. 322, from Oxyrhynchus in Egypt): Αὐρήλιος Ἐ̣νίας Ἐμπ̣ρανίου μη(τρὸς) Οὐαλερίας ἀπὸ Βόστρων Συρίας[53].

Areios: On this name's association with both Ares and the corresponding Nabataean deity Arsû, see the recent study by G.W. Bowersock.[54]

Bakhros: On this as a clan name, see MacAdam (1986: 139 # 36).

Gauthos & *Goththos*: Sartre has convincingly laid to rest any chance that these two names are variants of each other. Gauthos transcribes *Ghwt* or *ʿwt*, both attested in Nabataean and

48 De Saulcy (1874: 365 # 2).
49 Wessely (1905: 36-37).
50 Sartre (1985: 200-201 and n. 29 with fig. 2).
51 Wüthnow (1930: 23); Harding (1971: 207).
52 MacAdam (1986: 193 # 8). Other variants noted there are *Anios*, *Anēos* and *Aneos*.
53 The capital city is identified as (ἀπὸ) Βόστρας τῆς Συρίας in P. Oxyrh. 3054 l. 1 (see above). This "popular geography" is reflected also in P. Oxyrh. 1722 l. 3 where the Palestinian city of Eleutheropolis is identified as ἀπὸ Συρίας.
54 Bowersock (1986).

Safaitic inscriptions. Goththos means a Goth. Sartre has missed Speidel's discussion of this latter name.[55]

Dalsoum(ē)s: There is an excellent discussion here of the difficulties inherent in onomastic studies.

Eunomos: A major printing error on this page (Nar. 200) has conflated the beginning of the discussion of this name with commentary on the name Hermola[os] of Ins. # 9336. The entry for Eunomos is repeated on that same page, but the entry under Hermolaos was lost. Hopefully this can be rectified in the addenda for IGLS XIII/1 to appear in XIII/2.

Thetas: Sartre could offer no certain etymology for this name, if indeed it is a proper name. Years ago I met a young lady named Alpha; the name was given by her classicist father. Her younger sister was named Beta. A child named Theta would therefore be probable (and have many siblings!) if Theta(s) was taken as a variant spelling of Thêta. But Θέτις (*Iliad* I: 413) is a more likely protonym.

Iamleeilus: This name appears in the only Latin inscription from Bostra in which indigenous names are attested.

Oualēs: The discussion of the Graeco-Roman/Semitic contexts in which this name and its variants appear is a model of lucid exposition (Nar. 225-227); cf. also the commentary to the name *Ouaros* (Nar. 227) which follows.

Seouēros: This name is attested (in its Greek form) no fewer than seven times at Bostra; add the appearance of a Septimius Severus (again in Greek) in P. Oxyrh. 3054 1. 24.

Soleos: Sartre rejects, without good reason, Wüthnow's (1930: 111) identification of this name with Semitic Ṣlḥ.

Philadelphos: Like Arsinoē, it is the sole attestation of this Ptolemaic name in southern Syria.

Phraētos: Perhaps a variant of Persian *Phraates,* but Jean Starcky thinks it may be a transliteration of *'frht* in an unpublished Nabataean inscription from Bostra.

Kheilōn: Sartre believes this is not an exact transliteration of Semitic *khl* but an attempt to find a Greek name similar in sound. Cf. the parallel with the name Marinus.

* Among the new names to appear at Bostra, many of them unknown anywhere, I note Boudaē, Eupatis, Ekharos, Zēnobris, Iekoumos, Itmero(s), Katarkhos, Mazarathē, Nenemakhos, Neikeratos, Neikias, Othika, Orasia(s)?, Otaianēs, Oukhos, Rhadē and Tarmos.

The Corpus of Inscriptions

When Sartre undertook the formidable task of revising the corpus of basalt inscriptions from Bostra, only 211 had previously been published. The total now stands at 472 (Ins. 29). There are, by my count, 112 instances where the notation *perdu* appears in the *lemmata,* and all but six of these apply to previously published inscriptions. Five of the half-dozen now lost but never published were found in the papers of Jean Mascle, who had copied them during the 1930's and one, copied by Moughdad in 1944, appears in the papers of René Mouterde. Sartre himself was never less than diligent in his search for previously reported texts. In one instance, described in the commentary to # 9403, Sartre actually dug up a sarcophagus near the birkit al-Hāj in the search for a funerary inscription seen by Savignac and Abel and the Princeton expedition in the same year (1904/05). The sarcophagus turned out to be anepigraphic.

[55] Speidel (1977: 712 and n. 100).

About forty of the inscriptions from the new corpus can be specifically dated, but a large number of these have disappeared without being photographed or measured. I offer below some comments on various inscriptions which caught my attention for one reason or another:

9001: The two Greek texts on sides of a small altar dedicated to the "Zeus of Ṣafā" remain as enigmatic as they did when first published by Mordtmann a century ago. To the various parallel dedications throughout the Near East noted by Sartre (Ins. 74 and n. 4) add a dedicatory text from the central Negev in Israel, part of which reads: **Ἀγαθῇ Τυχῇ (καὶ?) Ζεῦ Ὄβοδα**[56].

9004: From two strips of text inscribed on either side of a bas-relief sculpture Sartre has read **Ṃαλεχος Βọρḍου Ῥουεὺς θεῷ ἀνέθηκεν.** *Rhoueus* he then took to be a tribal name or an ethnic. Would it not be more likely to read instead **Μαλεχος Βọ[δ̣]ουρου εὐσ(εβῶν) θεῷ ἀνέθηκεν,** with a close parallel in 9005? Sartre's reading of the patronymic is far from certain, but Boderos is a name already attested in Greek epigraphy from the Ḥawrān,[57] and *Bodouros* would be an acceptable variation. The Semitic name behind it might be akin to Arabic Bdr, very commonly attested.[58]

9005: An unknown deity, Ed. non, appears in a new dedication.

9011: This fragmentary Latin dedication to Jupiter Hammon was one of two texts from the Ḥawrān brought to Princeton University by the expedition of 1904/05 (cf. 9320 below). Littmann's publication of it was uncharacteristically unsatisfactory. I have seen the stone at Princeton's archaeology museum, thanks to the kind efforts of Dr. Robert Guy, Assistant Curator. The text is actually complete except for the initial I in *Iovi* and the left vertical of the H in *Hammoni*. The entire text is set within a recessed panel on the stone. A photo of the inscription will be published in the addenda of IGLS XIII/2.

9017 & 9018: As Bowersock noted[59] in his own commentary on these two abbreviated dedications to Caracalla and Geta, "*damnatio* by erasing one letter is an interesting phenomenon." To his parallel references add CIL III 3668 (= ILS 4349) in which the *damnation* is accomplished by erasing one "d" and one "n".[60]

9029: The last line of this Latin dedication is still problematical. Sartre has slightly modified Littmann in expanding CI **V** DD as *ci(v) (itas) d(ono) d(edit)*. V for Λ or A is rather an unhappy solution. I would prefer to see the first three letters as the date in Greek, i.e. CIA = 211 (of the Arabian era) which is A.D. 316/317, a date which accords well with a civic dedication involving *quaestores*. The subject of *dedit* would be understood. For another Latin inscription of similar date (in Greek) see PAES # 228 (A.D. 306) from Dayr al-Kahf, farther east in the Ḥawran.

9071: To the bibliography, add Speidel (1977: 716).

9089: This is the second attestation of Ulpius Philippus, *praepositus* of the public prison at Bostra.

9101: Sartre's reasoning that this milestone represents a terminus point (Ṣalkhad) of the road from Tiberias through Capitolias, Adraa and Bostra is intriguing. The mileage distance (93 MP) certainly corresponds: *Hamatha* as the designation for Tiberias at this date (early third century?) is still problematical.

9107: To the bibliography add Speidel (1977: 723).

9128-9137: This represents the collection of building inscriptions dating to the reign of Justinian. The commentary that follows (Ins. 209-219) is well worth the attention of anyone interested in the Byzantine history of Bostra.

[56] Negev (1981: 15 # 3 [undated]).

[57] Wüthnow (1930: 36).

[58] Harding (1971: 97). Cf. Bḏr, ibid. 98, less well-attested.

[59] Bowersock (1985: 141).

[60] This can best be seen in Češka and Hošek (1967: 12 and the accompanying plates). I am indebted to Prof. Michael Speidel for bringing this to my attention.

9143: Fragment of an architrave, previously unpublished, attesting the cult of Roma and Augustus at Bostra. Undated.

9167-9168: Two abbreviated notations from the theater specifying which *centuria* was in charge of raising and lowering the *velum*.

9170: To the bibliography add Speidel (1977: 721).

9174: A Latin dedicatory text attesting a *numerus M(aurorum) Ill(yricanorum) Constan(tium)*, otherwise unknown. The *Notitia Dignitatum* (Or. 37.17) attests a unit of *equites Mauri Illyriciani* at Aereopolis (Rabba) in south-central Jordan under the command of the *dux Arabiae* and a unit of exactly the same name stationed across the Dead Sea at Aelia (Jerusalem); cf. *ND* Or. 34.21. There is no reason to suggest, as Sartre does, that Aelia is a mistake for Aereopolis, since some unit had to replace the *Legio X Fretensis* when the latter was moved from Jerusalem to Aila (ʿAqaba); cf. *ND* 34.30. Recent (1986-1987) archaeological work at ʿAqaba by Donald Whitcomb of the Oriental Institute, the University of Chicago, has begun to shed some light on the pre-medieval history of that port. See his report to be published in the *Proceedings* of the Bilād al-Shām conference (October, 1987) in Amman, Jordan. I owe this information to the author.

9177: Sartre read this badly-worn Latin text as: *D(is) M(anibus) S(acrum) Chresto sanctissimo M. ṇato Corinthias dulcissima uxor bene merenti fecit.* The editors of AE (1982: 906 bis) read the letters following *sanctissimo* as *ṃaṛito* and suggested that "Corinthias ne designe pas une femme 'originaire de Corinthe' [Sartre's interpretation]; c'est le nom de l'épouse très chère." Sartre's photograph of this stone demonstrates only that either reading is possible.

9184: The Dacian name "Ocibocus" read by Mouterde (*MUSJ* 25 [1942/43] 54-56) has become the more probable *Oc(tavius) Procu(lus)* in Sartre's re-reading of the stone.

9188: An unpublished funerary text which Sartre read *T(itus) Quintus/P̣ẸTRVLLO/(centurio) leg(ionis) III Cyr(enaicae),/dom(o) Britạn(nia),/*etc. This is problematic in a number of ways. I do not see *CYR* in Sartre's photo. *Domo Britannia* looks odd indeed; one would expect "*origo*" instead. *Brit*..... is more likely to be the name of a town or city, and if the cognomen is restorable it may help to identify which region was the man's home.

* 9223: The letters AKR at the bottom of this gravestone may simply represent the date, i.e. 121 (= A.D. 226/227).

9284: To the bibliography add Speidel (1977: 712).

9320: This was the second of two stones brought to Princeton by Littmann et al.; cf. my comments on # 9011 above. Littmann read it as 'Αντώ/νιος / Μαρῖο/(νος) [ἐ]τ̣(ῶν) ο̣. But Sartre rightly notes that the majuscule text printed by Littmann doesn't justify this. That there was a fourth line of text I confirmed when viewing the stone at Princeton's archaeology museum. My reading is Α̣ΝΙ̣Ω / ΝΙΟC / ΜΑΡΙΟ / - - - Τ̣Γ̣. A photograph of this inscription will be published in the addenda of IGLS XIII/2.

9358: At issue in Sartre's commentary on this funeral text is whether Palladis (the deceased) or his father Maximus is to be associated with the *legio III Cyrenaica*. Palladis' age is given as 16 in Magie's copy. Sartre believes, therefore, that the father must be the soldier. But in his own corpus Sartre has two instances on record of early enlistments. Ins. # 9194 attests a Thracian aged 38 at death with 21 years of military service; Sartre accepted his age at enlistment as 17. Ins. # 9187 is the tombstone of an Umbrian who died aged 39, also with 21 years in service. Enlistment age: 18.

9396: There is much left unsaid in Sartre's commentary on this famous but long-lost tombstone of Flavius Maximus, who as a soldier in the *legio III Cyrenaica* was killed in battle in Mesopotamia and his remains brought back to Bostra. The Swedish traveler J. Berggren, as Sartre notes, was the only one to have produced a complete copy of the text. But Berggren's facsimile drawing, published in the Swedish[61] but not the German[62]

[61] *Resor i Europa och Osterlanderne*, Vol. III Part IV: Inskrifter, Plate III (Stockholm, 1828).

[62] *Reisen in Europa und im Morgenlande* (Leipzig, 1834).

edition, was not available to Sartre, who used Waddington's copy of Berggren. Berggren's facsimile, available to me in Firestone Library, indicated that Waddington's copy was accurate in all but a few details. Berggren's laconic notes relate that the text was engraved on upper and lower parts of a stone, and his drawing implies that four lines of text at the end. are missing. Berggren also states that he saw the stone *outside* the citadelle (utanför fästningen),[63] one of several inscribed blocks that he copied. Waddington diligently looked for the stone *inside* the citadelle "à cause de son intérêt historique". He failed to find it. What is taken to be the date is shown in Berggren's (and Waddington's) drawing on either side of line 2: **EΠ** to the left, and **EIE** to the right. The former was read as **ETI** , and the latter was taken to be either **EIP** or **CIE** , i.e. 115 or 215 (A.D. 220/221 or 320/321). Sartre's reproduction of Waddington's text moves the date down to the last line, and takes the later date as a given. Speidel's re-publication (1977: 721) of the text indicates that he preferred the earlier date, which Bowersock observes accords with "the Parthian war of Caracalla and Macrinus".[64]

9412: Sartre has included this Nabataean-Greek bi-lingual in the corpus, even though it was found by Milik in the nearby village of Jimarīn, five km north. Thus a bi-lingual from Bostra itself has yet to appear. The two texts do not exactly translate each other, which seems to be a constant feature of Arabian bi-linguals. For comments on both texts see Bowersock (1985: 142).

9428: Once again Sartre could not consult Berggren's copy of this inscription, of which only the last four lines survive today. Once again he reproduces Waddington's copy of Berggren, which is accurate. Since the last line of Berggren's facsimile and the last line(s) of the text copied by Sartre don't match, it seems that two different inscriptions (albeit with essentially the same message) were cut.

9439: An unfortunately damaged inscription of A.D. 352/353 which attests *dioikētai* in charge of fig-sales at Bostra, and a *hiereus,* empowered (by the city council? by the church?) to purchase workshops (*ergasteria*) presumably connected with the marketplace. On the duties of *dioikētai* in villages throughout the lava-lands, see MacAdam (1986: 165-167).

9451: One of numerous fragments. Sartre restored this as a dedication to Julia Domna by the *legio III Cyrenaica.* It has now been reinterpreted, by analogy with others of similar nature, as a dedication to a *praefectus castrorum* of that legion.[65]

Conclusion

The early history of Bostra was already obscure by the time of John Malalas (c. 570), even though the city would continue as a provincial capital for another five and a half decades. Malalas[66] believed that Bostra came under Roman control in the time of Augustus, and was actually named for the commanding general who conquered Arabia. This statement has been interpreted by all commentators, including Sartre (Nar. 49), to mean that Malalas had inadvertently referred to Augustus when he should have mentioned Trajan. While we may dismiss an eponymous "Bostros" as founder of the Roman city, it is now more difficult to dismiss an Augustan province of Arabia, however briefly it may have been within the empire. Sartre shows in a notational reference (Nar. 54 n. 91) that he is aware of Bowersock's[67] proposal of a temporary (3-1 B.C.) annexation of Nabataea during the unstable period immediately following the death of Herod the

[63] Prof. Bengt Thomasson kindly helped me translate the Swedish notes.

[64] Bowersock (1985: 141).

[65] Christol and Demougin (1986).

[66] *Chronographia* 9 (ed. L. Dindorf, CSHB Vol. 28, p. 223).

[67] Bowersock (1983: 53-57).

Great. Sartre was unable, inevitably, to discuss this important issue. However that may be, it is *Nea Traianē Bostra* with which he begins the Roman history of the city.

Bostra ultimately rose from the status of *polis* to that of *colonia* under the first Arab emperor (Elagabalus) and *mētropolis* under the last (Philippus Arabs). All three titles are attested abundantly on the coinage of the city, and there are numerous inscriptions in Sartre's corpus which designate Bostra as *polis*. There is, as Sartre notes (Ins. 129), only one epigraphic attestation of Bostra as *colonia*.[68] But in his brief (Nar. 78) discussion of Bostra as *mētropolis* Sartre overlooked the only epigraphic attestation of that title. This appears not in the inscriptions from the city, nor even from the province, but in the epigraphy of the great oasis of Khargah in west-central Egypt. Since the only publications of this short text are rather obscure, I will take the opportunity to re-publish it in an appendix to this article.

Ironically, Bostran coinage comes to an end shortly after the city was elevated to the status of *mētropolis*. The last issues appear under Herennius Etruscus and Hostilianus (251/252). (Nearby Adraa was the only city of *provincia Arabia* to coin later than Bostra, and at that only until 256/257.) At some point in the city's history Nabataean epigraphy comes to an end; the latest dated inscription that I know of is A.D. 148 (RES 676). Sometime in the reign of Diocletian, perhaps c. 300, Arabia was partitioned,[69] and Bostra was thereafter the capital of a province only one-third its original size. But its subsequent status as the seat of an archbishop may have helped to compensate for the loss of territory. The Christian aspect of the city remained predominant throughout the last three centuries of its Romano-Byzantine history. The Muslim conquest was evidently a bloodless affair. Bostra's legendary association with the Prophet Muḥammed and the arrival of the Qur'an made it a place of early pilgrimage. The recent discovery of an Umayyad farmhouse in the western tell area[70] also demonstrates a peaceful transition, a phenomenon now paralleled at numerous sites in northern and central Jordan. In the late twelfth or early thirteenth century the site of Bostra became a formidable military base with the construction of the Ayyubid fortress[71] that still encapsulates the theater. The medieval history of Bostra is quite obscure,[72] and by the time the first European travelers described it in the early nineteenth century it was the home of only a few hundred families. The first photographs of Bostra were not taken until the American Palestine Exploration Society's expedition in 1875. The panoramic view presented here (fig. 3) has never been published; it is a tribute to the keen eye and technical skill of the French-born photographer Tancrède Dumas (1830-1905).[73] Since that time the site has been transformed by a substantial growth of the town during this century, and most recently as parts of the old quarter of Buṣrā are gradually being abandoned by the inhabitants for more modern housing in newer quarters so that full-scale excavation may proceed.

[68] Ins. #9057, a Greek dedication to Gordian III in 238/239.

[69] On the partition see the comprehensive article by Y. Tsafrir (1986). What the detached southern portion was initially named is problematical. A short-lived province designated "*Nea Arabia*" is attested in P. Oxyrh. 3574 of A.D. 314/317. Mayerson (1983, 1986) has argued that this "new" Arabia refers to that portion excised from "old" Arabia. Bowersock (1984) insists that "new" Arabia is the old *nomos* of Arabia in the Egyptian delta raised to the rank of province.

[70] Seeden (1983). The farmhouse was damaged and abandoned in an earthquake, perhaps that of 18 January 746. Other portions of the city might also have been affected. See also *Berytus* 32: 19-147. *

[71] Abel (1956). These defenses were in response to the Third Crusade.

[72] The architecture of Islamic Bostra has been recently reviewed by M. Meinecke, *Berytus* 32 (1984) 181-190.

[33] On Dumas and his contribution to Near Eastern photography see MacAdam (1986: 234-238 and plates 4a-6b).

The preparatory stages of Maurice Sartre's learned and readable volumes actually overlap this latter transitional period in the city's modern history. Most of the 261 previously unpublished inscriptions Sartre presents have come to light only in the past twenty years. There is every reason to believe that the corpus total of 472 could be doubled in that same amount of time given controlled, systematic excavation. The narrative history of Bostra is still sketchy, but that is for lack of evidence rather than lack of research. The study of Bostra — its inscriptions and its monuments — is unusually demanding of the epigrapher and historian. Basalt does not yield easily to the inscriber's chisel, and the information imprinted there long ago is notoriously difficult to decipher. Other references to the city and its peoples are widely scattered in the ancient sources. Such evidence creates immediate restrictions on the researcher. As both epigrapher and historian Sartre has extracted much of value from the bits and pieces available. What is seen emerging from his portrait are the outlines of the once-living city through which the anonymous author of the *Expositio* may have walked, and from whom we have a verbal snapshot c. 350: *deinde iam de dextris iterum Syriae supra invenies Arabiam, cuius civitas maxima est Bostra, quae negotia maxima habere dicitur, propinqua Persis et Saracenis, in qua publicum opus tetrapyli mirantur* (XXXVIII). The near-contemporary remarks of Ammianus are worthwhile juxtaposing here: *haec* (i.e. the province of Arabia) *quoque civitates habet inter oppida quaedam ingentes, Bostram et Gerasam atque Philadelphiam, murorum firmitate cautissimas* (XIV.8.13). The contrast is striking: the casual visitor remembers the tetrapylon of Bostra; the military historian notes the strength of the walls. The gates, the baths, the cryptoportico, the theater and the hippodrome are taken for granted. We are fortunate to have a more three-dimensional portrait of the city which elicited such epithets as "far-famed" (ἐπικυδής [Ins. # 9410] and allowed one banal building inscription to be garnished with the phrase Χάρῃ Βόστρα (Ins. # 9106)! "Bostra la Noire devait, n'en doutons pas, faire belle figure parmi les villes de l'Orient syrien" (Nar. 97). BOSTRA GLORIOSA!

POSTSCRIPT

While this article was in press, two new publications appeared which discuss aspects of the history of Bostra. The first is an article by J.-M. Dentzer, "Les Sondages de l'Arc Nabatéen et l'Urbanisme de Bosra", *CRAI* (1986) 62-87, see also *Berytus* 32 (1984) 163-174. Apart from dating the arch itself (and its adjoining streets) to the late first century A.D. by ceramic analysis, the discovery of the ground-level outline of a second "cathedral" is the most important revelation. The second publication is Patricia Crone's *Meccan Trade and the Rise of Islam* (Princeton University Press, 1987). However controversial the major argument of the book (i.e. that Mecca was not the great trade emporium we are accustomed to believe), there is a useful survey of trade relations between Bilād al-Shām and the Ḥijāz. In particular the author calls attention to references in early Islamic literature to the Nbṭ or Anbāṭ ahl al-Shām who regularly traded grain and oil at Medina — the sūq al-nabṭ in that city was named for these "Nabataean" merchants (p. 139 n. 31). There is also a reference to "the qūṣur and aswāq (enclosures and markets) of Buṣrā" (p. 163 n. 72), confirmation that the *Expositio's* description of the city some two or three centuries earlier was not fanciful! For the meaning of qaṣr/quṣūr see L.I. Conrad, *Abḥāth* 29 (1981) 7-23; on the transformation of eastern Byzantine cities see H. Kennedy, *Past and Present* 106 (1985) 3-27.

APPENDIX

A Greek Inscription from the Khargah Oasis in Egypt

This slightly-damaged inscription was first published just over a century ago as one of a group of largely Coptic inscriptions and graffiti from the Christian Necropolis near the northern end of the Khargah Oasis, some 200 km west of the Nile. The Necropolis is called locally al-Baqawāt, apparently a metathesis of al-Qabawāt ("The Domes"), a reference to the many chapels within the cemetery area. The earliest publisher of the short text did not specify where it was found, but a later visitor noted that it was scratched on the inner surface of a chapel dome. No details of letter-size or other measurements are available, and I do not know of any photograph of the inscription *per se*. I believe that the four publications noted below are the only accounts of this inscription.[74]

BIBLIOGRAPHY

1. H. Brugsch, *Reise nach der Grossen Oase el Khargeh in der libyschen Wüste Beschreibung ihrer Denkmäler* (Leipzig, 1878) 60-61 and Tafel 20 # 6.
2. W. de Bock, *Matériaux pour servir à l'archéologie de l'Égypte chrétienne* (St. Petersbourg, 1901) 13 fig. 18.
3. G. Lefebvre, *Recueil des inscriptions grecques-chrétiennes d'Égypte* (Cairo, 1907) 359 # 355.
4. F. Preisigke, *Sammelbuch griechischer Urkunden aus Ägypten* (Strassburg. 1915) Band I: 629 = 5727.

Text

The text was copied twice, neither time by anyone skilled in epigraphy. Below I reproduce the two facsimiles. The texts are essentially the same, though the religious symbols surrounding each vary somewhat. This is no doubt due to the fact that the entire interior of the chapel is covered with graffiti. The drawing on the left appeared in Brugsch, and the one on the right in de Bock. The texts of Lefebvre and Preisigke are based on the two drawings:

[73] The Necropolis has often been described, e.g. by Hoskins (1837: 122-130) and Hauser (1932: 38-50, with photographs) in addition to Brugsch and de Bock (see the bibliography in the appendix). But even when individual chapels are discussed by Lythgoe (1908: 203-208) there is no mention of inscriptions. Photographs of the chapel interiors (ibid. figs. 3-6) show clearly the bewildering array of graffiti and short inscriptions scratched into the walls, arches and domes. More recent surveys of the Khargah Oasis have focused on the Temple of Hibis and its inscriptions, cf. Jouguet (1936) and White and Oliver (1941).

Fig. 3: Panoramic view of Bostra. The four photographs joined here edge to edge were taken from the top of the Ayyubid citadelle, looking north-east. On the skyline are the mountains of the Jebal Drūz (Jebal Ḥawrān or Jebal ʻArab). The distinct conical crater of Jebal Kulayb (elev. 1760m) can be seen to the far left (top), and the flat-topped tell of Ṣalkhād (anc. Salcha) to the far right (bottom). The photographs were taken in October, 1875 by Tancrède R. Dumas of Beirut, the official photographer for the American Palestine Exploration Society (1870-1884). An account of the visit to Bostra is given in S. Merrill, *East of the Jordan* (London & New York, 1881: 53-58). The photographs were made available to society members in an album produced by the APES in 1876. An account of that Society and its expeditions is given in MacAdam (1986: 234-238), with a re-publication of the photograph catalogue (ibid. 257-276). These photos appeared as Nos. 38-41 in that catalogue. A recent but much more circumscribed view of Bostra from the citadelle appears in Sartre, *Bostra*, Plate 2. (*The Dumbarton Oaks Center for Byzantine Studies, Photograph Collection, has on file copy negatives of all photographs of the APES album. Their negatives were made from photographic prints owned by Speer Library at Princeton Theological Seminary, and are reproduced here with the permission of both institutions.*)

6

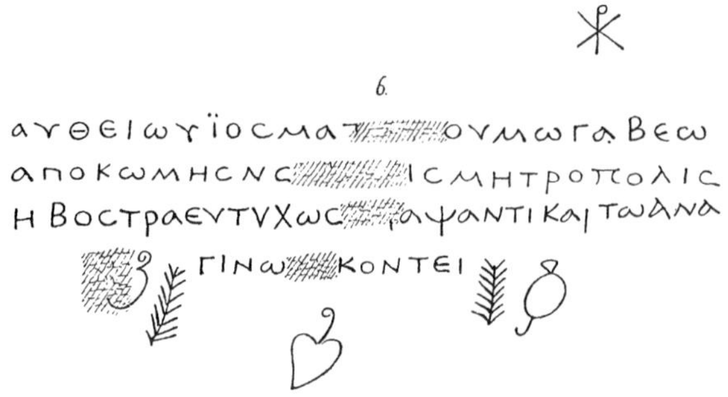

6.

18. (cf. Brugsch. Taf. XX. 6)

1. Αὐθειὼ υἱός Ματ̣[.?.]ου Μωγάβεω
2. ἀπὸ κώμης Νω̣[..?..]ι̣ς μητρόπολις
3. ἡ Βόστρα. εὐτυχῶς [τῷ γρ]άψαντι καὶ τῷ ἀνα-
4. γινώ[σ]κοντει.

Commentary

* **Line 1:** The names are Semitic. The first and last names would appear to be in the nominative case if the final *omega* is taken to represent a terminal *waw* (as in Nabataean personal names). There is an almost exact parallel to this from Bostra itself: Sartre's Ins. # 9027 which attests the donor of a small altar as Αουαθω. Both Αυθειω and Αουαθω undoubtedly transcribe Nabataean *ᶜwtw*; see Sartre's comments on this (Nar. 180). The same phenomenon is at work in another Bostran inscription (# 9301), a funeral stele of a young man named Σιθρο, where the *omicron* rather than an *omega* represents a *waw*; the Nabataean would be *Str(w)*, so far unattested (Nar. 238). The patronymic is likely to be the Ματ̣[θαι]ου (Matthaios) which Lefebvre restored; this name is known in Egypt (Wüthnow [1930] 74) and in related forms (MTN', MTNY) at Palmyra (Stark [1971] 38, 98), but it is otherwise unattested in the Ḥawrān. The patronymic could also be restored Ματ̣[ιηλ]ου (Matiēlos = Mattī'ēl), again known from Egypt (Ruozzi Sala [1974] 27). There is certainly no reason to accept Preisigke's grotesque joining together of this name and the name following as the patronymic. Μωγαβεω is a puzzle. It is either a given name, an ethnicon (Μωγαβεύς) as Lefebvre guessed, or a tribal name. If it is a personal name, it is either a second name for Autheio(s) the son of Mat...., a papponymic in the genitive, or the name of a third individual. Wüthnow (1930: 80) took it to be the genitive of a personal name, just as he had taken the ending of Autheio(s) to be dative. But he clearly saw Mōgabeos as Semitic, i.e. (M)ᶜgb (Muᶜgabî — ibid. 154). The *mu* in Greek would represent the common Semitic *mim*-prefix which intensifies the roots of personal names. But I have found no parallel for this in Cantineau (1932), Ryckmans (1934), Stark (1971) or Harding (1971). I think it most likely to be a tribal name, not with the normal Greek suffix *-ēnos* or *-ēnōn* but with the same *omega*/*waw* termination as the proper name. An example in Nabataean would be the tribal name *Qsyw* (Qasiu) attested in a religious dedication at Bostra (CIS II 174).

Line 2: The village name is quite uncertain since four or five letters in the middle are missing. The village is clearly associated with "Bostra the mētropolis", but the fact that the latter appears in the nominative is indicative that it was added for its geographic value, with no concern for grammar. The village actually may have lain within the *territorium* of Bostra. Whether it did or not, Autheios used the Arabian capital to specify his place of origin. Certainly this narrows the possibilities to places in the Ḥawrān plain or its vicinity.

Long ago Waddigton re-published a Greek inscription (Wadd. #2431) which he copied on two occasions at Nejrān in the Lejā (Trachōnitis). It records the construction of a sanctuary (*naos*) for Saint Elias in A.D. 563 by "Sergius (the son) of Samaathus, [κ]ώ(μης) Νορεράθης, of the tribe Soboṛēnoi". Whether the restoration is valid is unimportant; the word that follows is a place-name: Norerathē. Both the Khargah inscription and that from Nejrān follow a similar pattern: personal name, patronymic, tribe and village (or village and tribe), then a dedication, prayer or whatever. See the numerous examples of Greek inscriptions attesting villagers, tribes and clans, and village names in the region of Bostra (MacAdam 1986: 119-146). *

Waddington hesitantly identified the village-name Norerathē with Nejrān but René Dussaud (1927: 378) sensibly rejected this identification on the grounds that the dedicant would not name his village in such an inscription if he himself was from Nejrān. Norerathē is thus to be located elsewhere, perhaps in the Ḥawrān plain. What matters here is that the name Νω[ρεραθ]ης *could* be restored in the Khargah inscription. Thus the village from which Autheios came is at least conjecturally known.

Line 3: The *epsilon* at the beginning of εὐτυχῶς is clearly seen in Brugsch's facsimile, but was missed by de Bock. This closing invocation identifies the inscription as Christian even if the surrounding monograms do not belong to it.

BIBLIOGRAPHY

Abel, A. 1956. La citadelle Eyyubite de Bosra Eski-Cham, *AAS* 6: 95-138.

Alt, A. 1951. Das Territorium von Bostra, *ZDPV* 68: 235-245.

Bowersock, G.W. 1983. *Roman Arabia,* Cambridge (Massachusetts), Harvard University Press.

— 1984. Naming a Province: More on New Arabia, *ZPE* 56: 221-222.

— 1985. Review of M. Sartre, IGLS XIII/1 (Bostra) in *AJP* 106: 139-142.

— 1986. An Arabian Trinity in *Christians among Jews and Gentiles: Essays in Honor of Krister Stendahl on his Sixty-Fifth Birthday,* Philadelphia, Fortress Press, 17-21.

Braemer, F. 1984. Prospections archéologiques dans le Ḥawrān (Syrie), *Syria* 61: 219-250.

Butler, H.C. 1919. *Publications of the Princeton University Archaeological Expeditions to Syria in 1904/05 and 1909,* Division II, Architecture: Section A, Southern Syria, Leiden, E.J. Brill.

Brulet, R. 1986. Estampilles de la IIIe Légion Cyrenaique à Bostra, *Berytus* 32 (1984): 175-179.

Cantineau, J. 1930, 1932. *Le Nabatéen* (2 vols.), Paris, Librairie Ernest Leroux.

Češka, J. and Hošek, R. 1967. *Inscriptiones Pannoniae Superioris in Slovacia Transdanubiana Asservatae,* Brno, Universita Filosofická Fakulta.

Christol, M. and Demougin, S. 1986. Un préfet de camp de la Légion Troisième Cyrenaique, *ZPE* 64: 195-199.

Creswell, K. 1924. *The Origin and Plan of the Dome of the Rock at Jerusalem* (Bulletin of the British School of Archaeology at Jerusalem, Supplementary Paper No 2), London.

Dentzer, J.-M. (ed.) 1985, 1986. *Hauran I: Recherches archéologiques sur la Syrie du sud à l'époque hellénistique et romaine* (I F A P O, B A H Vol. CXXIV), Paris, Librairie Orientaliste Paul Geuthner.

Dussaud, R. 1927. *Topographie Historique de la Syrie Antique et Médiévale* (B A H Vol. 4) Paris, Librairie Orientaliste Paul Geuthner.

Gatier, P.-L. 1982a. Inscriptions Grecques et Latines en Jordanie: Quelques Aspects du 1er au IVe Siècle. *Le Monde de la Bible* 22: 10-11.

— 1982b. Un témoignage de Libanios sur Bostra, *Journal des Savants:* 163-167.

— 1983. Corpus des Inscriptions grecques et latines de Jordanie, *Syria* 60: 324-326.

— 1983-1984. La préparation du Corpus des Inscriptions Grecques et Latines de Jordanie (IGLJ), *AfO* 29/30: 277-279.

Golding, M. 1948. The Cathedral at Bostra, *Archaeology* 1: 150-157.

Grabar, O. 1959. The Umayyad Dome of the Rock in Jerusalem, *Ars Or* 3: 33-62.

Hadidi, A. (ed.) 1985. *SHAJ* II, Amman, Department of Antiquities.

Harding, G.L. 1971. *An Index and Concordance of Pre-Islamic Names and Inscriptions* (Near and Middle East Series No 8), Toronto, University of Toronto Press.

Hauser, W. 1932. The Christian Necropolis in Khargeh Oasis, *BMMA* 27 (March): 38-50.

Hill, S. 1975. The 'Praetorium' at Musmiye, *DOPap* 29: 347-349.

Hoskins, G.A. 1837. *Visit to the Great Oasis of the Libyan Desert,* London, Longman et al.

Humphrey, J.H. 1985. *Roman Circuses and Chariot Racing,* Berkeley, University of California Press.

Isaac, B. 1981. The Decapolis in Syria: A Neglected Inscription, *ZPE* 44: 67-74.

Jouguet, P. 1936. Observations sur les inscriptions grecques de l'oasis de Khargeh: l'edit de Vergilius Capito, (Atti del IV Congresso Internazionale di Papirologia), *Aegyptus* (Seria Scientifica) 5: 1-22.

Lythgoe, A.M. 1908. The Oasis of Kharga *BMMA* 3: 203-208.

MacAdam, H.I. 1986. *Studies in the History of the Roman Province of Arabia* (British Archaeological Reports, International Series No 295), Oxford.

— and Munday, N. 1983. Cicero's Reference to Bostra: *Ad Quintum Fratrem* II.XI.3.21, *CP* 78: 131-136.

Mayerson, P. 1983. P. Oxy. 3574: Eleutheropolis of the New Arabia, *Zeitschrift für Papyrologie und Epigraphik* 53: 251-258.

— 1986. Nea Arabia (P. Oxy. 3574): An Addendum to ZPE 53, *ZPE* 64: 139-140.

Mercati, J.M. 1895. Stephani Bostrensis nova de sacris imaginibus fragmenta e libro deperdito "kata Ioudaion", *Theologische Quartalschrift* 77: 663-668.

Miller, D.S. 1983. Bostra in Arabia: Nabataean and Roman City of the Near East, in R.T. Marchese (ed.), *Aspects of Greek and Roman Urbanism* (British Archaeological Reports, International Series No 188), Oxford: 110-136.

Mouterde, R. 1926. Sur le Recueil des Inscriptions Grecques et Latines de la Syrie, *MUSJ* 11: 177-182.

Negev, A. 1981. *The Greek Inscriptions from the Negev* (Studium Biblicum Franciscanum, Collectio Minor No 25), Jerusalem, Franciscan Printing Press.

Parker, S.T. 1986. *Romans and Saracens: A History of the Arabian Frontier (ASOR* Dissertation Series No 6), Winona Lake, Indiana, Eisenbrauns.

Peters, F.E. 1983. City-Planning in Greco-Roman Syria: Some New Considerations, *DaM* I: 269-277.

Ruossi Sala, S.M. 1974. *Lexicon Nominum Semiticorum quae in Papyris Graecis in Aegypto Repertis ab anno 323 a.Ch.n. usque ad annum 70 p.Ch.n. Laudata Reperiuntor* (Testi e Documenti per lo Studio Dell'Antichità Vol. 46), Milano, Cisalpino-Goliardica.

Ryckmans, G. 1934-1935. *Les Noms Propres Sud-Sémitiques* (3 vols.). Louvain, Bureau du Muséon.

Sartre, M. 1979. Rome et les Nabatéens à la fin de la République (65-30 av. J.-C.), *RÉA* 81: 37-53.

— 1981. Le territoire de Canatha, *Syria* 58: 343-357.

— 1982a. Tribus et clans dans le Ḥawrān antique, *Syria* 59: 77-91.

— 1982b. *Trois études sur l'Arabie romaine et byzantine,* Bruxelles: Collection Latomus No 178.

— 1985, Le peuplement et le développement du Ḥawrān antique à la lumière des inscriptions grecques et latines, in Dentzer (1985: 189-202).

De Salcy, F. 1874 (1976). *Numismatique de la Terre Sainte* (photographic reprint of the Paris edition), Bologna, Arnaldo Forni.

Sauvaget, J. 1949. Le plan antique de Damas, *Syria* 26: 314-358.

Savignac, M. and Abel, F.-M. 1905. Chronique: Glanures Épigraphiques, *RB* 2: 93-98; 596-606.

Seeden, H. 1983. Busra 1983: An Umayyad Farmhouse and Bronze Age Occupation Levels, *AAAS* 33: 162-173.

— 1984. Busra eski-Shām (Ḥaurān), *AfO* 31: 126-128.

Seeden, H. and Kadour, M. 1983. Busra 1980: Reports from a South Syrian Village, *DaM* 1: 77-101.

Shahid, I. 1984a, *Rome and the Arabs: A Prolegomenon to the Study of Byzantium and the Arabs,* Washington, D.C., the Dumbarton Oaks Press.

— 1984b. *Byzantium and the Arabs in the Fourth Century,* Washington, D.C., the Dumbarton Oaks Press.

Speidel, M.P. 1977. The Roman Army in Arabia, *Aufstieg und Niedergang der Römischen Welt* II.8: 687-730.

Starcky, J. 1966. Petra et la Nabatène, in *SDB* 7: 886-1017.

— 1985. Les Inscriptions Nabatéennes et l'Histoire de la Syrie Méridionale et du Nord de la Jordanie, in Dentzer (1985: 167-181).

Trimingham, J. S. 1979. *Christianity among the Arabs in Pre-Islamic Times,* London and New York, Longman.

Tsafrir, Y. 1986. The Transfer of the Negev, Sinai and Southern Transjordan from Arabia to Palestine, *IEJ* 36: 77-86.

Van Rengen, W. 1977. L'épigraphie grecque et latine de Syrie: Bilan d'un quart de siècle de recherches épigraphiques, *Aufstieg und Niedergang der Römischen Welt* II.8: 31-53.

Wessely, C. 1905. *Corpus Papyrorum Hermopolitanorum* (in Studien Palaeographie und Papyruskunde [photographic reprint of the Leipzig edition]), Amsterdam, A. M. Hakkert.

Wild, S. 1973. *Libanesische Ortsnamen: Typologie und Deutung* (Beiruter Text und Studien, Band 9), Beirut and Weisbaden, Franz Steiner Verlag.

Wilkinson, J. 1984. What Butler Saw, *Levant* 16: 113-127.

Winlock, H.E., White, H.G. & Oliver, J.H. 1941 (1973). *The Temple of Hibis in El Khargeh Oasis,* New York, Arno Press (photographic reprint of the original edition published by the Metropolitan Museum of Art).

Wüthnow, H. 1930. *Die Semitischen Menschennamen in Griechischen Inschriften und Papyri des Vorderen Orients* (Studien zur Epigraphik und Papyruskunde I.4), Leipzig, Dieterich'sche Verlagsbuchhandlung.

VIII

CITIES, VILLAGES AND VETERAN SETTLEMENTS: ROMAN ADMINISTRATION OF THE SYRIAN HAWRAN

Prefatory comments

My thanks go to the organizers of this conference for allowing a Roman historian to venture some observations on parallel patterns of regional development in Roman and Ottoman Syria. I am fully aware that what I say about one region of the Ottoman Near East may some * somewhat naïve to an audience of specialists in all aspects of Ottoman and Turkish history. Nevertheless I have learned much in the preparation of this paper, both from the sources and the coments of my colleagues. If you will indulge me I will begin with a broad but brief sketch of the transition from Roman to Ottoman rule in Constantinople, and then move immediately to the more narrow confines of Roman/Ottoman rule in southern Syria.

In the eighth and final volume of his famous *The History of the Decline and Fall of the Roman Empire,* first published in 1788, Edward Gibbon lamented the fact that so little reliable information was available to him as he assessed the impact of the Ottoman dynasty on the history of the eastern Roman Empire. Gibbon was particularly concerned that he knew of the work of no Turkish historian, living or dead, to whom he could turn for a connected narrative history and some perspective on the conquest of the Byzantine Empire (Gibbon, 1887; 22 note 41).

It is interesting to me to realize that Gibbon blamed the demise of Byzantium as much on the Greek proclivity for factionalism and rivalry as on the unity of purpose of the Turks (Gibbon, 1877: 25). He in fact devoted numerous pages (index, s.v. Ottoman Empire") of his final volume to the Ottoman regime, at one point (Gibbon, 1887: 72-76) tracing its rise and development from the thirteenth century to his own day.

The following statements are typical of his prise for the Ottoman military leaders who established and maintained a durable imperial system:

> ... [T]wo hundred and sixty-five years... from the elevation of Othman to the death of Soliman [are characterized] by a rare series of warlike and active princes, who impressed their subjects with obedience and their enemies with terror. Instead of the slothful luxury of the *seraglio*, the heirs of loyalty were educated in the council and the field, from early youth they were intrusted by their fathers with the command of provinces and armies; and this manly institution... must have essentially contributed to the discipline and vigour of the monarchy... While the transient dynasties of Asia have been continually subverted by a crafty vizir in the palace or a victorious general in the camp, the Ottoman succession has been confirmed by the practice of five centuries, and is now incorporated with the vital principle of the Turkish nation (Gibbon, 1877: 72-73).

It would almost seem that Gibbon saw beyond the Ottoman regime to a time when the values he praised in the Turkish peoples would sustain them in the aftermath of their own imperial eclipse. It is a subject ripe for discussion in and of itself, but I can do no more here than mention it.

Introduction

Rome was the first — and last — imperial power to bring the entire Mediterranean basin under a single geo-political system. Roman historians continue to debate the issue of whether and when Rome developed an imperial "policy" of territorial expansion in the Mediterranean (MacAdam, 1992: 272). By the Augustan age (27 B.C. — A.D. 14). Rome was the dominant power west of the Euphrates River, and remained so until the Islamic conquest. But expansion of the empire continued, especially eastward. The aggressive wars of Trajan in the eastern Danube region and Mesopotamia, coupled with the conquest of the Nabataean Kingdom, have prompted some modern historians to postulate a Roman version of a later German *Drang nach Osten* or *Ostpolitik* (e.g. Bowersock, 1983: 82-5).

Whether or not Rome ever formulated an "Eastern policy" is not at issue here. My concern is to explore the stages through which one portion of the Roman Near East, the Hawran, was transformed from a sparsely settled, unstable district into an agriculturally productive and intensely urbanized region. The Hawran lay outside the bounds of most Near Eastern kingdoms until the Hellenistic period, and played only a marginal role in Biblical history. The term *Au-ra-na* (the "Hollow

Land") appears in Babylonian records of the ninth century and after, but except for epigraphy from the region itself the ancient sources have little to say. Systematic archaeological excavation in the Hawran is a phenomenon only of the past twenty years (Dentzer, 1985-86; MacAdam, 1986a: 10-19).

The Roman role in the development of the Hawran was a gradual but deeply influential process evolving over the better part of seven centuries. It began in the first century B.C. with gradual annexation of the disintegrating Greek kingdoms in the eastern Mediterranean, founded by Alexander's successors three centuries earlier. The new province the Romans called Syria embraced all the territory from the Euphrates to Damascus, and from the Taurus Mountains to Tyre. The Hawran lay just outside the southeast border of Roman Syria, in the lava-lands between Damascus and Amman. Because this region was particularly important to the economic and social history of both Roman and Ottoman Syria, and because the documentation is unusually abundant for the two imperial periods, it might be instructive to look to them for parallel patterns of regional development.

Rome and the client-kings

In the Hawran Rome established indirect rule through a client-state relationship with the Herodian dynasty of Palestine and the Nabataean kingdom of Transjordania. Between them the two dynasties neutralized the Ituraean Arabas, warlike tribesmen from the Phoenician mountains. *
Damascus itself was threatened, and Herod the Great, Rome's Jerusalem-based client-king, was given *carte blanche* to undertake a process of pacification. The northern Hawran, known in the Greek and Latin sources as Trachonitis ("Rough-Land") and Auranitis, was administrered by Herod and his descendants until the end of the first century A.D. The ancient city of Bostra (Busra al-Sham) and the southern Hawran were ruled by the Nabataean kings of Petra until the beginning of the second century A.D. Between the two lay a wedge of territory in the central Hawran plain (called Batanaea in the sources) belonging to the equally ancient city of Canatha (Bowersock, 1983: 1-58; Sartre, 1985, 43-62).

That tripartite division of the Hawran into Herodian, Roman and Nabataean sectors, under the aegis of Rome, obtained until the very beginning of the second century A.D. It was a policy similar to that of the Ottomans, who until the 19th century governed the Hawran indirectly through the powerful political families of Damascus. Damascus-based chieftains or *aghawat* controlled local Hawrani *shaykhs* who oversaw the details of policing and tax-collecting. Clientage offered Romans and Ottomans the opportunity of intervening directly in the affairs of the Hawran when circumstances deemed it necessary. Indeed, in both instances the impetus was toward direct imperial rule (e.g. Schilcher, 1981; 1991).

The agricultural potential of the Hawran, particularly viniculture, is celebrated in the art and architecture of the region is discussed by Doris Miller elsewhere in this volume. It is my intention instead to demonstrate that Roman rule in the Hawran, indirect and direct, encouraged the development of the region's agriculture, and fostered steady and measurable urbanization.

The Roman Hawran

Direct and permanent Roman administration of the Hawran occurred with the annexation of the last Herodian kingdom at the end of the first century A.D., followed shortly by the creation of a new Roman province (Arabia) from Nabataea, at the very beginning of the second century. The reasons for this transformation are not yet clear, but it is likely that the death of the Herodian and Nabataean monarchs within a decade of each other provided the opportunity for swift absorption of their kingdoms.

A major highway, the *Via Nova Traiana*, was constructed between Aela (Aqaba) in the south to Bostra (and eventually on to Damascus) in the north. Like the Ottoman-sponsored Hijaz railway (Isaac, 1990: 120-121), it served both military and commercial functions, firmly linking the Hawran to regions north and south. A second road bisected the Hawran from east to west, from Salkhad to Adraa via Bostra. The roads were imperial projects, and their maintenance was the responsibility of the provincial government. Along them moved civilian and military traffic, and the imperial post (Bowersock, 1983: 59-109; Sartre, 1985: 62-98).

Bostra became the capital of the new province and the headquarters of its military garrison. Within a century it boasted a theater, a hippodrome, a tetrapylon, two public baths, an assortment of government buildings, colonnaded streets, and recently-discovered portions of what may be an amphitheater (Mougdad et al., 1990). Military outposts were established at key points in northern Trachonitis, on the eastern slopes of Auranitis, along the southern road to Philadelphia (Amman), and at the Azraq

Oasis in the southeast. Signal stations and watchtowers linked the major military garrisons. It is worth noting that Turkish troops were later stationed at some of those same Roman sites; the Turkish term for watchtower (*burç*) is very reminiscent of Latin *burgus* (Isaac, 1990: 114 note 59). French garrisons replaced their Ottoman and Roman predecessors during the Mandate period following World War I.

When the road-system was completed c. 200 the northern Hawran was administratively detached from Syria and joined to Arabia. For the first time since the Hellenistic age the Hawran in its entirety came under one administrative system. The road network and the settlements it linked were the framework upon which the economic and social infrastructure of the region was built (Bauzou, 1985). Secure towns and safe, well-maintained roads meant that internal and external commerce could flow freely. The wine and grain of the Hawran were marketed, we may assume, far and wide.

The governor's staff, his *officium*, would have included a procurator responsible for financial affairs. Other personnel (some selected from the military) oversaw the routine administrative duties. We know of one person, a native of the area, who served as official translator (*hermeneus* in Greek) for the procurator (MacAdam, 1983: 106). This at first seems odd given the abundance of Greek inscriptions from the cities and villages of the Hawran (some 2,000 published to date, perhaps half that many awaiting publication). The indigenous spoken languages throughout the Roman/Byzantine period were Aramaic and an early form of Arabic. Though it is probable that a large number of inhabitants could read simple Greek, this should not be taken to imply widespread facility regarding the arcane and bureaucratic language of tax-registers and imperial decrees. Interpreters provided the specific skills to render comprehensible the endless stream of information which flowed back and forth between the government and the governed (Gehman, 1914). Latin, and to a lesser extent Greek, were the languages of what I term the "inner" imperial system and would have been spoken by the governor and his closest officials, as they were by the military forces (legionnaires and auxiliaries). Greek was the linking language of "inner" and "outer" realms of the imperial system, the language of contact between rulers and ruled. Aramaic was the language of field and farm, the language of the hearth. This dichotomy between "official" and "unofficial" languages also obtained in Ottoman Syria, with Turkish and Arabic in place of Latin/Greek and Aramaic, respectively.

1. The cities

The major cities of the Hawran, Bostra, Canatha and Adraa, functioned according to the normal constitutional pattern: a council administered everyday affairs, appointing magistrates to fulfill the various civic functions and oversee routine and special activities (Jones, 1971: 281-294). The city councillors represented the various tribes from which its members were selected. Each city administered the affairs of its *territorium*, i.e. those villages and lands within its jurisdiction. All three cities minted coins until the mid-third century. Thanks to the research of Maurice Sartre we know much more about the history of the provincial capital, Bostra, than we do about any other urban community in the Hawran (Sartre, 1982a; 1985). Bostra became an ecclesiastical *see* from the fourth century on. There is evidence of strong commercial relations between the Hawran and the Hijaz in the sixth and early seventh centuries. Accordingly the *suqs* of Bostra were justly famous in pre-Islamic Arabic sources (Crone, 1987: 139 note 31). The Hijaz-Hawran link is also evident upon the completion of the railway line to Mecca during the late Ottoman period.

2. The villages

There is no evidence that villages of the central or southern Hawran plain developed formal institutions of government, nor any other aspect of individualized existence. They were very much subsidiaries of the lands owned and administered by the three big cities. They therefore had no "independent" existence. In contrast the villages in the lava-flows and the fertile hills of the northern Hawran appear to have been autonomous. This was in part because of their inhabitants' very recent transition from pastoralism (and banditry) to sedentarization, with the concomitant retention of strong tribal identities and more independent traditions. In villages of both areas the military played a prominent role, either through the actions of serving soldiers, or of veterans. The role of the latter is examined separately below.

The Northern Hawran

In what once had been the wildest and most backward region of the Hawran we can witness a rather extraordinary social transformation within a remarkably short period of time (MacAdam, 1986: 47-99).

Numerous village inscriptions attest a strong Roman military presence throughout the second century A.D. This, in conjunction with the Roman road which cut diagonally across the lava plateau, is fundamental to our understanding of how this transformation took place. Soldiers of several legions, including those stationed in Syria and Arabia, left testimonies to their presence in many villages. Named centurions, specifically acting on behalf of the Syrian governor, served as military attachés between the imperial administration and the villages (MacAdam, 1986: 91-96). In his contribution to this panel of papers, Norman Lewis addresses the history of this portion of the Hawran in Ottoman times.

One aspect of urbanization which characterizes the northern Hawran is the numerous *metrocomiai* ("mother-villages") attested by the epigraphy (MacAdam, 1986: 79-84). The would appear to have been villages * within the lava-field chosen for their proximity to the fertile land in the Hawran plain. Other, interior villages were somehow subordinate to a *metrocomia* but we do not know what the formal relationship meant. I suspect, though I cannot yet prove it, that *metrocomiai* were designated as such for the fundamental purpose of administering communal agricultural lands. How and why this "system" was inaugurated is not clear. One suspects imperial encouragement of this experiment in civic organization, though it is extremely doubtful that it was *imposed* upon the indigenous inhabitants. It is attested only where the villages were not subordinate to a city.

The Central and Southern Hawran

Epigraphy from the villages of the central and southern Hawran confirms the preoccupation of the inhabitants with matters agricultural. Several villages shared a common threshing-ground, announced as such in a formal Greek inscription of uncertain date. A metrical epitaph honors a man who was "wealthy from farming". Another man built and dedicated something "from his own farming labors". In a collective enterprise the "farmers" (*georgoi*) set up and dedicated a statue "at their own expense" (MacAdam, 1984: 53-54).

Other communities attest the construction of cisterns and reservoirs in which to store the seasonal rains. A funerary inscription witnesses provisions made for a man's property (including a fig-orchard) to be administered by his widow. Communal upkeep of a sacred area is noted by inhabitants of four named villages. Villagers undertake extensive repairs in the aftermath of some calamity, probably an earthquake, "for the good of the *polis*" (in this case the village in question belonged to the territory of Bostra) to which their community belongs (MacAdam, 1984: 50-55; MacAdam, 1986a: 107-112).

South of Adraa and Bostra were a belt of villages and several substantial towns which stretched from the Roman highway in the west to the Azraq Oasis at the desert edge in the east (MacAdam, 1986a: 16-19; MacAdam et al. 1986; MacAdam & Graf, 1989). Most show traces of continuous occupation from the first century A.D. through the Umayyad period. The largest settlements were also garrisons for units of the Roman army in provincia Arabia. Most, perhaps all, of the villages of the southern Hawran lay within the political and ecclesiastical orbit of Bostra, perhaps as far south as the territory of the small city of Arbela (Irbid).

Several additional and important military stations dating to the late Roman period were established on the edges of that central band of towns. * Much of this region is, and presumably was, the Roman army are well-attested throughout the empire. Upon retirement these soldiers would be granted farmsteads. Many had undoubtedly married locally. Where they were especially numerous (such as Beirut) veterans made a colonial impact upon the region. This is doubtful regarding the Hawran, where the overall number of soldiers was far below than that of less secure frontier areas like the Euphrates, the Rhine, the Danube, and Britain.

Even so, what appear to be remnants of "centuriation"-type field patterns can be seen on aerial photographs in the central Hawran (Kennedy, 1985). These are especially clear in the hinterland of three villages southeast of Bostra, precisely where the epigraphy attests ethnic units. So far there has been no ground-level investigation of these formal field-patterns. Very recently French archaeologists have become interested in the field-patterns near Damascus, where aerial photographs reveal what appear to be ancient, and geometrically regular, land divisions (Dodinet et al., 1990).

Perhaps connected with this phenomenon is the evidence of a cadastral land-survey conducted in the early Byzantine period. Boundary-stones with formulaic inscriptions have been recovered from sites in almost all sectors of the Hawran (MacAdam, 1986a: 109 note 32). All delineate established boundaries between land belonging to two villages, or between a village and a city. In addition several land-demarcation inscriptions imply the existance of imperial estates bordering on privately-owned property. Such estates were doubtless confiscated by the Romans from Herodian or Nabataean royalty at the creation of provincia Arabia.

The Hawran in Late Antiquity

There is some evidence, archaeological and literary, to suggest a fall in population in the Hawran area in the late Roman and Early Byzantine periods. Lawrence Conrad has recently called attention to recurrent plagues as a factor in the demographics of late antiquity, particularly for the Near East (Conrad, 1989). He has traced sporadic, epidemic outbreaks of bubonic plague from its first identifiable appearance in 541/542 (the "Plague of Justinian") through the end of the Umayyad caliphate in 749. It is clear that northern Syria was especially hard hit. We cannot yet assess the full impact of the plague upon the communities of southern Syria.

The historical *tradition* testifies to the severity of plagues in Syria/ Bilâd al-Shâm, but is specific only in noting that certain cities (e.g. Jerusalem, Damascus) were affected (Conrad, 1989: 151-154). For rural areas like the Hawran the evidence is even sketchier. Conrad cites passages in pre-Islamic Arabic poetry for references to fear of the plague among Ghassanid forces (Conrad, 1989: 151 & note 56; 156). The latter were, of course, deployed in the Hawran and Golan areas, and we may infer that those regions were affected. Yet it is a given of plague dynamics that centers of densest population are the most affected. Therefore it seems odd that the provincial capital, Bosra, is never mentioned. Nor is any other urban center of the Hawran. All that may be said at present is that for most of those ancient communities of the Hawran in which some archaeological work has been done, there is evidence of continuity of habitation c. 550-c. 750. But for several sites, particularly the military bases, there is no trace of Umayyad occupation. We cannot know at present why this was so.

Worth noting at this chronological juncture is what I might term the "parabolic" pattern of Roman rule in the Hawran. Roman involvement began indirectly through the Herodian and Nabataean client-dynasties in the first century B.C. Five centuries later Rome once again turned to clients, first the Lakhmids and then the Ghassanids, to effect control of a region that was no longer firmly welded to the imperial system. Herodian and Nabataean hegemony lasted almost a century * and half and paved the way for gradual and non-destructive Roman annexation. Ghassanid control also endured for about 150 years. The transition from Byzantine to Islamic rule occurred with the minimum of disruption.

Conclusion

When Roman historians look to other imperial systems for the sake of comparison and contrast (wether specific or general) their eyes inevitably turn westward, toward Europe. In particular the great empires of Spain, France, Britain and Germany (to note them in the chronological order of their appearance in history) are investigated for parallels of development. The example of this blinkered vision which comes most readily to mind is Sir Ronald Syme's slender volume, based on a series of lectures, entitled *Colonial Elites* (Syme, 1958). In the introduction to that book Syme noted:

> "The world has seen three empires notable for their wide extent and long duration — Rome, Spain and England… it may be instructive in different ages and civilizations to study the origin, composition and behaviour of provincial or colonial elites" (Syme, 1958: 1; 4).

Syme was of course mistaken to identify only three great empires, to identify them only in western Europe, and to look only forward in time for comparisons. Inexplicably omitted by Syme were the ancient empires of China, Persia, Mesopotomia, and Egypt, as well as the imperial regime of the Ottoman Turks which for five centuries rivaled the greatest powers of western Europe. Syme also narrowed his study to just one facet of comparative research: the emergence of an aristocracy within the colonial setting. Nevertheless his essays in this collection are insightful, and historians of any period can learn something from them.

The organizers of this panel on Roman-Ottoman rule have noted in passing several recent articles and books which explore aspects of trans-epochal studies. Linda Schilcher's contribution draws attention to the splendid new volume *City States in Classical Antiquity and Medieval Italy* (Molho et al., 1991) as a prime example. By way of contrast may I mention a recent volume of *The Journal of Peasant Studies* (Vol. 18, 1991), which has devoted the entire issue of some 300 pages to the subject of "New Approaches to State and Peasant in Ottoman History". Some of the articles are: "The Ottoman State and the Question of State Autonomy: Comparison and Perspectives"; "The Search for the Peasant in Western and Turkish History/Historiography"; and "Ottoman History by Inner Asian Norms". In particular I note the study by Halil Berktay, "Three Empires and the Societies They Governed: Iran, India and the Ottoman Empire", which offers comparisons and contrasts among three eastern imperial systems.

Also worthy of note, though not a full study of trans-epochal proportions, is Benjamin Isaac, *The Limits of Empire: the Roman Army in the East* (Isaac, 1990). This traces Rome's occupation of the eastern Mediterranean from Augustus through the Islamic conquest, and draws upon many Ottoman sources for comparisons and contrasts of troop deployment, provisioning, routing and the like. I believe it is the first attempt by a Roman military historian to utilize in any systematic way the Ottoman military material presently available.

Perhaps there is the need now for a parallel assessment of "The State and Peasant in Roman/Byzantine History". This trans-epochal study may be one small step in that direction. What I hope will occur ultimately is a shift in focus from the urban world of the central Mediterranean (the "City States" volume) to the rural world of the eastern Mediterranean (the "State and Peasant" volume), from city to countryside, in an effort to explore several topics, in two different but not completely unalike historical eras. The focus of this comparison is a particular landscape familiar to anyone knowledgeable about the physical geography of the Near East: the lava-lands of the Syrian Hawran between Damascus in the north and Amman in the south.

BIBLIOGRAPHY

BAKHIT (M.A.) & SCHICK (R.) eds., 1989, *The Fourth International Conference on the History of Bilad al-Sham*, University of Jordan, Amman.

BAUZOU (T.), "Les voies de communication dans le Hauran à l'époque romaine", in Dentzer, 1985, 137-165.

BOWERSOCK (G.W.), 1983, *Roman Arabia*, Harvard University Press, Cambridge (U.S.A.)

CONRAD (L.), 1989, "The Plague in Bilad al-Sham in Pre-Islamic Times" in Bakhit & Schick, 1989, 143-163.

CRONE (P.), 1987, *Meccan Trade and the Rise of Islam*, Princeton University Press, Princeton.

DENTZER (J.-M.) ed., 1985-86, *Hauran I Pts. 1 & 2: Recherches Archéologiques sur la Syrie du Sud à l'Epoque Hellénistique et Romaine*, Librairie Orientaliste Paul Geuthner, Paris.

DODINET (M.) et *al.*, 1990, "Le Paysage Antique en Syrie: L'exemple de Damas", *Syria*, vol. 62, 339-355.

GIBBON (E.), 1887, *The History of the Decline and Fall of the Roman Empire* in eight volumes (new edition by Wm. Smith), John Murray, London.

ISAAC (B.), 1990, *The Limits of Empire: the Roman Army in the East*, Oxford University Press, Oxford.

JONES (A.H.M.), 1971, *Cities of the Eastern Roman Provinces*, 2nd ed., The Clarendon Press, Oxford.

KENNEDY (D.L.), 1985, "Ancient Settlements in Syria", *Popular Archaeology* (september), 42-44.

KEYDER (C.) & TABAK (F.), eds., 1991, *Large-Scale Commercial Agriculture in the Ottoman Empire*, State University of New York Press, Albany, N.Y.

KHALIDY (T.) ed., 1984, *Land Tenure and Social Transformation in the Middle East*, American University of Beirut, Beirut.

MACADAM (H.I.), 1983, "Epigraphy and Village Life in Southern Syria During the Roman and Early Byzantine Periods", *Berytus*, vol. 31, 103-115.

—, 1984, "Some Aspects of Land Tenure and Social Development in the Roman Near East: Arabia, Phoenicia and Syria" in *Khalidy*, 1984, 45-62.

—, 1986a, *Studies in the History of the Roman Province of Arabia*, British Archaeological Reports, Oxford.

—, 1986b, "Bostra Gloriosa", *Berytus*, vol. 34, 169-192.

—, 1992, "Rome and the Eastern Provinces", *Topoi*, vol. 2, 247-273.

MACADAM (H.I.), KENNEDY (D.L.) & RILEY (D.N.), 1986, "Preliminary Report on the Southern Hawran Survey, 1985", *Annual of the Department of Antiquities of Jordan*, vol. 30, 145-153.

MACADAM (H.I.) & GRAF (D.F.), 1989, "Inscriptions from the Southern Hawran Survey, 1985", *Annual of the Department of Antiquities of Jordan*, vol. 33, 177-197.

MOLHO (A.) et *al.*, 1991, *City-States in Classical Antiquity and Medieval Italy: Athens and Rome, Florence and Venice*, Franz Steiner Verlag, Stuttgart.

MOUGDAD (R.) et *al.*, 1990, "Un amphithéâtre à Bosra?", *Syria* , vol. 67, 201-204.

SARTRE (M.), 1982a, *Inscriptions Grecques et Latines de la Syrie, tome XII: Bostra*, Librairie Orientaliste Paul Geuthner, Paris.

—, 1982b, *Trois études sur l'Arabie romaine et byzantine*, Collection Latomus, vol. 178, Bruxelles.

—, 1985, *Bosra: Des origines à l'Islam*, Librairie Orientaliste Paul Geuthner, Paris.

SCHILCHER (L.S.), 1981, "The Hauran Conflicts of the 1860s: A Chapter in the Rural History of Modern Syria", *International Journal of Middle East Studies*, vol. 13, 159-179.

— (L.S.), 1991, "The Grain Economy of Late Ottoman Syria and the Issue of Large-Scale commercialization" in Keyder & Tabak, 1991, 173-195; 224-228.

SPEIDEL (M.P.), 1977, "The Roman Army in Arabia", *Aufstieg und Niedergang der römischen Welt*, vol. II.8, 687-730.

SYME (R.), 1958, *Colonial Elites: Rome, Spain and the Americas*, Oxford University Press, London.

IX

Settlements and Settlement Patterns in Northern and Central Transjordania, *ca.* 550-*ca.*750*

Introduction

THE HISTORY OF human habitation east of the Jordan River has been continuous from prehistory to the present. There is now growing evidence that the Late Bronze and Iron Ages were the period of heaviest settlement in earliest antiquity. Several localities (e.g. Gerasa, Abila, Pella, Philadelphia) that would in time be numbered among the cities of the Decapolis were already in existence at the end of the second millennium.

The collapse or decline of various Bronze Age empires throughout the eastern Mediterranean affected inland as well as coastal cities. From the end of the Iron Age until the early Roman period there is evidence of urban decline and impoverishment throughout Transjordania. The intervention of Rome in A.D. 64/63, the creation of the Decapolis, and the recognition of the Nabataean Arabs as a client kingdom fostered a new period of urbanisation and wide-spread settlement. [1]

---

* Grateful thanks are due to Linda S. Schilcher, Department of History, Villanova University, for her valuable comments on all aspects of this paper. Remaining errors are my responsibility.

[1] An excellent summary of this period, including a review of evidence relating to the Decapolis, is given in G.W. Bowersock, *Roman Arabia* (Cambridge, Mass.,1983), Chaps. III-V. The role of the Roman/Byzantine military is fundamental in understanding the development of the Near East from the first century B.C. through to the Islamic conquest. See now Benjamin Isaac, *The Limits of Empire: the Roman Army in the East*

Nabataean independence ended with the annexation of that kingdom in A.D. 106. Most of it became the Roman province of Arabia. A paved highway (the famous *via nova Traiana)* connected Aela (al-'Aqaba) in the south with Bostra (Buṣrā al-Shām) in the north. Around A.D. 300 the entire portion of Roman Arabia south of the Wādī l-Ḥasā was administratively detached and joined to Roman Palestine.[2] Just under a century later (*ca* A.D. 390) another modification occurred with the tripartite division of Palestine into Prima, Secunda and Tertia (or Salutaris).[3] Cities of the Transjordanian northwest such as Pella, Gadara and Hippos (and their *territoria)* were now administratively part of Palestine II. The towns and villages of the old Peraea (Judaean territory across the Jordan) fell within Palestine I. Northeastern and central Transjordania, as well as Moab, remained within Roman Arabia.

In A.D. 451 Moab was detached and added to Palestine III.[4] For most of the next two centuries portions of Transjordania remained parts of four Byzantine provinces. It has been argued recently by Shahid[5] that another provincial modification occurred *ca* A.D. 628, when, he believes, Heraclius reorganized the east in the aftermath of the Persian occupation and created administrative/military provinces (*themata*), e.g. "Palaestina" and "Iordanes". Shahid maintains that these *themata* were subsequently incorporated as military districts (sing. *jund*, pl. *ajnād*), with Arabized names such as "Filasṭīn" and "al-Urdunn", into the earliest Islamic administrative scheme for Bilād al-Shām (Fig. 11).[6]

Recent research has pointed to recurrent plagues and devastating earthquakes (see below) in the late sixth and early seventh centuries as major factors undermining resistance to Muslim forces at the onset of the Islamic conquest. By the 640s, the entire Near East from Egypt to eastern Anatolia and to the Persian Gulf was within Islamic control. Again and

---

(Oxford, 1990) and David L. Kennedy and Derrick N. Riley, *Rome's Desert Frontier from the Air* (London, 1990).

2 Bowersock, *Roman Arabia*, 142-47.

3 Philip Mayerson, "'Palestina' vs. 'Arabia' in the Byzantine Sources", *ZPE* 56 (1984),223-30; id., "Justinian's Novel 103 and the Reorganization of Palestine", *BASOR* 269 (1988), 65-71.

4 Arabia's southern border was fixed at the Wādī l-Mūjib in A.D.451; see Albrecht Alt, "Die letzte Grenzverschiebung zwischen den römischen Provinzen Arabia und Palaestina", *ZDPV* 65 (1942), 68-76. This modification is clearly shown on Fig. 11.

5 Irfan Shahid, "The Jund system in Bilād al-Shām: its Origin", in M.A.Bakhit and M.Asfour, eds., *Proceedings of the Symposium on Bilād al-Shām During the Byzantine Period (1983)* II (Amman, 1986), 45-52.

6 There is still no agreement on the configuration of these "provinces", and Shahid seems uncertain as to their number.

again archaeology and epigraphy have demonstrated that the period directly following the Conquest was one of peaceful transition during which the non-Muslim communities of the region were comfortably integrated within the Islamic state. In central and north-eastern Jordan a group of elaborate palaces, estates and baths, popularly designated the "desert castles", arose on or near the sites of earlier encampments or fortifications. At al-'Aqaba in the far south, the site of the Umayyad port is being excavated. Extensive field surveys in Ammanitis and Moabitis have begun to illuminate the extent of settlement in those regions. Multi-national excavations of Pella, Gadara, Gerasa and other sites in northwest Jordan are beginning to illustrate the pre-Roman and post-Byzantine history of that region. Characteristic early Islamic ceramics until very recently were a feature of only northern Jordanian sites. But as field work in the south expands, more and more Umayyad and 'Abbāsid pottery is found associated with sites (e.g. Udhruḥ, al-Ḥumayma) attested in the early Islamic sources.[7]

A brief look at the characteristics of selected settlements, and the overall pattern of settlement during that transitional, two-century period (between the late years of Justinian and the establishment of the 'Abbāsid dynasty) are the objects of this paper. My survey will examine three areas of Transjordania: (l) the northeast (including the southern Ḥawrān, the al-Azraq oasis and several fortified sites), (2) the northwest (Gerasa, Abila, Pella, etc.) and (3) the central sector ('Ammān, Ḥiṣbān, Mādabā, Dhibān and the Umayyad "castles" from Qasṭal to al-Kharāna). Recent literature regarding the Roman/Byzantine and Early Islamic periods in northern and central Jordan is largely localized, *i.e.*, focused upon settlements in specific areas. For north-east Jordan, especially, the emphasis has been on sites of a military character (e.g. the studies by Kennedy and Parker, cited below), and although they cannot be ignored they are discussed here in association with non-military settlements. For north-west and central Jordan, the broader studies have focused on epigraphy and ecclesiastical art and architecture (e.g. Gatier and Piccirillo, cited below). It is time to draw upon the results of much new archaeological excavation and field surveys, casting the net as wide as possible for evidence of regional settlement

---

7 See in particular a number of fundamental studies by Donald S.Whitcomb, "Mahesh Ware: Evidence of Early Abbasid Occupation from Southern Jordan", *ADAJ* 33 (1989), 269-85; "Evidence of the Umayyad Period from the Aqaba Excavations", in M.A.Bakhit and Robert Schick, eds., *The Fourth International Conference on the History of Bilād al-Shām during the Umayyad Period* (Amman, 1989), II, 164-84; "Archaeology of the Abbasid Period: The Example of Jordan", *Archéologie islamique* 1 (1990), 75-85.

patterns. Accordingly, no apologies are offered for the amount of bibliography incorporated herein, though I have attempted not to duplicate the fundamental secondary sources cited elsewhere.

The publication of *Archaeology of Jordan* [8] makes available for the first time a comprehensive (albeit inevitably incomplete) register of archaeological work in Jordan from its beginnings in the early nineteenth century until the late 1980s. One may consult that in conjunction with a recent but uneven essay which outlines the broad developments of Jordanian archaeology and assesses the evidence of selected sites.[9] It is pleasant indeed to report that the editors of the *American Journal of Archaeology*[10] have just created an annual forum for Jordanian archaeology which will supplement the annual reviews in (e.g.) *Syria, Revue Biblique*, and *Liber Annuus,* as well as the preliminary reports which are a regular feature of *Annual of the Department of Antiquities of Jordan.* Less frequent but more comprehensive treatments appear in *Archiv für Orientforschung*,[11] the *I.F.A.P.O.* occasional reports in *Contribution française à l'archéologie jordanienne*, and the important series of publications which are generated by international conferences, *Studies in the History and Archaeology of Jordan.*[12] Much of interest contributed by philologists, archaeologists and historians may be found in the Proceedings of the first four gatherings (1974-87) of *The International Conference on the History of Bilād al-Shām.*[13]

In making the specific divisions noted above, I am following closely the regional schema laid out by the editors of the epigraphic series

---

[8] Denise Homès-Fredericq and J. Basil Hennessy, eds., *Archaeology of Jordan*, 2 vols. (Leuven,1986-90),.Vol. I, pt.1 (*Bibliography and Gazetteer of Surveys and Sites)* appeared as *Akkadica*, Suppl. III; its companion, Vol. I, pt.2 (*Bibliography of Classical Authors and Arabic Writers)* is in preparation.Vol.II, pts. 1 and 2 (Field Reports of Surveys and Sites A-K, L-Z) appeared as *Akkadica*, Suppl. VII-VIII. Other fascicles will appear as additional information accrues from sites already mentioned, or from new surveys and excavations.

[9] Lawrence T. Geraty and Lloyd A. Willis, "Archaeological Research in Transjordan", in L.T.Geraty and Larry G. Herr, eds., *The Archaeology of Jordan and Other Studies Presented to Siegfried Horn* (Berrien Springs, 1986), 3-72.

[10] Bert De Vries, "Archaeology in Jordan", *AJA* 95 (1991), 253-80. Cf. p. 253: "this is the first instalment of an annual newsletter on archaeology in Jordan". Early and late classical and Islamic sites are presented under the rubric "Hellenistic, Roman, Medieval", 268-80.

[11] See *AfO* 29/30 (1983/84), 242-92; *ibid.* 33 (1986), 148-308.

[12] Three volumes of *SHAJ* appeared between 1982 and 1987. A fourth, the proceedings of a conference held at Lyon, 1989, was published in 1992.

[13] See the extremely useful (despite several curious omissions) *Collective Index* (Arabic and English) prepared by Muhammed Darwish and Abdoul Salameh al-Bakhit under the supervision of Muhamed Bakhit (Amman, 1990).

Inscriptions de la Jordanie.[14] North-western and central Jordan are geographically separated by the Wādī Zarqā', between Jarash and 'Ammān. For north-western and north-eastern Jordan, there is also a geographical demarcation, but one less sharply defined. The dichotomy there is roughly along the line of the *via nova Traiana* from Zarqā' north-east to Khirbat al-Samrā'.[15] From there the line goes due north to al-Mafraq and eventually to the Syrian border, west of Jābir. Most of the cities and villages west of that somewhat arbitrary division belonged to one or another city of the Decapolis for the better part of two centuries. Gerasa, Capitolias and Dium later claimed foundation by Alexander or his general, Perdiccas.[16] Even if such a claim cannot be substantiated, the Hellenisation of those cities was far more developed than that of the towns and villages that lay along the southern approaches to the lava-lands to the north and east. The pre-Islamic settlements of central Jordan, south of the Wādī Zarqā', also combined elements of both Graeco-Roman and indigenous culture, but the Aramaic/Arab traditions appear to have been much stronger there and in the north-east.

1. North-eastern Jordan

This is the largest in area of the three sectors to be surveyed, but it was by no means the most densely populated. Much of the region is steppeland or basalt desert, and therefore unattractive to permanent settlement. The southern Ḥawrān[17] is the most fertile portion of the north-east, and subsequently has been the most populous. A band of towns and villages stretched from the *via nova* in the west to the line of the *Strata Diocletiana*

---

[14] Pierre-Louis Gatier, "La préparation du Corpus des Inscriptions Grecques et Latines de Jordanie", *AfO* 29/30 (1983/84), 277-79 (see esp. fig. 35). The northern limit of the *IJ* series is the modern Syrian-Jordanian border. For the purposes of this article, that division is artificial; thus I shall include the evidence of sites both south and north of the border, but not the northern Ḥawrān plain, the Lajā or the Jabal Durūz. Those areas have recently been the subject of important publications by the Institut Français d'Archéologie du Proche-Orient; see J.-M. Dentzer, ed., *Hauran I: recherches archéologiques sur la Syrie du sud à l'époque hellénistique et romaine*, Pt. 1 (Paris, 1985); Pt. 2 (Paris, 1986; BAH 124). The term "romaine" includes the Byzantine period up to the Islamic conquest.

[15] Al-Samrā' lies but a half-km. west of the *via nova*. Like the village of Riḥāb to the north-west, its ecclesiastical affiliation was with the metropolitan archbishops of Bostra. Nevertheless, both villages will here be considered within north-western Jordan.

[16] A.H.M. Jones, *Cities of the Eastern Roman Provinces* (Oxford, 1971), 237 and n. 15.

[17] The terms "Jordanian" and "Syrian" Ḥawrān are conventional modern designations of the areas on either side of the political border established in the post-Mandate period. No such division was in use before World War I. The Princeton University expeditions (see below) referred to both areas collectively as the "Southern Ḥawrān"; that inclusive term is also used here.

[18] in the east. Most, if not all, villages of the southern Ḥawrān lay within the political or ecclesiastical orbit of Bostra, the large and resplendent metropolis and bishopric whose history, epigraphy and institutions have been the subject of much recent scholarship.[19] South of the Ḥawrān, the Umayyads planted their desert palaces, from the al-Azraq Oasis in the east to Qasṭal, south of ʻAmmān, in the west. Both areas were studded with fortifications. Some of these were outposts anchored at strategic locations, such as Qaṣr Bāʻiq near the *via nova* and Qaṣr Burqūʻ in the black basalt desert far to the east. But in two instances military encampments are closely associated with large towns, i.e. Umm al-Jimāl, and (less certainly) Umm al-Quṭṭayn. Watchtowers and observation/signaling posts linked settlements and fortifications.[20] Several isolated sites (e.g. Bā'ir, far south of al-Azraq, and Dayr al-Qinn north-east of Umm al-Quṭṭayn) were probably abandoned before the Islamic period. Unlike Bāʻiq and Burqūʻ *(inter alia)* they outlived their usefulness and were not revived by the Umayyads.

Thus four categories of settlement may be identified: indigenous towns or villages (fortified or unfortified), military bases, villas/ monasteries, and sites of indeterminate character.[21] It would seem that the Roman and Byzantine authorities were concerned with either internal or external threats to the communities and trade routes of this area. At the beginning of the third century, and again in the fourth, sustained efforts were made to garrison large portions of Transjordania. From the late fifth century and thereafter, however, the imperial military presence evaporated when the federate Arab Ghassānids undertook the responsibility of tribal police for the desert frontier.[22] Christianity is strongly evident in town,

---

[18] For the meaning and history of the term see Maurice Dunand, "La Strata Diocletiana", *RB* 40 (1931), 227-48.

[19] Maurice Sartre, *Bostra* (*IGLS* 13.1, 1982; BAH 93), *id.*, *Bostra. Des origines à l'Islam* (Paris, 1985, BAH 97). See also my "Bostra Gloriosa", *Berytus* 34 (1986), 169-92.

[20] G.R.D.King *et al.*, "Survey of Byzantine and Islamic Sites in Jordan: Second Season report, 1981", *ADAJ* 27 (1983), 411-14.

[21] An example of the latter is the village of Umm Sanana south-east of Bostra, visited by the Princeton Expedition: "it is difficult to form an opinion as to the extent or character of this place in ancient times; for every block of dressed stone, and much other building material, has been carried away by the Druses for the building of the houses [in a nearby village]", H.C.Butler, *PPUAES 1904/5 and 1909, Division II, Architecture: Section A, Southern Syria* (Leiden, 1919), 107.

[22] Fred M. Donner, *The Early Islamic Conquests* (Princeton, 1981), 42.

village and fort alike from the fourth century on, and, in its Monophysite form, had been accepted by the larger Arab tribal groupings.[23]

In the past two decades the settlements within the southern Ḥawrān have once again attracted the interest of historians, archaeologists and epigraphers. Earlier archaeological surveys in the decades before World War I had indicated that this territory enjoyed a prosperous and peaceful existence in late antiquity.[24] Modern surveys and excavations confirm this, and extend the period of growth and development at many places through the Umayyad period.[25] Some seventy sites have been investigated, including three not noticed until 1980.[26] All lie within a region of volcanic soils and marginal rainfall (*ca.* 200 mm. per year) supportive of cereal crops and pastoralism.[27] Most lay on or near major trade routes from inner Arabia via Dūmat al-Jandal (al-Jawf), the Wādī al-Sirḥān, the al-Azraq Oasis and thence either northward to Bostra and Damascus, or directly westward to 'Ammān and Jarash. It is probable, as Maurice Sartre has observed, that in many of the smaller communities skilled artisans developed "cottage industries" which sold or bartered a variety of high-quality products in emporia such as Bostra, which reached markets as distant as Mecca.[28]

---

23 J. Spencer Trimingham, *Christianity among the Arabs in Pre-Islamic Times* (London and NewYork, 1979), esp. chap. 5.

24 Butler, *op. cit.*, 63-70, gives an excellent introduction to the region up to the time of his publication.

25 See e.g. Siegfried Mittmann, *Beiträge zur Siedlungs- und Territorialgeschichte des Nördlichen Ostjordanlandes* (Weisbaden, 1970), 196-207; G.R.D. King, "Preliminary Report on a Survey of Byzantine and Islamic Sites in Jordan, 1980", *ADAJ* 26 (1980), 86-95; *id.*, "Second Season Report", *ibid.* 27 (1983), 385-436; D.L.Kennedy *et al.*, "Preliminary Report on the Southern Hauran Survey", *ibid.* 30 (1986), 145-53.

26 King, "Preliminary Survey", 92; "Second Season", 409-10, records brief visits to Khirbat 'Amra/'Amīra, Sīrat Arnūb and Saba' Asīr, all east of Umm al-Jimal. The village named 'Amra/'Amīra resulted from the "unification" of two modern villages.

27 The 200 mm. isohyet is clearly marked in Maurice Sartre, *Trois études sur l'Arabie romaine et byzantine* (Brussels, 1982), carte 4.

28 M. Sartre, "Le Hawran byzantin à la veille de la conquête musulmane", in M. Bakhit, ed., *Proceedings of the Symposium on Bilad al-Sham During the Byzantine Period (1985)* III (Amman, 1987), 159-60. The role of commerce in the early history of Mecca is a hotly-debated issue since the publication of Patricia Crone's *Meccan Trade and the Rise of Islam* (Cambridge, 1987), where she underscored the lack of evidence for Meccan commercial prosperity before or during the lifetime of Muḥammad. Exactly the same conclusion was reached independently by Francis E. Peters,"The Commerce of Mecca before Islam", in Farhaz Kazemi and R. D. McChesney, eds., *A Way Prepared: Essays on Islamic Culture in Honor of Richard Bayly Winder* (New York and London, 1988), 3-26. See the sharp response to Crone's book by R.B. Serjeant, "Meccan Trade and the Rise of Islam: Misconceptions and Flawed Polemics", *JAOS* 110 (1990), 472-86.

In 1904/1905 the Princeton University survey team visited a total of sixty-six sites in the southern Ḥawrān.[29] They ranged in size and importance from Umm al-Jimāl, the largest and best-preserved of all the towns of the area, to Qawm Manāra, a solitary watchtower. Several sites (e.g. Qaṣr Bā'iq, Dayr al-Kahf) had been isolated military posts. Many places have not been re-visted since. Siegfried Mittmann copied inscriptions at several villages in the late 1960s,[30] and the King survey studied architectural features and took ceramic samples at several others in 1980 and 1981.[31] Multi-season archaeological work began at Umm al-Jimāl in 1972.[32] A multi-season survey of military sites in north-eastern Jordan was undertaken in 1976.[33] The Southern Ḥawrān Survey team spent a total of four weeks at and near the town of Umm al-Quṭṭayn in 1984-5.[34]

For the most part these sites are the remains of small villages, often no more than a few kilometres from one another. Almost all retained identifiable vestiges of late antiquity in spite of continuous habitation or use as quarries for modern constructions at nearby sites. Many produced epigraphy, ranging in date from Nabataean of the first century A.D. through Greek of the seventh century and Arabic of the eighth. It was often the epigraphy alone that determined the chronology of a site, since ceramic typology was unknown to the Princeton and other early surveys. Even the epigraphic evidence was speculative unless a dated inscription was found *in situ*. Inscribed stones of moveable size had decorative or constructional value to later settlers, and sometimes travelled with them to other localities. Material remains from the early Islamic period have been especially enigmatic for investigators. Only now are we becoming more confident about the identification of what is Umayyad or 'Abbāsid at any Near Eastern site.[35]

---

[29] Butler, *ibid.*, Pts. 1-2. That total did not include the town of Umm al-Jimāl, to which a separate fascicle (*PPUAES* II A, Pt. 3) was devoted in order to underscore its importance.
[30] Mittmann, *Beiträge*, 196-207, nos. 33-51.
[31] King, "Preliminary Survey", 85-95; "Second Season", 385-436.
[32] *AJ* II.2, 590-97.
[33] David L. Kennedy, *Archaeological Explorations on the Roman Frontier in North-East Jordan,* BAR Int. Ser. 134 (Oxford, 1982).
[34] *AJ* II.2, 612-14. See Kennedy, "Preliminary Survey", 145-53, with David F. Graf and H.I. MacAdam, "Inscriptions from the Southern Hawran Survey, 1985", *ADAJ* 33 (1989), 177-97.
[35] We are on much firmer ground with Umayyad pottery, but a recent assessment by Donald Whitcomb concludes that "the study of Islamic ceramics is perhaps less well developed than that of other Islamic artifacts, in spite of its importance for chronological, technological and functional interpretations of Islamic archaeological sites": see his "Khirbet al-Mafjar Reconsidered: The Ceramic Evidence", *BASOR* 271 (1988), 51-67,

Churches and chapels are a common feature of the civilian and military settlements alike.[36] But apart from inscriptions which date the construction or repair of a church, the use of the building into the seventh and eighth centuries can really only be determined archaeologically. At the few sites where careful archaeological work has been done, there is clear evidence for Umayyad occupation. The best example from the southern Ḥawrān is Umm al-Jimāl. To date it is the only town in north-east Jordan for which a coin-controlled stratigraphic sequence has been established.[37] Still visible are the remains of the town which saw an explosion of growth between the fifth and seventh centuries and perhaps beyond.[38] In all, some fourteen churches and two monasteries have been identified from physical remains and epigraphy. All these are fourth century or later; most probably date from the last two centuries of the Byzantine era.

The Umayyad period at Umm al-Jimāl is represented by several archaeological discoveries. De Vries notes that the floor of the "praetorium" , and that of a nearby house, were cobbled and overlaid with plaster. One segment of the plastered floor of the "praetorium" is painted, reminding the archaeologist of similar features associated with Umayyad palaces further south and east.[39] The town's "East Gate" was rebuilt in the late seventh or early eighth century, perhaps to accommodate large wooden doors. The major ground-level aqueduct which channelled water along the eastern side of the town was extended to the south-east corner, just inside the walls. The interior of the "North-east Church" was enhanced by reflooring the chancel area and then screening it.[40]

It is unfortunate that dated epigraphy from Umm al-Jimāl later than the fifth century is almost non-existent. Only the date of A.D. 556-57

at 51. On the refinement of Islamic ceramic typology see Denis Pringle, "The Medieval Pottery of Palestine and Transjordan (A.D.636-1500): An Introduction, Gazetteer and Bibliography", *Medieval Ceramics* 5 (1981), 45-60, with James A. Sauer, "The Pottery of Jordan in the Early Islamic Periods", *SHAJ* 1 (1982), 329-37; *id*., "Umayyad Pottery from Sites in Jordan", in *The Archaeology of Jordan and Other Studies*, 301-30.

36 G.R.D. King, "Some Churches of the Byzantine Period in the Jordanian Ḥawrān", *DM* 3 (1988), 35-75.

37 Khirbat al-Samrā', south-west of Umm al-Jimāl, is here considered to be within north-west Jordan (see above).

38 Continuous occupation of the site apparently begins in the late Nabataean period; see Bert De Vries, "Umm al-Jimal in the Third Century", In P.W.M. Freeman and D.L. Kennedy, eds., *The Defence of the Roman and Byzantine East*, BAR Int. Ser. 297 (Oxford, 1986), 227-52.

39 Bert De Vries, "Urbanization in the Basalt Region of North Jordan in Late Antiquity: The Case of Umm al-Jimal", in A. Hadidi, ed., *SHAJ* II (1985), 249-56, at 251.

40 *Ibid.*

remains from what was a Greek dedicatory or building inscription.[41] There are also several undated but clearly sixth or early seventh century Greek inscriptions alluding to the Blue and Green racing factions.[42] However cosmopolitan the latter may seem, the hellenization of the community was only surface-deep. The funerary epigraphy is extensive (though mostly undated) and attests to the solidly Arab identity of the inhabitants.[43] The numismatic evidence from the site still awaits publication.

Some diminution of the population during the Umayyad period was evident to the excavators, who noted the "abandonment and collapse" of buildings in the southern quarter of the town.[44] The reasons for this are far from clear. Throughout the seventh century the "praetorium" was the dominant structure in the west-central part of Umm al-Jimāl. Its "rather deluxe refurbishing" led the excavator, Bert De Vries, to look to nearby Qaṣr al-Ḥallābāt and other desert palaces for parallels to its interior form and function.[45] The Diocletianic *castellum* was robbed of much of its stonework in the sixth century, and a bakery installed in a former barracks.[46] There is later evidence of severe seismic damage to the town, plausibly associated with the great earthquake of A.H. 129-30/A.D. 747-48.[47] No attempt was made to repair and resettle Umm al-Jimāl, which thereafter lay abandoned until the decades immediately following World War I.

With Umm al-Jimāl in mind as a "type-site" for the region, we may look for parallel or similar features at other places that will argue for or against continuity of habitation through the Islamic period. The Princeton Expedition found remains of churches and chapels virtually everywhere,

---

[41] Enno Littmann *et al.*, *PPUAES Division III, Greek and Latin Inscriptions: Section A. Southern Syria* (Leiden, 1913), 151, no. 260.

[42] *Ibid.*, 148, no. 256; 154, no. 266. The stones may well have come from nearby Bostra, * which boasted a hippodrome (still unexcavated) in the south-eastern sector of the vity.

[43] Maurice Sartre, "Le peuplement et le développement du Hauran antique à la lumière des inscriptions grecques et latines", in Dentzer, *Hauran* I.1, 201-2 and *passim*.

[44] De Vries, "Urbanization", 251.

[45] *Ibid.*, 255.

[46] S. Thomas Parker, *Romans and Saracens: A History of the Arabian Frontier*, ASOR DS 6 (Philadelphia, 1986), 161.

[47] The traditional date assigned has been January, A.D.747 or 748; see Zuhair El-Isa, "Earthquake Studies of Some Archaeological Sites in Jordan", *SHAJ* II (1985), 234, and for a broader survey, Kenneth W. Russell, "The Earthquake Chronology of Palestine and Northwest Arabia from the 3rd through the mid-8th Century A.D.", *BASOR* 260 (1985), 37-59. Yoram Tsafrir kindly informs me that the date can be fixed as January, A.D. 749: see Yoram Tsafrir and Gideon Foerster, "The Dating of the Earthquake of the Sabbatical Year of 749 C.E.", *BSOAS* 55 (1992), 231-35.

not only in towns and villages,[48] but as an integral part of military architecture as well.[49] Exclusive of the fourteen at Umm al-Jimāl, they number about two dozen and range in date from the mid-fourth century to the mid-sixth century. Monasteries/convents are also well-represented. Besides the two at Umm al-Jimāl, Butler identified another seven. Where dates can be assigned the range is *ca* 350-624-25.[50] We are also fortunate to possess, for the province of Arabia, a partial list of Monophysite monasteries in a document dated to *ca* 575.[51] Some eleven names appear in that portion of the list devoted to the Ḥawrān. [52] Very probably many of these monasteries continued to function as such well into the early Islamic period. At Samā (north-west of Umm al-Jimāl)[53] a Greek lintel inscription dated to A.D. 624-625 was found *in situ* within the courtyard of a building associated with that village's monastery.[54]

In several villages the transition from Byzantium to Islam may be evident in the re-use of a church as a mosque. The Princeton architect and classicist Howard Crosby Butler noticed that churches in Samā[55] and Umm al-Surab (slightly south-east of Samā)[56] had square towers associated with them. In both cases he ascribed the towers to the Byzantine period, though at Umm al-Surab he recognized that the tower had been re-used as a minaret.[57] The King survey[58] revisited both villages, examined the churches, and ascribed both towers to the Islamic period. King's argument for Samā is more secure, since the eastern side of the tower "rests on top of

---

48 Butler, *PPUAES* II A Pts. 1-3, *passim*; *id.*, *Early Churches in Syria: Fourth to Seventh Centuries* (Leiden, 1929), 17-24 [4th c.]; 41-47[5th c.];115-27 [6thc.]). It should be noted that these summaries include churches from areas north and east of the southern Ḥawrān, as well as those associated with military structures.

49 E.g. Butler, *PPUAES* II A, 80-83 (Qasr Ba' iq); 145-48 (Dayr al-Kahf).

50 Butler, *Early Churches*, 84-93.

51 This "Letter of the Archimandrites" is referred to in a wide-ranging discussion of monasticism in the Ḥawrān by François Villeneuve, "L'économie rurale et la vie des campagnes dans la Hauran antique (Ier siècle av. J.-C.-VIIe siècle ap. J.C.): une approche", in Dentzer, *Hauran* I.1, 118-21. The fundamental study is still that of Th. Nöldeke, "Zur Topographie und Geschichte des damascenischen Gebietes und der Haurangegend", *ZDMG* 29 (1875), 419-44, esp. 433-40 on place-names in southern Syria and northern Jordan.

52 Villeneuve, "L'économie rurale", 118, n. 160. Only a few of these appear on the map of Monophysite monasteries in Sartre, *Trois Etudes*, carte 5.

53 *AJ* II.2, 552-53.

54 Littmann, *PPUAES* III A, 45-46, no. 27.

55 Butler, *PPUAES* II A, 83-87.

56 *AJ* II.2, 621-24; Butler, *PPUAES* II A, 94-99.

57 *Ibid.*, 96 and illus. 78.

58 King, "Preliminary Survey", 89-91; *id.*, "Two Byzantine Churches in Northern Jordan and their Re-Use in the Islamic Period", *DM* 1 (1983), 111-36.

a wall of the monastery".[59] That monastery, as noted above, was constructed in 624-25. In neither case is there clear evidence for a *miḥrāb* within the church/mosque, though the south wall of each church is damaged approximately where one might expect to find the niche for a *miḥrāb*. There is also uncertainty about which period (Umayyad or Ayyūbid/Mamlūk) to date the transformation from church to mosque. Though sherds of both periods were collected at the sites by his survey, King suspects that the growing evidence of a strong Umayyad presence in the area favours the earlier era.[60]

Even where the case for a church transformed into a mosque is indisputable, the question of date is still vexed. In the village of Muta'īya, north of and almost equidistant from Samā and Umm al-Surab, Butler[61] examined and described in detail a rather extraordinary structure. The building exhibited distinct traces of Nabataean architectural features which he thought late in date (early second century, or even late third), and secular in nature. Transformation into a mosque was demonstrated by a *miḥrāb* precisely where one would expect to find it, and a square-tower minaret. Oddly, there was no apparent intervening use of the building as a church. Butler himself confused the issue by referring to the building as the "temple-mosque" and terming the earlier style of architecture "pre-Christian" rather than "pre-Constantinian".[62] He was unable to date the transformation other than to say that it occurred when "architecture was an art among [Muslims]."[63] In her article on the decorative arts of the Ḥawrān, Jacqueline Dentzer-Feydy[64] published a striking photograph of the main entrance to that mosque, thus assuring us that it still exists.[65] She notes that it is one of several regional structures for which "seule une étude complète avec quelques sondages nous renseignera sur leur fonction et leur date".[66]

Like Umm al-Jimāl, these are all agricultural/pastoral communities, subsisting on dry farming and animal husbandry. Large and sophisticated

---

[59] King, "Preliminary Survey", 89.
[60] *Ibid.*, 92.
[61] Butler, *PPUAES* II A 88-91. The spelling of the site is there given as Umta'iyeh, which reflects local pronunciation.
[62] *Ibid.*, 88.
[63] *Ibid.*, 91.
[64] "Décor architectural et développement du Hauran dans l'antiquité", in Dentzer, *Hauran* I.2, 261-309.
[65] *Ibid.*, 304, pl. XXIIId.
[66] *Ibid.*, 307.

monastery complexes, such as al-Dayr,[67] south of Bostra, also must have grown and harvested much of their own food, as did the villas. Modern farms have all but obliterated any vestiges of the ancient. While it is almost impossible to identify traces of the ancient fields from ground-level examinations, "centuriation" outlines do appear in aerial photographs of three sites in the southern Ḥawrān.[68] These regular field divisions are most probably the result of large-scale Roman veteran settlement, perhaps one or more ethnic units (Thracians, Illyrians, *Gothi gentiles*) attested near Imtān (ancient Motha) in the third century.[69] Block enlistments of ethnic groups into the Roman army are known, and upon retirement those soldiers would be granted farmsteads. Whether they were numerous enough to make a "colonial" impact is doubtful. Many would have married locally and become part of the Ḥawrān communities in which they settled.

In an area of minimal rainfall the villages and towns relied on extensive water catchment techniques to ensure an adequate supply for human and animal consumption: "... the countryside around [Umm al-Jimāl] was ... extensively subjected to hydraulic engineering. A variety of water diversion, diffusion and storage installations, similar to those in the [Israeli] Negev, for irrigation of fields and watering of flocks, are to be found everywhere in and near the wadis in the country between Umm al-Quttein to the east and Summa to the west. In addition, there are extensive agricultural installations like terraces, corrals and, possibly, barns".[70]

Subsidiary or supplemental cisterns within the town, many of which are still in use, were also a common feature of these communities. Many had vaulted roofs to minimize evaporation and maximize above-ground construction space. That strong and sophisticated tradition of water conservation continued into the Umayyad era. An Arabic inscription of *ca* 730 from Rāmat Ḥāzim attests the construction of a *birka* during the

---

67 Butler, *PPUAES* II A 101-5. Villeneuve, "L'économie rurale", 118-19, notes that the site today is in such a ruined state that only its toponym and Butler's publication could identify it as a convent and not just a "village tardif pauvre".

68 D.L.Kennedy,"Ancient settlements in Syria", *PA* (Sept. 1984), 42-44 (west of Imtān); Villeneuve, "L'économie rurale", pl. VIIb, opp. p. 137 (north of Imtān); Kennedy, "Preliminary Survey", 151-53 and Fig. 2 (Umm al-Quṭṭayn). Contrast those with the field-patterns shown in M. Piccirillo, *Chiese e Mosaici della Giordania Settentrionale* (Jerusalem, 1981), photos 46 (Samā); 47 ((Umm al-Surab) and 51 (Umm al-Jimāl).

69 Kennedy, "Ancient settlements", 44.

70 De Vries, "Urbanization", 254. The hydrological history of Umm al-Jimāl has been the subject of an M.A. thesis (July, 1990) at Yarmouk University, Jordan: Atef M. Kuwaireh, *The Water System at Umm al-Jimal*. An abstract is given in *The Newsletter of the Institute of Archaeology and Anthropology, Yarmouk University* 10 (1990), 13.

caliphate of Hishām.[71] It was noted above that the Roman/Byzantine aqueduct at Umm al-Jimāl was later lengthened and directed to another quarter of the Umayyad town.[72]

The place of farm animals in village life is also well-attested archaeologically. The lower rooms of many houses were used as stables for various species of livestock, with the family resident in an "upper" room. At the very least, the living quarters would be on a raised dais above the area where the livestock were kept.[73] But in at least one instance a two-storey building constructed exclusively for animals has been identified.[74] In that particular case the upper floor was for the storage of grain and fodder. The owners of this "barn" were no doubt residents of a nearby villa, as yet undiscovered. François Villeneuve[75] has drawn attention to two such villas, both within a few kilometres of Bostra. He sees them as characteristic of the Roman period, and monasteries as distinct features of the Byzantine era. That may be so, but given the secure economic conditions which apparently obtained in Byzantine Transjordania, the villas must have been continuously inhabited.[76]

This raises at once the question of property ownership and land tenure in this region. Very little is known about "private" and "public" property. Numerous boundary-stones from the beginning of the Byzantine period have been found in and near villages in the Ḥawrān, and also the Golan immediately to the north-west.[77] These for the most part designate

---

[71] A.K. Rihaoui, "Découverte de deux inscriptions arabes", *AAS* 11/12 (1961/62), 207-8.

[72] De Vries, *op. cit.*, 251.

[73] The nativity scene at Luke 2:7 assumes such a structure; the *kataluma* there mentioned refers to a "guest room", not an "inn". See Kenneth E. Bailey, "The manger and the inn", *Near East Theological Review* 2 (1979), 33-44.

[74] Butler, *PPUAES* II A, 111-12 describes in detail one such stable or barn. Other buildings which Butler identified as churches may well be farm structures; see John Wilkinson, "What Butler saw", *Levant* 16 (1984), 115-16.

[75] Villeneuve, "L'économie rurale", 76.

[76] This was Butler's conclusion regarding the villas at Jimārīn and Burd. He added, "It seems probably that they were either the country residences of the citizens of the metropolis [Bostra], or the homes of a wealthy farming class dependent upon the city for the disposal of their produce" (*PPUAES* II A, 106).

[77] H.I. MacAdam, *Studies in the History of the Roman Province of Arabia*, BAR Int. Ser. 295 (Oxford, 1986), 109, n. 32, for the known boundary-stones. Surveys in the Golan Heights region have revealed three stages (prehistoric, Roman, Ottoman) of agricultural development and one stage (Ghassānid) of pasturage. See Shimon Gibson and Claudine Dauphin, "Landscape archaeology at Er-Ramthaniyye in the Golan Heights", in *Archéologie et espaces. Rencontres internationales d'archéologie et d'histoire*, Éditions APCDA (Juan-les Pins, 1990), 35-45. Fig. 4, p. 41, is a sketch-map of the area presumably based on aerial photos; there is no evidence of centuriation among the field-patterns depicted.

the territorial limits of adjoining villages, or of a village and a city. More of interest, but unfortunately very cryptic, are two boundary-stones which delineate property belonging to a private owner, and imperial property. One is from the village of Samā,[78] the other from nearby Jābir, only six kilometres distant.[79] Both contain the official Greek designation *engaion tamiakon*, i.e. *ager fiscalis*. Villeneuve points to the reign of Justinian for the widespread use of this term.[80]

This is precisely the period in which the Ghassānid phylarchs controlled the region as Byzantine *foederati*. It would be interesting to know what effect their presence had upon the local population. Their main encampments were at al-Jābiya and other sites in or near the Golan and north-western Jordan.[81] A recent archaeological survey of Ramthanīya in the Golan Heights[82] identified a *martyrion* of A.D. 377 dedicated to S. John the Baptist. Some rebuilding, incorporating a mosaic floor, took place in the sixth century. The *martyrion*, probably the focus of an annual pilgrimage, was part of a building complex including a monastery and funerary chapel. The nearby Ghassānid encampment "consisted of clusters of curvilinear [stone?] enclosures serving as tent bases".[83] In the southern Ḥawrān only the monastery at al-Dayr is closely associated with the Ghassānids.[84]

There is some evidence to suggest a fall in population in the Ḥawrān area, given the tentative archaeological evidence from Umm al-Jimāl noted above. Support for this comes from available literary sources. Lawrence Conrad[85] has recently called our attention again to recurrent plagues as a factor in the demographics of late antiquity, particularly for the Near East.

---

[78] Littmann, *PPUAES* III A, 46, no. 28.

[79] G. Lombardi, "Nuove inscrizioni di Jaber", *LA* 6 (1955-56), 312-13, no. 10. Even though Lombardi was aware of the Samā boundary-stone, he misread this damaged inscription as a funeral stele. Correctly restored, it duplicates the Samā inscription: see *SEG* 17 (1960), no. 760. *Archaeology of Jordan* does not register this site.

[80] Villeneuve, "L'économie rurale", 114.

[81] Sartre, *Trois études*, 185, doubts (*contra* Heinz Gaube, *Ein arabischer Palast un Südsyrien: Hirbet el-Beida* [Weisbaden, 1974], BTS 6) that the palace-complex at Khirbat al-Bayḍa is Ghassānid precisely because of its eccentric location far to the east in the Ṣafā' desert.

[82] Gibson and Dauphin (n.77), 43-44.

[83] *Ibid.*, 44.

[84] Sartre, *Trois Études*, 177-88, collected the evidence then available for Ghassānid sites in the area: for al-Dayr see p. 183.

[85] Lawrence I. Conrad, "The Plague in Bilād al-Shām in Pre-Islamic Times", in *Bilād al-Shām* 1986 II, 143-63, based in part on his unpublished doctoral dissertation, *The Plague in the Early Medieval Near East* (Princeton University, 1981).

He has traced sporadic, epidemic outbreaks of bubonic plague from its first identifiable appearance in 541-542 (the "plague of Justinian") through to the end of the Umayyad caliphate in A.D. 750. For evidence of the chronology, distribution and intensity of these various plagues Conrad has consulted the relevant Byzantine, Syriac and Arabic sources. It is clear that northern Syria was especially hard hit. That would help explain the abandonment of so many towns and villages (the "villes mortes") in the limestone massif region made famous by the field surveys of Georges Tchalenko.[86] That area has recently been the focus of archaeological exploration undertaken by the I.F.A.P.O.[87]

The historical tradition testifies to the severity of plagues in Syria/Bilād al-Shām, but is specific only in noting that certain cities (e.g. Jerusalem, Damascus) were affected.[88] For rural areas like the Ḥawrān the evidence is even sketchier. Conrad cites passages in pre-Islamic Arabic poetry for references to fear of the plague among Ghassānid forces.[89] The latter were, of course, deployed in the Ḥawrān and Golan areas, and we may infer that those regions were affected. F.M. Donner[90] has pointed to the plague originating at ʿAmwās[91] in 639 as an underlying cause of the abandonment of al-Jābiya. It is a given of plague dynamics that centres of densest population are the most affected. Therefore it seems odd that the provincial capital, Bostra, is never mentioned. Nor is any other urban centre of Transjordania. All that may be said at present is that for most of those ancient communities of the southern Ḥawrān in which some archaeological work has been done, there is evidence of continuity of habitation *ca.* 550-*ca.* 750. But for several sites, among them Dayr al-Qinn, Saba' Asīr, and Bā'ir, there is no trace of Umayyad occupation. We do not know at present why this was so.

We must now move to the area immediately south and east of the Ḥawrān, a region with an annual rainfall level below 100 mm. Apart from Roman/Byzantine fortifications at Dayr al-Kahf, Qaṣr Burqūʿ, at the al-Azraq Oasis, and at Qaṣr al-Ḥallābāt, no attempt was made to establish permanent civilian settlements. Nor is there proof as yet that those forts

---

86 *Villages antiques de la Syrie du Nord I-III*, BAH 50 (Paris, 1953-58).
87 J.-P. Sodini *et al.*, "Déhès (Syrie du Nord). Campagnes I-III (1976-78): Recherches sur l'habitat rural", *Syria* 57 (1980), 1-305, and see Gatier in this volume.
88 Conrad, *art. cit.*, 151-54.
89 *Ibid.*, 151 and n. 56; 156.
90 Donner, *First Islamic Conquests*, 245 with n. 16.
91 Emmaeus/Nicopolis, 32 kilometres north of Jerusalem; see EI^2 I, 460-61.

were manned beyond the reign of Justinian. But with the Islamic conquest there is evidence (in some cases very limited) that all four fortifications were reactivated, and an elaborate bath was constructed at Quṣayr 'Amra, south-west of al-Azraq. Farther south, in east-central Jordan, half a dozen major palace-complexes were built or were in the process of construction by the time of the 'Abbāsid revolution. Those palaces are not unique, since similar structures are known at other Near Eastern sites, e.g. the "Palace of Hishām" (Khirbat al-Mafjar) on the West Bank, and (perhaps) Qaṣr Abyaḍ on the edge of the Ṣafā' desert in eastern Syria.[92] Several explanations of this "desert castle" phenomenon have been proferred, [93] and to date there is no consensus as to which (if any) is correct.

Geographically and functionally these structures fall into two broad categories: those that are identifiably pre-Islamic with later modifications (Dayr al-Kahf, Burqū', Qaṣr al-Azraq and Qaṣr al-Ḥallābāt in the north-east) and those constructed in the Umayyad period where nothing had stood before (Qasṭal, al-Mshattā, al-Muwaqqar, al-Mushāsh and al-Kharāna further south). Accordingly this survey will examine them in turn within the relevant sections. Also worth noting is their lack of uniformity in design and function. Stephen Urice[94] has pointed out that the *raison d'être* for these installations varies from agricultural to political to recreational to mercantile.

Dayr al-Kahf still awaits excavation.[95] Its size, shape and the associated Greek and Latin epigraphy clearly identify it as an early Byzantine *castellum.* Ruins of ancient field walls, ancient buildings, and a cistern, have been noted in the area surrounding the fort. The place-name Dayr al-Kahf is modern and implies that it was, or was associated with, a monastery "of the caves". Neither the monastery nor the caverns has been identified. It may be that the former related to the Byzantine chapel on the western side of the fort's central courtyard, and the latter to the covered underground cisterns (beneath the court) which, when dry, might have reminded the casual visitor of grottoes or caves.[96] The fort is anepigraphic

---

92 Gaube, *Hirbet el-Beida*, argued that the buildings were Ghassānid, but this seems unlikely (above, n.81) also in view of the Umayyad structures (perhaps including a mosque) at nearby Jabal Says.

93 See e.g. R. Hillenbrand, "*La dolce vita* in Early Islamic Syria: the Evidence of Later Umayyad Palaces", *Art History* 5 (1982), 1-35.

94 *Qasr Kharana in the Transjordan* (Durham, N.C., 1987), 87-88.

95 The site is recorded only as part of the Jawa epigraphic survey in *AJ* II.1.59.

96 Butler, *PPUAES* II A, 145-48; Parker, *Romans and Saracens*, 21-24. Because of the Arabic appellation *Kahf* ("cave"), the site was identified with the Byzantine garrison-post

beyond the late fourth century. There is no identifiable architecture from the Umayyad or any later Islamic period. The pottery sequence from Dayr al-Kahf suggests that the fort was abandoned by the sixth century, but the largest number of sherds is Umayyad, perhaps indicating reactivation of the site.

Qaṣr Burqū'[97] lies some 130 km. northeast of Dayr al-Kahf in the "black desert" of modern Jordan's upper panhandle. It is a walled enclosure with a tower and capacious cistern. Two kilometres to the north-west is a large, seasonal pond created by a dam across a *wādī*. Parker[98] has expressed scepticism that the site was occupied before the late Byzantine period, when it perhaps served only as a forward watch-tower. An Arabic inscription of *ca* A.D. 700 [99] mentions the construction of rooms, and it is probable that the main enclosure was built then, encapsulating the earlier tower. The inscription specifically credits the new construction to al-Walīd, Caliph 'Abd al-Malik's son and successor. Evidence that Burqū' was of major importance to the Umayyads at once raises the question of why. I think Geoffrey King's answer to that is compelling. After his visits to the site in 1980 and 1981 he commented that the "... re-use of Burqū' ... might have had less to do with a princely desire for solitude in the basalt wasteland [as some have held] than with command of the route between northern Arabia and central Syria, and with the political relations of tribes with the Caliphate."[100] A joint Edinburgh University-British Institute ('Ammān) team is beginning to publish its first season's findings (of a three-season survey and excavation) at Burqū'. [101] Results of soundings at the Qaṣr during the 1988 season are still awaited.

---

of *Spelunca* in the early fifth-century provincial register known as the *Notitia Dignitatum* (Oriens, 37). I have suggested recently that the long-accepted equation is unfounded: see "Epigraphy and the *Notitia Dignitatum*," in D. French and C. Lightfoot, eds., *The Eastern Frontier of the Roman Empire*, BAR Int. Ser. 553 (Oxford, 1989), 302.

[97] The site is registered but not discussed in *AJ* II.1.196.

[98] *Romans and Saracens*, 21.

[99] A. Shboul, "On the Later Arabic Inscription in Qasr Burq' ", *ADAJ* 20 (1975), 95-98.

[100] King, "Second Season Report", 416. There is no mention of Burqū' in his "Preliminary Report".

[101] A. Betts, 'The Edinburgh University/B.I.A.A.H. Expedition to Qasr Burq'/ Ruweishid", *Syria* 67 (1990), 471-73, and for more detail, A. Betts et al., "The Burqu'/Ruweishid Project: Preliminary Report on the 1988 Field Season", *Levant* 22 (1990), 1-20. See most recently A. Betts et al., "The Burq'/Ruweishid Project: Preliminary Report on the 1989 Field Season", *ibid.*, 23 (1991), 7-28.

The al-Azraq Oasis[102] lies some hundred kilometres directly east of 'Ammān.[103] Its huge spring-fed, perennial pools and abundant vegetation have been attractions for humans and animals since remote pre-history. It has always been a major stop on the trade route from inner Arabia to Jordan and Syria, and therefore had great strategic value throughout antiquity. A complex of Romano/Byzantine military installations were centred on a Severan *castrum*, later a Diocletianic *castellum*, at Azraq al-Durūz.[104] A few kilometres south, at Azraq al-Shishān, gigantic masonry reservoirs or channels (?) lie partially exposed. They are still undated. Like Dayr al-Kahf to the north, the Azraq fort and its subsidiary installations were almost certainly abandoned by the end of the fifth century.

No sondage or excavation has been undertaken at al-Azraq's main fort, nor anywhere else at the oasis. The ceramic sampling, as Parker admits,[105] is so meagre that no conclusions can be drawn. Most of the sherds were either Late Roman/Early Byzantine or Ottoman, with some Umayyad and Ayyūbid/Mamlūk specimens represented. The only Arabic epigraphy from the fort is Ayyūbid.[106] The small mosque within the courtyard was probably built then. There is nothing identifiably Umayyad in the architectural features of the fort, but it seems inconceivable that such a structure would not have been occupied immediately after the Islamic conquest. Very probably the rebuilding commemorated by the Ayyūbid inscription removed the surface evidence of Umayyad date, but only excavation will confirm this. Within the fort are a series of basalt bas-relief sculptures of wildlife and vegetation, presumably representative of the flora and fauna of the oasis. These have yet to be published in their entirety. I would venture to guess that they date to the Umayyad period, and are perhaps contemporary with the vivid, recently-restored representations of animals and humans in the frescoes of nearby Quṣayr 'Amra[107] and Qaṣr al-Ḥallābāt.[108] An Umayyad presence at the fort and

---

[102] The site is mentioned but not discussed in *AJ* II.1, 183.
[103] Parker, *Romans and Saracens*, 21-37.
[104] A British aerial photograph of 1928 clearly shows the outline of the larger, earlier fortification; see Bowersock, *Roman Arabia*, pl. 12.
[105] *Romans and Saracens*, 20.
[106] Kennedy, *Archaeological Explorations*, 77. The text records the (re)construction of the fort in 1237.
[107] Oleg Grabar, "La palace de Qusayr Amrah dans l'art profane de Haut Moyen Age", *CA* 36 (1988), 75-83.
[108] Ghazi Bisheh, "Qasr al-Hallabat: A Summary of the 1984 and 1985 Excavations", *AfO* 33 (1986), 158-62, at 160, fig. 23.

interest in developing the oasis may explain the elaborate "reservoirs" at al-Shishān.

The westernmost of these fortifications is Qaṣr al-Ḥallābāt,[109] twenty kilometres north-east of 'Ammān. A Latin military inscription attests the rebuilding of a fort in the early third century. A Greek inscription of Justinianic date (529) also attests rebuilding, but it is not at all certain that either stone belongs to al-Ḥallābāt.[110] It has long been clear to investigators that much Umayyad building now obscures the earlier, and much smaller, Romano/Byzantine fortifications. It is unclear how long the fort remained garrisoned, as later constructions all but totally obscured it. Since 1979, ongoing excavations have identified the extent and purpose of the Umayyad settlement at al-Ḥallābāt.[111] The main structure does not owe its form or function to any earlier building. The mosque which stands just without the fort, and a bath complex (Ḥammām al-Sarākh)[112] two kilometres to the east, are characteristically Umayyad. These new structures were central to a large farmstead which depended upon an elaborate hydrological system of dams, cisterns and aqueducts, somewhat reminiscent of the water catchment system at Umm al-Jimāl to the north.[113] There is no evidence of occupation at al-Ḥallābāt in the 'Abbāsid period or later.

2. North-western Jordan

North-western Jordan (Fig. 12) is distinctly different from its north-eastern counterpart. It is not the sharp contrast one encounters moving from desert to oasis, but remarkable nonetheless. The flat Ḥawrān plain with its characteristic basalt architecture, and a skyline against which

---

109 *AJ* II.1, 245-51. To the bibliography there and in *AJ* I.1, 209 add Parker, *Romans and Saracens*, 30-32, and see n. 110 below.

110 H.I.MacAdam, "Some Notes on the Umayyad Occupation of North-East Jordan", in P.M.W. Freeman and D.L. Kennedy, eds., *The Defence of the Roman and Byzantine East*, BAR Int. Ser. 297 (Oxford, 1986), 540 with n. 10. Bisheh, "Qasr al-Hallabat", 161-62, suggests al-Jimāl or al-Samrā' as the origin of the inscriptions.

111 The earlier seasons' work is summarized in G. Bisheh, "Qasr al-Hallabat: an Umayyad Desert Retreat or Farm Land?", in *SHAJ* II (1985), 263-65, and in R. Khouri, *The Desert Castles (Amman, Al Kutba)*, Jordan Guides Series, 27-30; see also his "Enigmas in Stone", *Aramco World* (Sept./Oct., 1990), 34-35.

112 Ghazi Bisheh, "Hammam al-Sarah in the Light of Recent Excavations", *DM* 4 (1989), 225-29.

113 What had been described as a Roman "fortlet": at Qaṣr 'Ayn Sūl, two kilometres north-east of al-Azraq, is probably a mini-version of the al-Ḥallābāt agricultural estate; see Parker, *Romans and Saracens*, 20, with Khouri, *Desert Castles*, 31-32. The third-century Roman milestone reused as a millstone pivot came from the Roman road between al-Azraq and Dayr al-Kahf; see D.L. Kennedy and H.I. MacAdam, "Latin Inscriptions from the Azraq Oasis, Jordan", *ZPE* 60 (1985), 105.

volcanic craters are silhouetted, gives way to a plateau of rolling hills, shaded valleys and more abundant water. Farther west the plateau makes a steep descent to the Jordan River Valley, the central portion of which is some 300-400 metres below sea level.

The plateau proper, the Gilead of the Old Testament, is a landscape of verdant valleys and hillsides tinged with shades of soft green.[114] This is apparent to the traveller whether one approaches from the east, e.g. from al-Azraq and al-Ḥallābāt, or from the north (e.g. Damascus and Dar'a). That belt of vegetation extends from the southern edge of the Golan and the Wādī Yarmūk south to the Wādī Zarqā' between Jarash and 'Ammān. This profusion of natural beauty was noted late in the Hellenistic period by the poet Meleager of Gadara (fl. *ca* 90 B.C.) in his "Song of Spring".[115] Meleager's epitaph (which he composed himself) bears witness to his multicultural background. Its final invocations are justly famous: "If you are Syrian, *salaam*!; if Phoenician, *naidius*!; and if Greek, *khaire*! All say the same."[116] Had he lived two and a half centuries later, in the full flower of the Antonine period, he might have added "And if Roman, *ave*!"

Within Meleager's lifetime or shortly thereafter this region became one of urban communities, cities each of which boasted a constitution, coinage, calendar and a *chora* (*territorium*). All those aspects bespeak, by the onset of the Byzantine age, a long tradition of Graeco-Roman culture. It is no accident that six of the ten Decapolis communities were to be found here: Gerasa, Gadara, Pella, Abila, Hippos, and Dium.[117] Of these six, only Pella and Hippos are not situated on the high plateau. Pella lies in the foothills of the northern sector of the central Jordan Valley at sea level, with Hippos on the valley floor just east of the Sea of Galilee. The location of Dium alone has not yet been settled.

---

[114] Rainfall average ranges from 300 mm to 600 mm per year depending on altitude; see Peter Beaumont, "Man Induced Erosion in Northern Jordan", *SHAJ* II (1985), 291-96, esp. 291-93 and the isohyet chart on p. 293.

[115] *Anth. Pal.* IX.363 – a marvellous mosaic of vernal images: meadows, flowers, birdsong, bees, berries, shepherds, flocks, swans afloat and ships asail. While the poem may of course reflect a literary *topos*, everything evoked in it is nevertheless visible from Meleager's hometown on the great bluff overlooking the confluence of the Yarmūk and Jordan rivers, just south of the Sea of Galilee.

[116] *Anth. Pal.* VII.419, ll.6-7.

[117] Philadelphia, Damascus, Canatha and Raphana round out the list of ten given by Pliny, *NH* 5.74. If Raphana is to be identified with Capitolias/Bayt Rās, this would be the seventh city in the north-western region. Coins of Capitolias attest an era beginning in A.D. 98/99, which is perhaps best interpreted as a refoundation date, the significance of which is as yet unknown.

It is probable that the territories of the six were contiguous, incorporating all the settlements of the region. Since the 1960s, and to a much greater degree since the 1970s, archaeological and epigraphic surveys, and major excavations, have transformed our knowledge of this area's history. I shall briefly review the latest publications generated by these activities, and then assess the evidence pertaining to late antiquity and early Islam. Because this region was highly urbanized, and partly because some of the cities had biblical associations, much money, time and effort has been expended in large-scale, multi-team excavations at certain sites. But several towns and smaller settlements have also been investigated, and that evidence, plus the results of regional surveys, must also be considered. In all cases, sites discussed are a representative selection.[118]

The cities belonging to the Decapolis, naturally, have received the lion's share of scholarly attention.[119] At Pella (Ṭabaqāt al-Fiḥl), teams from Wooster College in the U.S.A (since 1967), and from the University of Sydney (since 1979) have begun full-scale excavations of several sectors at the site.[120] The Jerash Archaeological Project brought multi-national teams together on that site in the early 1980s, but subsequent funding problems have limited the scope of operations and drastically reduced the number and nationality of participants.[121] Gadara (Umm Qays) has been the scene

---

[118] One may note in passing that many promising sites in the central Jordan Valley, surveyed in the 1950's, were threatened by inundation. See James Mellaart, "Preliminary Report of the Archaeological Survey in the Yarmuk and Jordan Valleys for the Point Four Irrigation Scheme", *ADAJ* 6/7 (1962), 126-57. Mellaart registered ninety-one sites, sixty-nine on the east bank and the remainder on the west.At my count, twenty-eight of the east bank sites yielded evidence of Byzantine/Islamic settlement (see the map of sites following Pl. XXXII). These were either farmsteads, villages, fortresses or "unidentified". Only a few (e.g. Tell Dayr Allāh) were later excavated. For additional notes on selected sites see Henry Contenson, "The 1953 Survey in the Yarmuk and Jordan Valleys", *ADAJ* 8/9 (1964), 30-46.

[119] For a general survey of research into the history of the Decapolis up to the early 1960's, see H. Bietenhard, "Die Dekapolis von Pompeius bis Traian", *ZDPV* 79 (1963), 24-58 (repr. with minor revisions and a map, in *ANRW* II.8 (1977), 221-51). For research up to the mid-1970's, see E. Schürer, *The History of the Jewish People in the Time of Jesus Christ II* (Edinburgh, 1979), 130-32 (Hippos); 132-36 (Gadara); 135-37 (Abila); 137-38 (Raphana); 145-48 (Pella); 148-49 (Dium); 149-55 (Gerasa). For an assessment of one facet of the plastic arts in the region, see Thomas Weber, "A Survey of Roman Sculpture in the Decapolis: Preliminary Report", *ADAJ* 34 (1990), 351-55.

[120] *AJ* II.2, 406-41. To the bibliography there add Robert H. Smith, "Trade in the Life of Pella of the Decapolis", *SHAJ* III (1987), 53-58, with R.H. Smith and Leslie Preston Day, *Pella of the Decapolis* 2 (Wooster, 1989), and P.C.Edwards *et al.*, "Preliminary Report on the University of Sydney's Tenth Season of Excavations at Pella in 1988", *ADAJ* 34 (1990), 57-93.

[121] To the bibliography in *AJ* II.1, 316-37 and I I.1, 214-17, add Carol Meyer, "Glass from the North Theater Byzantine Church, and Soundings at Jerash, Jordan, 1982-1983", in Walter E. Rast, ed., *BASOR* Suppl. no. 25 (Baltimore, 1988), 175-222. The account in

of intense and prolonged investigation since 1974 under the aegis of the German Evangelical Institute in Jerusalem, and from 1976 by the German Protestant Institute for Archaeology ('Ammān), Liebieghaus (Frankfurt-am-Main), and the German Archaeological Institute (Berlin).[122] From 1977 to 1983 the Foundation for Danish Research in Palestine undertook excavation and restoration of the Roman baths.[123]

Abila was the subject of a field survey in 1980, and excavations every two years since then by a team from Covenant Theological Seminary (St. Louis, U.S.A.).[124] Hippos (Qal'at al-Ḥuṣn/Susīya) was partially excavated by the Israel Exploration Society in the late 1950s.[125] As noted above, the

---

AJ II.1 is inadequate for understanding the aim and scope of present activities at the site. Large-scale work at Jarash was initiated in 1975-76 by the Department of Archaeology at the University of Jordan, and the Jordanian Department of Antiquities. For a preliminary report see Asem N. Barghouti, "Urbanization of Palestine and Jordan in Hellenistic and Roman Times", *SHAJ* I (1982), 209-29, esp. 218-28. A final report of that truncated project has not been published. The "Jerash International Project for Excavation and Restoration" was launched in 1981 with teams from Australia, Britain, France, Italy, Jordan and Poland. Two major publications have since appeared: Fawzi Zayadine, ed., *Jerash Archaeological Project: 1981-1983* I (Amman, 1986) and *Jerash Archaeological Project: 1984-1988* II, IFAPO 18 (Paris, 1989), with a preface by F. Zayadine. The latter is a reprint of related articles which appeared in *Syria* 66 (1989), 1-261. Nearly all of *MB* 62 (1990), is devoted to Jarash. A recent comprehensive account of the city's history for the non-specialist is R. Khouri's *Jerash: A Frontier City of the Roman East* (London, 1986).

[122] *AJ* II.2, 597-611. To the bibliography there add Thomas Weber and Rami Khouri, *Umm Qais: Gadara of the Decapolis* (Amman, 1989); Birgit Mershen and Ernst Axel Knauf, "From Gadar to Umm Qais", *ZPDV* 104 (1988), 128-45; Thomas Weber and Adolph Hoffmann, "Gadara of the Decapolis: Preliminary Report of the 1989 Season", *ADAJ* 34 (1990). 321-42. The modern habitations that are bonded into the ancient site have been succumbing to archaeological intrusions since the early 1980's. Happily, the architecture and other important features of the living village have been recorded; see Heinz Gaube, "Nabi Hut/Umm Qais/Sattana", *AfO* 33 (1986), 177-78, with Seteney Shami, "Umm Qais: A Northern Jordanian Village in Context", *SHAJ* III (1987), 211-13.

[123] Svend Holm-Nielsen *et al.*, "The Excavation of Byzantine Baths in Umm Queis", *ADAJ* 30 (1986), 219-32. The final report by the Danish team is to appear in the series *Abhandlungen des deutschen Palästinavereins.* Other baths associated with Gadara (within its *territorium*, which extended north-west to the Yarmūk River) were excavated by an Israeli team in the late 1970's; see Y. Hirschfeld and G. Solar, "The Roman Thermae at Hammat Gader: Preliminary Report of Three Seasons of Excavation", *IEJ* 31 (1981), 197-219.

[124] *AJ* II.2, 472-86. See also W. Harold Mare, "Quwailiba: Abila of the Decapolis", *AfO* 33 (1986), 206-9 and the bibliography there cited; idem, "Abila", *AJA* 95 (1991), 272-74.

[125] The Israeli Department of Antiquities announced that it had "undertaken exploratory work at Hippos" in *IEJ* 1 (1950-51), 121, and later reported the discovery of a nymphaeum, a large basilica (sixth century) a cathedral and six short Greek inscriptions ("Notes and News", *ibid.*, 3 [1953], 133). Thereafter the focus of the excavations shifted to the Iron Age sector of the site; see Benjamin Mazar *et al.*, "Ein Gev: Excavations in 1961", *IEJ* 14 (1964), 1-49, esp. 32. Excavation continued until at least the late 1970s; see "Notes and News", *IEJ* 28 (1978), 262. On a religious aspect of the site see A. Ovadiah, "Was the Cult of the God Dushara-Dusares Practised in Hippos-Susitha?", *PEQ* 113 (1981), 101-4.

location of Dium is not settled.[126] Capitolias (Bayt Rās) and Arbela (Tell Irbid) also ranked among the important regional *poleis*. They were recently surveyed together by a team from the Institute of Archaeology and Architecture at Yarmuk University (Irbid).[127] The modern, expanding village of Bayt Rās is so firmly imbedded upon the ancient site of Capitolias that only piecemeal, rescue archaeology has been attempted.[128] Some of the vaulted street-front shops in the *sūq* of the ancient city have been exposed. This is also a feature at Gadara and Jarash.[129] Capitolias' fourth-century church, described by Schumacher a century ago, has been partly excavated. Structural modifications were made between the seventh and ninth centuries. This may reflect a general alteration of the city plan at that time. On the Rās itself, the city's acropolis, frescoes found *in situ* on interior walls of a yet-unidentified structure date to the eighth or ninth century.[130] Surveys of Tell Irbid and its immediate surroundings began in the 1960s. By the mid-1980s, the expansion of the modern city began to destroy areas of the southern edge of the Tell, and rescue archaeology was undertaken by the Jordanian Department of Antiquities and Yarmuk University.[131]

There are no natural springs at any sites within the Irbid-Bayt Rās survey area, so that the water catchement systems must be carefully examined. The modern villages of Kafr Ghāyīz and Tubqul, close to the secondary Roman road, were probably villas or farmsteads in late antiquity.[132] Just five kilometres south of Irbid, but outside the survey area, is Ham.[133] The modern village spreads up facing hillsides, and all but obscures the remains of the ancient site. The perennial spring west of the village may be its *raison d'être*. A 1984 survey produced late Roman,

---

[126] Schürer, *History* II, 148-49 discusses the various modern sites proposed as its location. To the bibliography there cited add Christian Augé, "Sur le monnayage de Dion 'de Coelé-Syrie'", in Gatier *et al.*, *Géographie Historique*, 325-41.

[127] Cherie J. Lenzen, "Tall Irbid and Bait Râs", *AfO* 33 (1986), 164-66, with bibliography. The area to be surveyed is approximately five kilometres in circumference and incorporates subsidiary sites. By 1985 some twelve square kilometres had been investigated. See also *AJ* II.1, 55-56; *AJA* 95 (1991), 271-72.

[128] Alison McQuitty, "Bait Ras", *AfO* 33 (1986), 153-55; C.J.Lenzen and E.A.Knauf, "Beit Ras/Capitolias: A Preliminary Evaluation of the Archaeological and Textual Evidence", *Syria* 64 (1987), 21-46; C.J. Lenzen, "Beit Ras Excavations: 1988 and 1989", *ibid.* 67 (1990), 474-76.

[129] Weber and Khouri, *Gadara*, 24. For comparative purposes see Khaled As'ad and Franciszek M. Steppniowski, "The Umayyad Suq in Palmyra", *DM* 4 (1989), 205-23.

[130] Lenzen, "Beit Ras Excavations", 474.

[131] C.J. Lenzen and E.A. Knauf, "Irbid (Jordanie)", *RB* 95 (1988), 239-47, with bibliography at 239-40, nn. 1-8.

[132] Lenzen, "Tall Irbid and Bait Râs", 164.

[133] *AJ* II.1, 252-53.

Byzantine and Umayyad ceramics, and a late Roman tomb. Additional excavation is planned by the Department of Antiquities. The site of Yasīla, about eight kilometres east of Irbid, yielded remains of a fifth-sixth century church which continued in use at least through the Ayyūbid/Mamlūk period.[134]

East and south of Jarash is a scatter of small villages, several of which are identifiably Byzantine[135] Riḥāb and Khirbat al-Samrā'[136] are * perhaps the best known. Both are vivid examples of the Byzantine predilection for church-building which is so evident throughout Transjordania. Each town boasts no fewer than eight such structures. Well-preserved mosaic inscriptions at Riḥāb attest that all the churches were built within the last century (533-635) before the Islamic conquest.[137] Mosaic inscriptions at three churches in Samrā' can be dated to the first half of the eighth century. Though the churches antedate the epigraphy, their construction cannot be earlier than the first half of the seventh century.[138]

The marked difference in span of habitation of the two towns is worth noting. Riḥāb demonstrates no Hellenistic or Roman history; the Byzantine settlement must look back to the Iron Age for its predecessor. Al-Samrā' would seem to have been continuously inhabited from the Nabataean period onward, and owes its transformation from obscure village into prosperous town to the nearby Roman road. Another contrast is the purely civilian aspect of Riḥāb and the clearly military aspect of al-Samrā'. The latter boasted not only a Byzantine fortress within the town, but an auxiliary fortlet beside the Roman highway.

Apart from mosaic inscriptions, the epigraphy of Riḥāb is sparse. Al-Samrā's cemetery, however, has been an epigraphic harvest for the

---

134 See the MA thesis (Yarmouk University) by Maysoun F. al-Khoury, *Mosaic Pavements of the Church of Yasileh: A Comparative Study with Some Mosaic Pavements of Northern Jordan Churches* (December 1990); abstract in the *Newsletter of the Institute of Archaeology and Anthropology, Yarmouk University* 10 (1990), 14.

135 Piccirillo, *Chiese e Mosaici*, 97-101.

136 *AJ* II.2, 554-57. To the bibliography there add Jean-Baptiste Humbert and Alain Desreumaux, "Khirbet as-Samra'", *CFAJ* (1989), 113-21; *idem*, "Huit campagnes de fouilles au Khirbet as-Samra (1981-1989)", *RB* 97(1990), 252-69. I am indebted to Fr. Humbert for providing offprints of recent articles on this site and for a comprehensive bibliography of publications relating to it. Al-Samra's ancient name was spelled Aditha or Hatita; see Parker, *Romans and Saracens*, 30. A variant of the former, Adeitha, is now attested in a Greek inscription found near the site: "Huit campagnes", 254. For the first of several volumes of full reports on this site see *Hirbet es-Samra I: Voie Romaine et Documents Épigraphiques* (Paris, 1992).

137 Piccirillo, *Chiese e Mosaici*, 67-90.

138 J.P. Humbert, "Khirbet es Samra: la route et questions de chronologie", *SHAJ* III * (1987), 309.

excavators. Noteworthy are the approximately seventy Melkite Aramaic or Syro-Palestinian funeral *stelai* inscriptions so far discovered, which the excavators would date by palaeographic means to the seventh or eighth century.[139] Thirty tombstones inscribed in Greek attest to the bi-lingual * character of the community. There is a distinct (but naive) Egyptian influence in the mosaic art from Khirbat al-Samrā', a feature it shares with Jarash and several other village mosaics from the northwest of Jordan.[140] For reasons still obscure Riḥāb was abandoned about the time of the Islamic conquest, but al-Samrā' flourished for another century.

West and north-west of Jarash, in the district of which the great Ayyūbid castle at 'Ajlūn is the central feature, more than two dozen villages and several hundred isolated sites have been surveyed.[141] The Byzantine period is well-represented, and Piccirillo[142] has already catalogued some of the more important ecclesiastical remains. At Umm Manābi' an attractive floor mosaic from a Byzantine church depicts a stylized representation of Egypt (labelled in Greek *Egyptos*) in conjuction with a Nilotic scene featuring a boat, a fish and a calibrated Nilometer![143] Listāb [144] lies just five kilometres north-west of 'Ajlūn. Several surface surveys indicate continuous habitation of the tell between the Roman period and the present, with abundant Byzantine and Islamic ceramics. Between 'Ajlūn and Pella, recent field surveys centered on the Wādī Yābis[145]

---

139 Humbert and Desreumaux, "Huit campagnes", 266. The Greek (and a few Latin) inscriptions will appear in *IJ* Vol. I (northern Jordan), now in preparation by P.-L. Gatier, who dates the Greek inscriptions to the sixth and seventh centuries, but suggests that the Aramaic inscriptions may be later. The Aramaic texts will be published by Desreumaux; see the latter's preliminary report, "La naissance d'une nouvelle écriture araméenne à l'époque byzantine", *Semitica* 37 (1987), 95-107; *idem*, "Les araméens melkites: vie et mort d'une communauté chrétienne à l'époque byzantine", *CANAL INFOS* 6 (1989-90), 9-30. I wish to thank the author for bringing these publications to my attention.

140 Humbert, "Khirbet es-Samra", 310.

141 A. Augustinovic and R. Bagatti, "Escursioni nel dintorni di 'Ajlun", *LA* 2 (1951), 227-314. See the bibliography for this site in *AJ* I.1, 193; it is not recorded among the register of surveys in *AJ* II.1, 12-97. On more recent work in the area see Jean Sapin, "Prospection géo-archéologique de 'Ajloun oriental", *CFAJ* (1989), 30-35. Thirty "secteurs" were explored and mapped, yielding evidence of settlements from prehistoric times through to the Islamic era.

142 *Chiese e Mosaici*, 16-27.

143 *Ibid.*, 21-23, with the sketch facing p. 23. The attraction of Egyptian themes is undoubtedly Biblical.

144 *AJ* II.2, 368-73 with bibliography.

145 AJ II.1, 91-97 (the 1987 season). Twenty-nine Roman and sixty-two Byzantine sites were identified; this was "an all-time pre-modern peak in population and agricultural production ... in the wadi basin" (*ibid.*, 96). See now Gaetano Palumbo *et al.*, "Survey in the Wadi el-Yabis, 1989", *Syria* 67 (1990), 479-81; *idem*, "The Wadi el-Yabis Survey: Report on the 1989 Season", *ADAJ* 34 (1990), 95-118. The latter report concentrates on

recorded scores of sites in the 186 km^2 area. An unspecified number date to the Late Roman, Byzantine and early Islamic periods. Noted in passing was an "early mosque [at Khirbet 'Usaym] recently cleared by the Jordanian [University's] Department of Religion."[146] Nothing more is presently known.

Several sites in the central Jordan valley are worth noting. Abū Sarbūt and Abū Ghurdān lie just a few kms. from each other on the northern bank of the Wādī Zarqā'. Abū Ghurdān[147] is in fact situated just across the modern road from the famous Bronze/Iron Age site of Tell Dayr Allāh, and Abū Sarbūt [148] is just under two kilometres south/south-west of there. Both sites are *ca* 200-*ca* 250 m. below sea level. Abū Ghurdān seems to have been an Umayyad foundation which may have served as an administrative centre until its abandonment in the 'Abbāsid period. Abū Sarbūt was a Byzantine foundation which lasted through to the end of the Umayyad period. The nature of the settlement is unknown, since no sub-surface archaeological work has been done. Both sites were resettled in the Ayyūbid/Mamlūk period. Tell Nimrīn [149] (perhaps Biblical Beth-Nimrah) lies on the edge of the central Jordan Valley floor, sixteen kilometres east of Jericho. Though the site's occupational profile extends from the Middle Bronze age through to the late Islamic period, the upper portions of the tell (3-5 m. of material, from Roman to Ayyūbid/Mamlūk) was levelled due to recent military activity. Fr. Piccirillo has published the remains of a Byzantine church discovered at the south-west corner of the tell in the early 1980's.[150]

Among the major military sites of north-west Transjordania is Fidayn,[151] on the *wādī* of the same name. The ancient castle dominates the Mafraq plain, at the juncture of the Roman road from Gerasa to Adraa (Dar'a) and a branch road to Bostra. Fidayn is attested by that name as a

---

the Palaeolithic/Bronze Age sites, which are scattered throughout a 20 km^2 portion of the survey area.

146 Palumbo, "Wadi el-Yabis", 480.

147 *AJ* II.1, 99-101.

148 *Ibid.*, 118-20.

149 James W. Flanagan and David W. McCreery, "First Preliminary Report of the 1989 Tell Nimrin Project", *ADAJ* 34 (1990),131-52, with Rudolph H. Dornemann, "Preliminary Traditions at Tell Nimrin", *ibid.*, 153-81.

150 M. Piccirillo, "A Church at Shunat Nimrin", *ADAJ* 26 (1982), 335-42.

151 *AJ* II.1, 22124. To the bibliography there add J.-B. Humbert, "El-Fedein/Mafraq", *CFAJ* (1989), 124-31.

Monophysite monastery early in the reign of Justin II (*ca* 571),[152] and portions of a Byzantine church (perhaps part of a monastery complex) have been uncovered. The strategic value of the site was not utilized until the time of the Umayyads; the transformation from fortress to palace probably took place under al-Walīd II. Major damage to the structure may have been due to the earthquake of 747-48. Repairs were made by the ʻAbbāsids, and the site remained a major stop on the pilgrim route to the Ḥijāz.

We may now return briefly to assess the evidence for this transitional period among the "Decapolis" cities. Let us begin with the largest and most splendidly-adorned of those communities. Jarash boasted at least fifteen churches by the early seventh century, but that number is likely to continue to grow as the site is excavated. The most recently discovered church is that dedicated to Bishop Marianus,[153] built in 570. The small bath complex built by Bishop Placcus in 454-55 was restored in 584.[154] But in spite of the ongoing ecclesiastical construction, the archaeological evidence so far indicates a period of economic decline and perhaps a shrinking of population. This is most evident in the northern sector of the city, where shops and public buildings of the Roman period were later used as stables. The North Theatre, now nearly completely excavated, had not been in use since the fifth century. The effect of the Sasanian occupation of the city (614-28) is difficult to assess.

It is clear that Jarash experienced a revival under Umayyad rule. The southern portion of the city was developed as a residential area *ca* 660, following the disastrous earthquake of 648. The fallen Romano/Byzantine structures were cleared (some to bedrock) and a complex of houses erected near the south *decumanus*. Polish excavations there in 1982-83 [155] revealed the ground plan of the project. Some structures stand to a height of four and a half metres. One Umayyad house, "a rare example of domestic urban architecture of this period", has been restored.[156] The one mosque so far discovered is modest both in size and design. The eight Umayyad kilns built into sections of the North Theatre are probably contemporary with the

---

[152] Nöldeke, "Topographie", 433 with n.1. Nöldeke cites Sozomen, *HE* VI.33 for the Greek spelling *Phadana*.
[153] Michael Gawlikowski and Ali Musa, "The Church of Bishop Marianus", *JAP* I (1986), 137-62. Only the church of Genesius (611) is later in date.
[154] Khouri, *Jerash*, 116-7.
[155] M. Gawlikowski, "A Residential Area by the South Decumanus", *JAP* I (1986), 107-36.
[156] *Ibid.*, 111-14; cf.120, and see also 108, fig. 1.

residential complex.[157] They are best interpreted as evidence for a substantial Umayyad ceramics industry at Jarash, although apart from "exporting" to its neighboring cities of Pella and Gadara it is not clear what the extent of the market actually was. Another indication of the city's pre-eminent status is the recent discovery that Gerasene coins were struck under the aegis of a minting official, first in the late Byzantine period, and then again in Umayyad times.[158] But the period of renewed prosperity had peaked by the onset of the 'Abbāsid age, even though Jarash was spared seismic damage in the earthquake of 747/748. To date there is no evidence of occupation beyond the eighth century from the excavated areas of the city.[159] The circumstances of this abandonment are presently not clear.

Archaeologically, Pella is one of the richest sites in Transjordania, with attested occupation from Palaeolithic to modern times.[160] The evidence to date demonstrates that the peak of Pella's population and prosperity was reached in the Byzantine period. Three churches are so far known, one of which was part of a monastery complex. All are of fifth or sixth-century date.[161] The Sydney team excavated a 1,700m^2 portion of the city's residential sector. The Byzantine pottery sequence continues through to the mid-seventh century, by which time the city limits had expanded to the summit of nearby Tell Ḥuṣn.

Pella surrendered peacefully to Islamic forces in 635.[162] The city was thereafter a district capital of al-Urdunn.[163] Umayyad pottery of Jarash type eventually superseded the Byzantine ware. The impoverishment of the churches stands in puzzling contrast with the evidence of prosperity

---

157 See Vincent A. Clark, "The Jerash North Theater Part II: The Archaeology of the Roman Theater", *JAP* I (1986), 235-39, with Jerome Schaeffer, "An Umayyad Potter's Complex in the North Theater, Jerash", *ibid.*, 411-59.

158 Aïda Naghawi, "Umayyad Filses minted at Jerash", *JAP* II (1989), 219-22.

159 Gawlikowski, "Residential Area", 115-17.

160 The literary sources referring to Pella are conveniently collected and translated in Robert H. Smith *et al.*, *Pella of the Decapolis* 1 (Wooster, 1973), 23-82; for the Byzantine and Early Islamic period see esp. 57-76.

161 Piccirillo, *Chiese e Mosaici*, 15-16. Piccirillo's plan of the site (Pl. 3, Fig. 3) is remarkably different from that in *AJ* II.2, 416, despite that fact that both were drawn by expedition staff. Compare both with the site-plan given in Smith and Day, *Pella* 2, Fig. 1, p.3. The excavation of the "civic complex" is described in detail in the latter volume.

162 Al-Balādhurī, *Futūḥ al-buldān*, 114-15 (ed. De Goeje) (= Philip K. Hitti, *The Origins of the Islamic State* I [New York, 1916], 176-77). The "fierce and bloody battle" here described took place in the hinterland of Pella and does not seem to have affected the city itself. This and other Arabic sources on the capture of Pella are given in Smith, *Pella* 1, 69-72.

163 Alan G. Walmsley, "Pella/Fihl after the Islamic Conquest (A.D. 635-ca. 900): A Convergence of Literary and Archaeological Evidence", *MA* 1 (1988), 142-59.

elsewhere in the city.[164] The decline of the churches may reflect a reduction of the Christian population, perhaps through conversion to Islam, since there is no indication that the overall population declined. From the 1985 season, the excavations produced ʻAbbāsid material, especially new styles of ceramics (plates, lamps, bowls, bottles) which show a revival of the city following the devastating effects of the earthquake of 747-48.

The German excavations at Gadara concentrated on several fields between the upper and lower sectors of the city. Remains of a sixth century church of the "central type" came to light. Among the most recent finds are an underground rock-cut water channel (similar to that at Abila), and evidence that the city's monumental gate (third century) was so poorly planned and constructed that "part of [it] collapsed soon after completion".[165] An Islamic necropolis came to light near the so-called Tiberias Gate. Fifteen tombs have so far been uncovered, dating from Umayyad through to Mamlūk times.[166]

The Danish team spent four seasons excavating and restoring sections of a public bath flanking the *decumanus*. The baths fell into disuse *ca* 600-650. Whether this was due to the Persian or Islamic occupation is unknown. In the Umayyad period the baths were converted into residential quarters. In one room a semi-circular niche may delineate a *miḥrāb*. The baths were levelled by the earthquake of 747/748 and thereafter abandoned until the Mamlūk period. Israeli excavations of the Gadarene baths *extra muros* (at Ḥammat Gader in the Jordan Valley) have yielded more spectacular results, particularly the epigraphic discoveries.[167] A Greek dedication of 5 December, 662, records that a Gadarene Christian official named John oversaw the restoration of the *clibanus* (furnace) for the *thermae* "by provision of" the Caliph Muʻāwiya and "under the direction of ʻAbdullah̄ the son of Abū Hāshim, advisor (*sumboulos*)".[168]

---

[164] "The overall impression gained from the excavations ... is one of respectable wealth and an easy, if provincial, lifestyle in Umayyad Fihl" (*AJ* II.2, 438).

[165] Weber and Hoffmann, "Preliminary Report", 330. On the water channel, *ibid.*, 323-24. The authors have provided a new and excellent topographical map of Gadara, *ibid.*, 322, fig. 1.

[166] *Ibid.*, 331-32.

[167] Judith Green and Yoram Tsafrir, "Greek Inscriptions from Hammat Gader: A Poem by the Empress Eudocia and Two Building Inscriptions", *IEJ* 32 (1982),77-96, esp. 94-96. See also two associated articles: Joshua Blau, "The Transcription of Arabic Words and Names in the Inscription of Muʻawiya from Hammat Gader", *ibid.*, 102; Isaac Hasson, "Remarques sur l'inscription de l'époque de Muʻawiya à Hammat Gader", *ibid.*, 97-101.

[168] *SEG* 30 (1980), no. 1687.

Our knowledge of the history of Abila in the late Byzantine and early Islamic periods is still quite sketchy. Two basilical churches have come to light, both of the sixth century. The residential area of the city is so far unidentified. A recent report notes "a large Umayyad building in the *cavea* area [of the theatre] with a well-paved street in front of it."[169] An elaborate hydraulic system brought water by ground-level aqueduct some 1.4 kilometres from the nearest source ('Ayn Quwāliba). A painted Greek inscription in the upper aqueduct testifies that the system was cleaned in Sept./Oct. of 568.[170] There seems to be no break in occupation until the earthquake of 747-48. According to its excavator,[171] the site was not resettled until the Ayyūbid period: "Abila is not mentioned along with Pella, Gadara and Capitolias as flourishing after the Islamic conquest." The source cited for that statement is so far unavailable to me; nevertheless, it is difficult to reconcile it with the list of towns belonging to the *jund* of al-Urdunn said by Ibn Khurradādhbih (d. ca. 900) to be surviving in the 'Abbāsid period.[172] The cities listed are seven of the traditional Decapolis cities: Baysān (Scythopolis, west of the Jordan), al-Fiḥl (Pella), Jarash (Gerasa), Bayt Rās (Raphana/Capitolias), Jadar (Gadara), Abila and Sūsīya (Hippos). For an assessment of sites in the northwest surveyed by King we must await the publication of a preliminary report.[173]

3. Central Jordan

Central Jordan (Fig. 13) is considered here to be the region between the Wādī Zarqā' in the north and the Wādī Mūjib to the south, and from the Jordan Valley in the west to the desert edge in the east. The plateau area was the core of what Arab geographers called al-Balqā',[174] the ancient districts of Peraea, Ammanitis and Esbonitis combined. Several large portions of the plateau (the Baq'a Valley[175] and the Mādabā Plain) are agriculturally rich and well-watered. Accordingly, such urban centers as 'Ammān (Philadelphia) and Ḥisbān (Esbous), and dozens of lesser settlements, flourished throughout most of antiquity. The export of

---

169 W.H.Mare, "Abila", *AJA* 95 (1991), 273.
170 *Ibid.*
171 *AJ* II.2, 476.
172 *Kitāb al-masālik wa-l-mamālik* (ed. De Goeje, Leiden, 1889), 78.
173 Announced in King, "Second Season Report", 385, n.1.
174 On the various uses of Balqā', see the entry in *EI*² I, 997-98; the etymology is uncertain.
175 Not to be confused with the Lebanese Biqā' Valley between the Lebanon and Anti-Lebanon ranges.

domestic and wild livestock (e.g. horses and onagers)[176] and a lively slave traffic[177] are attested in the Hellenistic era and were undoubtedly viable factors in the economy of the Roman and Byzantine periods.

Philadelphia was a charter member of the Decapolis, and became (with Bostra and Gerasa)[178] one of the more prominent cities of Roman Arabia.[179] Knowledge of its history and institutions in the Byzantine period is still sketchy, but with the help of archaeology and epigraphy the broad outlines are clear. That is also true for other major settlements of the region: Ḥisbān, Mādabā, Ma'īn and Dhibān. The Greek and Latin inscriptions from those towns, and others throughout the central sector of modern Jordan, have recently been published.[180] I shall examine in turn the results of surveys and excavations of the major archaeological sites before turning to 'Ammān. This portion of the paper will conclude with a brief look at recent developments in the history of the Umayyad desert palaces.

Several areas of Jordan's central plateau have been extensively surveyed in the past twenty-five years. A single-season (1977) Belgian expedition concentrated on the area between Ḥisbān and al-Karak in Moab.[181] In subsequent years the same team undertook excavation at Lehūn on the northern edge of the Wādī' l-Mūjib.[182] Since 1968 Andrews University Seminary (Michigan, U.S.A.) has sponsored multi-season surveys and excavations centred on Tell Ḥisbān[183] and Tell al-'Umayrī in

---

[176] See H. Hauben, "'Onagres et Hémionagres' en Transjordanie au IIIe siècle avant J.-C.", *AS* 15 (1984), 89-111.

[177] A papyrus document of *ca* 280 B.C. (*PSI* 406) specifically attests regular slave-trade between "Rabbatamana", i.e. 'Ammān, the Ḥawrān and the Palestinian coast. This memorandum is republished with full commentary (including references to related sources) by David H. Graf and Henry I. MacAdam, "*PSI* 406", as an appendix to Graf's "The Origin of the Nabataeans", *Aram* 2 (1990),68-75.

[178] Ammianus Marcellinus (14.8.13) noted precisely these three cities in his own day as possessing "mighty walls" (*murorum firmitate*).

[179] For a comprehensive account of Greco-Roman and Byzantine 'Ammān, see my chapter on "The History of Philadelphia in the Classical Period", in Alastair Northedge, ed., *Studies on Roman and Islamic 'Amman I: History, Site, Architecture*, British Academy Monographs in Archaeology 3 (Oxford, 1992). For a popular recent account of the city from prehistoric times to the Umayyad period, see Rami Khouri, *Amman: A Brief Guide to the Antiquities* (Amman, 1988).

[180] Pierre-Louis Gatier, *Inscriptions de la Jordanie* 2, *IGLS* 21, *BAH* 114 (Paris, 1986).

[181] Denyse Homès-Fredericq, "Prospections archéologiques en Moab", in A. Théodorides et al.,eds., *Archéologie et philologie dans l'étude des civilisations orientales* (Leuven, 1986), 81-100.

[182] *AJ* II.2, 349-59, with bibliography. The King Survey's "Fourth Preliminary Report" will summarise a later survey of this area: see *ADAJ* 27 (1983), 385, n.1.

[183] Fourteen volumes of Ḥisbān-related studies are projected, of which three have appeared. A register of titles and authors for each volume is given in *AJ* II.1, 267-68. Of

the Mādabā plain, and sites west of Ḥisbān to the edge of the plateau.[184] For more than a decade French teams have conducted excavations and surveys at and near the site of 'Araq al-Amīr west of 'Ammān.[185] Roughly sixty per cent (83 out of 145) of the sites investigated by the French expedition showed signs of habitation in the Roman/Byzantine era. That figure fell to twenty per cent in the early Islamic era, with only thirty sites occupied. Nearly total abandonment of the area occurred in the mid-eighth century.[186]

The Belgian survey recorded Byzantine material from just over half (16 out of 30) of the sites investigated. Since twenty-one sites had produced Roman-period finds, the indications were that during the Byzantine era the region underwent a twenty per cent decrease in settlement. Over a period of five campaigns (1968-76), Andrews University recorded 155 sites, most (125) within ten kilometres of Tell Ḥisbān, and the rest between Ḥisbān and 'Ammān. This is one of the most fertile regions of Transjordania. Roman-period material was evident at only ninety-nine of the sites, but 133 showed traces of Byzantine occupation, and eighty-one of Islamic.[187] The Byzantine sites were not differentiated according to period (i.e. early or late). Twenty-nine sites were identifiably Umayyad, and four 'Abbāsid.[188]

The Andrews team undertook a separate survey of Tell al-'Umayrī and the surrounding area in 1984, collectively called the Mādabā Plains

---

particular interest here will be J. Bjornar Starfjell, *Hesban 8: Byzantine and Early Islamic Strata: A Study of the Stratigraphy of Tell Hesban from the Fourth to the Tenth Centuries A.D.* The literary evidence for the history of Ḥisbān is reviewed by Werner Vyhmeister, "The History of Heshbon from Literary Sources", *AUSS* 6 (1968),158-77; for the Byzantine/Early Islamic period, see esp. 168-71.

184 *AJ* II.1,261-69; add to the bibliography there and in *AJ* I.1,210-12 Lawrence T. Geraty, "The Andrews University Madaba Plains Project: A Preliminary Report on the Second Season (1987)", *AUSS* 26 (1988), 217-52; Randall W. Younker *et al.*, "The Joint Madaba Plains Project: A Preliminary Report of the 1989 Season, including the Regional Survey and Excavations at El-Dreijat, Tell Jawa and Tell el-'Umeiri", *ibid.* 28 (1990), 5-52.

185 *AJ* II.1, 280-97. To the bibliography there and in *AJ* I.1, 212-13, add François Villeneuve, "Prospection archéologique et géographie historique: la région d'Iraq al-Amir (Jordanie)", in P.-L. Gatier *et al.*, eds., *Géographie historique au Proche-Orient* (Paris, 1988), 257-88.

186 Villeneuve, *art. cit.*, 282. There is at present no clear explanation for the abandonment of these sites, though one may suspect seismic damage associated with the earthquake of *ca.* 749.

187 Robert D. Ibach, "Expanded Archaeological Survey of the Hesban Region", in R.S. Boraas and Lawrence T. Geraty, *Heshban 1976* (Berrien Spring, 1978), 201-213, at 212 and Table 1 (= *AUSS* 16 [1976]). See also the final report of the earlier surveys by R.D.Ibach, *Hesban 5: Archaeological Survey of the Hesban Region* (Berrien Spring, 1987).

188 Ibach, "Archaeological Survey", 202-5.

Project.[189] That and two subsequent seasons' work have now been published. The 1984 survey registered another fifty-five sites. Ceramic samplings indicated continuous settlement from the early Roman to the Umayyad period, with scant evidence for the 'Abbāsid period.[190] A similar summary was given in one of the second season (1987) reports.[191] Fifty-five more sites were identified, of which (by my count) twenty-one yielded Byzantine ceramics, but at only one were Umayyad sherds registered.

During the 1989 survey twenty-five new sites were recorded, with the emphasis given to those which illuminated the area's system of food production.[192] Wādī Bishāra, two kilometres west of al-'Umayrī and near a large Roman/Byzantine town, was one such location. On the evidence of water diversion and storage, terraced gardening, and abundant pottery associated with the remains of the nearby town, the suggestion was made that "when the ancient [food producing] system was at its peak [in Roman/Byzantine times], the wadi and the surrounding slopes could have provided tenfold its modern production in vegetable and food crops."[193] No mention was made of this settlement's survival into the Islamic era.

Mādabā[194] lies fifteen kilometres directly south of Ḥisbān. Systematic excavations within the town have been limited to the Roman/Byzantine period. Mosaic inscriptions from Mādabā's eleven churches have provided the names and dates of Byzantine bishops from the sixth and seventh centuries.[195] The churches date to those same centuries. Fr. Piccirillo has published a Greek funeral stele found within Mādabā village, inscribed on the very eve of the Islamic conquest.[196] He also discussed the significance

---

[189] Mention is made of this project in the register of surveys in *AJ* II.1, 13-97, but it receives only a brief notice in the entry on "Hesban", *AJ* II.1, 268-69.

[190] Geraty, "First Season", 100-101.

[191] Geraty, "Second Season", has no summary. See instead L.T. Geraty et al., "The 1987 Season at Tell el-'Umeiri and Vicinity", *ADAJ* 33 (1989), 145-75, esp. 165-74.

[192] Earlier concern for this aspect of the region's history was outlined by L.T.Geraty and Oystein LaBianca, "The Local Environment and Human Food-Procuring Strategies in Jordan: The Case of Tell Hesban and its Surrounding Region", *SHAJ* II (1985), 323-30.

[193] Younker, "Third Season", 9-10.

[194] *AJ* II.2, 374-75.

[195] The dates range from 562 to 663. Most of the inscriptions concern church activities, but several commemorate the building or repair of cisterns. See *IJ* 2, 131-32; 135; 140-41; 145; 147; see M. Piccirillo, *Chiese e Mosaici di Madaba* (Jerusalem, 1989). One undated Greek inscription (*IJ* 2, 137) substitutes for *lakkos* a transliteration of the Aramaic term for cistern, *goubba*.

[196] M. Piccirillo, "Un' iscrizione imperiale e alcune stele funerarie di Madaba e di Kerak", *LA* 39 (1989), 114, no. 10 (Fig. 13); the date is 633.

of a building which he classified as "il primo caso di architettura civile de Madaba bizantina".[197]

Mādabā's most famous relic of the Byzantine age is the damaged but still-spectacular mosaic map[198] discovered a century ago in the Church of S. John. Yoram Tsafrir[199] has compared the Latin text of the first portion of Theodosius' *De Situ Terrae Sanctae* (*ca.* 518-30) with many of the Greek captions on the Mādabā map. He suggests that the mosaic cartographer translated segments of the *De Situ*, and also used a pilgrim's guide (or guides) available to Theodosius. Until recently a late sixth-century date for the mosaic map found wide acceptance. But Pauline Donceel-Voûte[200] has now argued for a date in the first half of the seventh-century, based on stylistic features, iconography, propagandistic tendencies, and the prominence of the Transjordanian bishoprics at that time. Though her modified dating is not convincing, the critical examination of the religio-political motives in the creation of the map deserves consideration, not least for the light it sheds on the socio-economic status of even so modest a town as Mādabā.

Ma'īn[201] lies some eight km. southwest of Mādabā. The town has long been identified with the Ba'al Ma'on of the Old Testament (Num. 32; 38; Josh. 13; 17), but there is to date no evidence from the site of settlement at any other period than the Byzantine. Fr. Piccirillo has excavated the ruins of a monastery (Khirbat Dayr) and the town's Western Church. Mosaic inscriptions (one of which is dated 719-20) from the church on the acropolis not only show the Christian community flourishing, but have yielded a number of Palestinian/Jordanian place-names.[202] Remains of a *xenion* (inn) and of a *pribaton* (bath) were found just north of Ma'īn, and the artifacts from a tomb dating to *ca.* 600 have been published.[203]

---

197 M. Piccirillo, "Il palazzo bruciato di Madaba", *LA* 36 (1986), 317-34, at 326.

198 The literature on the Mādabā map is extensive and still growing: see e.g. the bibliographies by Herbert Donner and Heinz Cüppers, *Die Mosaikkarte von Madaba* (Weisbaden, 1977), xi-xvi, and Gatier, *IJ* 2, 148-49.

199 "The Maps Used by Theodosius: On the Pilgrim Maps of the Holy Land and Jerusalem in the Sixth Century C.E.", *DOP* 40 (1986), 129-45.

200 "La carte de Madaba: cosmographie, anachronisme et propaganda", *RB* 95 (1988), 519-42, esp. 536-40.

201 *AJ* II.2, 376-77.

202 Roland DeVaux, "Un mosaïque byzantin à Ma'in (Transjordanie)", *RB* 47 (1938), 227-58; M. Piccirillo, "Le antichita bizantine di Ma'in e dintorni", *LA* 35 (1985), 344-45 (the dated inscriptions); ibid., 345-49 (the place-names inscriptions). See also *IJ* 2, 157-60. The final place-name is Belemoun(im), i.e. Ba'al Ma'on.

203 Dan Barag, "Finds from a Tomb of the Byzantine Period at Ma'in", *LA* 35 (1985), 365-74. The tomb is identifiably Christian.

Dhibān [204] lies just a few kilometres north of the rim of the Wādī Mūjib, some sixty-four km. south of ʻAmmān. The town has always lacked a dependable source of water, so in compensation it boasts a large number of rock-cut cisterns, many of which date to the Iron Age. When rainfall is sufficient, the outlying land is quite arable. The Byzantine remains include two churches (probably sixth century), a basilica (?) and numerous tombs. There is an Umayyad residential sector which includes a large building with vaulted rooms. The site appears to have been inhabited through to the Ayyūbid/Mamlūk period.

In richness of soil, adequacy of rainfall, moderation of climate, and the abundance of springs, the Baqʻa Valley[205] just north of ʻAmmān is generously endowed with the natural resources needed to sustain plant, animal and human life. Since 1977, the University of Pennsylvania has been conducting wide-ranging surveys in selected sectors of the fifty square kilometres of the Baqʻa. The north-western region was of particular interest, since that area "has more springs and visible ancient remains than any other sector of the valley."[206] It is quite remarkable that to date the physical evidence for the Late Roman, Byzantine, Umayyad and ʻAbbāsid periods is virtually lacking anywhere in the Baqʻa. Since late antiquity is precisely the time when central Transjordania reached its peak of population, and therefore when demand for food would have been greatest, it seems odd indeed that such an agriculturally rich region has not left traces (e.g. of field-systems, farmsteads, villas) associated with intensive farming, such as those in the Mādabā Plain and the Southern Ḥawrān. So far no satisfactory explanation is at hand; we may at least hope that future surveys will shed some light on the mystery.[207]

ʻAmmān/Philadelphia[208] was central Jordan's largest urban complex throughout antiquity. Its defensible acropolis, several springs creating a

---

[204] *AJ* II.1, 206-10.

[205] *AJ* II.1, 25-44.

[206] *AJ* II.1, 29. The site of Khirbat Umm Dadānīr in the central Baqʻa yielded ceramics, coins, jewellery and architecture of the "early Roman III" (4th c. B.C.-A.D.73) period. The only dated artifacts of a later period are Mamlūk (*ibid.*,42). The site was therefore abandoned at the very time when less fortunate areas of Ammanitis experienced a renaissance under the Antonine emperors.

[207] During discussion at the Workshop, Pierre-Louis Gatier suggested that the Baqʻa might have been an imperial estate in late antiquity, while Michael Whitby proposed that the agricultural centre may have shifted south to the Mādabā Plain when the soil of the Baqʻa was exhausted from overproduction.

[208] Considering the wealth of information now available from intensive archaeological investigation, the entry on ʻAmmān in *AJ* II.1, 154-56 is completely inadequate for any period of the city's history beyond the Bronze and Iron Ages, and especially so for the

perennial stream, and adequate arable land nearby, were partly responsible for its rise to prominence in both Biblical and classical times. Equally important was the city's fortunate position at the juncture of north-south and east-west trade routes. 'Ammān's visible ancient remains are predominantly of Roman and Umayyad date. Archaeology, epigraphy and numismatics all point to the late first century A.D. for the transformation of a then-modest town into a substantial *polis*. By the Byzantine period both the acropolis and the area beneath the citadel were resplendent with paved streets, arcades, temples, baths, a forum, a gymnasium,[209] basilicas and the other civic or religious structures so typical of major urban centres throughout the Roman east.[210]

But the peak of the city's expansion and prosperity seems to have passed by the fourth century. Byzantine Philadelphia allowed its fortifications to deteriorate, and with few exceptions, the six churches so far known, including the city's cathedral, were poorly constructed.[211] Agricultural over-development apparently eroded the existing soil-cover of the surrounding region. Taxes, earthquakes and plagues, the latter two afflictions briefly documented above, also took their toll. In short, the cumulative evidence indicates that the city and its hinterland experienced a progressive decline long before its capture by Muslim forces in 635. This was, perhaps, symptomatic of the general impoverishment of other urban centres in the Byzantine east in the last century or so before Islam.[212]

Islamic period. Khouri's *Amman* is both more comprehensive and, for the Roman/Byzantine period, far more accurate. See also Northedge, *Studies on Roman and Islamic 'Ammân*, particularly for the Umayyad period (with the emphasis on archaeological remains), and *EI*[2] I, 447-48 for the later Islamic period (based on literary sources). Some recent developments are noted in Fawzi Zayyadine, "Amman", *AJA* 95 (1991), 274-76 (the central city); 276-77 (Quwaysama).

209 *IJ* 2,29 (undated) attests a *gymnasiarchos* honoured by the "council and people" of Philadelphia. The city's gymnasium has not yet been identified.

210 Among recent discoveries see M. Piccirillo and 'Abd al-Jalil 'Amr, "A Chapel at Khirbet el-Kursi-Amman", *LA* 38 (1988), 361-82. Two of the mosaic inscriptions (which record church repairs) are Greek, and three are in "Christo-Palestinian Aramaic". None is dated, but all are late sixth-century, based on the mosaic style.

211 Butler identified as churches only two structures during his field investigations at 'Ammān. The "apsidal structure" he noted (*PPUAES* II A,69) is now believed to be the cathedral. The second church, near the northern end of the *cardo*, was identified as such by Conder during the 1881 British Survey. The best modern study is B. Bagatti, "Le antiche chiese di Filadelphia-'Amman (Transgiordania)", *LA* 23 (1973), 261-85.

212 The case for general social and economic decline has been made by Hugh Kennedy, "The Last Century of Byzantine Syria", *BF* 10 (1985), 141-83. The evidence for the areas treated in this paper indicates that prosperity or impoverishment were regional phenomena only and that generalizations beyond that are presently premature.

Epigraphy neither refutes nor supports the archaeological and literary evidence of this malaise. At Quwaysma, on the southern edge of today's city, three undated mosaic inscriptions on the floor of a Byzantine church (designated B) attest a wealthy patron and members of his household as benefactors of a holy edifice which may be the very structure in which the sumptuous mosaic was discovered.[213] A Greek inscription in a nearby church (designated A) records major repair work carried out in the year 780 of the Pompeian era (A.D.717-18). Presumably the repairs were associated with the great earthquake of January, 717.[214] By that time 'Ammān had shed its Greco-Roman name, and become the capital of the Balqā' district under the Caliphate. The ruins of the Umayyad congregational mosque and the great civic hall on the acropolis attest 'Ammān's importance as a major administrative centre.[215] But the shift of imperial power to Baghdād in the late eighth century led to another, and far more protracted, decline. Whether the earthquake of 747-48 had any effect on the city is not yet clear.

It remains now to review briefly the desert palaces which are known to be Umayyad in concept and construction. The westernmost two, Qasṭal and al-Mshattā, are on the periphery of modern 'Ammān, thirty-two kilometres south and south-east respectively. Until recently Qasṭal[216] was considered to be a Roman/Byzantine *castellum* in origin,[217] with an overlay of Umayyad buildings. One part of the site (Zubāyir Qasṭal, about one kilometre to the south-west) may well have been a farmstead in an earlier era, but there is now no doubt that the palace, baths, cemetery, mosque (with circular minaret), domestic buildings, and a sophisticated hydrological system, all clustered at the main site, are Umayyad in origin

---

[213] *IJ* 2, no. 54 a-c.

[214] *IJ* 2, no. 53.

[215] On the decorative arts connected with those structures see Heinz Gaube, "'Ammân, Harâne and Qastal", *ZPE* 93 (1977), 53-63. Northedge, *Studies on Roman and Islamic 'Ammân*, chaps. 4-7, 10-11, is now the fundamental study of the architecture of Umayyad 'Ammān.

[216] *AJ* II.2, 458-65. To the bibliography cited there add Sylvie Bacquey and Frédéric Imbert, "La nécropole de Qastal", *ADAJ* 30 (1986), 397-404; Parker, *Romans and Saracens*, 39-41; Patricia Carlier and Frédéric Morin, "Qastal al-Balqa': un site omeyyade complet (685/705 ap. J.-C.)", *CFAJ* (1989), 132-40. A preliminary report on the Arabic funerary inscriptions from the site (three of which date to the late ninth century A.D.) is given by S. Bacquey and F. Imbert, "Épigraphie islamique en Jordanie", CFAJ (1989), 141-42.

[217] The (unfounded) derivation of the Arabic toponym from the Latin term, just as al-Lajjūn (east of Karak in the Moabite plain) was derived from Latin *legio*, was first suggested by H.B. Tristam, *The Land of Moab* (London, 1874), 221.

and are probably attributable to the Caliph 'Abd al-Malik (685-705). A surface survey[218] in 1967 was followed by several seasons (1983, 1985, 1987) of excavations.[219] Though Qasṭal remained inhabited throughout the 'Abbāsid period and later, it became more rural and isolated as the number and population of neighboring settlements diminished.

Qaṣr al-Mshattā,[220] often attributed to the Caliph Walīd II (743-44), is the largest and most splendid of the Transjordanian desert palaces. There is no need to dwell here on its form or function; whatever its purpose, it was unfinished at the time of its abandonment *ca.* 750. Its ornate, sprawling grandeur is a study in contrasts with the compact and functional complex at Qasṭal, only ten kilometres to the west. A late Umayyad date for its creation is strengthened by several discoveries within al-Mshattā. Two are of especial interest. One is an inscribed brick, yielding portions of an Arabic letter (in Kūfic script) from an Umayyad official, and the other is an Umayyad coin.

Both discoveries were recently published by Ghazi Bisheh.[221] The fragmentary letter mentions Sulaymān ibn Kaysān, whom Bisheh argues forcefully should be identified with the homonymous and prominent late Umayyad official in the service of several caliphs until his death at the onset of the 'Abbāsid revolution.[222] The coin is one of two bronze *fulūs* found in the débris of a palace room, part of a series minted at al-Ramla in Palestine and known to have been struck no earlier than 719/720.[223] Though neither the inscription nor the coin by itself offer any conclusive evidence as to the date of construction of al-Mshattā, when taken together with what Creswell called the developed style of the site's architecture and strong Mesopotamian influence, a date in the last decade of Umayyad rule is not

---

218 Gaube, "'Ammân, Harâne und Qastal", 76-84.

219 Pauline Carlier, *Qastal: château omeyyade?* 2 vols. (Aix-Marseilles, 1984), an unpublished doctoral dissertation not yet available to me.

220 *AJ* II.2, 396, notes the site, but there is no entry for it. See the partial bibliography in *AJ* II.1, 223-24. The standard account of al-Mshattā is still that of K.A.C. Creswell, *Early Muslim Architecture: The Umayyads* I^2 (Oxford, 1969), 578-606; 614-41, and the extensive bibliography at 604-06.

221 "Qasr al-Mshatta in the Light of a Recently-Found Inscription", *SHAJ* III (1987), 193-97.

222 Bisheh, *art. cit.*, 195-96, summarizes what is known of the Kaysān family and the colourful career of Sulaymān.

223 *Art. cit.*, 196-97, with figs. 4-5.

unlikely. Some newly-discovered but undated Arabic graffiti from al-Mshattā may be mentioned in passing.[224]

The date and purpose of Qaṣr al-Muwaqqar,[225] some ten kilometres north-east of al-Mshattā, have always been clear. A dedicatory Arabic inscription from a reservoir depth-gauge credits the caliph al-Yazīd (719-24) with the construction of al-Muwaqqar's palace. Moreover, it is known that the caliph Walīd II was reared at al-Muwaqqar. The extensive ruins at the site, where excavation has just begun,[226] suggest a substantial Umayyad settlement and its continuation into the ʿAbbāsid period.[227] It is to be hoped that the domestic quarter of this site will be given proper archeological attention.

The vast ruins of Qaṣr al-Mushāsh,[228] spead over an area of some three or four square kilometres, lie about twenty kilometres north-east of al-Muwaqqar. It is the only Umayyad desert installation which has yielded enough Byzantine pottery (from the Qaṣr itself and the nearby bath) to suggest a modest settlement (of unknown purpose or duration) on the site before Islam. In addition to *wādī* water in the rainy season, al-Mushāsh depended on storage in reservoirs (eleven are known) linked to a series of *qanawāt* (ground-level aqueducts). The King Survey visited the site in 1980 and 1981. Excavations began soon thereafter, with the emphasis on the *qaṣr* (which is *not* a palace) and the baths. The standing structures at the site are Umayyad, but have so far proved to be anepigraphic. The pottery sequence indicates the site was abandoned *ca.*750, with no resettlement until the Mamlūk era.

Qaṣr al-Kharāna,[229] thirty kilometres east of al-Muwaqqar, is unique among the Umayyad desert structures in its two-storey height, its arrow-slit flanks, and its remarkable state of preservation. Until the past decade its function has been particularly enigmatic. Four seasons of excavation

---

[224] F. Imbert and S. Bacquet, "Sept graffiti arabes du palais de Mushattâ", *ADAJ* 33 (1989), 259-67.
[225] *AJ* II.2, 402, notes the site, but there is no entry for it. See *AJ* I.1,224 for a partial bibliography, and the additions noted below.
[226] M. Najjar *et al.*, "Preliminary Report of the Excavations at al-Muwaqqar", *ADAJ* 33 (1989), 5-11 (in Arabic).
[227] M. Najjar, "Abbasid Pottery from el-Muwaqqar", *ADAJ* 33 (1989), 305-21.
[228] *AJ* II.2, 391-96, with bibliography.
[229] Al-Kharāna is noted in *AJ* II.1, 348. To the very incomplete bibliography in *AJ* I.1, 218, add Parker, *Romans and Saracens*, 21 and what is now the fundamental study of the site, Stephen Urice, *Qasr Kharana in the Transjordan* (Durham, NC, 1987) and the extensive bibliography cited there.

(1979-81) and access to unpublished photographs[230] depicting details of construction now obscured or obliterated have established with credible accuracy that there were two phases to the building's construction, the probable dates of those phases, and the building's likely use for each phase. An eleven-line grafitto from an interior room yields a date: "the year [A.H.] 92" (= 710).[231]

The excavator of al-Kharāna, Stephen Urice, believes this inscription not only provides a *terminus ante* for the initial construction of the *qaṣr*, but also indicates that the building's original purpose was modified. Urice maintains "that Kharāna was called into being by a Sufyānid order (i.e. before 684) to serve as a meeting ground for Umayyad and tribal leaders in the latter's territory."[232] This formal, political purpose of the *qaṣr* was suggested some years ago by Heinz Gaube,[233] who advocated a similar political basis for all the desert palaces. But the shift of power to the Marwānids after 685, according to Urice, was responsible for a second building phase "associated with a general program of construction and economic development in the region under Yazīd and his family."[234] For parallels, Urice has pointed to Quṣayr 'Amra and Khirbat al-Mafjar for contemporary second-phase construction. Whatever the scenario, al-Kharāna was abandoned *ca* 750 before the rebuilding programme was complete.

Conclusion

The extent and sophistication of excavations and field surveys in Jordan has increased dramatically in the past twenty-five years. Happily, the sheer volume of investigation is accompanied by a growing refinement of techniques. This has led to a resurgence of interest in the early Islamic era and ultimately to the realization that Islamic archaeology (and not just reliance on the literary sources) is essential to an understanding of the world of late antiquity. The focus in this paper is the Near East, but one must bear in mind that the Islamic conquest went west to Spain and east to

---

[230] The photographs were taken on 20 July, 1940, and credited to G. Lankaster Harding, who bequeathed them to the Jordanian Department of Antiquities; see Urice, *Kharana*, 22 and figs. 14-10.
[231] Three fragmentary and unreadable Greek inscriptions, apparently brought to al-Kharāna from elsewhere, have no historical value for the site.
[232] Urice, *Kharana*, 88.
[233] "Die syrischen Wüstenschlosser: einige wirtschaftliche und politische Geschichtspunkte zu ihrer Entstehung", *ZPDV* 95 (1979), 182-209, esp. 205.
[234] Urice, *Kharana*, 88.

Indonesia as well. There is much to be done within the entire geographic range.

The refinement of techniques in identifying and classifying Umayyad[235] and 'Abbāsid[236] ceramics is among the most exciting prospects in Islamic archaeology. This is not only true for ceramic analysis based on excavations presently undertaken, but (retrospectively) for reviewing analyses in published reports from bygone years as well. Donald Whitcomb has demonstrated the potential of the latter point. His careful, analytical review of Dimitri Baramki's excavations at Khirbat al-Mafjar a half-century ago brought him to the realization that the great palace complex of Hishām was not, as Baramki believed, abandoned *ca* 750 before its completion. While there may be evidence at al-Mafjar of seismic damage from the earthquake of 747-748, Whitcomb believes that the major damage occurred during a subsequent tremor, perhaps in the mid-ninth century or even as late as the early eleventh century.[237] Furthermore, numismatic studies of the early Islamic period are scarce and seldom comprehensive. An attempt to redress that situation was made recently at a Jordanian conference.[238] Much more needs to be done.

Among the type of sites omitted from this report are those which are essentially shrines, e.g. Mt. Nebo/Siyāgha in central Jordan. Although there would be a small community of resident monks who maintained such holy places, the transient population of pilgrims cannot be counted as a settlement. It may seem that I have compensated for that omission by giving churches, chapels and monasteries an undue amount of attention. That was not intentional, but merely reflects the fact that civic religious structures are very often given priority when excavation schedules are decided. One special benefit, of course, is that mosaics, particularly *inscribed* mosaics, are so frequently found in Byzantine (or later)

---

[235] E.g. Abdel-Jalil 'Amr, "Umayyad Painted Pottery Bowls from Rujm Kursi, Jordan", *Berytus* 34 (1986), 145-59. Thirty-four decorative bowls are described and illustrated. All were found in association with two Umayyad copper coins of 'Abd al-Malik (685-795). Ceramics with precisely this decorative motif have been found at Baysān (Scythopolis) and Khirbat al-Mafjar in Palestine, and can now be dated with accuracy.

[236] E.g. Nabil Khairy and A.-J. 'Amr, "Early Inscribed Pottery Lamps from Jordan", *Levant* 18 (1986), 143-53; A.-J. 'Amr, "More Islamic Inscribed Pottery Lamps from Jordan", *Berytus* 34 (1986), 161-68. The majority of these, made in Jarash, date to the early ninth century.

[237] Whitcomb, "Khirbet el-Mafjar Reconsidered", 64 and *passim*.

[238] R.J. Hebert, "The Early Coinage of Bilâd al-Shâm", in M. Bakhit, ed., *Proceedings of the 2nd Symposium on the History of Bilad al-Sham during the Early Islamic Period (40 A.H./640 A.D.)* I (Amman, 1987), 133-54.

ecclesiastical contexts. These can often pinpoint not only the date of construction, but reveal the names of local church officials and lay benefactors, and in so doing illuminate aspects of that community's social or economic structure.

It was tempting to omit as well the Umayyad desert palaces as anomalies, i.e. specialized creations with no functional or organic relationship to the settled communities of the region. Perhaps that might be true of those (e.g. al-Kharāna) which were occupied only on a seasonal basis. Otherwise, the same reasons for excluding the palaces might also be applied to monasteries. Certainly the sites of Qasṭal and al-Ḥallābāt were nuclei of what became agrarian settlements of some substance and importance, and indeed, were doubtless planned as such. At the very least the whole phenomenon of the Umayyad palace-estates cannot be ignored. They should be seen as a major aspect of Umayyad relationships with the nomadic and sedentary portions of Transjordania.[239]

Several generalities emerge from this review of the evidence for settlements and settlement patterns in Transjordania during late antiquity. One is that the number of sites showing continuity of occupation into the Umayyad age continues to increase. Whenever we see clearly that a settlement's Byzantine and Islamic phases are smoothly interlinked it should remind us that the once-traditional image of serious disruption and social dislocation at the time of the Islamic conquest no longer obtains. Theodor Mommsen's harsh dictum that "Islam was the executioner of Hellenism"[240] sounds very hollow today. It has been said more recently, and will be stated more forcefully in the future, that the Umayyad period in particular represents in the plastic arts the last full flowering of Hellenism.[241] Indeed, the very smoothness of this transition is indicative that the peninsular tribes

[239] One may hope that the public can be made aware of the heritage that these sites represent through a comprehensive display of important artifacts such as that devoted to the "desert castles" of Syria. See the splendid publication prepared by the Institut du Monde Arabe, *Chateaux omayyades de Syrie* , Collections du Musée National de Damas (Paris, 1991). I wish to thank Linda S. Schilcher for bringing this to my attention.

[240] *Römische Geschichte* 5 (Berlin, 1885), 611. The full statement reads "Die grosse Halbinsel [i.e. Arabia] ist in der ganzen Kaiserzeit, abgesehen von dem nördlichen und nordwestlichen Küstenstriche, in derjenigen Freiheit verblieben, aus welcher seiner Zeit der Henker des Hellenenthums, der Islam hervorgehen sollte".

[241] E.g. Philip K. Hitti, *History of the Arabs*^{9} (London, 1968), 174-75; Peter Brown, *The World of Late Antiquity* (London, 1971), 197.

were themselves imbued with a long tradition of Helleno-Arab culture and were familiar with the basic tenets of both Judaism and Christianity.[242]

Another aspect is that of the grouping of settlements. Those in the southern Ḥawrān lay at or near the southernmost edge of the great agricultural belt which stretched from the Jabal Durūz in the east to the Golan in the west. Not until the Umayyad period was any attempt made, as seems to be the case at al-Ḥallābāt and al-Mushāsh, to develop the agricultural potential of less than marginal land farther south through large-scale, intensive hydrology. We know far less about the villages of northwest Jordan. The Arabic sources are clear that viniculture was a major feature in the economy of Capitolias/Bayt Rās and, by logical extension, the settlements within its *territorium*.[243] Jarash developed a distinctive ceramic tradition. For the other cities and their dependencies we are (thus far) less informed. In central Jordan the Mādabā plain and its settlements grew wealthy from agriculture and the widespread traffic in Christian piety. Where evidence of major agricultural production would be expected, in the Baq'a Valley north of 'Ammān, it is so far inexplicably missing. The villages of the old Peraea, that extension of Palestine across the Jordan, are another natural group of which we have little evidence for the period of late antiquity.

Eventually we should be able to produce demographic charts of settlement patterns throughout Transjordania, not only for late antiquity but for all earlier periods as well. Claudine Dauphin[244] has shown in a recent study what can be done, in a limited way, for Palestine. We may be mindful, also, that publications of surveys and excavations over the past few decades have shown an increased awareness of the modern, living environment in any locality and not just the ancient artifacts on or in the ground. This has been vividly demonstrated by my former colleague Helga Seeden[245] in her ethnoarchaeological project at Bostra, by a study of the

---

242 For Hellenic influence see the chapter entitled "Hellenism and Islam", in G.W.Bowersock, *Hellenism in Late Antiquity* (Ann Arbor, 1990), 71-82, and pll. 12-16. On Christianization see I. Shahid, "Byzantium and South Arabia", *DOP* 33 (1980), 22-94.

243 The Arabic texts attesting the high quality of the wine are collected and discussed in Lenzen and Knauf, "Bayt Ras", 35-39.

244 "Les 'kômai' de Palestine", *POC* 37 (1987), 352-67; see especially the charts depicting settlements north-west and north-east of the Dead Sea and Lake Tiberias in figs. 1-6 between pp. 252-53. Her chronological parameters are Roman to Byzantine only. See also her related study, "Le catalogue des sites byzantines de la Palestine: buts, méthodes et limites d'une étude démographique", *Eretz-Israel* 19 (1987), 2-9. She is presently preparing a major publication on the demography of Byzantine Palestine.

245 Numerous articles have appeared in *Berytus* between 1984 and 1987. See also H. Seeden, "Busra 1983: An Umayyad Farmhouse and Bronze Age Occupation Levels", *AAS*

continuity of local pottery traditions in northern Jordan,[246] and by the Andrews University team in their Mādabā Plains Project.[247] Such sensitivity regarding the ways in which the present can instruct us in how we might interpret the past will hopefully become a standard feature of all field investigations. If so, the future of archaeology in Transjordania, and elsewhere, looks very bright indeed.

Abbreviations

In most cases, abbreviated titles are given in full on their first appearance. Note however the following:

ARCE	*American Research Center in Egypt*
ANRW	*Aufstieg und Niedergang der römischen Welt*
BASOR	*Bulletin of the American Schools of Oriental Research*
BSOAS	*Bulletin of the School of Oriental and African Studies*
EAEHL	*Encyclopaedia of Archaeological Excavations in the Holy Land*
ESI	*Excavations and Surveys in Israel*
IEJ	*Israel Exploration Journal*
FEPR	*Fustat Expedition: Preliminary Report*
IGLS	*Inscriptions grecques et latines de la Syrie* (Paris, 1929– , Bibliothèque archéologique et historique)
INJ	*Israel Numismatic Journal*
JAP	Fawzi Zayadine, ed., *Jerash Archaeological Project I, 1981–83* ('Ammān, 1986)
JARCE	*Journal of the American Research Center in Egypt*
RBK	*Reallexikon zur byzantinischen Kunst*
TAPA	*Transactions of the American Philological Association*
Villages	Georges Tchalenko, *Villages antiques de la Syrie du Nord. Le massif du Bélus à l'époque romaine, 3 t.* (Paris, 1953–58).

33 (1983), 162-73; H. Seeden and Muhammed Kadour, "Busra 1980: Reports from a South Syrian Village", *DM* 1 (1983), 77-101.

246 Birgit Mershen, "Recent Man-Made Pottery from Northern Jordan", *Berytus* 33 (1985), 75-87.

247 For the stated aims of this project see L.T.Geraty *et al.*,"Madaba Plains Project: A Preliminary Report of the 1984 Season at Tell el-'Umeiri and vicinity", *BASOR* Suppl. 24 (1986), 117-19.

X

Some Aspects of Land Tenure and Social Development in the Roman Near East: Arabia, Phoenicia and Syria

I. Introduction

The aftermath of World War I, including the Great Depression, was at least partly responsible for focusing scholarly attention on the economic substructure of ancient societies. The classical world of Greece and Rome received its share of this attention; between 1925 and the outbreak of World War II a number of fundamental studies appeared in print or were nearing publication. Among these were the two magisterial monuments of research undertaken by the Russian-born scholar Mikhael Rostovtzeff, *The Social and Economic History of the Roman Empire* (two vols, 1926)[1] and *The Social and Economic History of the Hellenistic World* (three vols, 1941).[2] In between the publication of these now-standard studies an equally massive and erudite six-volume series edited by Prof. Tenney Frank appeared: *An Economic Survey of Ancient Rome* (1933–1940).[3]

The Roman Near East received its share of discussion in both Rostovtzeff's and Frank's survey of imperial domains, but the treatment of individual areas was, inevitably, uneven. One may note, for instance, that in Prof. Frank's study Roman Egypt was allotted a separate volume of some 733 pages; Roman Syria (including Mesopotamia, Phoenicia, Arabia and Palestine as well as *provincia Syria*) occupies fewer than 140 pages in a volume containing surveys of three other regions of the Empire.[4] That same proportion of space held for Rostovtzeff's survey, but on a much more modest scale. It is not difficult to see why this was so.

In the preface to a recent article summarizing certain aspects of research into the history of Roman Syria, Prof. Jean-Paul Rey-Coquais states bluntly: "*Sur la Syrie Romaine, nos informations sont aujourd'hui vastes, lacunaires et dispersées.*"[5] This follows on forty years of research and new discoveries since Prof. F.M. Heichelheim published his survey of Roman Syria for Frank's *Economic Survey of Ancient Rome.*[6] Heichelheim had conveniently (and for the most part, accurately) noted a division of Syrian land into four categories: (1) military lot-land, (2) farmland, (3) sacred land and (4) imperial or crown-land.[7] However, his subsequent treatment of the economic history of Roman Syria demonstrated that he had oversimplified the issue by treating the vast and varied territories as a monolithic whole. Rostovtzeff had earlier issued a stern *caveat* against such a tendency.[8] Heichelheim also relied heavily on the Babylonian and Jerusalem *Talmuds*, as well as Josephus and the *Mishna*, for information on land tenure. This led, unfortunately, to a very unbalanced view of the Roman Near East, since only its north-eastern and south-western extremities were represented in any detail. Rostovtzeff's less detailed survey is also distorted, not geographically but through compression of the material on Syria into less than twenty pages (including notes) and placement of it within a chapter devoted to developments under the Flavian and Antonine dynasties.[9] Syria was entirely omitted from later chapters.

It is now possible to redress this situation. In the forty-six years since Heichelheim's *Roman Syria* appeared a number of documents (largely epigraphic but some on paper) have been published which shed light on aspects of land tenure and social development in various portions of the Roman Near East. This new material has not yet been evaluated in a comprehensive manner, although the individual publications hint at its potential value. It is not my intention to attempt a broad-based synthesis here. But perhaps by focusing upon several of the more recent and valuable publications, and by re-examining some older evidence with a different emphasis in mind, it will be possible to indicate in a necessarily limited way the direction which a later and more thorough study might be encouraged to go. The provinces of the Roman Near East I wish to examine are Arabia, Phoenicia and Syria. Within each I shall concentrate on an aspect of land tenure and/or social development.

II. Arabia

Land ownership, or more broadly speaking, *property* ownership, figures strongly in some, perhaps many, of a remarkable collection of papyrus documents discovered in the early 1960's in caves near the south-eastern end of the Dead Sea.[10] An Israeli survey team discovered *in toto* fifty documents ranging in date from A.D. 93–135. Fifteen related directly to the activities of Bar Cochba during the second Jewish revolt. All of *those* were utilized with customary alacrity.[11] The remaining thirty-five documents include twenty-six in Greek, six in Nabataean and three in Aramaic. For reasons known only to their discoverers, just three of these have subsequently been published (and re-published).[12]

If the three which are available for study are any indication, this small archive (which includes all of the other 32) could shed some very bright light on property ownership and social customs in a remote corner of Roman Arabia. The three are written in Greek; all date from A.D. 123–132. Two have signatures in Nabataean and Aramaic as well as Greek. One is a legal proposal by a widow who wants a business arrangement legalized whereby the guardians of her son (young, but of indeterminate age) would receive three times a certain sum of money for the boy's maintenance. Another paper is a receipt issued by the same widowed mother to one of the two guardians for three month's maintenance money. The third paper appears to be a Greek version of a Roman legal document, an *actio tutelae* or formal contract for guardianship. These three form part of what has become known as the 'Babatha archive.'[13]

All three of these documents were written in or near the old Nabataean city of Petra, which only a generation earlier had been occupied by Roman military forces during the seizure of the kingdom. The widow is an illiterate Jewess from an unidentified village southeast of Petra. Apparently upon her husband's death, the son (who is referred to throughout the documents as an orphan), through a decree of the council or senate of Petra, was placed under the guardianship of two local men, one a Jew and the other a Nabataean. A fund of some sort had been established to pay for the child's maintenance, but something had gone wrong. Represented by *her* male guardian, the widow brings legal action against the *child's* guardians through her petition to the Roman governor himself, in person, at Petra. The widow insists that the son's trust fund be turned over to her; this includes some unnamed property. She will guarantee the full value of the fund by arranging a mortgage of equal value on her *own* property, and in this way will treble the amount of the maintenance payments. The document in which the details of this transaction are given (in duplicate) is unfortunately damaged so that its interpretation is not always clear. It was to be signed by seven witnesses, but only five names are appended. The document itself was written by a man referring to himself as a *librarius* or a *libellarius*; an unfortunate spelling mistake which makes his title uncertain. If the former term is correct, the man * must have been an official on the staff of a Roman legion commander, no doubt stationed nearby, who earned extra income by acting as a notary public in his off-duty hours.[14] But because his name, and his patronymic, are Semitic, *libellarius* would appear to be the correct title and he would be one of numerous public servants hired to draw up legal documents.[15]

It becomes obvious that we are dealing with the affairs of a family of some substance. Although the word used for property *(ta hyparchonta)* is collective rather than specific, it certainly includes land of some sort—perhaps real estate in Petra, or some cultivable land nearby—plus additional valuables of unknown type. As the one document demonstrates, this property could be mortgaged when necessary, and the widow is certainly not reluctant to use the value of her property as surety for administering a trust fund herself. She is also not too shy to call upon the Roman governor as an advocate for her cause. This means that he regularly traveled from the provincial capital, Bostra, to preside at legal hearings within each *conventus* or judicial district under his authority.[16] Where and how this widow wished to invest the fund of money is unknown, but the fact that she is willing to pay three times the legal limit of interest indicates that investment capital was scarce in this region. At some point during or just after the Bar Cochba revolt the widow and her family undoubtedly fled from Petra or her native village across the Wādī ᶜAraba and north, where she and her son and others took refuge in the caves at Naḥal Ḥiver above the Dead Sea. Perhaps they joined, or were joined by, remnants of the insurrectionist army led by Bar Cochba. Whatever the case, the documents left there became a historical legacy to yet another episode of political unrest in the Near East. It is disappointing that 22 years have passed without full publication of the archive—but one may hope that good sense and an obligation to the scholarly community at large will prevail. It is time to examine the documents—*all* of them—from a more humanistic point of view, for their true value lies in the realm of social relationships.

III. Phoenicia

In the second century A.D., when Lebanon was firmly under Roman control, the Emperor Hadrian late in his reign designated the forests of coastal Phoenicia as imperial domains, and announced this by ordering Latin inscriptions to be cut into the exposed rock surfaces (in irregular intervals at varying altitudes) along the limits of the forest. These inscriptions and groups of inscriptions, first recorded by the French consul H. Guys in 1846, and now numbering nearly 200, have been found as far south as the Matn and Kisrawān, and as far north and east as the hillsides above Hirmil in the Biqāᶜ. In a remarkably thorough and very recent monograph, Jean-François Breton has collected, annotated, mapped and commented on the known examples of these texts.[17]

The inscriptions are not simply carbon copies of each other, even though they were all cut within a short period of time. There is enough variety to indicate that certain segments of the forest were accorded a special status, and Breton has demonstrated that a supervised program of cutting and replanting in rotational sequence was observed. One text will serve to illustrate this unique genre of epigraphy; it comes from the Nahr Ibrāhīm valley near the source of the Adonis River:

IMPHADAVG
DFSAGIVCP

IMP (ERATORIS) HAD (RIANI) AVG (USTI)
D (E) F (INITIO) S (ILVARUM) A (RBORUM) G (ENERA) IV C (ETERA) P (RIVATA)
"BOUNDARY OF THE FORESTS OF THE EMPEROR HADRIAN AUGUSTUS; FOUR SPECIES OF TREES; THE REMAINDER (ARE) PRIVATE."[18]

According to Breton's analysis, which I think is sound, these four species (which he identifies as cedar, oak, juniper and spruce) were the direct monopoly of the Emperor, to be used exclusively for naval ship-building; the other varieties were available for commercial exploitation in accordance with imperial regulations.[19]

These inscriptions are not to be equated in any way with the milestone texts so familiar from all parts of the Roman Empire. The motivation for this particular project was very specific, and as far as we know, the forest area thus designated was to remain *in perpetuam rei memoriam:* a permanent, private, protected preserve. There was, of course, some precedent for this. Other 'royal forests' were placed under special protection.[20] The *Epic of Gilgamesh* reminds us that 'the cedar forests' were under the semi-divine protection of the guardian Humbaba.[21] There may have been a long tradition of a royal preserve on Mt. Lebanon during the Hellenistic or Persian periods or even earlier, but we have no specific evidence for it. We may therefore ask why this project was conceived by Hadrian, and why more exactly in A.D. 134. The answer to both is most probably Hadrian's last tour of the provinces in the 130's, culminating in the Bar Cochba war already mentioned. The testimony of an obscure (but not necessarily unreliable) source indicates that Hadrian visited Byblos, most probably during that final provincial tour.[22] It would follow logically that the forest preserve was the result of personal observation by the Emperor, and his subsequent concern that its resources be maintained. But it cannot be taken as an act of what we would term today 'environmental' or 'ecological' protection; Hadrian's motivation was far more pragmatic and expedient.

Yet beyond this is the aspect still uninvestigated—what was the economic and social impact of this imperial decision? Obviously a good portion of the territory encompassed by the forest preserve belonged to individuals or villages already in existence. Large numbers of the inscriptions were found near present-day Lebanese villages, e.g. Baskinta, Bsharrī and Tūla. Are we to believe that these enticing localities were uninhabited in Hadrian's day? It is this aspect that Breton did not investigate in his otherwise admirable study—i.e. the full implication of a vast area of ancient Lebanon, once the private preserve of mountain families, suddenly claimed by imperial authority. What about the livelihood of landowners in the villages? Were the inhabitants now restricted by enforced regulations regarding the harvest and sale of timber from the forest? Or did they simply become the indentured servants of the imperial procurators appointed to Phoenicia? And by extension, what about the economic impact on the coastal cities of Lebanon, within whose territory the mountain villages lay? Roman Beirut, for instance, may have had a territory so extensive that its easternmost portion was contiguous with the territory of the temple-city of Heliopolis/Baalbek. Once the revenues from this vast tract of land were channeled to the imperial *fiscus*, was some form of compensation offered to the landowners and merchants of Beirut for the financial losses incurred? We may perhaps want to look again at the available historical sources for some hint of the reverberations—social, economic and political—of Hadrian's far-reaching decision.[23]

IV. Syria

I wish now to move to an area of the Near East where forests are non-existent, trees are few, but the volcanic soil is fertile and water is abundant—namely the region of ancient Auranitis and Trachonitis near the modern Syria-Jordan border—i.e. the region known today as the Jebel al-ᶜArab (or Jebel al-Drūz) and the Lejā.

It is precisely here, and nowhere else in Roman Syria, that we can study in some detail, and for a period of more than two centuries, the transformation of a region wealthy in viniculture but politically unsophisticated which developed gradually and steadily a most remarkable system of social organization which was paralleled nowhere else in Syria, and indeed, in the Roman Empire.

The inhabitants of the Lejā and the Jebel al-ᶜArab were, I think, always aware that they lived in a border area. This was partly a geographical fact—the mountainous Jebel al-ᶜArab and the lava wastelands of the Lejā were a natural barrier between the plain of Damascus to the north and the Ḥaurān plain extending to Irbid in the south.[24] When the Nabataeans demonstrated economic if not political dominance in the first century B.C., the Jebel al-ᶜArab was already inhabited by a sedentary folk who practiced viniculture and could justifiably boast that their chief city of Canatha (mod. Qanawāt) was numbered among the ten important commercial cities of the Decapolis.[25]

But the Lejā (Trachonitis) had long been a refuge for dissident and/or predatory peoples who constantly represented a threat to the settled communities nearby. Herod the Great, who was given dominion over these territories by his patron Augustus, at one time settled a colony of militant Babylonian Jews near the Lejā in an attempt to pacify the region; when this failed he founded another colony at or near Nawā (Neve) in the western Ḥaurān.[26] His son, grandson and great-grandson continued the pacification program, and as long as the Herodian dynasty lasted, Rome was content to leave the burden of administering this difficult territory in its hands. But the dynasty died out, and southern Syria as well as the Nabataean kingdom passed to Roman rule by the early second century A.D. The Lejā and the Jebel al-ᶜArab were initially attached to the province of Syria; the remainder of Nabataean territory and the Decapolis became the new province of Arabia.

Thus began the social transformation of the villages in the lava lands along the border. They remained politically a part of Syria for about two centuries, and then passed under the jurisdiction of the governor of Roman Arabia for another three centuries. There are few historical sources to aid us for any part of this period, but the entire region is rich in epigraphy and it is from these inscriptions that we can trace, with some precision, the social and political development of these villages at least from the second through the fourth centuries.[27] I wish here to focus on three aspects of this development which were overlooked or under-emphasized by previous studies: (1) the autonomous nature of the villages, (2) the emergence of *mētrocōmiai* or village-complexes and (3) local patterns of land tenure.

The first of these points is the easiest to account for, and the one to which most attention has been paid. Trachonitis and northern Auranitis contained a proliferation of small villages and no cities whatsoever at the time it passed under Roman rule. The villages of southern Auranitis, and those of northern Batanaea (the Nuqra) belonged to Canatha.[28] Villages in the western and eastern Ḥaurān most probably belonged to Adraa (Derᶜā) and Bostra respectively.

As noted above, Herodian policy toward the backward regions of Trachonitis and Auranitis was to administer them as military districts under the supervision of mercenary units stationed at strategic points. This was only partially successful. The Romans also saw the need for a military administration, not through proxies but by the selection of centurions who acted as district military governors directly responsible to the consular legate of Syria.[29] The Roman presence in the Lejā is definitely manifested by the extant remains of a massive roadbuilding project which testifies to the completion of a military/commercial link between Damascus and Bostra in the late second century.[30] This welded the once wild territory of Trachonitis firmly to the economic and social life of the two adjacent provinces, and it is only then that we begin to notice the rapid urbanization of the region.

The military presence in Trachonitis is also attested through epigraphy from the individual villages. Dozens of dedications made by individual soldiers of Syrian (later Arabian) legions and sub-units are known.[31] Many demonstrate the active involvement of military or ex-military personnel in local village affairs.[32] One village at the northern entrance to the Lejā was forced to house and feed military and civilian officials. The villagers protested to the provincial governor, since there was no city to intercede on their behalf. No doubt the complaint was channeled through the centurion acting as district governor. Whatever the procedure, the village (styled a *mētrocōmia* in the inscription) won redress for its grievance.[33] The whole affair is indicative that a major social transformation was underway, fostered by direct Roman intervention. The appearance of the term *mētrocōmia* in village inscriptions is therefore not purely coincidental. This brings us to the second of the three points.

There are in all five inscriptions from this region which mention *mētrocōmiai*.[34] Four are located within the Lejā; the fifth is only just outside the western edge of the Lejā. They range in date from c. 186–326 A.D. It is not yet certain if this title of 'mother-village' was honorary or constituted some legal entity, i.e. a federation of villages under the headship of one. All the indications are that this was *not* a legal fiction but represented an attempt by the Roman authorities to minimize their direct involvement in the governing of these communities. How many of these *mētrocōmiai* were in existence at any one time is unknown; it is certainly significant that no village inscription bearing this title has yet been found in the Jebel al-ᶜArab or the central Ḥaurān itself.[35] This is undoubtedly due to the fact that villages in these regions were dependent politically on the larger cities nearby—Bostra incorporated the villages of the southern Ḥaurān, Canatha those of the northern Ḥaurān and part of the Jebel al-ᶜArab, and Shuhbā incorporated nearby villages in the northern Jebel al-ᶜArab when it was raised to city-status by its native son Philip the Arab c. 245 A.D.[36] But the villages of the Lejā remained outside the orbit of these urban centers. At some time in the fourth century, one or more of them may have achieved city status. This undoubtedly occured under Constantine I, and marked the ultimate step in the process of urbanization within a once ungovernable region.[37]

It is also in the fourth century that the machinery of village self-government reached its peak of sophistication. As I have shown elsewhere,[38] inscriptions from dozens of communities—once again primarily in the Lejā—demonstrate clearly that they are emulating the cities of Syria in every detail except that of possessing a city constitution. This included the election or appointment of officials, management of village finances (including various projects of a public nature), and maintaining beneficial relations with the bedouin whose migratory pattern brought them within the 'territory' of a certain village or group of villages. Land regulation, whether it be lease, sale, transfer, inheritance or common use, does figure in certain inscriptions from southern Syria. This brings us to the third and last of the considerations noted above, the issue of land tenure in the process of social transformation.

It was mentioned that the extent of territories within the jurisdiction of *mētrocōmiai* was uncertain (presumably limited by the trans-Lejā highway). However this may have been, we can infer from the location of the known *mētrocōmiai* in the Lejā (Phaena, Zorava and Borecath Sabaōn) that part of their '*territorium*' included fertile farmland in the areas immediately adjacent to their position in the lava-fields. The Princeton expeditions carefully observed that the smallest inhabited villages visited by their team in the Lejā utilized the tiny parcels of arable soil trapped in pockets of the volcanic plateau surrounding them.[39] While this might sustain an individual * there were hardly enough of these to supply the needs of a community. It may also be safe to say that the villages of Trachonitis had little to offer by means of barter or sale to secure the agricultural staples necessary—with the possible exception of volcanic grist which might have been the major component of a compound used by the Roman authorities as the final stage in road surfacing.[40] It therefore seems probable—and even necessary—that the *mētrocōmiai* be situated on or near the edge of the lava-field so that the produce of communal farmland could be distributed to the individual villages in the interior. That at least is the interpretation I give to three inscriptions which mention farmers or farming within the Lejā or the central Ḥaurān to the south. One is undated and honors a certain Diomedes who became "wealthy from farming;"[41] another is a late second or early third century dedication by "the farmers of Zorava" (Ezraᶜ) who erected a statue of victory.[42] Another text is from Nahita in the north-western Nuqra, and commemorates a structure built in 385 by someone "from his own farming labors."[43]

Related to these is an enigmatic inscription found in Zabire in the west-central Lejā and dated precisely to 213 which may be interpreted as meaning "... the (clan) Aris and the (clan) Yachfir—those (leasing?) the land owned *(epoikion)* by (villagers) of Habiba and (its patron?) Bassus, built the temples to *Tychē* in the consulate of Severus (4) and Balbinus (2)."[44] My assumption is that the named clans are acting jointly. The village of Habiba (modern Khābeb) is on the western edge of the Lejā, just four km from where the stone was found by Waddington. *Epoikion* could mean estate, or even village, but here it seems reasonable to take it as property (pasture or farmland). The two clans (?) may have leased/rented the *epoikion* on a regular basis, or they may have simply guarded crops or livestock owned by the village.[45] The construction of the temple was certainly a joint venture, one in which members of this community took great pride.[46]

Another such instance of common ownership of secular land is a much more explicit, but damaged, text the extant portions of which translate:

> It seemed best to those from the village of Cō.inus, in favorable agreement among them (–selves?), that no one from their community [trespass?] upon the common property which is near (?) the (sacred?) mound of those from (the village?) Danaba: neither the threshing floor *(halōnion)* nor any other of the fenced areas (shared in the customary fashion?). And even if someone (?)....... (rest of text missing).[47]

Waddington is almost certainly correct here in stating that "*le but du décret paraît être de défendre aux habitants d'établir leurs aires pour battre le grain sur un terrain communal.*"[48] The village in which the inscription was found, Shaqra, is just five km north-west of Zorava/Ezra^{c}, on the western edge of the Lejā. Here is an instance in which Trachonite villages apparently owned land in the fertile adjacent territory to the west, and that a problem of sharing the commonly owned property led to the posting of this rather formal decree.[49]

Communal village property was not used exclusively for secular purposes. A series of inscriptions from Dayr al-Laban, barely two km from the south-eastern edge of the Lejā, testify that at least three named villages within the Lejā itself agreed to undertake a common project. The sanctuary at Dayr al-Laban was jointly owned and maintained by these villages, one of which (Borecath Sabaōn) was a *mētrocōmia.* Building projects dating to c. 320 and dedicated to a local solar deity were overseen by men from the various villages who were also identified by tribe.[50] It is quite probable that the sanctuary itself was not all that these villages owned in common; the temple territory surely included adjacent farmland. Three villages in association with a fourth, designated a *mētrocōmia*, may indicate the extent of territory within such a limited polity. Even so, the specific relationships among the villages are not clear, and no conclusions can be drawn. What *is* clear, once again, is the dependence of villages within the Lejā on the farmland immediately adjacent. There can be no doubt that this remained a constant factor in the public aspect of land tenure.

Private property ownership, and the transmission of property, is even more difficult to assess. The epigraphy from Trachonitis records the construction of many houses, many or all of which were privately owned. Funerary dedications note that tombs and monuments were constructed and maintained by families from private funds. But it is only a rare text which speaks of property ownership in any detail, or the transference of this property from one generation to another. Such an inscription was discovered and recorded by Waddington (and others) in the village of Damit-al-Alyā (Damatha) in the central Lejā.[51] Part of one line is damaged, but most of the inscription is legible and can be translated: "Aurelius Ouranius, (the son) of Ouabelus (Wahb-ēl), from his personal labor, (built) the monument and the court-yard and the pool within, and planted the fig-tree grove, and made provision for transfer (of these) to his sons and (left these matters?) in the care of Masakhnē, his wife." While this is obviously a family grave plot, the implication is clear that its value as property goes far beyond the tomb itself, even though the pond or pool and the fig-orchard may not have represented an extensive area of property. That the wife is given authority to supervise these affairs, if indeed she is, may indicate that the sons had not yet come of age.[52]

Beyond this there is nothing specific to note. Private affairs of individual families were normally not the subject of public inscriptions, and it would only be by chance that information of this type would appear. We must be grateful for the little that we have.

V. Conclusion

The standard social and economic histories of the Roman Empire published earlier this century are now somewhat dated. This can be demonstrated by a re-evaluation of the sections or chapters that survey developments in the provinces of the Near East. Choice of source material and the chronological structures incorporated imposed limitations on the original publications. More recently published material, especially that relevant to land tenure and social transformation, must now be considered. A re-evaluation of older material, especially epigraphic, is also necessary.

Documents relative to social and economic affairs in the Nabataean kingdom and *provincia* Arabia were discovered more than two decades ago. The few so far published shed much light on legal matters obtaining in the newly-created province of Arabia. Their social importance has not yet been evaluated.

A recent analysis of the forest inscriptions from Roman Phoenicia demonstrates that planned conservation and harvesting were of primary concern to the imperial authorities. The question of what effect the creation of a 'royal preserve' had on the indigenous population of the Lebanese mountains is yet to be considered.

The social transformation of Trachonitis and Auranitis from lawless and undeveloped areas of southern Syria to model districts displaying complex civic organization has often been remarked upon. But the role of the road system, the encouragement of communal village government *(mētrocōmiai)*, and the available evidence for land tenure have yet to be investigated.

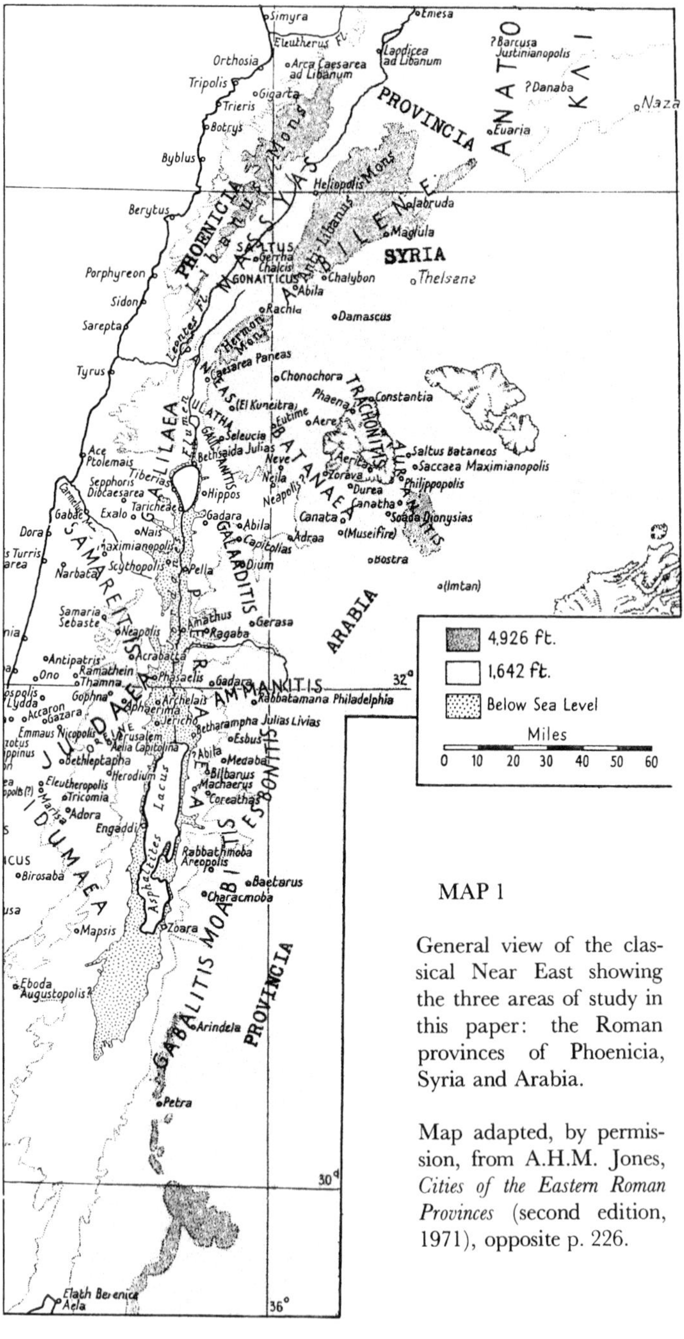

MAP 1

General view of the classical Near East showing the three areas of study in this paper: the Roman provinces of Phoenicia, Syria and Arabia.

Map adapted, by permission, from A.H.M. Jones, *Cities of the Eastern Roman Provinces* (second edition, 1971), opposite p. 226.

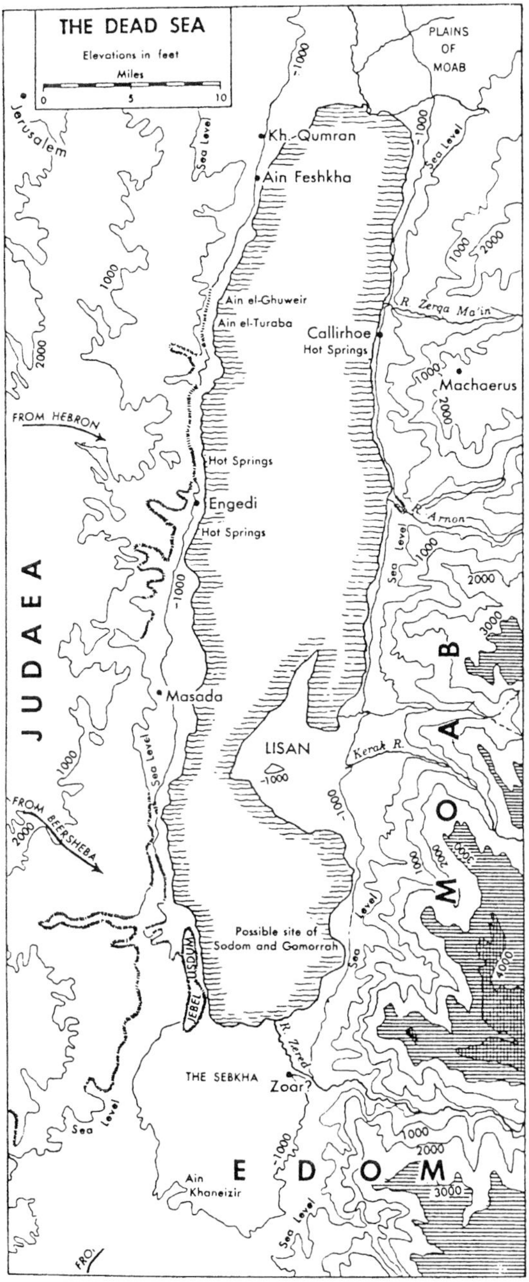

MAP 2

The regions of Zoar and Nahal Hiver (En-Geddi) where Babatha lived and where her archive was found. Map adapted, with permission, from D. Balay, *The Geography of the Bible* (London 1957), p. 203, fig. 39.

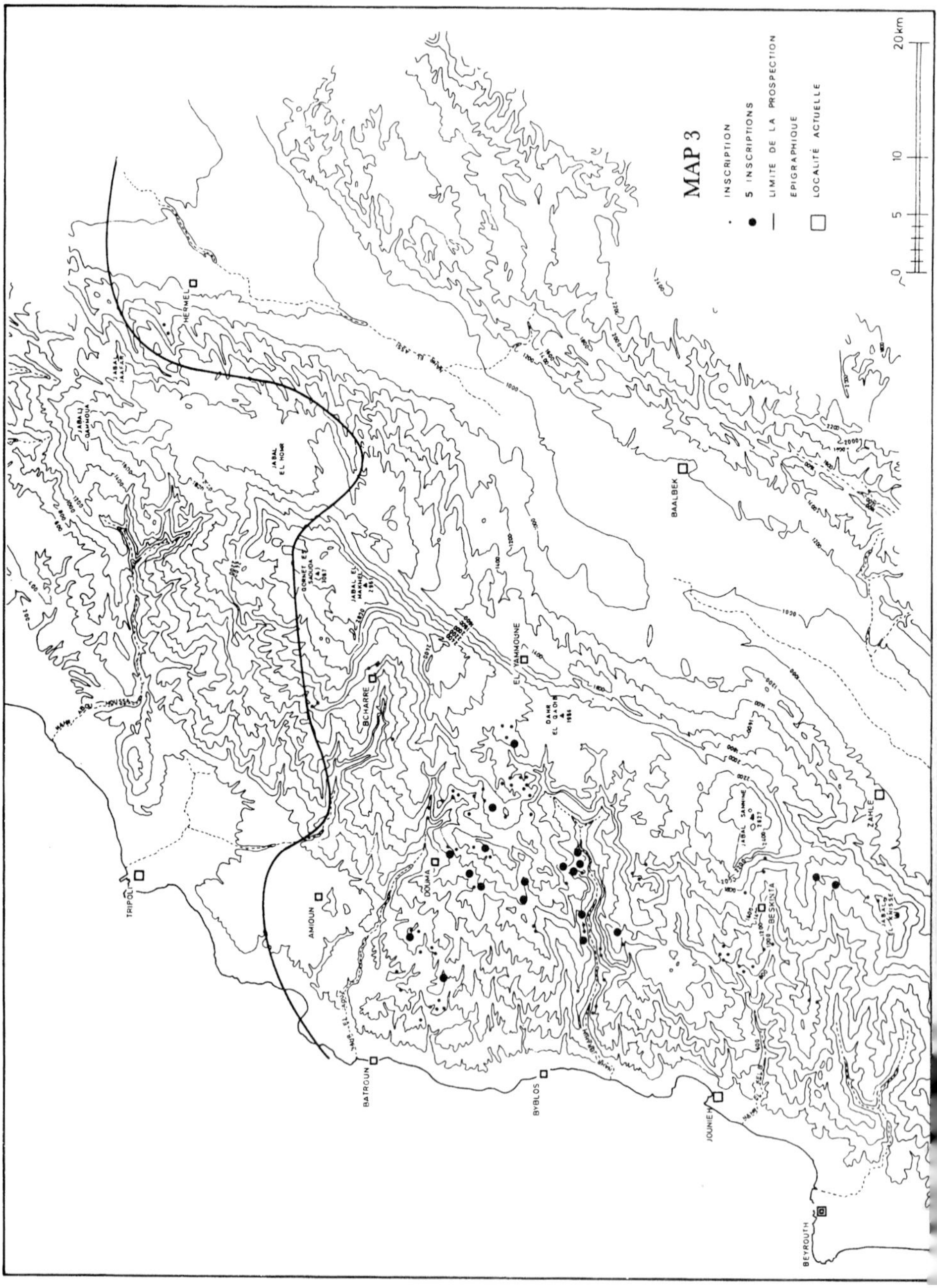

The Lebanese forest and the location of the Latin forestry inscriptions found there. Map reproduced, with permission, from J-F Breton, *IGLS* Vol. VIII Pt. 3 (1980), Carte I.

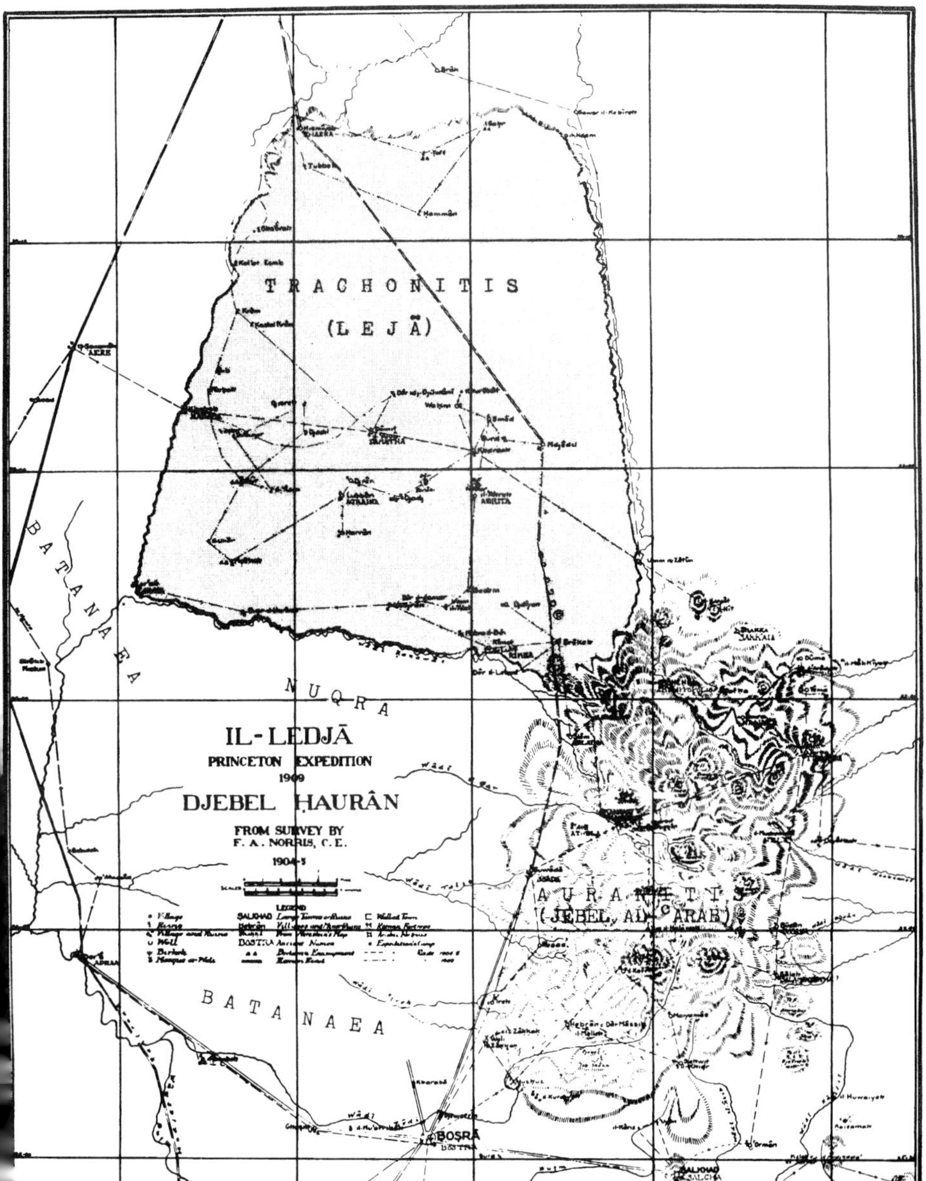

MAP 4

Roman Trachonitis, Auranitis and Batanaea in southern Syria. Map adapted from *Princeton Archaeological Expeditions to Syria, 1904–05 & 1909*, III A.

NOTES

Abbreviations used in this paper are:
AJ—Antiquities of the Jews.
ANET³—Ancient Near Eastern Texts (Relating to the Old Testament), third edition.
ANRW—Aufstieg und Niedergang der Römischen Welt.
BAH—Bibliothèque Archéologique et Historique.
BAR—British Archaeological Reports.
ESAR—Economic Survey of Ancient Rome.
ICS—Illinois Classical Studies.
IEJ—Israel Exploration Journal
IGLS—Inscriptions Grecques et Latines de la Syrie
IGR—Inscriptiones Graecae ad Res Romanas Pertinentes.
JAOS—Journal of the American Oriental Society
JRS—Journal of Roman Studies.
MAIBL—Mémoires présentés à l'Académie des Inscriptions et Belles-Lettres.
PAES—Princeton Archaeological Expeditions to Syria.
PEFQS—Palestine Exploration Fund, Quarterly Statement.
RIDA—Revue Internationale des Droits Antiques.
SEHRE²—Social and Economic History of the Roman Empire (second edition).
Wadd.—W. H. Waddington, Recueils des Inscriptions Grecques et Latines de la Syrie.

1. Oxford, The Clarendon Press. A second edition in English, revised by P.M. Fraser, appeared in 1957. Fraser's 'revisions' were translations of additions made by Rostovtzeff in the Italian edition of 1933. The work is thus very much a contemporary of the other 'Depression Studies' noted below.
2. Oxford, The Clarendon Press.
3. The Johns Hopkins Press. A reprint of all volumes was published by Pageant Books, Inc. in 1959.
4. Frank's note in the 'Preface' helps to explain the brevity of *Roman Syria*: "That this section has less space than it deserves is the editor's fault, for the assignment was not made until [the year before publication], after the first volunteer had resigned" (*ESAR* IV p. v.).
5. *Syria* 68 (1978) p. 44.
6. Vol. IV was originally published in 1938.
7. *ESAR* IV p. 145.
8. *SEHRE* 2 Vol. I p. 261: "It is no easy task to form a correct idea of social and economic life in the Syrian lands. To begin with, a warning must be uttered against generalizing and speaking of the Syrian lands as a single unit."
9. *SEHRE*² Vol. I pp. 261–273; Vol. II pp. 660–666 (notes 19–36).
10. The first comprehensive report was by H.J. Polotsky, "The Greek Papyri from the Cave of the Letters," *IEJ* 12 (1962) pp. 258–262.
11. In addition to related documents found earlier (e.g. S. Yeivin, "Some Notes on the Documents from Wadi Murabbaᶜat Dating from the Days of Bar Kokh'ba", *ᶜAtiqot* I [1955] 95–108), these formed the basis for Y. Yadin's *Bar Kokhba* (New York 1971).
12. On the history of publication, see G. W. Bowersock, *Roman Arabia* (Harvard 1983), p. 75 note 55; p. 76 notes 1 & 2.
13. The *actio tutelae* is represented by two copies. Bowersock (see above, note 12) has skilfully managed to synthesize the available information from the published and unpublished documents; see his Chapter 6 (pp. 76–89) of *Roman Arabia*.
14. So N. Lewis, "Two Greek Documents from Provincia Arabia," *ICS* 3 (1978) p. 105.

15. Thus H-J Wolff, "Le droit provincial dans la province romaine d'Arabie," *RIDA* 23 (1976), p. 276; See now the full study by Wolff, "Römische Provinzialrecht in der Provinz Arabia," *ANRW* II. 13 (1980) 763–806.

16. On this see G. P. Burton, "Proconsuls, Assizes and the Administration of Justice under the Empire," *JRS* 65 (1975) 92–106.

17. "Les inscriptions forestières d'Hadrien dans le Mont Liban," *IGLS* VIII. 3, 1980 (= *BAH* Vol. CIV).

18. *Ibid.* 5059 pp. 54–55. Breton failed to note that this had been published by J.P. Brown, *The Lebanon and Phoenicia: Ancient Texts Illustrating their Physical Geography and Native Industries*, Vol. I: *The Physical Setting and the Forest* (Beirut 1969) p. 153.

19. *IGLS* VIII. 3, pp. 17–22; pp. 30–34.

20. Brown, *op. cit.* pp. 152–153; *IGLS* VIII. 3, pp. 15–17; *ESAR* IV, pp. 134–135 and notes 67–75.

21. J. B. Pritchard (ed.), *ANET*³ (Princeton 1969) pp. 78–81.

22. F. Jacoby, *Die Fragmente der griechischen Historiker* (vol. XV, 792 p. 825) reproduces the reference to Aspasius of Byblos from the *Suda* (s.v.). Aspasius is said to be "a contemporary of (Aelius) Aristedes and Hadrian" and to have written an *Encomium* of that emperor "and certain others." This is hardly an explicit reference to an imperial visit to Byblos, but it certainly hints at such (noted by Brown, *op. cit.* p. 153).

23. R. Mouterde and J. Lauffray, *Beyrouth ville romaine* (Beirut 1952) is an excellent short survey of the administrative, economic and social history of Roman Beirut.

24. F. E. Peters, "Regional Development in the Roman Empire: The Lava-Lands of Syria," *Thought* 55 (1980) pp. 110–121.

25. F.E. Peters, "The Nabataeans in the Hawran," *JAOS* 97 (1977), pp. 263–271.

26. Josephus, *AJ* XVII 2, 1–3 (23–29); cf. *AJ* XVI 9, 2–3 (282–286).

27. The *IGLS* series (ongoing since 1929 and now under the aegis of the Institut Fernand-Courby, Lyon) has recently produced the first volume on southern Syria (Bostra, Vol. XIII/1) edited by Maurice Sartre. In the coming years the following volumes are scheduled to appear: XIII/2 (the Ḥaurān); XIII/3 (the Lejā); XIII/4 (the Jebel Drūz); XIII/5 (the Golan). I owe this information to Prof. Sartre.

28. M. Sartre, "Le territoire de Canatha," *Syria* 60 (1983) forthcoming. I wish to thank Prof. Sartre for providing a typescript.

29. The first to notice this was A.H.M. Jones, "The Urbanization of the Ituraean Principality," *JRS* 21 (1983) p. 268. These seven texts will be republished, with commentary, in my forthcoming *Studies in the History of the Roman Province of Arabia* (*BAR*, Oxford) 1984/1985.

30. A. Poidebard, "Reconnaissance aérienne au Ledja et au Ṣafā," *Syria* 9 (1928) pp. 114–123; M. Dunand, "La voie romaine du Ledja," *MAIBL* 13 (1933) pp. 521–557.

31. See, e.g., the collection of military inscriptions from the village of Masmiya (anc. Phaena) in *IGR* III, 1113–1123.

32. Jones, *JRS* 21 (1931), p. 270.

33. *IGR* III 1119 (c. A.D. 185).

34. *IGR* III 1112, 1119; 1155; *Wadd.* 2396b; *PAES* III A 797.²

35. Four of the five were found in the Lejā; *IGR* III, 1112 is from ʿAqrabā in the western Ḥaurān.

36. For a sampling of inscriptions found there, see *IGR* III, 1195–1202. On the historical circumstances, see Bowersock, *Roman Arabia*, pp. 122–125.

37. The Trachonite village of Burāq seems to have been elevated to city-status under the the name *Constantia;* for this see the epigraphic evidence in *Wadd.* 2537 a & b.

38. "Epigraphy and Village Life in Southern Syria during the Roman and Byzantine Periods," *Berytus* 31 (1982) forthcoming.

39. H.C. Butler, *PAES* II A p. 404.

40. D.L. Kennedy, *Archaeological Explorations on the Roman Frontier in North-East Jordan (BAR* 134) 1982 pp. 144–145, incorporating earlier observations by H.C. Butler.

41. R. Dussaud and F. Macler, *Voyage Archéologique au Ṣafā et dans le Djebel ed-Drūz* (Paris 1901), p. 203 No. 88.

42. *IGR* III 1154.

43. *Wadd.* 2412 l.

44. *IGR* III 1132.

45. Butler (*op. cit.* note 39) p. 407 described an instance of bedouin either hired or suborned to look after Drūz-owned cattle in the Lejā at the time of his architectural survey in 1909.

46. M. Sartre, "Tribus et clans dans le Hawran antique," *Syria* 59 (1982) p. 83.

47. *Wadd.* 25Q5 (undated).

48. Waddington's commentary to 2505 (see preceding note).

49. On threshing-floors (Latin *areae*) in this period, see the comments in K.D. White, *Roman Farming* (London & New York 1970) p. 426. For a description of threshing in the same region at the end of the 19th century, see W. Ewing, "A Journey in the Hauran," *PEFQS* (1895) p. 165; That grazing-land in some areas of Herodian territory was rented by the crown to local 'Arabs' is attested by Josephus, *AJ* XVI 9, 3 (292).

50. *Wadd.* 2392–2398.

51. *PAES* III A 800[6], with an improved reading on earlier copies.

52. There are some parallels here with the legal proceedings involving the son of Babatha discussed in Part II of this paper. This inscription is unfortunately undated.

EPIGRAPHY AND THE NOTITIA DIGNITATUM (ORIENS 37)*

Several toponyms in the Notitia Dignitatum Oriens **37 (Roman Arabia) have long been identified with certain Near Eastern sites: Diafenis with Masmiyah, Speluncis with Dayr al-Kahf and Asabaia with Zuberat or Qal'at Daba'a. These identifications can now be challenged by utilising epigraphic discoveries in eastern Jordan. Proposals are made in this paper for the identification of Diafenis with Qasr Azraq, Speluncis with Umm al-Quttayn and Asabaia with Dayr al-Kahf. The central core of the discussion is the road-terminus inscription from Qasr Azraq and its implication for the strategic role of that fort and its surrounding military installations in and near the Azraq oasis at the southern end of the strata Diocletiana.** *

Among the list of military forces and installations *sub dispositione viri spectabilis ducis Arabiae* the *Notitia Dignitatum* ([*or.*] 37.23) notes a unit of native (Arab) mounted archers stationed at Diafenis:

Equites scutarii Illyriciani, Motha.
Equites promoti Illyriciani, Tricomia.
Equites Dalmatae Illyriciani, Ziza.
Equites Mauri Illyriciani, Areopoli.
Equites Promoti indigenae, Speluncis.
Equites promoti indigenae, Mefa.
Equites sagittarii indigenae, Gadda.
Praefectus legionis tertiae Cyrenaicae, Bostra.
Praefectus legionis quartae Martiae, Betthoro.
EQUITES SAGITTARII INDIGENAE, DIAFENIS.

Et quae de minore laterculo emittuntur

There follows a list ([*or.*] 37.25-35) of *alae* and *cohortes* (Seeck 1876: 81).

For the purpose of identification it has become customary for editors and commentators to divide the placename Diafenis into two elements. Böcking (1839: 368) was the first to note that (Dia)-Fenis might be identified with either Phaeno (mod. Faynân) just south of the Dead Sea or Phaena (mod. Masmiyah) between Bostra and Damascus. Such correlations were based on the similarity of those placenames to the second element of the Notitia's toponym. Böcking immediately saw that the equation Dia-Fenis = Phaeno / Faynân was impossible. The latter was known from Eusebius / Jerome (*Onomasticon s.v.* Daidan; Phainôn) to be a town of Edom, which at the time of the Notitia was part of the province of Palaestina Tertia. The case for Dia-Fenis = Phaena / Masmiyah was thus enhanced by default, and strengthened by the fact that inscriptions recording dedications and benefactions by centurions of named legions had been found at the site (for example, *CIG* 4542-46, 4548).

In spite of some inherent difficulties, for example, explaining the element *Dia-* and admitting that none of the military inscriptions was later than the reign of

Commodus, the identification of Dia-Fenis with Phaena was advocated by Waddington (1870: 574), Seeck (1876: 81), Domaszewski (1898: 68), Vailhé (1898/99: 93), Benzinger (*RE* 5.1: 309) and Thomsen (1906: 127; 1907: 55). But by the time Brünnow and Domaszewski (1909: 256) published the third and final volume of their *Die Provincia Arabia* that identification was modified by a question mark.

It is clear that the question mark had been set in place by Brünnow, who expressed serious doubts in an article which appeared that very same year. In it he argued for the identification of Diafenis with the Roman fort at Qasr al-Azraq in the eastern desert of Jordan. His reasoning is worth setting out in full:

> Dia-Fenis ist gewiss irgendwo im südlichen Haurân zu suchen und kann jedenfalls nicht Phaena, das heutige el-Mismîye am Nordrand der Legâ sein, wie Domaszewski [1898] p. 68, meint, denn diese Stadt gehörte bereits schon von Severus ab zur Phoenice. Man dürfte vielleicht den Militärposten bei Kasr el-Azrak darin erkennen; die Lage dieses sicher anzunehmenden Postens in der Wüste abseits von der Limeslinie würde auch die anormale Stellung der Garnison am Ende der Hauptliste verständlich machen.
>
> (Brünnow 1909: 71)

Brünnow's assertion here that Phaena / Masmiyah belonged to the province of Syria Phoenice "from [Septimius] Severus" is misleading because, if true, it would preclude its identification with Diafenis. His own recent research (Brünnow & Domaszewski 1909: 268-70) had convinced him that Phaena remained in Syria when Diocletian readjusted the Severan borders between Syria and Arabia. More recently, Kettenhofen (1981: 65) and Sartre (1982: 60-1) have demonstrated independently that the entire Lejâ plateau (including Phaena) was incorporated into Roman Arabia during, or even before, the reign of Diocletian. Brünnow's argument on that point collapses.

However that may be, Brünnow's dissenting opinion on the identification of Dia-Fenis was either overlooked or ignored in subsequent scholarship. In his magisterial *Topographie* Dussaud (1927: 377 n. 4) accepted without question that Dia-Fenis = Phaena, and that *idée fixe* was echoed by Hölscher (*RE* 19.2: 309), Abel (1938: 187) and Sourdel (1952: 9). Dunand's survey of sites along the *strata Diocletiana* includes a brief description of "Tell ‘Ezrâq" (Dunand 1931: 229-30) and even cites (1909: 229 n. 1) Brünnow's article but manages to avoid any discussion of Azraq's ancient toponymy. To my knowledge only Parker (1986: 20) has specifically called attention to Brünnow's equation of Dia-Fenis with Azraq. But Parker's reference to it as "pure speculation" would make it seem that Brünnow alone had hazarded a guess at the site's ancient name.

There is now good reason not to dismiss Brünnow's suggested identification. The Notitia's placement of Diafenis and its garrison after the legionary designations rather than with its proper unit category of *equites indigenae* is indeed odd, as he noted, and requires some explanation. Brünnow pointed out the abnormality of Azraq's location to the east of the central *limes*. In his day the fort (which he and Domaszewski did not include in their survey) may have seemed quite remote. But it had been visited by Huber in 1883 and by Dussaud and Macler in 1901 (Dussaud and Macler 1903: 30). The Princeton University expedition was unable to visit the site a few years later because of regional banditry. Alois Musil and Gertrude Bell were the last Europeans to reach Azraq before World War 1 and the famous sojourn there of T.E. Lawrence (Kennedy 1982: 69-71).

It has only subsequently become clear that the fort at Azraq was the hub of a complex of military fortifications dating from the time of Septimius Severus (Kennedy 1980), and that it was later re-activated as the southernmost point on the *strata Diocletiana* (Kennedy 1982: 75-96). Thus its physical distance from the main military and commercial artery in Roman Arabia, namely the *via nova Traiana*, is irrelevant to its placement in the *Notitia*. But the non-sequential entry of Diafenis and its unit may be attributed to editorial work on an earlier version of the *Notitia*. More specifically it would indicate an addition to the *exercitus Arabicus* by the time the *Notitia* in its present form was produced.

The epigraphical evidence added little weight to Brünnow's argument, which is probably why he did not cite it. At the time of his writing, the published inscriptions from the fort at Azraq consisted of several Safaitic graffiti of indeterminate date (Dussaud and Macler 1903: 205), an inscribed altar dating to the first Tetrarchy (1903: 268-269) and an Arabic inscription of a much later period (1903: 337). Since that time a number of Latin building inscriptions discovered at Azraq show continued Roman use of the fort late in the reign of Constantine (Kennedy and MacAdam 1985: 97-105; 1986: 231-2). Renovation work of 326-33 (*AE* 1974: 661 = Kennedy 1982: 90-91) and 333 (Kennedy and MacAdam 1986: 231-2) are evidence of planned operational use of the *castellum* later in the fourth century. How late is still uncertain, but one may note a Latin inscription from the fortress at Dayr al-Kahf, only 52 km to the north, attesting alterations between 367 and 375 (Littmann *et al.* 1910: 127-8, no. 229).

Qasr Azraq was one of several late Roman / early Byzantine sites in eastern Jordan for which the ancient name was unknown or conjectural. Brünnow (and others) failed to note that Aloys Sprenger (1875: 151) had already identified the oasis of Azraq with the placename Adra (in Arabia Petraea) of Ptolemy's *Geography* (5.16.4). Such an identification is extremely tenuous. It is just as likely that Ptolemy's Adra stood on the site of the later Ummayad baths at (Qusayr) Amra some 22 km west of Azraq (MacAdam 1988: 69).

Azraq's ancient name is more likely attested in the text of a Latin terminus-stone from the Diocletianic fort at the oasis. The inscribed stone was first seen by Sir Aurel Stein in 1939 but not published until the discovery of Stein's lost *Limes Report* (Kennedy 1982: 179-85; Kennedy and Gregory 1985: 268-70; 416-7). The stone disappeared at some point after Stein's visit and was not among the epigraphy recorded at the fort by Bowersock in 1970 (Bowersock 1971: 241-2) or by Kennedy on several visits between 1976 and 1981. The inscription recorded soldiers from several legions engaged in establishing a line of military outposts and communication links between the provincial capital at Bostra and other named sites. The text is not dated but the legions named and the use of singular pronouns in an imperial context suggest that it belongs to the period between Aurelian's conquest of Palmyra and the establishment of the first Tetrarchy. Kennedy (1982: 182) surmised that one of the placenames noted by the inscription was the ancient name of Azraq, but he was unable to decipher it from Stein's photo of an ink squeeze on the stone.

In 1983 the inscription reappeared at Azraq. Kennedy and I have since autopsied, photographed and made squeezes of the stone on two occasions (Kennedy and MacAdam 1985: 100-104; 1986: 232). A line or two at the top is missing and the first visible line (line 1) was badly broken. That and the remainder of the text (**Fig. 22.1**) we read as:

P̣ẸṚ[MỊ]ḶỊṬ.ỤṆỊḶ? SS SUOṢ
LEGG. XI KL. ET UII KL.
ET I ITAL. ET IIII FL. ET
I ILL. PRAETENSIONE
CONCATA MIL. SVIS EX
LEG. III KVR. A BOSTRA
DASIANIS M.P. LXUI ET
A BASIENISA M.P. XXX
ET A BAMATA DVMATẠ
MP CCVIII

We found no parallels for this type of inscription. Its missing preamble presumably gave its purpose. The extant portion is quite unlike standard milestone texts or military dedications. There are vague affinities with what Chevallier (1972: 52-54) terms "indicateurs routiers", but those were displayed in public for civilian benefit. "Terminus-stone" seemed the most appropriate designation. The relatively small size of the Azraq inscription is also disconcerting; the original height would not have been much more than 60-70 cm and the width is only 39 cm. How or where it would have been displayed is a puzzle. We interpreted the sequence of placenames and mileage distances as: "From Bostra to Dasianis 66 miles and from Basienisa (to Dasianis) 30 miles and from Bamata-Dumata (to Dasianis) 208 miles." Two placenames were readily identifiable: Bostra is Busra in the Syrian Hawran, the capital of Roman Arabia and headquarters of the provincial army, *legio III Cyrenaica* (**Fig. 22.2**). Dumata refers to the oasis-town of Dumat al-Jandal (Jawf) in north-western Saudi Arabia (**Fig. 22.3**).

The find-spot of the inscription pointed to a military detachment at Azraq for its creation, although the stone's size and weight do not preclude its transport to the fort from elsewhere. The sequence of names and distances also suggested Azraq since the fort is exactly 66 Roman miles (97 km) from Bostra measured along the known road via Umm al-Quttayn. The logical assumption, following Kennedy's earlier study of Stein's photograph, was that Dasianis was the ancient name of Azraq and that it was to Dasianis that all distances were computed. Presumably the toponym is an indeclinable locative or (less likely) an ethnicon in the dative or ablative plural.

The initial letter of Dasianis is squeezed against the letter which follows. It is also poorly formed. Certainly it would have been welcome to read a *C* and to transcribe the placename, with a very slight emendation, as *Çasṭ(rum)* or *Çasṭ(ra) Anis*. Alternatively one might hope to read an *O* and transcribe *Oasianis*. But the only letter that suggested itself was the distinctively delta-shaped *D* clearly seen in the penultimate line as the the initial *D* in Dumata. The various paper sqeeze impressions supported this conclusion.

As additional support I would now submit that the *Notitia*'s Diafenis is a corruption of Dasianis, a possibility which escaped me when the inscription was prepared for initial publication. Such a corruption is quite likely in a document that underwent several editions and in its present form features numerous variant readings. Not all of these variants were noted by Seeck. In the case of Diafenis Böcking (1839: 368) states that the *editio princeps* gave Diaphenis. That is a very minor variation, but perhaps indicates that the name was transcribed into Latin from Greek. In that case the original Greek spelling will have been ΔACIANIC or something quite similar. *CI* can easily be confused as Φ , and *A* as *H*, producing ΔAΦHNIC which became DIAPHENIS and DIAFENIS in the hands of Latin copyists. The element *Dia-* has been an embarrassment for those identifying the placename with Phaena. As such it was simply ignored. When an attempt to explain it was made the result was grotesque, leading one eminent biblical scholar to propose that Dia-Fenis was to be found "entre la ville de Dia (Dion [of the Decapolis]) et Phaena" (Abel 1938: 187). It would seem instead that Brünnow's conjecture was correct after all.

The final mileage distance is problematical. If the figure given is taken to mean Dumata to Dasianis (208 *MP* = 304 km), this does not accord with the known distance from Jawf to Azraq which is *c.* 450 km or *c.* 308 *MP*. Only by supposing that a third *C* was omitted can the Roman mileage be reconciled with the actual ground distance. Emending the text to *MP* CCCVIII was a possibility, but that left Amata or Bamata unexplained. It seemed better to resolve the discrepancy by supposing that the final placename was a compound, Bamata-Dumata (or Amata-Dumata), with the second element referring to the oasis-town of Dumat al-Jandal and the first element a site in the Wadi Sirhan leading to Dumata. Amata signified nothing, although admittedly it is a common enough placename. Bamata suggested the Semitic term (*bmt*) for "high-place", in this case qualified for identity by its proximity to Dumata.

The distance given to Bamata-Dumata, and the first element of the name, gave us a clue to the actual location of the site. They correspond closely to the position and name of Banatha, a toponym in Ptolemy of Alexandria's *Geography* (5.18). The substitution of *M* for *N* and *T* for *TH* is a common feature of placenames. On that basis it did not seem too speculative to posit a military outpost, perhaps no more than an encampment, at a place where caravan-tracks from Jawf and Tayma merged at the southern entrance of the Wadi Sirhan. That is precisely the spot, west and slightly north of Jawf, where Ptlolemy's co-ordinates place "Banatha" (Kennedy and MacAdam 1985: 102-103) among his list of "towns" in Arabia Deserta. I have tentatively identified Bamata / Banatha with the modern site of Nabak abu-Qasr, "the first source of abundant water after entering the southern mouth of the [Sirhan] depression, and the last source of water for someone traveling to Jawf from the Azraq oasis" (MacAdam 1988: 62).

A Roman outpost at such a remote spot can only have been temporary. Its purpose must have been specific: to monitor traffic utilising the Wadi Sirhan between the oases of Jawf and Dumata during the threat of invasion from that direction. As a forward "lookout" post it must have been in rapid communication-distance from other such posts along the Sirhan. There would be no need to name or give distances to those intermediate posts. Ptolemy notes several as yet unidentified placenames between "Banatha" and his frontier with "Arabia Petraea" to the north-west. Sources of water necessary to transit traffic are still found at about one-day intervals along the course of the Sirhan (MacAdam 1988; Potts 1988: 144 [itinerary Kaf to Hail]).

Identifying Basienisa also seemed possible. The mileage to it, 30 *MP* (44 km), excluded a number of otherwise promising sites in the vicinity of Azraq: Dayr al-Kahf directly north (52 km), Qasr al-Hallabat to the north-west (62 km) Qasr Asaykhin to the north-east (15 km), Qasr Uwaynid to the south-west (15 km), Umari (35 km) and Bayir (130 km) to the south-east, and sites such as Haditha, Kaf, and Ithra (*c.* 70 km) near the northern entrance to the Wadi Sirhan. But the site of Khirbet Manara, north-west of Azraq on the road to Umm al-Quttayn and Bostra, is exactly 30 *MP* distant. Moreover, a Latin inscription of 334 (*AE* 1948: 136) found near that site notes the construction of a *receptaculum aquarum* under the supervision of a certain Vincentius who is styled *protector agens Basie*. Basie would appear to be an abbreviated form of Basienisa, and both would logically refer to the outpost at Manara where today one may see an abandoned cistern, Romano-Byzantine potsherds and traces of an ancient building partially obscured by modern construction (Kennedy *et al.* 1986: 151).

Our scenario based on the Azraq inscription was a line of military outposts between Bostra and the eastern end of the Wadi Sirhan. The permanent fort at Azraq / Dasianis was the key link in this chain. Although it was important to know the ancient name of Azraq, no immediate connection with a toponym in the *Notitia* came to mind. The overall purpose of the military work was not clear, but it was evident that the route from inner Arabia to the Azraq oasis was to be monitored. We speculated that the outpost at Bamata, 208 *MP* from the main base, was probably manned by "a small garrison of *dromedarii*" (Kennedy and MacAdam 1985: 105). It seemed very unlikely that Roman interest in the route through the Wadi Sirhan would involve the military occupation of Jawf / Dumata. We were aware of the stone altar found there some years ago (Kennedy 1982: 190, no. 39) with a Latin dedication by a centurion of the *legio III Cyrenaica*. This suggested a Roman presence in the region (the altar may have come from elsewhere) but hardly indicated that Dumata was under direct Roman control. Beyond that we did not venture.

More recently Michael Speidel (1987) has republished this inscription. In several places he has improved on our initial reading (the line numbering is his):

[D. n. Diocletiano - - - - - - - - - /
- - - - - - - - - - - - - - - - - - -]
per mil(ites) **fortiss**(imos) **suos**
legg(ionum) **XI Kl**(audiae) **et VII Kl**(audiae)
et I Ital(icae) **et IIII Fl**(aviae) **et**
I Ill(yricorum), **praetensione**
coligata mil(itibus) **suis ex**
leg(ione) **III Kyr**(enaica). **A Bostra**
Basianis m(ilia) **p**(assuum) **LXVI et**
a Basienis Amat(a) **LXX**
et ab Amata Dumata
m(ilia) **p**(assuum) **CCVIII**

Most important is his reading of the verb *coligata* for our conjectural *conlata* and the consequent interpretation of *praetensione coligata mil(itibus) suis ex leg(ione) III Kyr(enaica)*. This clearly demonstrates that detachments of soldiers from the named legions (including the provincial garrison) participated in an orchestrated deployment of forces between Bostra and named posts in the desert region to the south and east. The specifics of their deployment and duties cannot be known until the missing portion of the text is found. Speidel's interpretation, like ours, presents a line of outposts from Bostra to Azraq and through the Wadi Sirhan. But his *praetensio* is extended to include Dumata itself (Speidel 1987: 219). The sequence given, from point A to point B, from point B to C, etc. appears attractive. It presents us with a transverse arm of the *strata Diocletiana* stretching from Bostra to Dumata and meeting the north-south *strata* at Azraq. Neither the text of the inscription nor the concentration of military bases at Azraq supports this interpretation.

Speidel's reading of a *B* instead of a *D* in front of the placename following Bostra would be more acceptable if there weren't already three other well-cut *B*'s in the text. Basalt is notoriously hard to inscribe, especially so for rounded or curved letters such as *O*, *C*, *G*, and *S* and partially-rounded such as *P*, *R* and *B*. But this did not present an insurmountable difficulty to the stonecutter who produced the Azraq inscription. One may note that the shape of *V* is alternatively *U* and *V* throughout the text, indicating no particular problem with the rounded form (**Fig. 22.1**). Even in the topmost line of the text, where Speidel persuasively reads *per mil(ites) fortiss(imos) suos*, the remnants of rounded and curved letters are quite distinct. This includes the initial *P* chiseled on the left edge, precisely where one might expect some difficulty. Surely a *B* at the left edge just six lines below would have been no more difficult to carve. The *B*'s of Bostra, Basienisa and Bamata are easily discernible and indeed look nothing like the letter at the beginning of line eight.

There are difficulties as well in seeing Speidel's *Amat(a) LXX* at the end of line nine. Among them are supplying a missing letter, accepting that *MP* is omitted before the mileage figure, and emending that figure to read 70. This seems, cumulatively, rather drastic. Amatha (or variations such as Amathus and Amathous) is a common Near Eastern placename (Thomson 1907: 20). Stephanus of Byzantium's *Ethnica* mentions an Amatha "in Arabian territory", but the vagueness of his testimony hardly permits us to pin-point it in the Wadi Sirhan. Reading *ab Amata* in the penultimate line, as noted above, is possible. But that does not allow us then to reverse the emphasis and maintain that "the mention of a place called Amat(a) in line [nine] is confirmed by its recurrence in line [ten]" (Speidel 1987: 218 and n. 22).

It also does not address the fact that Ptolemy's co-ordinates for "Banatha" and the location of "Bamata" at 208 *MP* from Azraq coincide nicely. Photos, slides and squeezes of the inscription show that the initial mileage cipher near the end of line nine is an *X* rather than an *L*. There are two small vertical scratches following the final *X* which we took to be blemishes on the edge of the stone. It may be that these represent the upper parts of two additional ciphers, *i.e. II*, or of only one cipher, *i.e. V*. The formulaic aspect of this portion of the inscription demands *MP* before the mileage figure. The photos and squeeze do indeed show a sequence of letters that we read as *MP* with the loop of the *P* squeezed against the *X* that follows. Between the right vertical of the *M* (which is deeply cut) and the vertical of the *P* (also deeply cut) there appears to be a shallow diagonal line. I do not believe that the line was intentional, although I am aware that the diagonal and the vertical of the *P* can be read as an *A*. But that produces a sequence of letters (*MAP* with *A* ligatured to *P*) which makes no sense. Basienisa followed by *MP* (however poorly formed) and then by a mileage figure of 30 or slightly more still seems the most plausible interpretation.

The similarity of the names Dasianis and Basienisa is merely coincidental, however attractive it may be to identify one with the other. The identity of *Basienisa* in the Azraq inscription and *Basie* in the Khirbet Manara inscription seems assured, although I cannot explain the use of "short" and "long" forms of the name. Our identification of Basie / Basienisa with Manara was based in large part on the mileage figure for Basienisa-Dasianis and the corresponding distance between Manara and Azraq (see above). There is now good reason to doubt that. Here we may profit from Speidel's acute analysis of the phrase *agens Basie* in the inscription found near Khirbet Manara:

> *Agens Basie* in army speech meant "on duty at Basie". Had * Vicentius been stationed where the inscription was set up [*i.e.* at Manara], he might not have made a point of saying so. He is likely, therefore, to have been stationed elsewhere in the area.
>
> (Speidel 1987: 217)

* For Speidel, the "elsewhere" was at Azraq since Vicentius is named in a contemporary inscription there (Kennedy 1982: 93-94, no. 15) and Speidel believes that "Basianis" and "Basienis" and "Basie" are three versions of the same name. I am now persuaded that Basie or Basienisa is not to be identified with Khirbet Manara in spite of the comfortable agreement of distance. But I am not convinced that Basie / Basienisa is Azraq.

A third alternative seems likely, and that is the *castellum* at Dayr al-Kahf. The latter has been identified as the *Notitia*'s Speluncis (*Or.* 37.18) ever since Brünnow (1909: 70) observed that Arabic *kahf* (cavern, cave) translates Latin *spelunca*. That is an attractive analogy and there is a fourth century fort on the spot. But the caverns or caves at or near the fort for which the site would be given that distinctive name have not yet been identified. Very probably the "Monastery of the Cave" has taken its modern name from the remains of underground, roofed cisterns within the ruined fort (Butler 1910: 148). These, long since dry and unused, could well have given the appearance of caverns to those who settled in or near the abandoned *castellum*, just as the ruins of the fort's Byzantine chapel evoked the image of a monastery. Moreover, Spelunca is no more an uncommon placename in antiquity (Philipp and Honigmann *RE* 3A.2: 1609-10) than Kahf is at present (Dussaud 1927: 139).

Dayr al-Kahf is well-situated and must have been a vital link in communications between the military sites at Azraq and their counterparts in the Hawran and Auranitis. It lies on the eastern branch of the known Roman road north from Azraq, at a distance within reasonable emendation of the 30 MP on the Azraq terminus-stone. If the two vertical scratches mentioned above (**Fig. 22.1**) are the upper struts of a damaged *V* or *U*, the mileage would read *XXXV*. That accords nicely with the 52 km ground-distance between Azraq and Dayr al-Kahf along the remnants of the ancient road.

Such an identification also eliminates one inherent difficulty of equating Basienisa with Khirbet Manara, *i.e.* measuring the distance from Bostra and Basienisa to Dasianis independently along the same road rather than listing those distances consecutively as Bostra-Basienisa-Dasianis. It also emphasises the central importance of the fort at Dasianis for the military installations in the Azraq basin. The terminus-stone would then commemorate a triangulation of routes from Bostra, Basienisa and Bamata which intersect at Dasianis.

The castellum at Azraq and its satellite fortifications and watchtowers in the area (Asaykhin, Uwaynid, Rujm Mudawwar, perhaps also the sites of Qasr Amra and Khirbet Umari), as well as the vast reservoirs at Shishan, underscore the strategic value of the Azraq oasis in the desert interior of Roman Arabia. The defences established there in the Severan period and the road-system (from which there are numerous Severan milestones) linking the forts and watch-towers were apparently not maintained in the difficult decades of the mid-third century. Hence the need to resuscitate them. At the earliest that occurred immediately following Aurelian's destruction of Palmyra; at the latest in the 290s in order to anchor the southern end of the *strata Diocletiana*. The work of renovation at Azraq was still in progress under Constantine, and at Dayr al-Kahf a portion of the fort was restructured more than a generation later. This argues strongly that all these military installations were in use at the time of the *Notitia*, although at present there is no epigraphic or ceramic evidence beyond the third quarter of the fourth century (Parker 1986: 19-24).

But if Basienisa is indeed Dayr al-Kahf such an identification immediately raises two questions: where is Spelunca and why is there no mention of Basienisa in the *Notitia*? For each I can only hazard a guess. The fields to the south of the important Romano-Byzantine site of Umm al-Quttayn ("Mother of the [Dried] Figs"), 25 km west of Dayr al-Kahf, are honeycombed with caves. These are underground chambers formed when bubbles of gas were trapped during one or more volcanic eruptions of nearby Tell (more accurately Jebel) Ku'ays. The bubbles lasted long enough for the liquids to solidify in dome-shaped cavities, many of five or six cubic meters in volume (Kennedy *et al.* 1986: 146). The largest shown to the Southern Hawran Survey team was a cavern beneath the eastern slope of Jebel Ku'ays just a few kilometres south of Quttayn. The interior was some 50-75 meters in length, consisting of several large chambers connected by passageways. Surely such caves and caverns were known in antiquity. The name Spelunca would be apposite to the town and may have translated its pre-Islamic name. How or why Quttayn received its modern, dialectical name is unknown (Bron 1985). Certainly it is not to be identified with the medieval (Crusader) placename Alcotain (Dussaud 1927: 389).

Two factors indicate that Quttayn was the site of a Roman garrison. One is a brief Latin inscription attesting a part-mounted cohort (MacAdam and Kennedy 1986: 234-236). There is also the strong probability that the northern sector of Quttayn was a Roman fort of some 1.86 ha (Kennedy *et al.* 1986: 148-149; Kennedy and Gregory 1985: 414 pl. 73/b). It should be said at once that the unit attested, the *cohors III* (?) *Augusta Thracum equitata*, was probably stationed at Quttayn in the second century. The date and circumstances of the fort are so far unknown. Milestones dating to the first Tetrarchy and the Constantinian era are known from the town, and only recently a made road in the style of the *via nova Traiana*, and a milestone of *c*. 300 beside it, have been found northwest of Quttayn (Kennedy *et al.* 1986: 150). The topography of the site, its location on the only direct road between Bostra and Azraq and the military aspect of the town combine to suggest, however tentatively, an identification of Quttayn with Spelunca. If so, its garrison at the time of the *Notitia* was the *equites promoti indigenae*.

If Basienisa or Basie is to be found in the *Notitia*, it must be one of the still unidentified placenames. The toponym Asabaia (*Or*. 37.32) is a likely candidate. The site has never been satisfactorily identified (Thomson 1906: 128; 1907: 27), although some guesses have been made. Seeck's equation of Asabaia with the *Notitia*'s Sabaia (*Or*. 34.23) is non-sensical, since the latter was located in Palestine III. The *Notitia*'s Asabaia could well be a corruption of Basie(nisa). If so, the unit stationed there was the *cohors prima Thracum*. That the garrison was infantry rather than cavalry was the guess of the editors (Littmann *et al.* 1910: 127-28, no. 229) of the Latin dedication (noted above) from the fort. They restored *Valen*[*t*]*iniano prae*[*fect*]*o* [*coh*](*hortis*) in the penultimate line. As Parker (1986: 22, 24) cautions, one might also read *praefecto* [*alae*] or *praefecto* [*equ*](*itum*). The remains of what might be mangers for horses offer some support for that view.

Note

* Grateful acknowledgement is made to Prof. Peter Brennan, Department of History, the University of Sydney, Australia for acute and helpful suggestions in the preparation of this paper. He is not responsible for the conclusions drawn.

Bibliography

ABEL, F.-M.	1938	*Géographie de la Palestine*. Vol. 2. Paris.
ADAMS, R.McC. *et al.*	1977	Saudi Arabian archaeological reconnaissance - 1976 preliminary report on the first phase of the comprehensive archaeological survey program. *ATLAL* 1: 21-40.
BÖCKING, E.	1839	*Notitia Dignitatum et Administrationum Omnium tam Civilium quam Militarium in Partibus Orientis et Occidentis*. Vol. 1. Bonn.
BOWERSOCK, G.W.	1971	A report on *Arabia provincia*. *JRS* 61: 219-242.
BRON, F.	1985	Sur un emprunt sémitique en Grec et Latin. *RPhil* 59: 95-6.
BRÜNNOW, R.	1909	Die Kastelle des arabischen *Limes*. In G. Maspero (ed.) *Florilegium Melchior de Vogüé*: 65-77. Paris.
BRÜNNOW, R. and DOMASZEWSKI, A.	1909	*Die Provincia Arabia*. Vol. 3. Strassburg.
BUTLER, H.C.	1910	Ancient architecture in Syria, Southern Syria (Southern Hauran). In *PAES 1904-04 and 1909*. Division 2, Section A, Part 2: 63-148. Leiden.
CHEVALLIER, R.	1972	*Les voies romaines*. Paris.
DOMASZEWSKI, A.	1898	Die Namen römischer Kastelle am *Limes Arabicus*. In *Beiträge zur alten Geschichte und Geographie: Festschrift für Heinrich Kiepert*: 65-9. Berlin.

DUNAND, M. 1931 La strata Diocletiana. *RBibl* 40: 227-248, 579-584.

DUSSAUD, R. 1927 *Topographie historique de la Syrie antique et médiévale*. Paris.

GREGORY, S. and KENNEDY, D.L. 1985 *Sir Aurel Stein's limes report*. Oxford (BAR International Series 272).

KENNEDY, D.L. 1980 The frontier policy of Septimius Severus: New evidence from Arabia. In W.S. Hanson and L.J.F. Keppie (eds.) *Roman frontier studies, 1979*: 879-888. Oxford (BAR International Series 71).

1982 *Archaeological explorations on the Roman frontier in North East Jordan*. Oxford (BAR International Series 134).

KENNEDY, D.L. and MACADAM, H.I. 1985 Latin inscriptions from the Azraq Oasis, Jordan. *ZPE* 60: 97-107.

1986 Latin inscriptions from Jordan, 1985. *ZPE* 65: 231-236.

KENNEDY, D.L. *et al.* 1986 Preliminary report on the Southern Hauran Survey, 1985. *Annual of the Department of Antiquities of Jordan* 30: 145-53.

KETTENHOFEN, E. 1981 Zur Nordgrenze der *provincia Arabiae* im 3.Jahrhundert n. Chr. *ZDPV* 97: 62-73.

LITTMANN, E. *et al.* 1910 Greek and Latin inscriptions in Syria: Southern Syria (Southern Hauran). In *PAES 1904-04 and 1909*. Division 3, Section A, Part 2: 21-129. Leiden.

MACADAM, H.I. 1988 Ptolemy's *Geography* and the Wadi Sirhan. In P.-L. Gatier and B. Helly (eds.) *Géographie historique au Proche-Orient*: 55-75. Paris.

PARKER, S.T. 1986 *Romans and Saracens: A history of the Arabian frontier*. Winona Lake, Indiana.

POTTS, D.T. 1988 Trans-Arabian routes of the pre-Islamic period. In J.-F. Salles (ed.) *L'Arabie et ses mers bordières* 1: 127-62. Paris.

SARTRE, M. 1982 *Trois études sur l'Arabie romaine et byzantine*. Bruxelles.

SEECK, O. 1876 *Notitia Dignitatum*. Frankfurt am Main (1962 reprint).

SPEIDEL, M.P. 1987 The Roman road to Dumata (Jawf in Saudi Arabia) and the frontier strategy of *Praetensione Colligare*. *Historia* 36: 213-221.

SOURDEL, D. 1952 *Les cultes du Hauran à l'époque romaine*. Paris.

SPRENGER, A. 1875 *Die alte Geographie Arabiens*. Bern.

THOMSON, P. 1906 Untersuchungen zur älteren Palästina literatur. *ZDPV* 29: 101-132.

1907 *Loca Sancta: Verzeichnis der im 1. bis 6. Jahrhundert n. Chr. Erwähnten Ortsschaften Palästinas*. Halle.

VAILHE, S. 1898/99 Les garnisons romaines de la province d'Arabie. *EchOr* 2: 89-95.

WADDINGTON, W.H. 1870 *Inscriptions grecques et latines de la Syrie*. Paris.

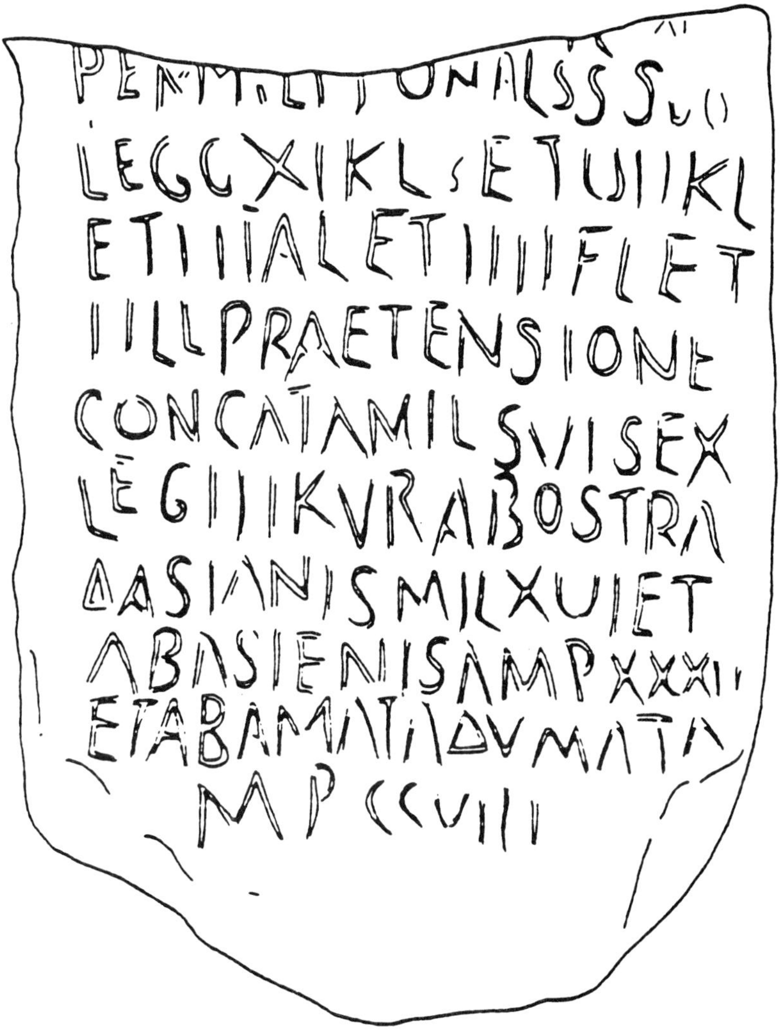

Fig. 22.1 Facsimile drawing of the Azraq terminus inscription,
as published in Kennedy and MacAdam (1985: 100)

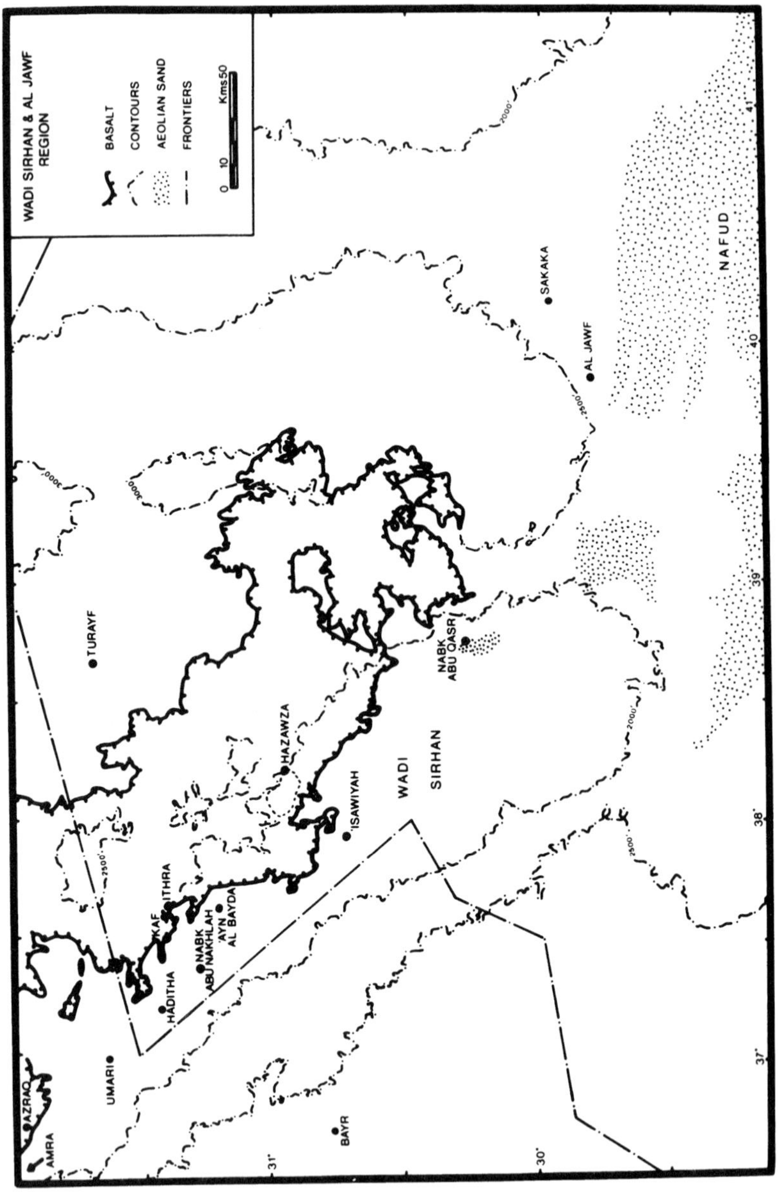

Fig. 22.2 The Wadi Sirhan and al-Jawf regions, adapted by Julie Kennedy from Adams *et al.* (1977: pl. 4) with permission from the publisher

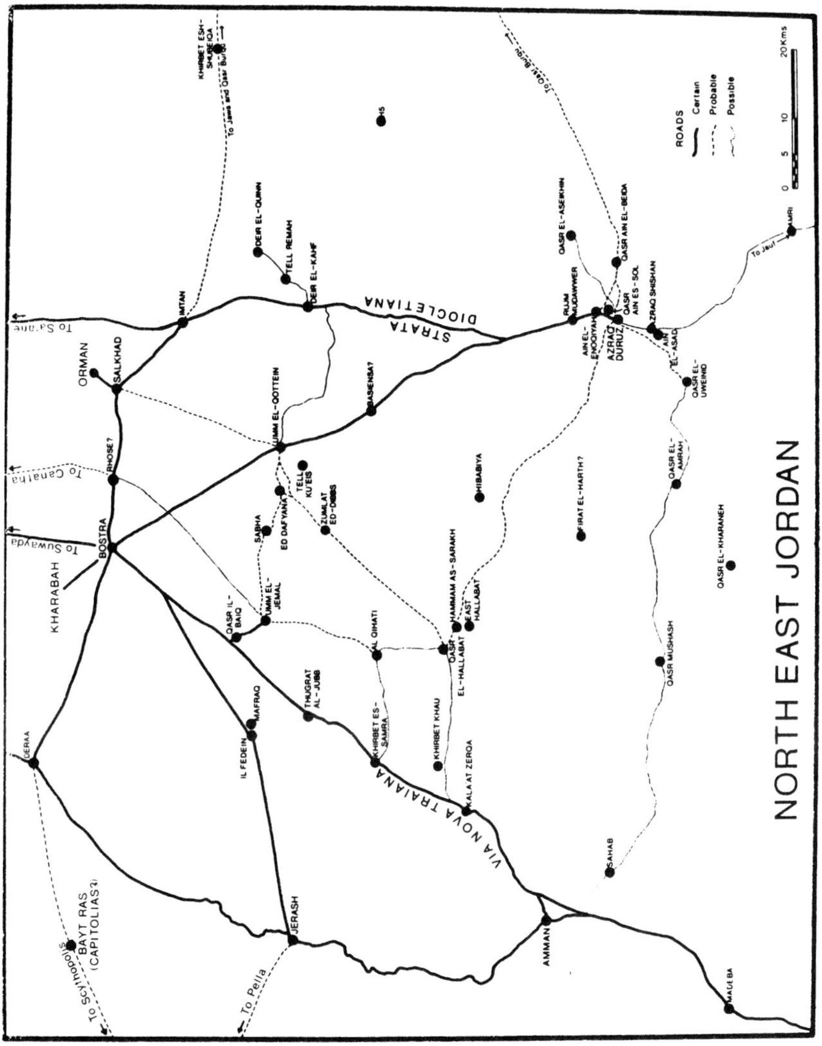

Fig. 22.3 Detail of the Roman road system in northern Jordan and southern Syria. The map is based on that appearing originally appearing as the end-map in Kennedy (1982), drawn by Julie Kennedy

XII

EPIGRAPHY AND VILLAGE LIFE IN SOUTHERN SYRIA DURING THE ROMAN AND EARLY BYZANTINE PERIODS

1. *Introduction*

On the morning of Tuesday, the fourteenth of May, 1861, the Anglo-French epigrapher W.H. Waddington departed from Damascus on horseback.[1] He took with him an assistant named Asad-Amer and a large quantity of blank notebooks. Within two years the notebooks contained facsimiles of over 1,000 inscriptions which Waddington hand-copied from stones imbedded in tombs, bridges, temples, arches, theaters, churches, houses, courtyards and a varied assortment of other buildings both private and public throughout southern Syria. These were published, with others copied in Lebanon and north Syria, as the *Recueils des inscriptions grecques et latines de la Syrie* in 1870.[2] It remains, more than a century later, the fundamental source of Greek and Latin epigraphy from southern Syria, and a monument to the energy and erudition of one of the 19th century's great orientalists.

In time, other collections of inscriptions — including Nabataean, Safaitic, Arabic and Syriac — were published after various surveys in this same region. Notable among those

[1] J.B. Chabot, "Le Voyage en Syrie de W.(H.) Waddington", *Mélanges Syriens offerts à René Dussaud,* Vol. 1 (Paris, 1939) 352. It is worth noting that for security purposes Waddington finished the first day's journey "avec l'escorte de 20 druzes..." (ibid).

[2] This was originally published in the third volume of a larger work, *Inscriptions recueillies en Grèce et en Asie Mineure par Philippe Le Bas,* which Waddington described as an "ouvrage que j'étais chargé de continuer après la mort de l'auteur, et dont elles forment le complément..." (iii). The separate volume will hereinafter be referred to as *Wadd.*

IL- LEDJĀ

PRINCETON EXPEDITION
1909

DJEBEL ḤAURÂN

FROM SURVEY BY
F. A. NORRIS, C. E.

1904-5

SCALES

LEGEND

SALKHAD	*Large Towns or Ruins*
Hebrân	*Villages and Minor Ruins*
Shakkâ	*From Wetzstein's Map.*
BOSTRA	*Ancient Names*
△ △	*Bedawin Encampment*
══	*Roman Road*

⊏	*Walled Town.*
⊠	*Roman Fortress*
⊠	*Arabic Fortress*
●	*Expedition's Camp*
— —	*" Route 1904-5*
—·— ·	*" 1909*

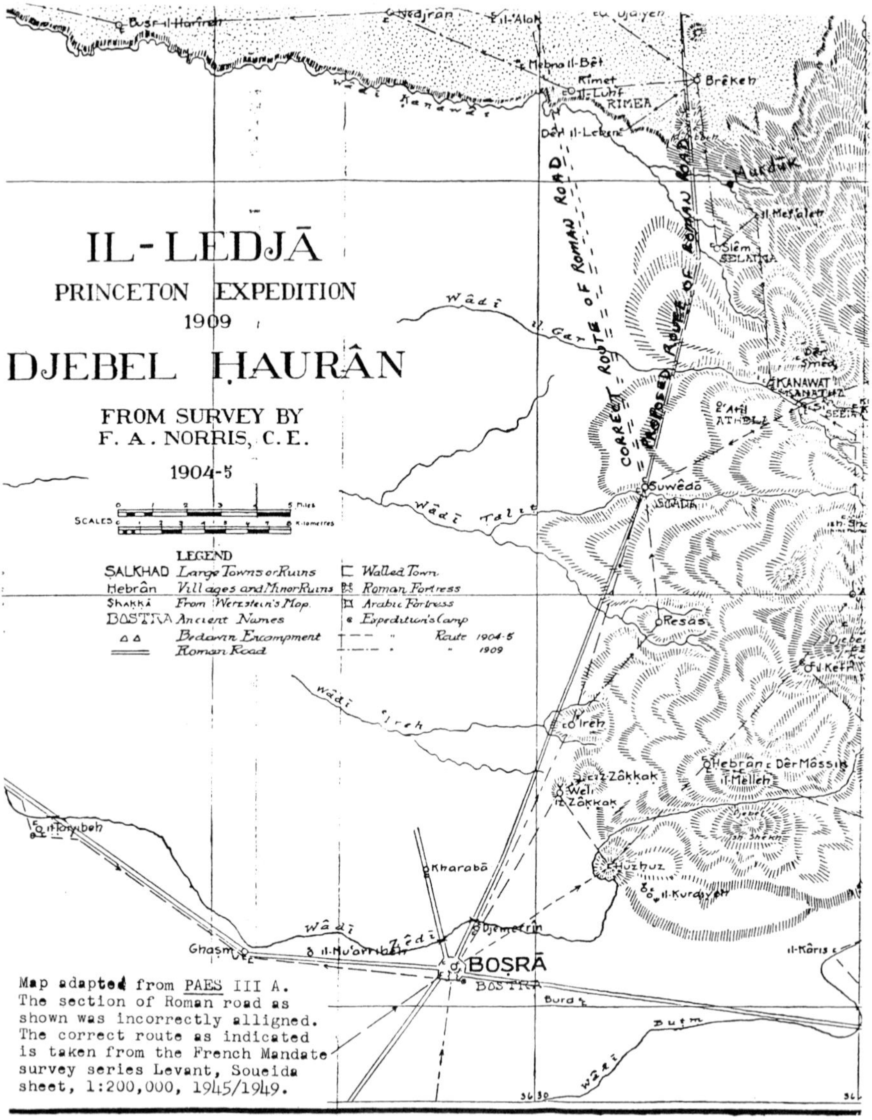

Map adapted from PAES III A.
The section of Roman road as
shown was incorrectly alligned.
The correct route as indicated
is taken from the French Mandate
survey series Levant, Soueida
sheet, 1:200,000, 1945/1949.

were the three expeditions from Princeton University between 1899 and 1909,[3] the survey by Dussaud and Macler at the turn of the century,[4] and the collection made by Maurice Dunand in 1925.[5] The Greek and Latin inscriptions alone now number more than 2,000. These are being re-edited and re-published as forthcoming volumes in the ongoing *Inscriptions grecques et latines de la Syrie* series presently undertaken by the Institut Fernand-Courby in Lyon, France.[6]

For many reasons, little archaeological work has been conducted in southern Syria. Even the once large and important cities such as Bostra (mod. Buṣrā ash-Shām) and Philippopolis (mod. Shubah) are only now beginning to attract the attention of serious field archaeologists. In lieu of archaeological evidence, the published inscriptions, together with the available historical sources, give some picture, however indistinct, of life in southern Syria during the first seven centuries A.D. Village life figures quite prominently in these texts, since it is from villages that the great majority of them come. Hence the subject of this paper.

By reference to specific inscriptions I will examine the following six topics: (1) the Hellenization process, (2) village government, (3) building activities, (4) inter-village activities, (5) tribal and clan activity and (6) occupations and professions. There are many other aspects which could be examined, and these will be noted in the concluding remarks.

My aim is to focus attention on matters often overlooked in the political histories of Roman and Byzantine Syria, i.e. how the indigenous communities reacted to and functioned within the Roman imperial system. It is the Greek inscriptions much more than the Latin, Nabataean or other that record the everyday affairs of the villages and their inhabitants. To a limited extent Profs. Heichelheim[7] and Rostovtzeff[8] showed the potential significance of such a study. A closer examination was made by A.H.M. Jones[9] and G.M. Harper,[10] but to date no full-scale, systematic study of village life in southern Syria has yet been attempted.[10a] A generation ago Georges Tchalenko showed what useful information could be gained by a careful study of villages in northern Syria.[11]. This paper is but a preliminary step in that direction, which I hope to expand upon in a larger work.

[3] W.K. Prentice, *Greek and Latin Inscriptions:* Part III of the *Publications of an American Archaeological Expedition to Syria in 1899-1900* (New York, 1908), hereinafter *AAES*; E. Littmann et al. *Publications of the Princeton University Archaeological Expeditions to Syria in 1904-05 and 1909,* Division III: Greek and Latin Inscriptions, Section A: Southern Syria (Leyden, 1910-21), hereinafter *PAES.*

[4] R. Dussaud and I. Macler, *Voyage Archéologique au Ṣafā et dans le Djebel ed-Drūz* (Paris, 1901) and the same authors' *Mission dans les régions désertiques de la Syrie Moyenne* (Paris, 1903), hereinafter *Voyage* and *Mission.*

[5] "Nouvelles Inscriptions du Djebel Druze et du Hauran", *RB* 41 (1932) 397-416; 561-580 and *RB* 42 (1933) 235-254; *Mélanges Syriens offerts à René Dussaud,* 2 vols. (Paris, 1939), II pp. 559-579; *Ar Or* 18 (1950) 144-164; collectively hereinafter *NIDH.*

[6] Vols. I-VII and VIII Pt. 2 as well as Vol XIII Pt. 1 (Bostra) are now in print; hereinafter *IGLS.* In addition, the following abbreviations should be noted: IGRRP: *Inscriptiones Graecae ad Res Romana Pertinentes;* Musée: *Le musée de Soueida;* Ewing: W. Ewing, "Greek and other Inscriptions Collected in the Hauran", *PEFQS* (1895); Fossy: C. Fossy, "Inscriptions de Syrie," *BCH* 21 (1897); SEG: *Supplementum Epigraphicum Graecum,* VII (1934).

[7] F.M. Heichelheim, *Roman Syria* in T. Frank (ed.), *An Economic Survey of Ancient Rome,* Vol. IV (New Jersey, 1959 — reprint) 121-258.

[8] M. Rostovtzeff, *The Social and Economic History of the Roman Empire* (2nd., Oxford, 1957), 270-273 and notes 661-666.

[9] "The Urbanization of the Ituraean Principality", *JRS* 21 (1931) 265-275 (hereinafter "Urbanization").

[10] "Village Administration in the Roman Province of Syria," *YCS* 1 (1928) 104-168.

[10a] See now note no. 103 below.

[11] G. Tchalenko, *Villages antiques de la Syrie du Nord,* 3 vols. (Paris, 1953).

2. The Hellenization process

Though the villagers of southern Syria spoke an Aramaic or Arabic dialect, they very often recorded their everyday affairs in Greek inscriptions. This in itself indicated some degree of Hellenization, even on the fringes of territory which had belonged to one or another of the Greek kingdoms created after Alexander's death. Three centuries of Macedonian rule established Greek as the new *lingua franca* of the eastern Mediterranean. Certainly some Syrian villagers spoke Greek, but the Hellenization process, at least linguistically, does not appear deep-rooted outside the large cities.

The Greek of the village inscriptions is often a *patois* of dubious meaning which makes the *koinē dialéktos* of the New Testament and papyri seem classical in comparison. But it is not always the spelling or grammar or syntax of an inscription, nor even the proper names of the villagers, which exposes the Semitic background of the inscribers. One illustration of this is the brief dedicatory text which Waddington copied at ʿAmra in the Jebel al-ʿArab:

Ἀουεῖδος Δάδου	Aoueidos (the son) of Dados
ἐποίησε τῇ Ἀθηνᾷ,	made (this) for Athēna,
σεννότου ρϟ΄.	(in) the year 190 (A.D. 295).[12]

Both the name of the dedicant (ʿAwīdh) and his father (Dād) are Semitic and well-attested in this region. Athēna was long ago identified with the Arabic goddess Allāt. It is the appearance of the term σεννότος which makes this text especially interesting. We should expect instead Greek ετος as in most inscriptions of this type. Waddington correctly identified *sennotos* with Semitic šnt; cf. Arabic *sana(tun)* and Syriac *šantā*.

One other inscription from the Jebel al-ʿArab demonstrates the process and the limits of hellenization. This text is from the village of Shaqqā (Saccaea/Maximianopolis):

(In memory of) Alexander (son) of	Ἀλέξανδρον Ἀκραβάνου
Acrabanus, pious high priest,	ἀρχιερέα εὐσεβὴν φιλό-
community-minded, interpreter for	πατριν, ἑρμηνέα ἐπιτρόπων,
the procurators; Namēlē his wife,	Ναμήλη [γ]υ[νὴ] α[ὐ]τοῦ,
Petran, and Rufus (his) son, laid	Πετραία, καὶ Ῥοῦφος υἱὸς,
(him) to rest among his own. [13]	ἐν ἰδίοις κατέθεντο.

This is a common funerary dedication, unfortunately undated. φιλόπατρις *could be* taken in its literal sense of "patriotic", but here the meaning seems closer to that of the term εὐεργέτης "benefactor". The wife's name is recognizably Semitic.[14] The patronymic is simply a rendering of ʿAqrabā(n), still today a place-name (cf. note 39) in the western Ḥaurān. Alexander was obviously a man of some social standing, since he combined a religious function with the duties of an interpreter (ἑρμηνεύς) for the financial officer attached to the governor's staff.[15] Apparently he traveled among the villages with the imperial officials, providing *viva voce* translations wherever needed. That the villages of this region required such a service is somewhat surprising in light of the sophisticated rural administrative system attested in Roman times. This is the subject of the next section of the paper.

---

[12] *Wadd.* 2081.
[13] *Wadd.* 2143
[14] H. Wuthnow, *Die semitischen Menschennamen in griechischen Inschriften und Papyri des Vorderen Orients* (Leipzig, 1930) 81, s.v.

[15] C. Clermont-Ganneau, "Les Epitropes de la Province d'Arabie", *BEHE* 230 (1921) 161-164; cf. A.H.M. Jones, *The Greek City* (Oxford, 1940) 290 and note 45.

3. *Village government*

Political stability in southern Syria was not initiated by the Romans. Herod the Great and his descendants, and the last few Nabataean kings, had effectively curbed the banditry and the Bedouin raids which must have impeded the social and economic development of the entire region. There is every reason to believe that Nabataean rule, had it continued to be effective beyond the first century, would have been just as beneficial as Roman rule. But the available evidence indicates that Nabataean control of internal and external affairs grew increasingly ineffective in the late first century.[16] This in turn jeopardized its long-standing client-kingdom status with Rome, and resulted in Roman annexation of the kingdom in A.D. 106.[17]

Villages which had been within Herodian territory (the Lejā and Jebel al-ᶜArab regions) were attached to the province of Syria; those within the Nabataean kingdom (eastern Batanaea and the Ḥaurān) were included in the new province of Arabia. Some of these villages were assigned to the territory of the few cities of the region. Those in the Ḥaurān fell within the territorial limits of Bostra or Canatha.[18] But many, especially those of the upland areas attached to Syria, did not take on the role of shadowy appendages of *poleis*. From the abundant evidence of the inscriptions, they assumed instead the form, if not the substance, of cities. Villages formed their own assemblies, elected or appointed boards of magistrates, managed a common fund, negotiated with the Bedouin in their vicinity, petitioned the governor for redress of wrongdoing, sent ambassadors to Rome, regulated the use of common land, undertook joint endeavors with other communities, and subscribed public works projects of every conceivable type;[19] some of these will be described in the next section.

Villages referred to their corporate or collective function by employing a remarkably diverse range of terms. Most notable among these are "the village" (ἡ κώμη), "the villagers" (οἱ κωμῆται), "those from the village" (οἱ ἀπὸ τῆς κώμης), "the people" (ὁ δῆμος), "the community" (τὸ κοινόν), and "the assembly" (ὁ ὄχλος).[20] Other collective terms were employed. A damaged Greek inscription from Junayn in the Jebel al-ᶜArab may indicate that the term τὸ συνέδριον (assembly or common-council) was used there instead;[21] this group, representing "the whole village" erected or dedicated some structure (a *propylon*?) under the supervision of magistrates elected by "the people". These "administrators" (διοικηταί) were but one example of the many village officials we find attested in the inscriptions. In addition we find the following titles: "village chief" (πρωτοκομήτης or στρατηγός); "trustees" (πιστοί); "planners" (προνοηταί); "commissioners" (ἐπιμεληταί); "overseers" or "supervisors" (ἐπισκοποί); "managers" (οἰκονομοί); lastly, "advocates" or "legal representatives" (ἔκδικοι and σύνδικοι).[22]

[16] F. Winnett, "The Revolt of Damasī: Safaitic and Nabataean Evidence", *BASOR* 211 (1973) 54-57.

[17] On the *motivation* for this, see G.W. Bowersock, "Syria Under Vespasian", *JRS* 63 (1973) 138-140. Arabia's annexation may have been only the penultimate stage of a Trajanic *Ostpolitik* designed to fix the Roman frontier at the Zagros mountains.

[18] A. Alt, "Das Territorium von Bostra", *ZDPV* 68 (1951) 235-245; M. Sartre, "Le Territoire de Canatha" *Syria* 58 (1981) 343-357, emending Alt's errors regarding Bostra's northern territory. Adraa (Derᶜā) undoubtedly incorporated villages in the western Ḥaurān.

[19] Jones, "Urbanization", 268-275; cf. his *Cities of the Eastern Roman Provinces* (2nd ed., Oxford, 1971) 282-287.

[20] Jones, "Urbanization" 272.

[21] *Wadd.* 2188 (undated). I wish to thank Mr. Francis Piejko, Utica, New York, for his suggestions regarding the restoration of parts of this text, and for comments on many other aspects of this paper.

[22] Jones, "Urbanization", 270-272.

All of this indicates that the villages emulated the cities in many details of administration. But there is as yet no compelling evidence that they usurped the ultimate authority of the city, the council (ἡ βουλή). The term "councillor" (βουλευτής) is attached to many men in village inscriptions, but as Jones pointed out long ago,[23] it is an honorary title designating one who had served (or was serving) on a city council. Likewise, the unique appearance of the city-council term *dekaprōtoi* in an inscription from Namra in the Jebel al-ᶜArab[24] is clearly an honorific title, since the two men so named are designated as village *pistoi* in the same text. The term *boulē* does not appear in any village inscription, nor is any variant of it known from rural epigraphy except *bouleutēs*.[25]

4. *Building Activity*

The known inscriptions demonstrate clearly that the villages of southern Syria undertook (normally at their own expense) public works projects of every conceivable kind. Among these I note the construction of baths, basilicas, stables, refectories, temples, hotels, reservoirs, theaters, aqueducts, courtyards, fountains and public buildings of uncertain character known by a variety of names. From the fourth century on some of the building inscriptions mention the erection of a significantly new structure: the watchtower (φρούριον). This apparently became a common feature on the skyline of many villages, especially those facing the desert frontier.

Perhaps the most common public structure of all was the inn or rest-house. Whether they were known as "the public guest-house" (τὸ δημόσιον πανδοχῖον) or "the common guest-house" (τὸ κοινόν πανδοχῖον), references to them are too numerous to warrant individual attention here. They normally included, or were built in conjunction with, stables and refectories. Some of these inns (built in northern Syria) have survived partially intact.[26]

Many village inscriptions refer to buildings which also have a public association, although in somewhat a more official capacity. Some examples of the terminology used will demonstrate this. In one instance "those from the village" of al-Ajaylat (anc. Egla) in the Jebel al-ᶜArab "dedicated to their god Ethaos (Ithaᶜ)" some kind of "public building" (δημόσιον τὴν οἰκοδομὴν) in an unknown year.[27] At Majdal-ash-Shur in the eastern Ḥaurān another "public house" (ὁ δημόσιος οἶκος) was built in A.D. 362 "by provision and under the direction of" three *pistoi* of the village.[28] In another instance, the southern Ḥaurān village of al-Muᶜarribah built in A.D. 336 "a common house" (ὁ κοὶνος οἶκος) by provision of two or more pistoi assisted by two or more *pronoētai*.[29] The exact function of these buildings is unknown. They may have been assembly-halls or public offices of some kind, even though the terminology of the inscriptions closely parallels that of the inns. Yet it isn't odd that a village would dedicate a hotel to a deity, as noted above, and the matter remains unsettled.

Even more obscure in meaning is the "vaulted hall of the people" (καμάρα τοῦ δήμου) built by the village of Busān (anc. Bosana) in the Jebel al-ᶜArab "under the advocacy of"

[23] Ibid, 272-273; cf. *CERP*² 286.

[24] *Voyage*, pp. 148-149 no. 12.

[25] *Wadd.* 2056 from Umm ar-Rūman in the southern Ḥaurān appears to be an exception to this, but only because Waddington very conjecturally restored the term *Koin]obouli(o)n* (common-council hall) in the last (?) line of a much- damaged text. I hope to republish this and show that the inscription simply refers to yet one more city councillor involved in village affairs.

[26] *PAES* III B no 1154.

[27] *Wadd*, 2209 (undated).

[28] *Wadd.* 2029.

[29] *Wadd.* 2070a.

one *syndikos* and two *pistoi* in an unknown year.[30] In the nearby village of al-Mushannaf (anc. Nela) a *syndikos* in association with a board of administrators built "the vaulted hall" (ἡ καμάρα).[31] Here also the meaning is uncertain, but some sort of public assembly-hall seems to be implied. Whether it had *political* use, like the council-hall (βουλευτήριον) in cities, is unclear. I am inclined to believe that καμάρα (Latin *camera*) here is synonymous with the more common term *basilica,* a covered public building normally placed in the vicinity of the market and used for a variety of functions. At least two villages in southern Syria noted the construction of just such a building.[32] At the very least, the importance of these buildings to the villages is demonstrably emphasized by the fact that high-ranking officials or boards of magistrates normally oversaw their construction.

5. *Inter-Village Activities*

At the site of a ruined monastery named Dayr al-Laban in the north-eastern corner of the Nuqrah, Waddington discovered and copied an unusual group of eight Greek inscriptions. All of them appear to be related, either in time or purpose or both. All are religious in nature and connected with the worship of a pre-Christian solar deity referred to in a number of texts as "Zeus-Aumos the Unconquered Sun-God".[33] Dayr al-Laban was not a village but a sanctuary or sacred area, later converted into a Byzantine and then an Islamic monastery. What is particularly significant is that the majority of these inscriptions are joint dedications by two or more individuals, villages or tribes.

The longest text, and the only one that is dated, begins with a preamble acknowledging Emperor Constantine and his son Constantinus (A.D. 320). It then goes on to note that:

> The courtyard and (something else) were (dedicated?) to the Lord and Unconquered Sun-God Aumos. Cassius Malichathus from the village of Rimea, of the tribe Khasetenoi, and Paulus Maximinus, from the village of Merdocha, of the tribe Audenoi, erected from the foundations (this) magnificent edifice and (its) roof, having generously donated their own time, by provision of Aumus and Amelathus (his) son, priests.[34]

Malichathus and Maximinus, again identified by village and tribe, appear in two other inscriptions. One notes the construction of "the enclosure wall of the courtyard"[35] and the other that "the altar was built".[36] In these latter two texts, the men are styled as *pistoi*.

On another large stone Waddington found two similar dedications obviously related to each other:[37]

[30] *Wadd.* 2240.

[31] *Wadd.* 2220 (undated).

[32] *Wadd.* 2044: "The basilikē *and* the door..." (A.D. 330); *Wadd.* 2189 (undated).

[33] D. Sourdel, *Les Cultes du Hauran à l'Époque romaine* (Paris, 1952) 54-56.

[34] *Wadd.* 2393.

[35] *Wadd.* 2394.

[36] *Wadd.* 2395.

[37] *Wadd.* 2396 a& b. Waddington hesitantly proposed translating the title ἱεροτομεύς as "sacrificateur", suggesting instead that it was a mistake in spelling for the commonly-attested title of * ἱεροταμιάς (temple-treasurer). To complicate matters, the term occurs as ωροτομης and οροτομης in *Wadd.* 2397 (see note no.38), obviously a contemporary text. Some support for Waddington's solution is found in *PAES* III A 765[11] (republishing Wadd. 2397). Prof. G.W. Bowersock has suggested to me that ἱεροταμιάς should be taken as the correct spelling, and translated as "sacred butcher" or some equivalent term. This is an attractive alternative, but I have not yet found parallels to support it. Sourdel, *Cultes* p. 54 surprisingly sidesteps the entire issue by failing to reproduce these particular texts from Dayr al-Laban.

(a)
Jul(ius) Maximus (the son) of
Oredanus, from the village of
Rimea, temple-treasurer(?)
(ἱεροτομεύς sic) of the tribe
Khasetēnoi, built (this).

(b)
Aur (elius) Avitus (the son) of
Atticus, from the *mētrocōmia* of
Borechath Sabaōn, temple-treasurer(?)
(ἱεροτομεύς — sic), of the tribe
Audēnoi, built (this).

One other text, inscribed by someone with scant knowledge of Greek, is worth noting:

Aur(elius) Gla(u)cus, (the son) of
Bernicianus, from the village of
Idnos (?), temple-treasurer? built
(this). Aur(elius) Montanus (the
son) of Ausus, from the village of
Rimea, temple-treasurer? of the
tribe Khasetēnoi, built (this).[38]

The significance of this group of texts was pointed out long ago by Jones, but only in a cursory fashion. Four villages and two tribes were involved in building projects at this sanctuary. No doubt they contributed to the maintenance of it as well. Not surprisingly, the villages which can be identified are very near Dayr al-Laban. Merdocha (mod. Murdūk) is eight km. south-east, in the foothills of the Jebel al-ᶜArab. Rimea (mod. Rimet al-Luḥf) and Borechath Sabaon (mod. Brākah) are a few km. north and northwest respectively — just within the southern edge of the Lejā. The name of the fourth village, Idnos, is quite uncertain, and hence its exact location is unknown. Like the others, it would have lain just east of the Roman road which ran north from Bostra, via Suweidā, and across the Lejā to Damascus. The sketch map will help to illustrate this.

From these texts, it is clear that certain villages near the sanctuary at Dayr-al-Laban were jointly responsible for major building projects at the site. It also appears that these villages participated in some sort of alliance, either through tribal affiliation or a more formal federation. The extent of this is unclear. The village of Borechath Sabaōn is referred to as a *mētrocōmia*, literally a "mother-village." This is normally taken to mean that it enjoyed a special status as the "capital" of a village league. If so, this might be understood as the in-between stage from village to city rank. But there is no evidence from these inscriptions that the other named villages were in any way subordinate to or dependent upon Borechath Sabaōn. Other inscriptions from this region demonstrate clearly that *mētrocōmia* was an honored privilege.[39] Moreover it is especially interesting that these references to *mētrocōmiai* are from villages formerly within the Herodian kingdom, and initially attached to the province of Syria following the death of Agrippa II in A.D. 93/94.

This collection of inscriptions may be unique, and therefore not representative of inter-village activities elsewhere in southern Syria. In spite of this, it is interesting to record that some villages undertook co-ordinated activities, and that tribal identification, even after two centuries of Roman rule, was still an important social distinction. Even so, the same texts bear witness that one tribe (the Audēnoi) split, and became part of the

[38] *Wadd.* 2397.

[39] Cf. *Wadd.* 2480 (Zorᶜah) and 2524 (Masmayah). Although an inscription from nearby Sūr (*PAES* 797²) yields the term *mētrocōmia,* it is by no means certain that the village of the inscription is Sūr. To the west of the Lejā, the village of ᶜAqrabā is styled a *mētrocōmia* in the Greek text of a boundary-stone found by Dussaud and Macler, *Mission* 298 no. 175.

population of two villages. This was no doubt a common pattern, and part of the urbanization process in this region.

6. *Tribal & Clan Activity*

The Greek inscriptions of southern Syria yield twenty-one names that are unquestionably tribal and another twenty which are doubtless clans or even smaller groupings.[40] This will come as no surprise since the same region today still has tribal and clan associations which play an important social role.

Only one of the tribal inscriptions is from a village in the Ḥaurān; the remaining twenty are almost equally divided between villages in the Lejā and the Jebel al-ᶜArab. These are the upland areas on the fringes of the desert, and the areas which would be a natural choice of Bedouin in the transitory stage from nomadism to urbanization.

It is also worth noting that all of these tribal names are recognizably Semitic, and that with only one exception all are from villages. By contrast, the known tribal names from Bostra are Greco-Roman and the tribes themselves, in keeping with other Hellenized cities, were no doubt artificial creations to conform with the needs of a city constitution. Only about half of the tribal inscriptions can be dated; the earliest is A.D. 170 and the latest is A.D. 560.

The clan inscriptions parallel the tribal texts in almost every way. Only two names are associated with the Ḥaurān, and three names with cities. Two-thirds of the remainder come from villages in the Jebel al-ᶜArab, and the rest from villages in the Lejā. Dates range from early second century to late fifth century.

Since the focus of this paper is on village life, it will be useful to briefly investigate the relationship between village and tribe based on what the inscriptions relate. This can best the done by grouping the inscriptions according to similarity of activity or purpose, and noting whatever patterns may emerge. Those inscriptions which emphasize community action will be of particular interest.

Fully one third of the tribal and clan inscriptions (taken collectively) testify to involvement in some kind of public work. These projects include the restoration[41] or construction[42] of houses and the building[43] or enlargement[44] of temples or parts of temples, e.g. an apse,[45] a dovecote[46] or just a door.[47] The "magnificent edifice" built jointly by two tribes at Dayr al-Laban and the "magnificent buildings" erected by tribesmen at Najrān in the Lejā may well have been temples.[48] In one case a wall[49] and in another a "public room" (ἡ καμάρα) [50] were built by provision of a clan and tribal *syndikos* respectively. A brief dedicatory inscription from Smād in the Lejā testifies that "the tribe of the Dabanēnoi made the public (speakers') rostrum;"[51] was this perhaps a reference to some local Hyde Park? On one occasion a city built and equipped some workshops; this task was supervised by "overseers" (*episkopoi*) of a named tribe.[52] On another occasion the same (?) city repaired aqueducts, and in this inscription the supervisors were

[40] M. Sartre, "Tribus et clans dans le Hawran antique," *Syria* 59 (1982) 77-91 and my "Notes on Tribal Names in Greek Inscriptions from southern Syria", *Proceedings of the Fourth Conference on the History of Bilād al-Shām* 1985, forthcoming.

[41] *AAES* 389 = *NIDH* 112.

[42] *Wadd.* 2481.

[43] *NIDH* 115 = *SEG* 1069.

[44] *Wadd.* 2366 = *AAES* 428a.

[45] *Wadd.* 2512.

[46] *Wadd.* 2173a = *PAES* 758.

[47] *Wadd.* 2483.

[48] *Wadd.* 2393b and 2427.

[49] *Wadd.* 2173.

[50] *Wadd.* 2220.

[51] *PAES* 786[3]

[52] *Wadd.* 2309.

"councillors" from another tribe.[53] In yet another community a man who was probably a clan spokesman paid for the construction of a "stable and two refectories."[54]

Only one tribal inscription is identifiably Christian; this commemorates that "Sergius (the son) of Samaathus, from the village of Norerathē (mod. Najrān?) of the tribe Soborēnoi, from his own funds built the sanctuary (for the church) to Saint Elias, in the year 455 (A.D.)."[55] St. Elias is also honored by the construction of a *martyrium* in a clan dedication found at nearby il-Jāj.[56] The other texts of a religious nature are surely non-Christian. One commemorates a feast held in honor of an unnamed god,[57] another is a dedication to an unnamed deity.[58] In other inscriptions a column,[59] a statue (?),[60] an altar base[61] and an altar[62] were all dedicated by clans or tribes or members of each. Only rarely are gods mentioned by name. Lycurgus was honored in some fashion by a tribe,[63] and two or more shrines to "Fortune" (Tychē) were built by two clans and a private (?) individual (a patron?).[65] A (temple?) façade dedicated "to the god Kronos of the (clan) Sokarathoi" was constructed in the village of Kafr in the Jebel al-ᶜArab "in the year 17 of Hadrianus Caesar" (A.D. 134).[66] In a unique text from ᶜOrmān in the Ḥaurān, three men of the tribe Konēnoi "had responsibility for the cleansing (of the temple?)".[67]

Surprisingly few tribal or clan dedications of a funerary nature have so far been discovered. Only one inscription is known in which a tribal patron is honored.[68] Likewise only one text has been published which commemorates a clan *stratēgos* (sheikh?).[69] Finally, there are two tribal inscriptions recorded which are so mutilated that their purpose remains, unfortunately, unknown.[70]

7. *Professions and Occupations*

The village inscriptions also offer information regarding the occupations of the inhabitants. Thus we learn that a certain Gabnes, who built an altar, was a sculptor.[71] The building profession itself is well-attested. The builder (οἰκοδόμος), partly out of pride and partly as free advertising, often notes his native village. In this way we hear of "Rabbus from Borechath Sabaōn", a *mētrocōmia* in the Lejā, who built a house at Ṣalkhād in the Ḥaurān in A.D. 403.[72] Likewise we know of Gadouos the son of Malechus "from the village of Egla" (mod. al-Ajaylat) in the Jebel al-ᶜArab who built a "memorial" and some other structure in Malaḥ aṣ-Ṣarrar in the eastern Ḥaurān.[73]

The successful builder might have assistants and apprentices[74] and could boast of his own skills: "the rafters of this house ʿAddus (the son) of Taroudus, far best of builders, joined, and the work was carried to completion."[75] These rafters were surely the basalt slabs still used today, which are often three or four meters long and may weigh one hundred kilos. Rapid completion of a building project was also acknowledged with favor; "the villagers" of Dayr-el-Mayas in the southern Ḥaurān bragged that "by

53 *Wadd.* 2308.
54 *AAES* 377.
55 *Wadd.* 2431.
56 *Wadd.* 2436 = *PAES* 791.
57 *Wadd.* 2370 = *PAES* 765[1]
58 *Wadd.* 2439.
59 *Wadd.* 2339 = *AAES* 413a.
60 *Wadd.* 2348 = *AAES* 421.
61 *Wadd.* 2537d.
62 Ibid; *Wadd.* 2173b (uncertain reading).
63 *NIDH* 76 = *SEG* 1102
64 *Wadd.* 2512.
65 *Wadd.* 2339 = *AAES* 413a.
66 Musée no. 198.
67 *PAES* 694 = *NIDH* 182a
68 *Wadd.* 2287 PAES 664.
69 *Wadd.* 2236.
70 *Mission* 243 no. 11 = *IGRRP* no. 1171.
71 *Wadd.* 2413n.
72 *PAES* 159.
73 *PAES* 713, 714.
74 *PAES* 787[8]
75 *Wadd.* 2244 = PAES 738.

provision of the builder Oenus, from the village of Bosana (mod. Būsān in the Jebel al-ᶜArab), the courtyard was completed in thirty-six days."[76]

Success in the building trade no doubt created a hierarchy among its practitioners. The most skilled (or least modest) builder might style himself as a "craftsman" (τεχνήτης)[77] or even an *architektos*.[78]

The agrarian basis of life in southern Syria did not pass unnoticed. Farmers took great pride in their work. One, named Diomedes, from Ghāriyyah ash-Sharkiyya near Bostra, was honored in a metrical epitaph as one who was "wealthy from farming."[79] Another, Masalemus Rabbus, from Nahita in the western Ḥaurān, built some structure in the year A.D. 385 "from his own farming labors."[80] We also have knowledge of collective enterprises. In one instance "the farmers (γεωργοὶ) of Zorava, at their own expense, set up (the statue of) Nikē."[81]

Not surprisingly, priests and temple-treasurers are too frequently attested to warrant individual references. However, there is mention at the great Nabataean sanctuary of Siᶜ of a "trumpeter" (βουκινάτωρ) appropriately named Triton.[82] This was undoubtedly a part-time job, as was that of an unnamed temple-sweeper (ὁ ναοκόρος).[82a].

Lawyers (*scholastikoi*) are known from inscriptions at Ghaṣm in the Ḥaurān[83] and Zorᶜah in the Lejā.[84] In the latter text the person named may have been attached to the provincial governor's staff (*officium*). Goldsmiths are known from two inscriptions. In one, a goldsmith named Moses (?) and his father built a memorial.[85] In the other something was built "through the generosity of Isakios (Isaac), goldsmith."[86] Waddington found this inscription "beneath the arch" at the opening of one of the numerous springs which flow from the hillsides near al-Kafr in the Jebel al-ᶜArab. The site is known in Arabic as ᶜAyn Mousa, "the Spring of Moses", and this led Waddington to guess that the place-name honored the Hebrew ancestry of its benefactor.

The military profession may also be noted here. There are few villages in southern Syria which do not honor veterans. Resident veterans, like retired city-councillors, were held in high esteem — and for much the same reason. Their experience, prestige and wealth were assets to any small community, whether or not the individual had been born there. Most veterans are known from their tombstones, but others are honored while still alive for their active participation in community activities. It is sometimes difficult to know if a person honored has actually retired from military service or whether he may still be on active duty. In either case the communities involved publicly acknowledged their gratitude.

An inscription from near the Lejā relates that a certain Julius Germanus, centurion of the *Legio III Gallica,* is "the benefactor and founder of the Aerisians";[87] Aera is modern as-Ṣanamāyn. A veteran named Rufus, a temple-treasurer in conjunction with two other men, made an offering "to Zeus" at Sahwat-al-Khudr near Bostra in 171.[88] A century later "the sanctuary was paved" at the nearby village of ᶜAyun by a veteran named Alexander (the son) of Bathourus.[89] A veteran named Bassus takes credit for building

[76] *Wadd.* 2053b.
[77] *Ewing.* p. 132 no. 51.
[78] *Wadd.* 2471.
[79] *Voyage* 203 no. 88.
[80] *Wadd.* 2412 1
[81] *Wadd.* 2479.
[82] *PAES* 772
[82a] J-M & J. Dentzer, *CRAI* (June, 1981) 92 note 9, also from Siᶜ. *Naokoros* is for *neōkoros.*
[83] *PAES* 618.
[84] *Wadd.* 2485.
[85] *PAES* 786[2]
[86] *Wadd.* 2295.
[87] *Wadd.* 2413f.
[88] *Wadd.* 1969.
[89] *Wadd.* 1984b.

(and financing?) a tower for the village of il-Mashqūq in the Jebel al-ᶜArab.[90] The villagers of Qrayah, just a few kms. northeast of Bostra, were proud to make a public announcement regarding a project important to their village:

> To Good Fortune! The reservoir was built in the year 190 (A.D. 295) at the common expense of the village, costing 15,000 denarii, by provision of Flavius Cornelius, primipilarius.[91]

In the Jebel al-ᶜArab village of Ḥabran the tribe Mozaidēnoi honored (with a statue?) as their patron a veteran named Aurelius Antonius Sabinus.[92] In the nearby village of Namrah another (?) Aurelius Sabinus described himself in a funerary inscription as a veteran and member of the tribe Askēnoi.[93] Two veterans served as "overseers" (*episkopoi*) of an unspecified project at Ṣalkhād in the Ḥaurān.[94] Even descendants of veterans benefit from a certain prestige, if the term οὐετρανικὸς is correctly understood in a number of inscriptions.[95] At Umm el-Zaytān in the Lejā two such οὐετρανικοὶ served as "planners" in the construction of a shrine (Kalybē).[96] The ease by which a man might pass from the military to a magistracy is exemplified by Theodorus Emmilis of el-Ghāriyah in the Ḥaurān, who distinguished himself in the careers of "soldiering and politicking."[97] He was only one of many who chose to make this particular transition. Obliquely related to the military profession is the occupation noted in a unique inscription from the village of Zayzān in the western Ḥaurān dated A.D. 485:

> Prosper, Zizios! (This) building of Malichus, engineer (μαγγάναριος) (was constructed) by authority of Antoninus, Anouneus and Anina (being village magistrates) in the year 380.[98]

A few professions remain to be noted. In the Lejā village of Sūr an enigmatic funerary text commemorates Aurelius Marcellus the son of Salus, "former steward (πραγματευτῆς) for thirty years in foreign lands;" his body was brought home and buried "in the forecourt" of his cousin's house.[99] Also in the Lejā, two men of Majadal who refer to themselves as surgeons (εἰατροτομεῖς) built something with money "from the common fund of the village."[100] The well-known Nabataean/Greek bilingual inscription from 'Umm aj-Jemal, just south of the modern Syrian-Jordanian border, notes that "Fihr, son of Shullai" had been a "tutor" (τροφεύς);[101] his pupil was Ghadīmat (al-Akrash?), king of the Tanūkh tribe and ancestor of the equally famous, and equally enigmatic, Imru' al-Qays, "King of *all* the Arabs." Lastly I should note the brief dedicatory inscription from Buṣr al-Ḥariri in the Lejā which reads: "May you live, Oaedos (Waᶜed), teacher (ὁ διδάσκαλος), may you live!"[102] One may hope to be so honored by his own students.

[90] *PAES* 177 = *Wadd.* 2053.

[91] *Wadd.* 1963.

[92] *PAES* 664.

[93] *PAES* 760.

[94] *Wadd.* 1989.

[95] *PAES* 765[13]; *Wadd.* 2227.

[96] *Wadd.* 2546.

[97] *NIDH* 230 = *SEG* 1217.

[98] Fossy, *BCH* (1897) 44 no. 19 = *IGRRP* 1165; cf. Heichelheim, *Roman Syria* 195 and note 76. The date given for this text in all three of these is incorrect. The exact meaning of *manganarios* is uncertain. F. Cumont, *L'Égypte des Astrologues* (Bruxelles, 1937) 85 and note 3 indicates that in context it can mean "prestidigateur", "machiniste", or "enchanteur". Liddell-Scott-Jones, *Greek-English Lexicon* (Oxford, 1966) s.v. note that "conjurer" or "mechanical engineer" could be correct. Neither source was aware of this inscription. The brevity of the text is of little assistance, but the context implies a building skill of some kind.

[99] *Ewing* 137 no. 64.

[100] *PAES* 787.

[101] *PAES* 238[1]. I cannot agree with the interpretation of *tropheus* given in M. Sartre, *Liber Annuus* 29 (1979) 253-258.

[102] *Wadd.* 2472 = *AAES* 432e.

8. *Conclusion*

The limited scope of this paper will, I hope, show the need for further research into the everyday affairs of these villages and their inhabitants. The aspects which I have briefly discussed are far from exhaustive. A full-scale investigation should include those inscriptions which deal with common ownership of property, the leasing of land for pasturage, management of what the texts refer to as "the common fund" (τὰ τοῦ κοινοῦ), private donations to villages, and constructions of a religious nature, both pre-Christian and Christian. Much of this would involve consulting the relevant Nabataean and Safaitic texts as well.

It should be clear that the evidence from Greek epigraphy is but one dimension of a more complete picture of village life in southern Syria. Careful archaeological excavations of some of the now deserted villages is absolutely essential.[103] This would constitute a second dimension. The third dimension can best be illustrated by Dr. Helga Seeden's recent ethnoarchaeological expeditions at Bostra.[104] By carefully co-ordinating a team of observers and recorders, she has demonstrated clearly how much can be learned of village life in antiquity by the systematic study of a living village.

Epigraphy alone serves only as a record of *what* was done, *when*, and *by whom*. It seldom answers the questions of *how*, or *why*. At best it is a supplement, although a valuable one, to what archaeology and anthropology can detect. In this sense it is an aid to understanding, and appreciating, the process of historical and cultural continuity in one uniquely interesting geographical area — that of southern Syria.

[103] Fundamental to the study of village architecture throughout southern Syria is the new study by François Villeneuve, *Recherches sur les villages antiques du Haurane: Ier siècle av. J.-C. — VIIème siècle ap. J.C.* (unpublished dissertation presented for the degree of Doctorat de 3ème cycle en archéologie, University of Paris, March, 1983). I wish to thank Dr. Villeneuve for providing me with a photocopy of this; I regret that it did not arrive in time to be utilized in this paper.

[104] On the 1980 season see the preliminary note in *Archiv für Orientforschung* 28 (1981/82) 214-215 and the preliminary report entitled "Busra 1980: Reports from a South Syrian Village", *Damaszener Mitteilungen* 1 (1983) 77-101. For reports, see *AAAS* 33, 1983 (in press) and *Berytus* 32, 1984 (in preparation). See also above pp. 13-26.

XIII

FRAGMENTS OF A LATIN BUILDING INSCRIPTION FROM AQABA, JORDAN*

Seven fragments of one or more Latin building inscriptions (plaques) were found in the port city of Aqaba on the Red Sea coast of Jordan during the spring of 1987. The discovery was made during clearance of debris on the surface in front of, and within a tower beside, the northwest gate (the Bab al-Misr or Egyptian Gate) of the medieval (7th to 12 cent.) city called Ayla.

Dr. Donald S.Whitcomb (Director of the excavation) and a joint University of Chicago / Department of Antiquities team recovered six fragments (locus no. E8a-2 a-f in the drawing) directly in front of the gate. The seventh fragment (E8d-5) was found within a tower abutting the gate to the left as one enters.

At the conclusion of that season's work Dr.Whitcomb contacted me for a preliminary reading of the text. He has since kindly asked me to make the initial publication of the fragments so far recovered and has agreed to allow Prof. Maurice Sartre (Université François Rabelais, Tours) to include them in the latter's forthcoming *Inscriptions de la Jordanie* Vol. IV (southern Jordan). Brief announcements of this discovery were made by Dr.Whitcomb at a conference on the history of Bilad al-Sham held in Amman, Jordan in October 1987 and in a recent publication.[1] Dr. Whitcomb is to be thanked for the drawing (traced from the stones) and the photograph (see Plate IX [Courtesy of the Oriental Institute of the University of Chicago]) which accompanies this presentation. I have not seen the fragments.

All seven fragments are wholly or partially inscribed. Portions of the surface of fragments a-d have been chiseled away. The work of erasure was quite thorough so that neither the tops or bottoms of letters, nor an underlying outline of letters in the stone, is visible. That information was made available by Dr. David Kennedy, who autopsied the fragments in June, 1988. The letters that do remain on the stone were inscribed with neatness and precision, are "V"-shaped in cross-section and were found to be filled with red paint.

---

* Grateful acknowledgement is made to Dr. Adnan Hadidi, Director General, Department of Antiquities, the Hashemite Kingdom of Jordan, for his enthusiastic support of the Aqaba excavations and permission to publish this inscription. I am also indebted to G.W.Bowersock, W.Eck, D.L.Kennedy, M.Sartre and D.S.Whitcomb for their acute and helpful comments.

[1] Aqaba: 'Port of Palestine on the China Sea', 1988, 16. The name *Aelana* will be used below to distinguish the Nabataean/Roman settlement from the Islamic town of *Ayla* .

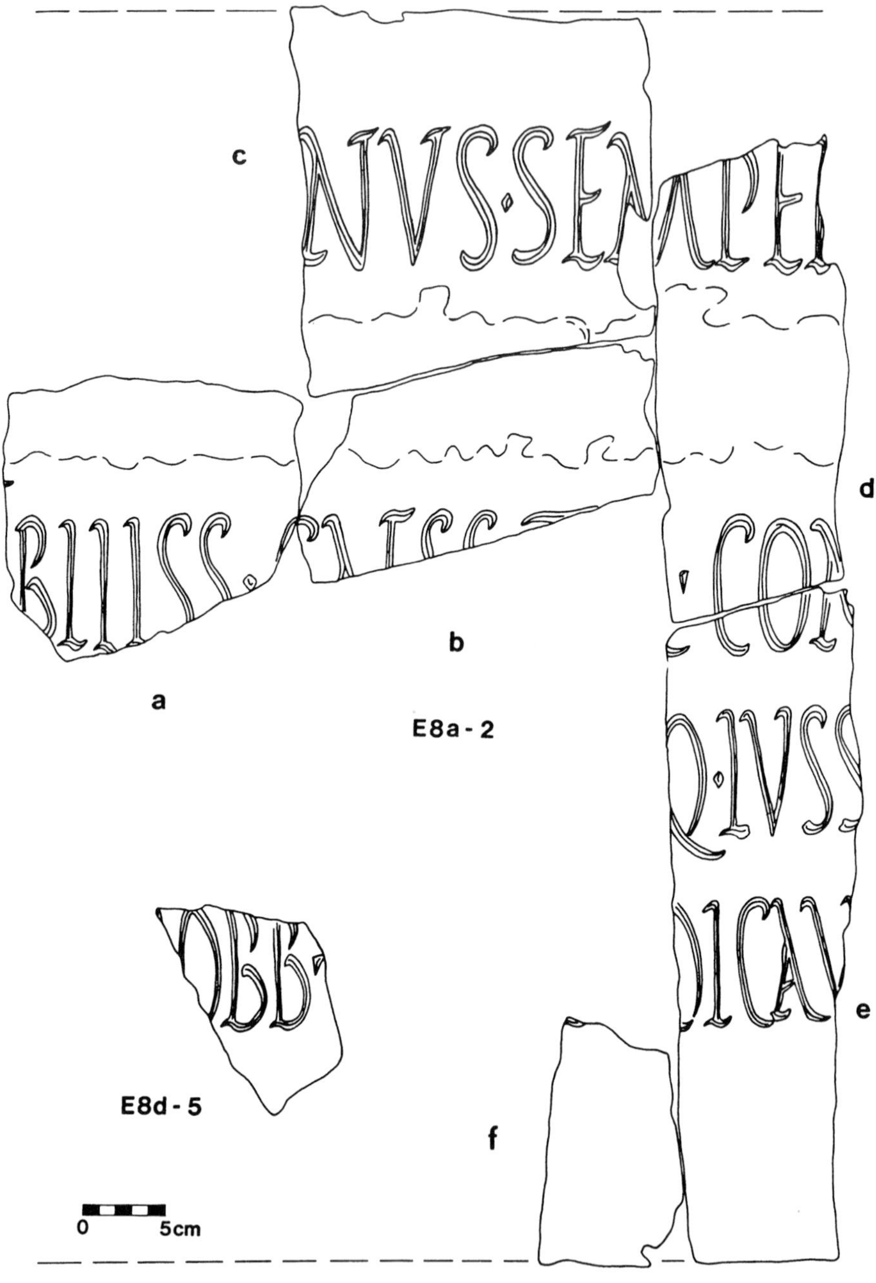
NVS·SEN
MPE
c
BIISS·
CAESS
d
·CO
CO
Q·IVS
DICAV
a
b
E8a - 2
OBB·
e
E8d - 5
f
0
5cm

The six fragments discovered together are clearly part of one plaque inscription. In spite of damage to the inscribed side the back surface of the stones shows that each and every piece joins perfectly in the position indicated. Fragment E8d-5 cannot be joined anywhere although its letter heights and shapes match closely those of the other fragments. It also (as will be shown) appears to be "odd" contextually and therefore should be set aside. It may be part of a second, matching inscription with slight variations in the text.

The blank but unchiseled space at the top of fragment c, and at the bottom of fragments e and f, indicate that the original text was probably no more than five lines. It is presently impossible to know how much text is missing to the left and right. Letters in the top line are 8 cm. in height, those in the remaining lines are 7,5 cm. The plaque is marble, measures 73,5 cm. from top to bottom, and is 2.7 - 2.9 cm. in thickness. No other Latin or Greek inscription has been recorded at Aqaba. The following observations may be offered:

1. SEMPER in line 1 as an element of imperial titulature does not appear until the time of the first Tetrarchy (293-305) and is far more common in the Constantinian period (312-337). The -NVS preceding *semper* cannot be restored as *aeter]nus* since that term is never found in conjunction with *semper*. If we are to restore the names of two emperors before -NVS then DD NN IMP CAES DIOCLETIANVS ET MAXIMIA]NVS SEṂPẸR [AVGG] would be likely. Constantine and Licinius cannot be candidates for a similar restoration in line 1 since Licinius' name invariably follows that of Constantine in the epigraphy and papyri.

2. The extant portion of line 2 was completely erased, and the erasure would appear to extend farther left and right (into missing segments of the text). It is possible that the name of a second emperor, e.g. Maximianus or Licinius, followed the titulature of the first and was later chiseled out. While this would make sense of the erasure, it would also mean that that second emperor's titulature and the names of several Caesars would have to be restored between the erasure and what remains of line 3. This would indicate that a far greater amount of text is missing than seems probable for a plaque.

3. It is more likely that the name of one or more Caesars had been erased from line 2. For the first Tetrarchy that would be Galerius, for the Constantinian period Licinius the Younger, Crispus, Constans or Dalmatius.

4. If we are to restore the name of only one emperor it must be Constantine. Depending, on the date, he may be associated with two, three or four Caesars. In line 3 NO]ḄILIṢṢ. ÇẠẸṢṢ implies only two but it could represent more. Fragment E8d-5, restored as N]ỌBḄ, is the first element of another version of this abbreviation. It would not be unusual to have it occur twice in the same inscription, but in one as short as this it seems out of place. It is perhaps best understood as part of a smaller plaque with essentially the same text and inscribed by the same hand.

5. What follows CAESS is also uncertain. There is sufficient space for two letters before the word-divider. The top of the first is rather flat and elongated compared to the top of an E. This is likely to be an F or a T. Only the tip of the foot of the second letter is visible in the upper left-hand corner of fragment e. This could belong to any number of letters but is probably an L or an I. After the word-divider one may read CON-, COM - or (less likely) COA-. Taken together it must be the beginning of another personal name rather than the start of a phrase.

6. IVSS[ERVUNT] and either DE]DICAV[ERVNT] or DE[DICAV[IT] are the likely restorations of the verbs in lines 4 and 5. Though the order or command may be seen as imperial, it is quite possible -- even probable -- that the dedication itself was not. *Iubeo* normally requires a complementary infinitive; sometimes two or more. The Q preceding IVSS[ERVNT] must therefore be the enclitic abbreviation Q[VE] rather than a pronoun, and was itself preceded by verbs of building or restoration such as *renovo*, *restauro, reficio, perficio. Dedico* usually terminates a building or rebuilding inscription unless the work was overseen and brought to completion by another official, in which case *curante* and that person's name would follow. This is unlikely here, but, it would be logical to assume that the name of the provincial governor (or dux) -- in this case of newly-expanded *provincia Palaestina* -- precedes DE]DICAV[IT].

7. The internal evidence of the plaque points to the reign of Constantine the Great for its creation. One clue is to consider the name following CAESS in line 3. The traces of letters strongly suggest FL CON[STANTIVS] or FL CON[STANTINVS] as a logical restoration. The prosopography of the period includes Flavius Constantius (PLRE I.225), *praefectus praetorio* of the East under Constantine (to whom he was probably related) from at least 16 December 324 (CTh 15.14.1) until he returned to Rome with the Emperor in 326.[2] The editors of PLRE (I.224) suggest this is the same Constantius who served in 315/316 as Constantine's envoy to Licinius the Elder. The only epigraphic attestation of Constantius is CIL III 6751 from Ancyra. In it he is *v(ir) c(larissimus) praefectus pretorii (sic)* in association with Constantine. The Emperor had then already taken the title of *victor*, which makes the terminus post of the Ancyra inscription the defeat and abdication of Licinius the Elder in September 324.[3] The latest attestation of Flavius Constantius is 11 June 327 (*CTH* 2.24.2), the year of his consulate. T.D.Barnes believes Constantius was one of two praetorian prefects who "operated independently of an emperor" and surmises that he was resident at Antioch from 324 to 326.[4] All of this argues for restoration of his name, but in the context of this inscription doing so also presents some difficulties. Prof.Eck has pointed out (in correspondence) the inherent peculiarities of an inscription "in dem der Kaiser und

---

[2] See also T.D.Barnes, The New Empire of Diocletian and Constantine, 1982, 131.

[3] Barnes, *ibid.* 24 following A.Chastagnol, Latomus 25, 1966, 543-550.

[4] Barnes, *ibid.* 139.

seine Söhne und ein pref. praetorio gemeinsam etwas anordnen." I am aware of no parallel example and it may well be that some other member of the imperial family was attested instead. The matter is best left open for further discussion.

8. We must next consider the name or names erased in line 2. On 1 March 317 Constantine and Licinius the Elder established their joint rule with three Caesars (Crispus, Licinius the Younger and Constantinus the Younger). This lasted until 19 September 324. Constantine then ruled as sole emperor until his death in 337. For just under two months (19.Sept.-8.Nov. 324) he was associated with two sons as Caesars, Crispus and Constantinus (AE [1977] 602; AE [1975] 135). From at least 8 November 324 until May 326 his Caesars were Crispus, Constantinus and Constantius, and from then until 333 only the latter two. From 25.Dec. 333 Constans joined his brothers as Caesar, and from 18 Sept. 335 Constantine's half-brother Dalmatius was a fourth Caesar. As noted above neither NO]BILISS CAESS in line 3 nor the redundant fragment N]OBB should limit the number of Caesars to just two. There are instances where similar abbreviations are clearly mistakes. In ILS 714 Crispus, Licinius and Constantinus are recorded as DD NN and NOBB CAESS (see Dessau's comment on the error). In AE (1978) 727 the same three are again Nobb. Caess; in AE (1978) 283 Crispus, Constantinus and Constantius are Nobb. Caesar. and in AE (1934) 158 all *four* Caesars are Nobb. Caess.

9. We may dismiss the date of 326-333 for the plaque, since the names of Constantinus and Constantius were never erased. Any date later than 333 is improbable for two reasons. One is that Constans' name would appear last in a listing of three Caesars (333-335) and therefore immediately precede NO]BILISS in line 3. His *damnatio* did not occur until January 350 and even if his full formal name had been inscribed here the erasure of it would not have extended back to the extant portion of line 2. We might conjecture that the erasure included Dalmatius as well as Constans. In that case the plaque would have been inscribed no earlier than Sept. 335. But if the restoration of F̣ḷ Coṇ[stantius] in line 3 is correct, and if this refers to the known PPO, it is highly unlikely that his name would appear in an inscription of 335-337 given his last attestation in 327.

10. The date of this plaque is therefore likely to be 317-326 when two sets of three Caesars, or two Caesars briefly, were associated with Constantine. Given the bits of the inscription so far available it is possible to offer three plausible restorations:

(a) In inscriptions of 1 March 317-19 Sept. 324 we would expect to find mention of both Constantine and Licinius the elder. For reasons given above this seems to be impossible here. It is worth noting in addition that when Constantine and Licinius appear together in inscriptions of Oct. 312-Sept- 324 the title *maximus* invariably distinguishes Constantine as the senior emperor. Its absence here following Constantine's name and before the term *semper* is significant.

I have not yet found an inscription of this date in which Constantine alone is attested with all three Caesars. There is a revised milestone text (AE [1969/70] 375b) in which only Constantine and Licinius the Younger are named. But milestone inscriptions are notoriously laconic and hardly to be taken as standards of epigraphy. ILS 8940, however, is a dedicatory text in which only Licinius and his son are mentioned, and Dessau was quick to point out the oddity of it. In light of that the Aqaba inscription would seem less unusual. If we accept that the elder Licinius' name was simply omitted it obviates the neccessity of a labored restoration involving his name and titulature and the name of his son. Allowing that Constantine alone is associated here with Crispus, Licinius the Younger and Constantinus in that usual order, a text is easily restorable in which the erasure could embrace the names of both Crispus and Licinius the Younger:

[D N IMP CAES FL VAL CONSTANTI]NVS SEMPER [AVGVSTVS]
[ET FL IVL CRISPVS ET VAL LICINIANVS LICINIVS IVN ET
[FL CL CONSTANTINVS NO]BILISS CAESS FL CON[STANTIVS ?]
[V C PRAEF PRAETORIO PERFICI ? REFICI ?]Q IVSS[ERVNT]
[. . . . ? . . . . ?. . . . ? . . . . ? . . . . ? . . . . ? . . . . ?. DE]DICAV[IT?]

This restoration inevitably associates Fl. Constantius with Licinius the Younger. If correct it would provide a new *terminus ante* for Constantius' elevation to the post of praetorian prefect, i.e. sometime prior to Sept. 324 (only three praetorian prefects are attested with certainty between 1 March 317 an 19 Sept. 324).

(b) If this inscription is from the period immediately following the fall of the elder and younger Licinius (late Sept. to early Nov. 324) the date is attractive for several reasons. One is that we would expect only Constantine to be mentioned. Another is that the names of only two Caesars need be restored. The name of Crispus would appear first and its erasure would be typical; in AE (1975) 135 (noted above) of precisely this date it was chiseled out. Restored thus the text would read:

[D N IMP CAES FL VAL CONSTANTI]NVS SEMPER [AVGVSTVS]
[PONTIFEX MAXIMVS ET DD NN FL IVLIVS CRISPVS ET FL CLA]
[VDIVS CONSTANTINVS IVN NO]BILISS CAESS FL CON[STANTIVS ?]
[VC PRAEFECTVS PRAETORIO PERFICI ? REFICI ?]Q IVSS[ERVNT]
[. . . . ? . . . . ? . . . . ? . . . . ? . . . . ? . . . . ? . . . . ?. . . . . DE]DICAV[IT?]

(c) In inscriptions of Nov. 324-May 326 Crispus' name also appears first and it alone was erased (e.g. ILS 708; 710). This date is attractive for the same reasons given in (b) above, though the name of a third Caesar must be added. We might also note that an attestation of Fl. Constantius (PPO) would be especially appropriate at this time:

[D N IMP CAES FL VAL CONSTANTI]NVS SEMPER [AVGVSTVS]
[PONTIFEX MAXIMVS PATER PATRIAE FL IVL CRISPVS FL CL CONSTA]

[NTINVS FL IVL CONSTANTIVS NO]BILISS CAESS FL CON[STANTIVS ?]
[VC PRAEFECTVS PRAETORIO PERFICI ? REFICI ?]Q IVSS[ERVNT]
[. . . . ? . . . . ? . . . . ? . . . . ? . . . . ? . . . . ? . . . . ? . . . . . [DE]DICAV[IT?]

11. It is of course possible to present variations of each of the above. The absence of *victor* in the titulature of Constantine is no reason for supposing that the inscription is prior to the the defeat of Licinius the Elder; its absence here means no more than it does in AE (1978) 283 of Nov. 324-May 326. I have found no certain example of *victor* ever following the title Augustus, though the editors of AE (1984) 434 have accepted G.Alföldy's restoration of *victor* following AVG. in CIL V 8269 of A.D. 326-?337.

If we are to assess what circumstantial evidence there is, it points to a date between late Sept. 324 (when Licinius abdicated) and May 326 (when Crispus was executed) for the creation of this inscription.

12. This plaque (and -- probably -- another like it) were removed from the Romano-Byzantine town of Aelana (like Ayla, now within the modern port of Aqaba) during the occupation of the Islamic settlement or some time thereafter. Presumably the inscription(s) commemorated a building project involving the military, perhaps reconstruction work. Qasr Azraq in eastern Jordan has produced a number of Constantinian building inscriptions, all associated with the Roman fort established there most probably in the Severan period and restructured during a major military buildup in the early fourth century.[5] One such inscription (AE [1974] 661) of A.D. 326-333 seems to describe the kind of rebuilding that the Aqaba inscription might commemorate:

[C]onsta[nt]ino M[a]xi[mo | pio uicto]re ac triumfatore se[mper | Augusto e]t Constantino et | [Consta]ntio nn(o)bb(ilissimis) Caess(aribus) | [aedem (?) inc]uria uetustate | [parietu]m ruina conlapsam | [refici (?) iu]ssit et [...].

D.L.Kennedy (1982: 91) read the final line as [refici ? iu]ssit Fl [Severinus], the personal name being that of "either the garrison commander or the provincial governor."

13. The Nabataean/Roman town of Aelana has been identified just a few hundred meters to the north-west of Islamic Ayla. Exploratory trenches are to be dug there in the autumn of 1988, but for the present the focus of the excavations will continue to be the Islamic city. Dr.Whitcomb has informed me (personal communication) that he saw at Aqaba in March, 1988 two marble column capitals exposed on the beach by winter storms. The opposing finished edge of each indicates that this is a matched pair, originally placed on pilasters at either side of a monumental gate. Though they may have been reused in the Byzantine or Islamic period Whitcomb has tentatively assigned them to the second century A.D. by

[5] D.L.Kennedy in Roman Frontier Studies, 1979 (BAR Int. Ser. 71, 1980), 879-888; idem, Archaeological Explorations on the Roman Frontier in North-East Jordan (BAR Int.Ser. 134, 1982), 75-96.

analogy with nearly identical stylistic features of monumental column capitals at Jerash in northwest Jordan.

14. Aelana stood at the southern terminus of the *via nova Traiana* which connected that Red Sea port with Petra, Philadelphia/Amman and Bostra. We know nothing of its history in that early period but the town must have served as the base for some as yet unattested military unit stationed there when the *via nova* was built (106-114) after the annexation of the Nabataean kingdom. That unit undoubtedly became the garrison of the port thereafter. There was no need to strengthen that garrison until at least the time of the Palmyrene revolt of 270-273.

15. Renewed military activity on the eastern frontier began with Aurelian, was augmented by Diocletian and continued under Constantine. At some point in the last quarter of the third century or the first quarter of the fourth a decision was made to transfer the *legio X Fretensis* from its former base in Jerusalem[6] to new headquarters in Aelana. The only record of that is a laconic and chronologically vague statement in Eusebius' Onomasticon,[7] s.v. Αἰλάμ (Gen. 14.1) ... νῦν [i.e. in Eusebius' lifetime] 'Αϊλά ... ἐγκάθηται δὲ αὐτοθι τάγμα 'Ρωμαίων τὸ δέκατον.

The date of composition of the *Onomasticon* has never been settled. Previous estimates have ranged from c.310 to as late as the 330's. Barnes recently made a strong case for a date of composition in the 290's.[8] Even if one accepts a date that early, the statement concerning the tenth legion which begins with νῦν could have been inserted during a later revision. *Legio X Fretensis* took part in the Persian campaign under Constantius II in 359 (Ammianus 18.9.3) but is was still attested at Aelana c.400 (*Not. Dig*. 34.30 [Seeck]). Its later history is unknown.

16. It is possible that the *legio VI Ferrata* was transferred from northern Palestine to Udhruh (near Petra) and the newly-raised *legio IV Martia* stationed at Lejjun (near Karak) as part of an orchestrated redeployment of the eastern military.[9] The motives for and timing of these moves have been discussed by S.T.Parker[10] who credits this major buildup to Diocletian and the first Tetrarchy c.300. The simultaneous stationing of the tenth legion at Aelana, as Parker and others would argue, remains a distinct possiblity. Should that hypothesis be proven correct, the Aqaba inscription might then relate to the renovation of a structure or structures already a quarter of a century old.

---

[6] The legion is now attested at Jerusalem with a new epithet: l(e)g(io) X Fr(etensis) *Fel(ix)* ; see AE (1985) 831.

[7] ed. E. Klostermann, 6 line 20.

[8] Constantine and Eusebius, 1981, 110-111.

[9] *VI Ferrata* : M.P.Speidel, ZPE 29, 1979, 172; *IV Martia* : J. Lander & S.T. Parker, Byzantinische Forschungen 8, 1982, 185-210.

[10] Romans and Saracans: A History of the Arabian Frontier, 1986, 137-142.

17. Until more of the inscription is found, however, the whole issue remains conjectural. That building activity of any kind was commemorated in this inscription is an assumption based on the two verbs in the text and by analogy with other inscriptions attesting construction work carried out elsewhere in the frontier regions of Roman Palestine and Roman Arabia within the years 324-337:

> " . . . there are [epigraphic] indications that the Arabian frontier was still of concern to Constantine. The *castellum* at Azraq may have been repaired between 326 and 333. [A fortified] reservoir [was] built in 334 northwest of Azraq by Roman soldiers for their own use ... . Milestone inscriptions indicate road maintenance in 334-35, including work on the central and southern *via nova Traiana* and roads in Palestine."[11]

What type of building activity and what official oversaw the work and dedicated its completion cannot be known until more of the Aqaba inscription is found. The restorations suggested here are admittedly quite tentative, especially so regarding the role of the praetorian prefect of the East acting in concert with the Emperor and certain of his Caesars. That raises important questions of imperial protocol. Another matter is the possiblity that this plaque is associated with the military base at Aelana. Latin inscriptions from any site along the route of the *via nova* are almost invariably related to the Roman army. Thus it is tempting to connect the arrival of *legio X Fretensis* at Aelana with this new inscription. In that case Eusebius' statement would reflect a revision of the *Onomasticon* c.325. But there is nothing to exclude the possibility of a civilian context for the plaque and whatever it commemorated. The ongoing excavations at Aqaba should eventually clarify some of these issues.

---

[11] Parker, *ibid. 145.*

POSTSCRIPT

Maurice Sartre has brought to my attention three fragmentary Greek inscriptions from Aqaba. Two are nothing more than proper names (?) carved on the upper edge of sculpted Byzantine capitals; see N.Glueck, Explorations in Eastern Palestine III (AASOR 18-19 [1937/39]) pp. 1-3 and figs. 1& 2 on p.2. The other is a brief Christian epitaph of A.D. 555; see M.Schwabe, HTR 46 (1953) 49-55 (= SEG 13.598). I am grateful to Prof. Sartre for allowing me to see the relevant entries in the typecript of his volume of inscriptions from southern Jordan. Donald Whitcomb has notified me that two inscribed milestones were uncovered near the marina at Aqaba in September, 1988. Both are Trajanic and date to c. 111/112.

Lateinische Inschrift aus Aqaba, Jordanien; zu H.I.MacAdam S.163ff.

XIV

A NOTE ON THE USAYS (JEBAL SAYS) INSCRIPTION*

In Irfan Shahîd's newly-published *Byzantium and The Arabs in the Sixth Century I* (Dumbarton Oaks Press, 1995) is a detailed discussion (pp. 117-24) of the Usays (Jebal Says) inscription, to which I drew attention in my review article based on that volume.[1] The four lines of text, in a lapidary proto-Arabic script, have not generated much scholarly attention since their initial publication more than thirty years ago.[2] I reproduce here the facsimile of the inscription, and the transliteration (including vowels) of that facsimile, which appear in Shahîd (*BASIC* I 118):

Ibrâhîm ibn Mighîra al-Awsî
arsalanî al-Ḥârith al-malik ^{c}ala
Sulaymân msylḥt/h (sanat 423)

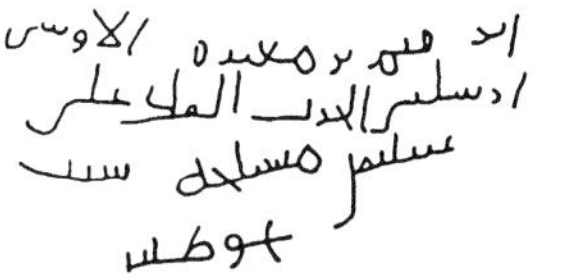

This commemorates a military expedition led by Ibrâhîm, a commander of the Ghassânid king Arethas (al-Ḥârith). The date given (of the Era of Provincia Arabia) corresponds to A.D. 528/529. The focus of Shahîd's discussion is the *crux* which occurs at the last word of the phrase *'ala Sulaymân msylḥt/h:*

> «There are two possible interpretations for the last three words of the inscription: either they refer to a federate rebel named Sulaymân Musayliha who revolted against the Ghassânid king Arethas, or they refer to a toponym, a frontier guard post named Sulaymân» (*BASIC* I 120).

* I am indebted to Michael Zwettler (Ohio State University) for a chance to discuss some philological aspects of this inscription, and to Brent Shaw (now at the University of Pennsylvania) for the opportunity to present a draft of this article to his Seminar in Late Antiquity at Princeton University.

Shahîd opts for the latter choice, understanding *msylḥt* as a diminutive form of the Arabic noun *maslaḥ(t)*, a fortlet or small military base, and that expression is «followed by the pronominal suffix *hi*, 'his'» (p. 121). Directly before *msylḥt* he takes *slmn* to be *Sulaymân*, which he believes was the name of the Jebal Says fortlet. As support he draws attention (p. 121 with notes 303 & 304) to several examples of toponyms derived from personal names. Unfortunately none of those cited can claim an association with a toponym of any real antiquity prior to the Islamic era. Shahîd finds additional help for his interpretation from the historical background: «[Arethas] would naturally have made administrative deployments like the dispatching of the commander Ibn Mughîra to Sulaymân, especially in a Ghassânid-controlled frontier region like that in which the inscription was found» (p. 122). I would agree that a toponymn *Slmn* is intended here, and I offer in what follows a suggestion regarding a much earlier attestation of that same place-name in the text of Claudius Ptolemy's *Geographia*.

Readers should note that there are uncertainties attendant upon every point I discuss, largely due to the methodology used in the initial publication of this inscription. While I have no intention of minimizing or sidestepping or even dismissing those difficulties, neither does it seem necessary to delay commenting until someone has completed a new autopsy of the inscribed stone, recorded all relevant data, created new drawings, made a squeeze of the text, and re-photographed it in great detail. I am also aware that the published texts of Ptolemy's *Geographia* are not without their own difficulties. That last point I have had the opportunity to discuss at length in an article to which I should draw the reader's attention.[3] With those warnings clearly in mind, let us proceed by examining the *crux* of the inscription.

Both terms, *msylḥt* and *Slmn*, are problematical because the letter-forms are not always clearly rendered, either in the photo accompanying al-ᶜUshsh's article, or in the photo reproduced in Adolf Grohnann's subsequent publication.[4] Indeed, * Grohmann's commentary (*Arab. Pal.* II 15-17) takes issue with several of the original readings by al-ᶜUshsh. Grohmann re-read the date as 423 of the Bostran or Arabian Era, and argued that the second word of line three, as Shahîd accepts, is to be read *msylḥt*. Importantly, however, Grohmann fully accepted al-ᶜUshsh's reading of *slmn*, and on that crucial point was followed by Shahîd. So the disagreement between Grohmann and Shahîd centers instead on *slmn* (which they understand to be *Sulaymân*) and whether it represents a personal name or a toponym.

But Michael Zwettler, who kindly read an earlier version of this article, has noted that the initial letter (from Grohmann's facsimile, reproduced by Shahîd) of what is taken to be the *samek* of *slmn* might be instead an *ᶜayn*. If that is so what follows must be, instead of the second and third loops of *samek*, yet another letter, perhaps a *bayt*, *taw*, or *thade*. One then must commence the task of working through a list of words derived from alternative spellings. Fortunately there is another initial *ᶜayn* in the text with which a comparison can be made. That occurs in the last word of line two, *ᶜala*. While I admit there is *some* resemblance, the two are not identical. I am persuaded that *slmn* is correct.

It is impossible to determine from the published photos if Grohmann's facsimile accurately renders what is on the stone. A new autopsy and/or a squeeze might resolve the issue. But it is clear that the resemblance between the initial letter of line three, and the other three occurrances of *samek* in the text, was enough to satisfy al-ᶜUshsh and Grohmann. Indeed, there was no doubt expressed by al-ᶜUshsh that the word *slmn* should be read (see his Arabic transcription in «*Kitâbât 'Arabîyya*» p. 302). Nevertheless it is discouraging that the provenance of the Usays inscription and the basic information regarding the text (such as letter-height and other measurements) are not available in the initial or any subsequent publication (see note # 2 and comments by Brisch, *MDAIK* 19 [1963] 166-7 regarding the «Inschriften»).

If *Slmn* is the correct reading it is then possible to find support for Shahîd's contention that it is a toponym, and not a personal name, in the context of this inscription. For such an identification we may look to a source from some four centuries earlier: Ptolemy of Alexandria's *Geographia* (c. A.D. 150). In it are two references (*Geog.* 5.14.6 & 5.14.20) to a mountain «in the Arabian desert» and/or «near the region of Batanaea». The name of that mountain is given in several variant forms in the Greek MSS: *Alsadamos*, *Alsalamos*, *A(l)salmanos* and even *Oualsadamos*. Scholars familiar with the text of the *Geographia* won't be surprised.

Alsadamos was the spelling favored by the German classicist Karl Müller, who prepared the very first (though unfortunately incomplete) critical edition of Ptolemy's *Geography* more than a century ago.[5] For reasons set out below, a slight modification in that spelling will resolve the MS variations. But first it is necessary to locate the mountain on a modern map. Ptolemy's vague designation «Arabian desert» could refer to any arid region of the Near East inhabited by Arabs. *Batanaea* helps us to narrow the search. That is the Graeco-Roman rendition of the Old Testament toponym *Bashan* (Arabic *Ard al-Bathaniyyah)*, a district or region south south-east of Damascus. This is not yet precise enough to identify *Oros Alsadamos* (?) = *Mons Alsadamus* (?) on a modern map of any scale. But there are additional clues.

Luckily, Ptolemy lists it among six prominent Near Eastern mountains,[6] and the map coordinates for each follows the name. Those given for *Mons Alsadamus* are, uncharacteristically, whole degrees: 71 east, 33 north. When that fixed point is plotted on a map-graph created from all of Ptolemy's Near Eastern coordinates, *Mons Alsadamus* appears east and slightly south of Damascus, about halfway between the cities of Bostra to the southwest and Palmyra to the northeast. The use of whole numbers for the coordiantes is a strong indication that Ptolemy could not «fix» with precision the mountain's location but knew that it lay on the desert edge.

Ptolemy's coordinates cannot be precisely equated with the latitude and longitude designations of modern maps. But beginning with Heinrich Kiepert,[7] scholars without exception have looked to the Jebal Ḥawrân (Jebal Drûz, Jebal Arab) range, or one of its peaks (Jebal Kulayb) for the true location of Ptolemy's enigmatic mountain. This included Müller, who followed Kiepert's suggestion of identification with the Jebal Ḥawrân, and Kiepert's proposed Semitic etymology of *Alsadamus* as (*al*)-*Ṣadam*, which he understood to mean «brennen», i.e. «burnt».

Müller died unexpectedly in 1894. Had he lived longer, he would have learned that Kiepert changed his mind. In his *Formae Orbis Antiqui* (Berlin: D. Reimer, 1907) p. 4 and Map VI, Kiepert rejected *Mons Alsadamus* as the correct reading and placed on the new map *Mons Asalmanus*. However, he still held that it was to be found within the Jebal Ḥawrân (ancient *Auranitis*), a range of once-volcanic hills directly east of the Ḥawrân Plain in southern Syria. The reason for locating it there seems to be convenience. Little was known then of the regions beyond the inhabited areas of Ottoman Syria, and no ancient map except for those created by Ptolemy himself (ironically) demonstrated familiarity with inner portions of the Graeco-Roman Near East. It is disturbing to note that subsequent scholarship did not question Kiepert's focus upon the Jebal Ḥawrân. Thus a geographical «factoid» was sustained.

Kiepert's preference for the reading *Mons Asalmanus* reflects his acceptance of Richard Benzinger's argument a decade earlier that behind this spelling one could clearly discern «... da sie dem hebräischen Namen Zalmon entspricht»[8]. Thirty years later, and with no reference to Benzinger, René Dussaud also proposed reading *Mons Asalmanus* and observed: «... si on peut l'appuyer par le Salmon de Psaumes LXI et suivant»[9]. Père Abel[10] shortly thereafter accepted *Asalmanus*, reckoned its etymology as «*slm*, être obscur», and located it (presumably following Kiepert) in the Jebal Ḥawrân. Neither Benzinger, Dussaud nor Abel made any attempt to plot the mountain's location according to Ptolemy's clearly-stated coordinates. Whether or not their identification with biblical King Solomon was correct, reading *Slm(n)* as the Semitic root of Ptolemy's place-name seems credible.

After reviewing these options in my *Studies in the History of the Roman Province of Arabia*[11], I suggested that Ptolemy's mountain might instead be identified with modern Jebal Says, 100km east and slightly south of Damascus[12].

Jebal Says is the crater of a now extinct volcano which rises some 700m above the flat basalt desert of the Ṣafa region. It was described in detail by several European voyagers in the nineteenth century, most notably by the Anglo-French epigrapher William Henry Waddington. He wrote:

> «Le Djebel Sès est un point très important pour le géographie du désert de Syrie, il est souvent question dans les récits des Bédouins du sable doré qu'on y trouve et des ruines qui existent au pied de la montagne.»[13]

At the time I was preparing my book for publication I was unaware that the *Slmn* of the Usays inscription might be a place-name referring to a site at the base of Jebal Says, or perehaps a reference to the mountain itself. Since neither Usays nor Says had been identified with any known ancient toponym, I concluded:

> «... no modern mountain or range of mountains in the lavalands [i.e. of modern Syria] bears a name which is closely reminiscent of any variant [spelling in the MSS of Claudius Ptolemy]» (*Studies*, p. 7).

The identification of Jebal Says with the biblical king named Solomon is perhaps due to a recurring belief from Flavius Josephus in the first century AD to John Malalas in the sixth) that King Solomon had founded the oasis city of Tadmor/Palmyra. Jebal Says lay directly along the inner desert route from the Arabian peninsula, via Bostra (Buṣra Shâms) to Palmyra. Shahîd inadvertantly strengthens the Tadmor/Sulaymân connection by noting that «Solomon's association with Palmyra is reflected in contemporary [sixth century] Arabic poetry, e.g. in the ode of Nâbigha, a panegyrist of the Ghassânids» (*BASIC* I p. 173 note 5). The epigraphy and other physical remains from Jebal Says attest to its use as a caravan and/or military post on the desert route between the Syrian interior (via the Ḥarra and Ṣafa regions) and the Euphrates River valley in the Umayyad period and later.[14] The Jebal Says inscription reinforces the importance of the site during the sixth century, and the reference to a mountain with a name similar to Solomon/Sulaymân in Ptolemy's *Geography* indicates that the volcanic crater was a landmark for cartographers of a much earlier era.

It seems very probable to me that Ptolemy's mountain and the frontier post of the Usays inscription refer to one and the same place: a remarkable physical feature which had both geographical and strategic importance. *Alsadamus* and *Alsalamus* must be the same toponym, with the Greek *delta* and *lambda* mistaken for each other by one or more copyists working with the handwritten text of Ptolemy over the centuries. Variant readings suggest that the original term was spelled with one or more *lambdas*. Therefore I would suggest that whatever toponym Ptolemy wrote when compiling his *Geography* lies behind the place-name *Slmn* of the Jebal Usays inscription. I would further suggest *A(l)salmanus* or *Alsalamus* as the correct spelling of Ptolemy's toponym. Either would represent that geographer's rendition of an original Semitic place-name for the volcanic mountain later known (today) as Jebal *Says*. Whether it is acceptable to render the Usays inscription's *Slmn* as *Sulaymân* is another matter. Accepting *Slmn* to be a place-name referring to a site at modern Jebal Says, and making the suggestion that *Slmn* also lies behind Ptolemy's *(Mons) Al-Salamus*, are all I hope to do here.

NOTES

1. *«Imperium et Arabes Foederati:* Constantinople and the Ghassânids», *Al-Abhâth* 43 (1995) 99-118, esp. 104-5.

* 2. The initial publication of the Jebal Says survey was that of Klaus Brish, «Das omayyadische Schloss in Usais», *Mitteilungen des Deutschen Archäologischen Institut (Abteilung Kairo)* Bd. 19 (1963) 141-89; K. Brisch, «Le château omeyyade de Djebel Seis», *Annales Archéologique de Syrie* 13 (1963) 135-58. See also his second report in *MDAIK* 20 (1965) 138-77. Brische did not devote any attention to the inscription discussed here but concentrated instead on the epigraphy directly connected with the Umayyad fort. Between Brisch's two publications the first full study of the text of this inscription appeared in this journal: Muhammad A. al-ᶜUshsh, «Kitâbât 'Arabîyya Ghayr Mansûra fî Jebal Usayss», *Al-Abhâth* 17 (1964) 302-3 # 107. References to all but one of these publications are given by Shahîd, *BASIC* I pp. 117-8 and notes #286, #287, #288.

3. See H.I. MacAdam, «Strabo, Pliny the Elder the Elder and Ptolemy of Alexandria: Three Views of Ancient Arabia and its Peoples» in T. Fahd (ed.), *L'Arabie Préislamique et son Environnement Historique et Culturel* (Travaux du Centre de Recherche sur le Proche-Orient et la Grèce Antiques 10, Leiden, E.J. Brill, 1989) 301-13, esp. 316-7.

4. Adolf Grohmann, *Arabische Paläographie II. Teil* (Wien, Hermann Bohlaus Nachf., 1971) Tafel I. 2. Grohmann attributes his photo to «Dr. K[laus] Brisch» who first discovered the inscription. Sadly, Grohmann chose to reproduce it on such a small scale that it is not possible to verify with confidence his or any other readings of individual letters or entire words. The stone is now in the National Museum in Damascus, but apparently in storage. I can find no reference to it in (e.g.) *Catalogue du Musée National de Damas* (1976).

5. *Claudii Ptolemei Geographia* (Vol. I Pts. 1 & 2 [text] plus a volume of maps (Paris: Fi. Didot, 1883 [text]; 1901 [maps]). It is worth noting that Müller did not have access to the Codex Urbinas Graecus 82, the oldest and the archetype of many texts of Ptolemy which he did examine. For the best publication of that see Josef Fischer, *Claudii Ptolemei Geographiae Codex Urbinas 82* (Leiden: E.J. Brill, 1932).

6. The others are Mt. Casius, Mt. Libanus, Mt. Anti-Libanus, Mt. Pieria and Mt. Hippus. The last-named cannot be identified with certainty.

7. H. Kiepert, *Lehrbuch der alten geographie* (Berlin: D. Reimer, 1878).

8. Pauly-Wissowa's *Realencyclopädie* I [1897] col. 1638.

9. *Topographie historique de la Syrie antique et médièvale* (Paris: Geuthner, 1927) p. 346-7.

10. Franz-Marie Abel, *Géographie de la Palestine* II (Paris: Lecoffre, 1938) 377-8.

11. Oxford: British Archaelological Reports (International Series #295), 1986 pp. 6-9.

12. See the photo I reproduced, *Studies* p. 8. For the original publication, see Antoine Poidebard, «Reconnaissance aerienne au Ledja et au Safâ», *Syria* 9 (1928) Planche LIV.

13. W.H. Waddington, *Academie des Inscriptions et Belles-Lettres, Comptes Rendus* (1865) pp. 86-7.

14. One looks in vain for some reference to this in Eugen Wirth, *Syrien: Eine Geographische Landeskunde* (Wissenschaftliche Länder-kunden Band 4/5, Darmstadt, 1971). Though Wirth does print a very striking photo (Bild 11) of Jebal Says, and his bibliography notes two articles by Brisch, there is no discussion of the site or its strategic/commercial importance in the text.

XV

SOME NOTES ON THE UMAYYAD OCCUPATION OF NORTH-EAST JORDAN

The available archaeological and architectural evidence, as well as written sources from a later period, attest a strong Umayyad presence in the Jordanian Ḥawrān and the Azraq Depression. The great "palaces" such as Quaṣayr 'Amra, Kharāna and Mashata have been * seen as rural retreats for Umayyad princes indulging in outdoor and indoor sports, or as rustic villas surrounded by Umayyad agrarian estates. Neither of these interpretations is satisfactory, and neither explains the remarkable absence of Umayyad military fortifications in the same regions. It is suggested in this paper that the Umayyad military control of north-east Jordan utilised the same methods employed by their predecessors, the Ghassānids, Kindites and Lakhmids - namely the federation of local tribal groups as auxiliaries. The bedouin encampments of these tribal forces explains why Romano-Byzantine military fortifications were not reactivated, and why new ones were not constructed. It also gives support to new views on the role and function of the desert "palaces".

I. Introduction

In a recent article with the evocative title "La Dolce Vita in early Islamic Syria: The Evidence of Later Umayyad Palaces", Robert Hillenbrand (1982) reviewed the various theories regarding the origin and purpose of theUmayyad "palaces" in Greater Syria (Bilād al-Shām). Hillenbrand points out that it was fashionable early this century to view these structures, particularly the ones in north-eastern Jordan, as pleasure-domes for hunting-happy bedouin princes who preferred life on the desert edge to the stricter mores of Damascus. This romanticised view was challenged more recently by an emphasis on economics. Oleg Grabar (1963) among others has been a proponent of the idea that hydrological techniques developed in the late Roman period - especially in Jordan - led to the creation of vast agricultural settlements which were simply incorporated into the Islamic state. These Levantine latifundia led the Umayyad regime to construct the palatial complexes nearby, all of which used the abundant water for the elaborate baths which are a common architectural feature.

Without rejecting either of these views, Hillenbrand suggests that:

> . . . the Umayyads were attracted to the desert for a variety of reasons: an instinctive hankering after a semi-nomadic life, a desire to visit the agricultural estates which they had taken over or created, and finally a desire to develop a sybaritic and ostentatiously royal life-style free from the moral and spatial constraints inseparable from city life (1982:4).

Hillenbrand then goes on to explore the rich literary sources for the early Islamic period, and to examine the most recent publications of architectural analyses at three famous sites: Quṣayr 'Amra and Mashattā in Jordan, and Khirbit Mafjar in Israel. The life and times of that merry monarch Walīd II (Caliph 743/744) are also scrutinized in some detail, and then set against the background of these enigmatic structures. Hillenbrand's survey of the period is certainly entertaining, but hardly enlightening. There is almost no attempt to investigate the history and archaeology of north-east Jordan for the period immediately preceding the Islamic conquest for clues to explain the Umayyad fascination with the area. It is precisely my intention to survey briefly what is now known of this area in late antiquity, and to concentrate particularly on the military aspect of the pre-Islamic sites. Perhaps this would serve as a more solid basis upon which to construct theories of why and how the Umayyad occupation of this region, brief though it was, left such a memorable legacy. As this paper appears in the Proceedings of a colloquium dedicated to the Defence of the Roman and Byzantine East, it may also be worthwhile to preface my remarks with a brief review of the Conquest and how it affected the two areas of north-east Jordan under consideration: the Hawran and the Azraq depression.

II. Conquest and Consolidation

It is commonly held that the consolidation of military strength in the newly-conquered Bilād al-Shām was to be focused on the well-established and strategic site of Jābiya on the eastern edge of the Golan.[1] This seems to have been an immediate - and perhaps emotional - decision, but it was shortly abandoned for more practical considerations. F. M. Donner (1981: 245 and n. 16) has pointed out that Jabīya was struck by the 'Amwās plague in AH 18/AD 639. The subsequent heavy loss of population no doubt contributed to the decision to abandon Jabīya - and perhaps also Ramla in Palestine - and to look to established Syrian cities (Damascus, Ḥomṣ, Aleppo) as more secure bases of operations inland, and to Palestinian and Phoenician coastal ports (Gaza, Caesarea, Acre, Tyre, Sidon, Tripoli) for defence against Byzantine reprisals by sea (Shaban 1971: I, 40-2).

A system of military districts (sing. jund) was established which simply reinforced or renewed a defensive policy perhaps initiated

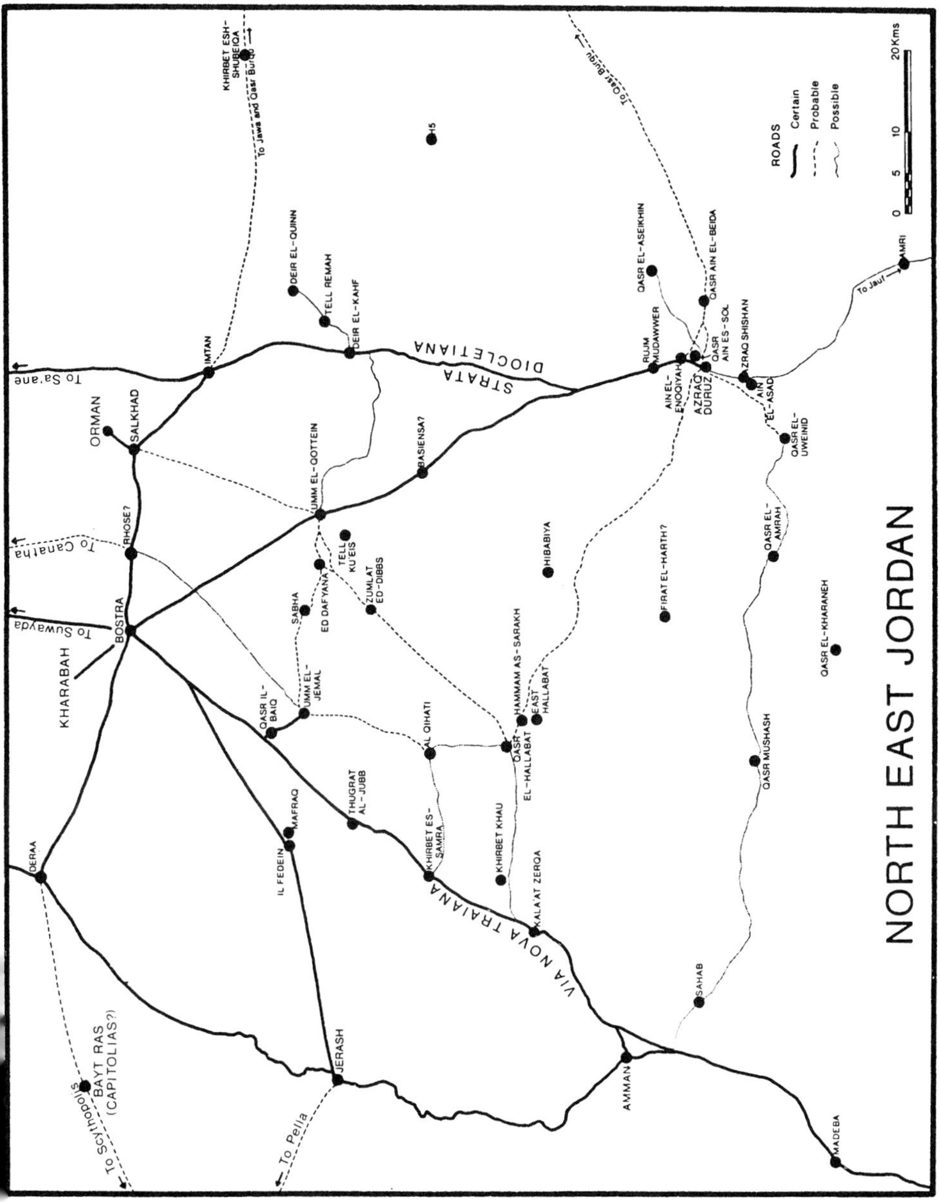

Fig. 31.1 Map of north-east Jordan based on Kennedy (1982) endpiece showing the sites discussed in this paper. Original and modifications given here were drawn by Julie Kennedy.

by Justinian c. 550 and modified by Heraclius c. 628/629 following the Byzantine re-conquest of Syria from the Persians.[2] This time, however, the focus of defence was to be the north-western rather than the north-eastern sector of Syria. Consequently tribesmen from the Arabian peninsula were settled in each of the five military districts: Qinnasrin, Ḥomṣ, Damascus, Jordan and Palestine. Under the governorship of Mu'āwiya, especially, the northern defences of Syria were reinforced, and from the junds of Qinnasrin and Ḥomṣ frequent raids were launched into Byzantine Anatolia. The conquest of 'Iraq in the east and Egypt in the west established complete Islamic control of Bilād al-Shām (H. Kennedy 1985b).

Mu'āwiya's succession from governorship to the Caliphate led to an openly aggressive policy against the Byzantines. Cyprus had been conquered as early as 24/649. Yearly raids into Anatolia were followed eventually by major campaigns resulting in the Arab occupation of Rhodes (52/672) and Crete (54/674). A sustained attack on Constantinople (54/674 to 60/680) ended in failure. Certain frontier garrisons such as Malaṭya (classical Melitene) on the upper Euphrates were reactivated to avoid surprise attacks by land from Byzantine forces (Shaban 1971:I, 81). Coastal cities such as Tyre became major naval strongholds and the port of Alexandria continued to guard the Nile Delta. Thus the outer parameters of the Islamic defensive system were established.

Jordan continued to be a vital commercial link between the interior of the Arabian penninsula and the coastal ports of the Levant. Recent archaeological work throughout the country demonstrates again and again that there was a peaceful transition from Byzantine to Islamic rule (King; 1983b; Piccirillo 1984). But the need for a defensive system within Jordan was minimal throughout the Umayyad period. Jordan was no longer a "frontier" region as it had been under Roman and Byzantine administration. Certainly the pilgrim route (formerly the Ṭarīq al-Sulṭanī or "King's Highway") from Damascus to 'Ammān to Ma'an and thence through the Ḥijāz to the Holy Cities of Mecca and Madina demanded protection for those who journeyed. But this route lies outside the concerns of this paper. Just as certainly, however, the ancient caravan road from Damascus to Bostra to Azraq and eventually to Dūmat al-Jandal needed protection. This was certainly the case in the pre-Islamic period and there is no need to believe that the situation changed following the Islamic conquest.[3] The defence of that route was centred on two areas - the Jordanian Ḥawrān and the Azraq depression - before and after the conquest. To each of these we must turn our attention.

III. The Jordanian Hawran

Recent interest in the towns and villages of the Jordanian Ḥawrān began with Siegfried Mittmann's epigraphic survey in the mid-1960's (1970: 166-207). Systematic archaeological work did not begin until the excavations at Jawa (Helms 1981) and Umm al-Jimāl (De Vries 1979, 1982, 1985, 1986). Work at the latter site is still in progress. Surveys of other sites in the area were published by Gaube (1974), Kennedy (1982), King (1982, 1983); a preliminary survey of Umm al-Quṭṭayn and vicinity is soon to appear (Kennedy and MacAdam 1986a & b).

A total of about twenty-five sites has been investigated, some more than once. Few sites to the west of the Via Nova are included, in large part due to the lack of interest in that area by survey teams. The eastern most site included in Qaṣr Burqu', on the edge of the Syrian desert. Many of these sites had been described and photographed by various expeditions early in this century, and it had been firmly established that the entire Jordanian Ḥawrān was populated by prosperous communities. Two considerations underlay this prosperity: the agricultural richness of the region, and what Maurice Sartre terms "un artisanat de qualite et varie"; both factors contributed to trade with the Hijaz (Sarte, 1985). Some settlements such as Umm al-Quṭṭayn and Umm al-Jimāl may have been garrisoned as early as the second century. The archaeological evidence for this is so far uncertain. The earliest dated walls at Umm al-Jimāl were constructed c. 176-180; ceramic and epigraphic evidence agree on this (De Vries 1982: 111). De Vries did not rule out the possibility of a smaller settlement in the period just preceeding Roman rule,for which he found some ceramic evidence (1982: 109). What he did not anticipate was the discovery of a Nabataean/Early Roman settlement slightly to the south-east of Jimāl, which was not investigated until the 1985 season; see his report on this in these Proceedings (De Vries 1986). Whether this early village had been fortified remains to be discovered.

A dated Nabataean funerary inscription of AD 93 (Dussaud & Macler 1903: 710 no. 5) at Umm al-Quṭṭayn remains the earliest epigraphic reference from that town: however, the walls and most of the buildings are undated. A careful examination of aerial photographs of the site and comparison with an investigation on the ground may indicate that the northern sector of the ancient community was an auxiliary fort. The evidence for this is summarised in two reports now in press (Kennedy and MacAdam 1986 a & b). Both Jimāl and Quṭṭayn lay along a major trade route between the Ḥawrān and Dūmat al-Jandal by way of Azraq, and the need to protect the major settlements along such a route is obvious. The construction of the Via Nova Traiana (106-114) was a major factor in their urban development. The Diocletianic fort recently discovered at Jimāl (De Vries 1985: 250; 1986) is further evidence that the town was considered to be a strategic link between the Via Nova to the west and the Strata Diocletiana to the east.

The fort at Dayr al-Kahf is also Diocletianic, as a building inscription of 306 testifies (Littmann 1921: no. 228). Another inscription from the site records alterations made to the earlier structure c. 370 (ibid: no. 229). There is as yet no evidence for an even earlier, perhaps Severan, fort at Kahf but the comments of Howard Crosby Butler, the Princeton architect and classicist who provided the first plan of the fortress, are worth quoting:

> In the walls [of the fortress] . . . are many blocks with draughted edges mixed with ordinary quadrated blocks . . . These draughted blocks, I believe, belonged to a building, probably a small military post . . . that was earlier than either of the dateable (sic) inscriptions here, and probably of the second century (Butler 1919:145).

Though the evidence is not certain, it does seem that the military character of these communities lapses in the fifth and sixth centuries and that some became monastic establishments.[4] Why this was so is also uncertain, but it may have something to do with the Ghassānid role in maintaining stability in this area (Knauf 1984: 579; Sartre 1982: 188; Parker 1986). Justinian's reactivation of military sites may have had some effect, but this did not avert the catastrophe of the Persian invasion in the early years of Heraclius or the permanent loss of Bilād al-Shām to the Islamic armies a generation later.

The peaceful transition to Muslim rule in Jordan cannot be overemphasised, and nowhere is it more evident than the Ḥawrān. This is just as true for sites on the Syrian side of the modern border as it is for the communities just discussed. The American University of Beirut's sondages at the tell in Bostra have uncovered substantial remains of an Umayyad farmhouse (Seeden 1983), and a recent report on the excavations at Umm al-Jimāl has expressed surprise at the extent of Umayyad occupation there (De Vries 1982: 113). The other sites to the east of Umm al-Jimāl have undergone no more than surface explorations, but this indicates clearly that continuous occupation of these communities was not interrupted until the onset of the 'Abbāsid era. Moreover, King's surveys demonstrate that the strategic value of the sites along this ancient trade route was not overlooked by the Umayyads; his comments on the Umayyad occupation of Qaṣr al-Burqu' are worth quoting:

> There seems to be good reason for thinking that Burqu' itself and the area in which it is situated was regarded by the Umayyads as of major importance since it was al-Walīd, eldest son and successor of the Caliph 'Abd-al Mālik, who rebuilt it according to the inscription in his name [Shboul 1975]. Burqu' was in a region that had belonged to the Bani Kalb, a tribe with whom the Umayyads had maintained close relations . . . al-Walīd's re-use of Qaṣr Burqu' with its water storage system might have had less to do with a princely desire for solitude in the basalt wasteland than with command of the route between northern Arabia and central Syria, and with the political relations of tribes with Caliphate (King 1983a: 416).

King's survey took him south-east of the Jordanian Ḥawrān to Azraq, and he noted carefully (1983a: 411-414) along the way those places which may have served as watch-towers and signalling-stations (Jebel al-Qis [Kuᶜays], al-Manāra and Jebal

Asaykhin). In all cases, there is a correspondence in the surface pottery sequence of Roman, Byzantine and Umayyad. There is also line-of-sight co-ordination from one site to another, and sometimes to more than one site; the place-name al-Manara ("light-house") itself may be indicative of the site's major function. Thus a line of rapid communication, especially at night,[5] could be maintained along the Wādī Sirḥān-Ḥawrān route. At Dayr al-Kahf this could go one of two directions - north to the Jebal Drūz along the Strata or west through Umm al-Quṭṭayn and Umm al-Jimāl to the Via Nova and thence to Bostra. The simplicity and utility of such a communication-system had undoubtedly been developed by the Nabataeans and the Romans, and its potential was not lost to the Umayyads. It is but one of many indications that this region constituted a vital link in commercial and military activity from the first through the eighth centuries AD (King 1983: 430).

IV. The Azraq Depression

The Azraq Depression represents more clearly than does the Ḥawrān Umayyad re-use of a military zone occupied in force by the Romans from the early third century to at least the late fourth century. Lying far to the east of the King's Highway and surrounded by desert, its perennial pools and vegetation attracted various forms of wildlife (including human) from remotest times. Though isolated, it was the nexus of trade routes to the east, north and west. It was (and still is) the major oasis of central Jordan, comparable to Damascus and Palmyra farther north but never the site of a permanent settlement of any appreciable size before this century.[6]

An Umayyad presence in the Azraq area has long been recognised, and indeed certain sites (Qusayr al-'Amra, Qaṣr al-Kharāna, Qaṣr al-Tuba, al-Muaqfar and al-Mashatta) are now closely associated with the early Islamic period (Tell, 1982) there as the nearby sites of Qaṣr al-Ḥallabāt, Qaṣr 'Uwaynid, Jebal al-Asaykhin and Qaṣr al-Azraq are associated with Roman and Byzantine occupation. The oldest oasis settlement of any kind may have been located at 'Ayn al-Asad, just south of Qaṣr al-Azraq at the north-western end of the remaining pools (Harding 1967: 155; Garrard & Price 1975). On or near these sites some Nabataean presence may be adduced, and it was at Qaṣr al-Azraq that the Romans constructed one of their earliest area fortifications. The oasis attracted the Umayyads, not only as a paradeisos in the Persian manner (al-faradīs in classical Arabic) but also because the location was clearly a strategic link with inner Arabia (via the Wādī Sirḥān), the Via Nova (through Ḥallabāt) and the Ḥawrān (via Asaykhin and Khirbet al-Manāra). In addition to the Umayyad sites already noted, King's survey included the lesser-known sites of Qaṣr Mushāsh and Umm al-Walīd. He also demonstrated that Qaṣr Bayēr, once thought to be Umayyad, is datable only to Nabataean, Roman and Early Byzantine times.[7]

From the time of the Princeton Expeditions (1904 and 1909) until now, much attention has been given to the fort at Ḥallabāt

(Butler 1919: 70-77). In contrast to other sites which are Umayyed in origin, Ḥallabāt is one of the few Romano-Byzantine forts yielding clear evidence of Umayyad modifications to the main military structure. There is also a mosque built just outside the eastern wall, and a bath (now reconstructed) known as Ḥammām al-Ṣarakh, about 2 km farther east (Butler 1919: xix-xxv). The remains of a large reservoir and cisterns have long been known, but not until the recent survey by Kennedy (1982: 17-65) and the excavations by Bisheh (1980; 1982; 1985) was attention drawn to the walled agricultural area and residential dwellings associated with the main structure.

On the basis of all the evidence to date, Ghazeh Bisheh is inclined to believe that Ḥallabāt had no military function under Umayyad rule, but served instead as a badiya (desert retreat) for one or more of the royal family. More importantly, Bisheh believes that the agricultural potential of Ḥallabāt was very limited, and what food was grown there was intended for local consumption. He believes the site's abandonment in the eighth century

> can be attributed neither to a deliberate 'Abbāsid destruction nor to climatic changes, but rather to human factors which are represented in the transfer of the seat of government to Baghdad and the concomitant lack of flow of funds (1985: 265).

These are extremely important considerations, since they cast doubt on both the military and economic raisons d'etre for the reoccupation of the site. We need now to look at other sites in the area.

At about the same time that Ḥallabāt was undergoing modifications in both form and function, the large and imposing structure known as Qaṣr al-Kharāna was built. G. L. Harding argued forcibly that Kharāna served primarily a military function; he described it as:

> . . . the only desert castle in Jordan which seems to have been built with a defensive purpose in mind . . . its commanding position . . . at a point where many tracks from all directions, including the Wadi Sirhan, meet makes the site a strategic one (1967: 159-160).

The multiple-storey height of Kharāna, the large interior courtyard, the two internal cisterns and the ground-floor rooms that could have easily served as stables, are all indicative that Harding was right. Like nearby Qaṣr al-Tuba and Mashatta, Kharāna was abandoned in the mid-eighth century; unlike the latter two, it was not left incomplete.

Dated building inscriptions demonstrate that the Azraq Depression was the focus of intense Umayyad interest in the first quarter of the eighth century. As all the sites were abandoned by the middle of that century, the 'Abbāsid takeover is obviously connected. Since none of the sites described shows major structural damage, one may rule out the possibility that the decision to abandon them was the result of earthquake activity.[8] Such was certainly the case for the contemporary Umayyad palace at Khirbet al-Mafjar (Qaṣr Hishām) just north of Jericho, damaged and abandoned in the earthquake of 18 Jan. 746 (El-Isa 1985: 234).

The fortifications at Qaṣr al-Azraq represent a more complex sequence. The structure that now stands, whatever its date, is certainly not the earliest. Aerial photos from the late 1920's show the outline (now not visible on the ground) of a sizeable castrum (c.250m²) which Kennedy (1982: 88-90) suggests may date to the Severan period. The standing fort he dates to the early fourth century on the strength of military building inscriptions now kept in the fort/museum, and the general plan of the fort itself. The similarities between the structure at Azraq and others in Jordan - notably the dated fort at Dayr al-Kahf - are readily evident (Kennedy 1982: 76 fig. 15). A Latin inscription of c.300 recently republished by Kennedy and me (1985) yields what is probably the ancient name of Azraq, Dasianis. The stone presumably was inscribed and set up in the fort. It records mileage distances between Azraq and three other place-names: Bostra (Buṣrā al-Shām), Basienisa (either Manāra or Dayr al-Kahf), and a hitherto unidentified site (Bamata or Amata) along the caravan track between Azraq and Dūmat al-Jandal (MacAdam 1986).

Nabataean and Roman interest in the Wādī Ṣirhān has been evident for some time, and one may reasonably assume that this factor lay behind the subsequent Umayyad interest in the Azraq area.[9] What dated inscriptions there are belong to the first half of the eighth century, and these are generally associated with structures which have no Roman or Byzantine predecessors (Qaṣr Burqu', an exception, is not in the Azraq area). Yet the two classical forts later re-used are so far anepigráphic for the Umayyad era. Ḥallabāt, however, has yielded large quantities of Umayyad pottery, and there are the mosque and bath of Umayyad architectural style. For the Azraq fort there is no parallel evidence. The earliest dated Islamic text is the Arabic inscription of 634/1237 commemorating the (re-)construction of the building (Kennedy 1982: 77). The small mosque within the courtyard of the fort must be contemporary with the inscription of 1237, though this is not certain. The absence of Umayyad evidence at Qaṣr Azraq is indeed remarkable, but this need not automatically constitute evidence of Umayyad absence. It seems unlikely that the strategic value of the fort would pass unnoticed had it been usable. Prior damage and decay may have been so extensive as to preclude occupation.

V. Conclusion

The evidence for an Umayyad military presence in north-eastern Jordan is very tenuous indeed. There are no pre-Islamic military sites which show indisputable evidence of military use in the Umayyad period. With the possible exceptions of Qaṣr Kharāna near Azraq and Qaṣr Burqu' far to the north east there are no Umayyad forts. There is as yet no evidence at all for Umayyad occupation, military or otherwise, of the Azraq oasis itself. Yet Azraq is associated with the Umayyad regime in early Islamic literature; in fact it is one of the few place-names in that literature which can be identified with certainty (Hillenbrand 1982: 26 n. 90 [Azraq]; 21-22 n. 9 [unidentified sites]). If the Azraq Oasis was important to the Umayyad regime regarding the * defence and monitoring of a major trade route into the Arabia peninsula, and if the old, established military towns of Umm al-Quṭṭayn and Umm al-Jimāl continued to guard the southern approaches to the Ḥawrān, how then can we explain the lack of garrisons at such points that were obviously part of the Roman and Byzantine defensive system for three centuries or longer?

The answer, I believe, lies in understanding the fundamental difference between Roman/Byzantine military deployment of auxiliary forces and the Arab counterpart to this. The fixed military position, especially within or near an urban area, is a feature of Roman military behaviour in the Near East. The stratopedon or * castrum represented an idee fixe in the military mind - a planned, defensive structure which served as a base of operations and which had a defined, physical presence. There is nothing even roughly equivalent to this concept in pre-Islamic Arab history, and little enough after the conquest until the medieval period. The Arabic term al-ḥīra is now well-established as meaning "encampment", but one of a moveable, semi-sedentary nature (Shahid 1984: 490-496). The Greek term parembolē was used to translate it; there is one undated attestation of a stratēgos parembolōn nomadōn from Taymā in the Jebal Drūz (Littmann 1921: 347 no. 752). This phrase was translated by the editors as "general of (the) armies of (the) nomads"; more correctly this would be "shaykh of the bedouin encampment", i.e. the commander of auxiliary forces which are encamped wherever they are needed.

A further clue to understanding the conspicuous absence of Umayyad military fortifications in north-east Jordan is the abandonment or re-use for other purposes of the Romano-Byzantine military structure so prominently attested in the region. This occurs in various places from the fourth century on; the last great register of military stations in Jordan before the Islamic conquest is the Notitia Dignitatum. Many of the place-names associated with units under the Dux Arabiae (Or. xxxvii) cannot be identified with any certainty, but some must be along the Strata Diocletiana in north-east Jordan. By the beginning of the sixth century there are almost no epigraphic references to Byzantine military activity in the region; the Ḥallabāt inscription early in the reign of Justinian is an exception.[10] The decline, decay or transformation of the "fortresses and castles" known to Ammianus Marcellinus[11] in the late fourth century is contemporary with the rise to prominence of the Ghassānids c. 500. There are no "Ghassānid forts" identifiable as such in Jordan. Perhaps if Jābiya is one day excavated we may learn something of what their Ḥawrānī stronghold actually was. The mobile military forces of the Ghassānid princes, as the Kindite and Lakhmid forces before them, left no permanent military structures behind. Their tent encampments moved with them where they were needed. The term ḥīra, as Lawrence Conrad demonstrated clearly in a paper at this Colloquium (Conrad 1986), became embedded in the Greek text of Theophanes' Chronographia as a place-name near Gaza. It is not. It refers to the federated bedouin parembolē near that city on the eve of the Islamic invasion of Jordan and Palestine.[12]

The situation obtaining in the Umayyad period must have been quite similar. The Umayyad regime simply adopted a military scheme already in existence, and maintained the security of towns and trade routes in north-eastern Jordan with the aid of allied tribal groups of long residence in the region. Bisheh's comments on the Umayyad settlement at Ḥallabāt are very apt indeed:

> Another likely reason for the development of Hallabat may have been the need to maintain close contacts with the tribes settled in the district [i.e. jund] of Jordan, especially the Belqa region, who were vehement supporters of the Umayyads (Bisheh 1985: 265).

The raison d'etre of the Umayyad "palaces" in Jordan now makes more sense. Their prominant, even ostentatious, presence was a constant reminder to the Arab tribes of Azraq in particular, that the old order had changed:[13]

> The excavations of later Umayyad palaces have disclosed decoration of hitherto unsuspected richness. These finds are enough to prove the existence of a conscious iconographic programme of royal themes, stressing not only majesty and dominion but also the pastimes of the ruler and his court (Hillenbrand 1982: 4).

"La dolce vita" it may have been, but the pragmatic aspect of the Umayyads in Jordan should not be disregarded. They ruled a vast territory from Damascus with only the minimum of military force. Their main armies waged war against the Byzantines in Antolia and took the Islamic conquest in the east as far as India. Whatever policing and patrolling of the desert routes was needed between the Ḥawrān and Dūmat al-Jandal was left to their bedouin allies - under the watchful eye of those who inhabited the badiyas of Jordan.[14]

Notes

1. On the location and history of Jābiya see Lammens and Sourdel-Thomine 1965. For an early appraisal of the site see Butler 1919: 311-312; his melancholy description indicates that he missed the actual site of the Ghassānid city.

2. Shaban 1971: I,41. See also Shahid 1985.

3. For a review of the early Islamic sources regarding the history of Dūmat al-Jandal (al-Jawf), see Musil 1927: 531-553.

4. De Vries (1982: 113; 1985: 251) believed that this was true for Jimāl, but King (1982: 94) expressed doubt about Butler's monastery/convent at Quṭṭayn. Whatever civilian settlement existed at Kahf must have been no larger than the *canabae* surrounding other military installations, and hardly *figures* here. On urban transformation in this period, see the important article by H. Kennedy (1985a). Paret (1960) discusses the large number of churches in Hawrānī communities and elsewhere in Arabia in the fifth and sixth centuries.

5. A recent experiment in night-time signalling between military posts and watchtowers in the Lejjūn area is vividly described in Parker 1985: 18-19.

6. Kennedy (1982: 69-136) is the best recent description of the oasis. For a study of the flora and fauna see Nelson (1985), and for the environmental history of the region see Garrard *et al.* (1985).

7. King 1983a: 386-391 (Mushāsh); 399-405 (Walīd) and 398-399 (Bāyer).

8. El-Isa 1985. See especially his comments (232) on Quṣayr 'Amra: "Contrary to expectations, the . . . 'Amra castle shows very little evidence of earthquake deformation despite the fact that it is built on the less firm Quaternary sediments . . ."

9. The evidence for the pre-Islamic period is conveniently collected in Bowersock 1983: 154-159 and in more detail in Sartre 1982: 19-22. For the use of this route during the Islamic conquest, see Musil 1927: 516-573 *passim*.

10. The excavator of Ḥallabāt, Ghazeh Bisheh, believes that this inscription was brought to Ḥallabāt at some later period from either Khirbit Samra to the north-east, or from Umm al-Jimāl directly north. I owe this information to a conversation with him. The Princeton University team which first recorded this text (Littman 1921: 22-23 no. 18) described the larger of the two fragments as being *in situ*. The inscription has since been removed according to Kennedy (1982: 40 no. 5). Whatever its origin, it attests military construction at the date given in the text.

11. Ammianus Marcellinus XIV 8.13: *castrisque oppleta validis et castellis*, which, he goes on to say, were built "to repel the raids of neighbouring tribes".

12. That the term al-hira *could* become a place name is demonstrated clearly by the Hira on the Euphrates, headquarters of the Lakhmids from as early as the late third century.

13. See Almagro and Olavarri (1982) for discussion of recent archaeological work on the Umayyad palace on the 'Ammān citadel. The numismatic, ceramic and stylistic evidence date the standing structure to 720-750, with a Byzantine predecessor incorporated.

14. The fact that so many of the sites associated with the Umayyads are qualified as qaṣr is also worthy of note. This does not mean, as commonly supposed, a "fortified" site as if the term qaṣr was derived from castrum. It means "enclosure" and could, of course, be used for security in times of danger. On the etymology of qaṣr (plural quṣūr) see the instructive article by Conrad (1981).

Bibliography

ALMAGRO, A. and OLAVARRI, E. 1982 A new Umayyad palace at the citadel of Amman. In A. Hadidi (ed.) Studies in the History and Archaeology of Jordan I: 305-321. Amman (Department of Antiquities).

BISHEH, G. 1980 Excavations at Qasr al-Hallabat, 1979. Annual of the Department of Antiquities of Jordan 24: 69-77.

1982 The Second Season of Excavation at Hallabat, 1980. Annual of the Department of Antiquities of Jordan 26: 133-143.

1985 Qasr al-Hallabat: an Umayyad desert retreat or farm land? In A. Hadidi (ed.), Studies in the History and Archaeology of Jordan II: 263-265. Amman (Department of Antiquities).

BOWERSOCK, G. W. 1983 Roman Arabia. Cambridge, Mass. (Harvard University Press).

BUTLER, H. C. 1919 Publications of the Princeton University Archaeological Expeditions to Syria in 1904-05 and 1909, Division II, Architecture: Section A, Southern Syria. Leiden (E. J. Brill).

CONRAD, L. I. 1981 The Quṣūr of Medieval Islam: some implications for the social history of the Near East. Al-Abhath 29: 7-23.

1986 The early Muslim campaign in southern Palestine. In P. Freeman and D. Kennedy (eds.) The Defence of the Roman and Byzantine East. Oxford (BAR, International Series).

DE VRIES, B. 1979 Research at Umm al-Jimal, Jordan, 1972-1977. Biblical Archaeologist 42: 49-56.

1982 The Umm al-Jimal Project 1972-1977. Annual of the Department of Antiquities of Jordan 26: 97-166.

1985 Urbanization in the basalt region of North Jordan in Late Antiquity: the case of Umm al-Jimal. In A. Hadidi (ed.), Studies in the History and Archaeology of Jordan II: 249-256. Amman (Department of Antiquities).

1986 Um el-Jemal in the third century. In P. Freeman and D. Kennedy (eds.), The Defence of the Roman and Byzantine East. Oxford (BAR, International Series).

DONNER, F. M. 1981 The Early Islamic Conquests. Princeton, (Princeton University Press).

DUSSAUD, R. and MACLER, F. 1903 Mission dans les régions désertiques de la Syrie moyenne. Paris (E. Leroux).

EL-ISA, Z. H. 1985 Earthquake studies of some archaeological sites in Jordan. In A. Hadidi (ed.), Studies in the History and Archaeology of Jordan II: 229-235. Amman (Department of Antiquities).

GARRARD, A.N. and PRICE, N.P.S. 1975 A survey of prehistoric sites in the Azraq Desert National Park in eastern Jordan. Annual of the Department of Antiquities of Jordan 20: 83-90.

GARRARD, A. N., HARVEY, P., HIVERNEL, F. and BYRD, B. 1985 The environmental study of the Azraq Basin. In A. Hadidi (ed.), Studies in the History and Archaeology of Jordan II: 109-115. Amman (Department of Antiquities).

GAUBE, H. 1974 An examination of the ruins of Qaṣr Burquʿ. Annual of the Department of Antiquities of Jordan 19: 93-100.

GRABAR, O. 1963 Umayyad 'Palace' and the Abbasid 'Revolution'. Studia Islamica 18: 5-18.

HARDING, G. L. 1967 Antiquities of Jordan (2nd ed.). Guildford (Lutterworth Press).

HELMS, S. W. 1981 Jawa: Lost City of the Black Desert. London (Methuen & Co.).

HILLENBRAND, R. 1982 La Dolce Vita in Early Islamic Syria: the evidence of Later Umayyad Palaces. Art History 5: 1-35.

KENNEDY, D. L. 1982 Archaeological Explorations on the Roman Frontier in North-East Jordan. Oxford (BAR, International Series 134).

KENNEDY, D. L. and MACADAM, H.I. 1985 Latin inscriptions from the Azraq Oasis, Jordan. Zeitschrift für Papyrologie und Epigraphik 60: 97-107.

1986a Latin inscriptions from Jordan, 1985. Zeitschrift für Papyrologie und Epigraphik: forthcoming.

1986b Preliminary report on the Southern Hawran Survey, 1985. Annual of the Department of Antiquities of Jordan: forthcoming.

KENNEDY H. 1985a From Polis to Madina: urban change in Late Antique and Early Islamic Syria. Past and Present 106: 3-27.

1985b The towns of Bilad al-Sham and the Arab conquests. In A. Bakhit (ed.), Proceedings of the Fourth Bilād al-Shām Conference: forthcoming. Amman, (University of Jordan).

KING, G. R. D. 1982 Preliminary report on a survey of Byzantine and Islamic sites in Jordan, 1980. Annual of the Department of Antiquities of Jordan 26: 85-95.

1983a Survey of Byzantine and Islamic sites in Jordan: Second Season report, 1981. Annual of the De-

		partment of Antiquities of Jordan 27: 385-436.
	1983b	Two Byzantine churches in northern Jordan and their re-use in the Islamic period. *Damaszener Mitteilungen* 1: 111-136.
KNAUF, E. A.	1984	Umm al-Jimal: an Arab town in Late Antiquity. *Revue Biblique* 91: 578-586.
LAMMENS, H. and SOURDEL-THOMINE, J.	1965	Djabiya. In the *Encyclopedia of Islam* (2nd ed.), II: 360.
LITTMANN, E., MAGIE, D. STUART, D.R.	1921	*Publications of the Princeton University Archaeological Expeditions to Syria in 1904-04 and 1909*, Division III, Greek and Latin Inscriptions: Section A, Southern Syria. Leiden (E. J. Brill).
MACADAM, H. I.	1986	Ptolemy's *Geography* and the Wādī Sirḥān. Proceedings of the Colloquium on *Geographie Historique au Proche Orient*: forthcoming Paris (C.N.R.A.).
MITTMANN, S.	1970	*Beiträge zur Siedlungs-und Territorial-geschichte des nördlichen Ostjordanlands* Weisbaden (Otto Harrassowitz).
MUSIL, A.	1927	*Arabia Deserta: A Topographical Itinerary*. New York (American Geographical Society).
NELSON, B.	1985	Azraq: A case study. In A. Hadidi, *Studies in the History and Archaeology of Jordan* II: 39-44. Amman (Department of Antiquities).
PARET, R.	1960	Les Villes de Syrie du sud et les routes commerciales d'Arabie a la fin du VIe siecle. In F. Dolger and H. G. Beck (eds.), *Akten des XI Internationalen Byzantinistenkongresses, München 1958*: 438-444. München (C. H. Beck).
PARKER, S. T.	1985	Preliminary report on the 1982 Season of the Central Limes Arabicus Project. *Bulletin of the American Schools of Oriental Research* Supplement No. 23: 1-34.

PARKER, S.T. 1986 The Arabian frontier after a decade of research. In P. Freeman and D. Kennedy (eds.) *Defence of the Roman and Byzantine East*: Oxford (BAR International Series).

PICCIRILLO, M. 1984 The Umayyad churches of Jordan. *Annual of the Department of Antiquities of Jordan* 28: 333-341.

SARTRE, M. 1982 *Trois études sur l'Arabie romaine et byzantines*. Bruxelles (Collection Latomus 178).

1985 Le Ḥawrān Byzantine à la veille de la Conquête Musalmane. In A. Bakhit (ed.), *Proceedings of the Fourth Bilād al-Shām Conference*: forthcoming. Amman (University of Jordan).

SEEDEN, H. 1983 An Umayyad farmhouse and the Bronze Age occupation levels at Buṣra (Ḥawrān). *Annales Archéologiques Arabes Syriennes* 33: 162-173.

SHABAN, M. A. 1971 *Islamic History: A New Interpretation*. Cambridge (Cambridge University Press).

SHAHID, I. 1984 *Byzantium and the Arabs in the Fourth Century*. Washington, D. C. (Dumbarton Oaks Press).

1985 The Jund-system in Bilād al-Shām: its origin. In A. Bakhit (ed.), *Proceedings of the Fourth Bilād al-Shām Conference*: forthcoming. Amman (University of Jordan).

SHBOUL, A. 1975 On the Later Arabic inscription in Qaṣr Burquʿ. *Annual of the Department of antiquities of Jordan* 20: 95-98.

TELL, S. 1982 Early Islamic architecture in Jordan. In A. Hadidi (ed.) *Studies in the History and Archaeology of Jordan* II: 323-327. Amman (Department of Antiquities).

ERRATA/CORRIGENDA/ADDENDA

Readers are again reminded that the maps which appear in some, not all, of these reprinted articles are for the purpose of general identification of the geographical areas and the toponyms referred to within the text. Readers needing detailed and accurate maps must consult the best available modern reference source for maps of the classical world, i.e. R.J.A. Talbert (ed.), *Barrington Atlas of the Greek and Roman World* (Princeton, NJ, Princeton University Press, 2000). HIM

I 257 lines 14–15: after 'with that in mind' add (see the following article for that study of Phoenician geography).
I 257 n. 10: remove 'I' after T. Ferris; italicize *Coming of Age in the Milky Way*.
I 260 n. 20: for 'Rhodes' read 'Rhodos'.

II 273 line 10: for 'Arabic' read 'Arab'

III 65 line 24: for 'symbolical' read 'symbolic'

VII pp. 180, 188: There are more than fifty personal names listed on these two pages, far too many to include in the Index to this volume. A note to this effect is made under the entry 'onomastics' in the Index.
VII 182, in the commentary to #9223: 'AKR' should read 'AKP'
VII 184: in footnote 70: the second citation should read '*Berytus* 32 (1984) 19–47'
VII 189, line 6: 'Waddigton' should read 'Waddington'

VIII 641, line 4: for 'some' read 'seem'; line 7: for 'coments' read 'comments'
VIII 643, line 23: for 'Arabas' read 'Arabs'
VIII 647, line 13: for 'The' read 'They'
VIII 648, line 16: The garbled sentence beginning 'Much of this region...' should be TWO sentences which read: 'Much of this region is, and presumably was, agriculturally important and therefore would benefit from the settlement of those veteran soldiers recruited locally and due for retirement. Veterans of the Roman army are well-attested throughout the empire. Etc.'
VIII 649, line 4 from bottom: 'and half' should read 'and a half'

IX 58, end of footnote 42: for 'vity' read 'city'
IX 73, line 7: after the word 'Byzantine' there should be a period

IX 73, footnote 138: for 'J.P. Humbert' read 'J-B. Humbert'
IX 74, line 5: for 'naive' read 'naïve'

X 47, line 5 from bottom: remove 'which' from that sentence
X 53, line 12: after 'individual' add the word 'family'

XI 295, line 11: for 'strata' read 'Strata'
XI 302, lines 11 & 14: 'Vicentius' should read 'Vincentius'

XII 109, footnote 37: the second occurrence of the Greek term '*hierotamias* should read instead *hierotomeus*

XIV 49, line 10: for 'ibn Mighīra' read 'ibn Mughīra'
XIV 50, line 3 from bottom: for 'Grohnann' read 'Grohmann'
XIV 56, footnote 2: for 'Brish' read 'Brische'

XV 531, line 5 of abstract: for 'Mashata' read 'Mashatta'
XV 537, line 21 from bottom: for 'Muaqfar' read 'Muwaqqar'
XV 540, line 9: for 'Arabia' read 'Arabian'
XV 540, line 21: for 'idee' read 'idée'

INDEX

NB: Every attempt has been made to ensure accuracy and consistency, especially with the tranliteration of Greek and Semitic proper and place-names (the Arabic definite article has been omitted with few exceptions). I have translated many Greek and Semitic words and/or phrases into English to assist those from other disciplines except where (e.g. Latin *canabae*) no equivalent term or expression exists for the concept. This index is extensively cross-referenced so that readers may easily find place names and/or proper names which are sometimes rendered differently in both ancient and modern sources.

There are more than fifty personal names (some incomplete) listed in Article VII pp. 180, 188, far too many to include in this Index. See the note to that effect in the Index entry 'onomastics.'

Ferro (island): I 258
Feudalherr: VI 9
Fidayn: IX 75
Fiḥl: IX 79; *see also* Pella, Tabaqāt Fiḥl
Fiḥr: XII 114
Filadelphia (variant of Philadelphia): VI 49
Filastīn: IX 50
Finance Minister (Ptolemaic): VI 5, 8–9; *see also dioiketēs*
Fischer, Kurt: V 309–10, 316
Fischer, Josef/Joseph: III 62; V 317; XIV 56 n. 5
fiscus ('treasury'): X 50
Fitzgerald, Ella: II 279
Flavia Ialla: VI 25
Flavian:
  dynasty: VI 26; X 46
  imperialism: V 295
Flavius Constantius (*praefectus praetorio*): XIII 166 and *passim*
Flavius Cornelius: XII 114
Flavius Josephus: V 305; VI 6, 12, 15–16, 21–5, 37; X 46; XIV 54
T. Flavius Longinus: VI 28
T. Flavius Marcianus: VI 25
Flavius Maximus: VII 182
Flavius Severinus?: XIII 169
Flood (Biblical): II 281
foederatus/foederati: IX 63; *see also* 'federated (Arab) tribes'
Forat: V 292
forests (Phoenicia, Lebanon): X 48–49; *see also* 'defoliation'
Forster, Charles: V 312
Fortunate Isles: I 258; V 304; *see also* Canary Islands, Islas Canarias
Foundation for Danish Research in Palestine: IX 71
Fourth Syrian War: II 278; IV 341; VI 12
France: VIII 650
Frank, Tenney: X 45–6, 60 n. 4
Frankfurt-am-Main: IX 71
frankincense: V 294–5
frankincense region: V 311
Fraser, P.M.: X 60 n. 1
French:
  archaeological surveys (Syria-Jordan): VI 40–41; VIII 648; IX 81
  garrisons (in Mandate Syria): VIII 645
  French-Jordanian excavations: VI 6
  Mandate (in Syria): VII 169; VIII 645
fulūs (bronze coin): IX 87

Gabalitis: VI 3
Gabinius: VI 17
Gabitha: VII 178
Gabnes: XII 112
Gadara (of the Decapolis): VI 11, 15, 16 (n. 61), 19–21 and nn. 80, 86; VI 22; IX 50–51, 69–70, 72, 77, 78 (and n. 165), 79; *see also* Umm Qays
Gadara (of the Jordanian Peraea): VI 16 (and n. 61), 19, 47; *see also* Tell Jadūr
Gadda: VI 38–39; XI 295
Gades: II 291; IV 343; *see also* Cadiz
Gadouos: XII 112
Gaius Caesar: V 293, 301, 311, 314
Galaaditis: VI 13 n. 49
Galatians (NT Book of): VI 42–3
Gallus expedition (to Arabia): V 292–3, 297, 299, 301, 314
Garis: II 295
Gatier, Pierre-Louis: V 305; VI 16, 20; VII 171, 177; IX 51, 84 n. 207
Gaube, Heinz: IX 89; XV 535
Gaulanitis: VI 3; VII 170; *see also* Golan (heights, region)
Gauthos (*Gwt*): VII 179
Gaza: V 292; VI 23; VII 177; XV 532, 541
Gazara: VI 13; *see also* Jazer, Yazer, Khirbat Sār?
Genesius, Church of: IX 76 n. 153; *see also* Byzantine chapels, churches
geographikos pinax ('geographical map'): V 297
Geography (of Ptolemy): I 254; II 286–8; III 58, 62; IV 343; V 289, 301–13; VI 22; VII 173; XI 297, 299; XIV 50 and *passim*
Geography (of Strabo): II 270 and *passim*; IV 342; V 289, 295–301
Georgian language: VI 44–5
Georgius Cedrinus: VII 178
georgoi ('farmers'): VIII 647; XII 113
Gerasa: III 59; V 306; VI 14–16, 18–19, 21, 27–8, 29 (n. 98), 31, 34, 45 and n. 153; VII 185; IX 49, 51, 53, 69, 75, 79–80
  oval forum at: VI 45 n. 153; *see also* Jarash, Jerash
Gerasa Gate (at Philadelphia): VI 45
Gerasenē: VI 15–16; IX 77
German:
  Archaeological Institute: IX 71